From Jeremia

From Jeremiad to Jihad

Religion, Violence, and America

———

Edited by

John D. Carlson and Jonathan H. Ebel

UNIVERSITY OF CALIFORNIA PRESS

Berkeley   Los Angeles   London

University of California Press, one of the most distinguished university presses in the United States, enriches lives around the world by advancing scholarship in the humanities, social sciences, and natural sciences. Its activities are supported by the UC Press Foundation and by philanthropic contributions from individuals and institutions. For more information, visit www.ucpress.edu.

University of California Press
Berkeley and Los Angeles, California

University of California Press, Ltd.
London, England

Portions of Eddie S. Glaude's essay "Religion and Violence in Black and White" originally appeared in his book *Exodus! Religion, Race, and Nation in Early Nineteenth-Century Black America* (Chicago: University of Chicago Press, 2000). Reprinted with permission of The University of Chicago Press and the author.

Library of Congress Cataloging-in-Publication Data

From jeremiad to jihad : religion, violence, and America / John D. Carlson and Jonathan H. Ebel, editors.
    p. cm.
  Includes bibliographical references and index.
  ISBN 978-0-520-27165-4 (cloth : alk. paper)—ISBN 978-0-520-27166-1 (pbk. : alk. paper) 1. Violence—Religious aspects. 2. Violence—United States. 3. United States—Religion. I. Carlson, John D. (John David) II. Ebel, Jonathan H., 1970–
  BL65.V55F77s 2012
  201'.763320973—dc23   2011050355

Manufactured in the United States of America

21 20 19 18 17 16 15 14 13 12
10 9 8 7 6 5 4 3 2 1

The paper used in this publication meets the minimum requirements of ANSI/NISO Z39.48-1992 (R 2002) (*Permanence of Paper*).

For
Sophia, Charlotte, and Beatrice
and for
James and Christopher

CONTENTS

Martin E. Marty

The contents of this book are strikingly diverse: Amalek, Iraq, and Ghost Dance; covenant, rights, and manifesto; schools and war; providence and cinema, Alma White and coercive interrogation. Can a topic as clearly focused as religion and violence in America be so hydra-headed as to yield a list of elements that differ so vastly? It can and it does. Consider the title's key terms, which ground this book in a dynamic American context.

The *jeremiad* is a rhetorical legacy of the colonial era, best understood as biblically informed and inflamed rhetoric intended to chastise a sinful people, enjoin humility, and call them to repentance. Yet this book limits the jeremiad neither to the colonial period in which it was prominent nor to the pulpits from which jeremiads were preached. Instead, the editors and authors use jeremiad as a trope for framing and interpreting religiously informed expressions of discontent with the state of American society, focusing on moments attended by calls for and acts of violence. Over time jeremiads and their variations urged Americans aspiring to communal piety or purity to focus on the "sins" of next-door neighbors who were irritants, threats, or competitors, whether they were witches, "heretics," schismatics, or simply "other." Preachers and self-styled prophets also called on Americans to demonstrate or recapture their virtue through violent resistance to global enemies such as "papist" Rome, marauding Mexico, militaristic Germany, and myriad other "foreign" specters. Proslavery jeremiads that equated racial tolerance with sinfulness and corruption provoked violence against African Americans in the form of intimidation, lynching, segregation, and more subtle but still damaging acts designed to snub, demean, and degrade in the name of God.

If jeremiad is a trope rooted in distant times, *jihad* is imported from distant places, chiefly, in today's instance, the world(s) of Islam(s). Conceived narrowly, jihad has come to be an all-purpose term for Islamic violence. The label rarely delineates domestic irritations and provocations. Many assume that jihad happens, most often, "out there." This book, though, recognizes that relevant features of jihad—including violence as purgation or holy war—overlap with jeremiads running through many features of American life, from colonial domestic scenes to postmodern global terrors.

Violence deserves more extended attention. A once long-neglected theme in social and religious history in America, violence has won a prime place on the agenda and, according to some critics, has become a voguish subject that demands criticism. (As evidence, there are a growing number of institutes, centers, disciplines, and publications devoted to study of religion and violence.)

Americans have only recently come to recognize violence as a part of American culture and life, aided by historians, the media, film, and popular culture. At least through World War II, Americans perceived violence primarily in the form of wars, often, but not always, fought in places far away: Europe, East Asia, Africa. This gave the impression that violence was something perpetrated or threatened—out there—by others against our peaceful nation, and to which Americans responded reluctantly but justly. A more complex understanding developed as Americans, aided by the growth of mass media and communication, witnessed the violence of the second half of the twentieth century. It was one thing for publics in 1943 to read about or see pictures in *Life* magazine of soldiers fighting and dying in Europe or clashes and race riots in Detroit. It was another to experience racial violence, riots, and war on television in one's living room (and eventually one's computer). These phenomena—both modern events and modern media—forced citizens to recognize that violence is part of their putatively nonviolent society. In other words, violence, many now see, is integrally bound up with ideas and identity signified by "America." As Americans—and their popular culture, news, and entertainment—conceived violence differently, the nature of historical research and teaching developed, inspired by new approaches to "doing history" (for example, cliometrics, social history). Today, as this book shows, a different kind of story is being written, which reckons with how violence interconnects with religion.

Religion has been deeply implicated in American violence both at home and abroad. American clergy of all stripes—from colonial-era preachers inveighing against the Crown to twentieth-century pastors who cultivated fear of "Godless" Communism—have preached the importance of spreading divinely ordained concepts of freedom and democracy. The klaverns of the Ku Klux Klan favored chaplains and bannered the Bible to advance their causes of physical intimidation and violence. But the picture was not only bleak. Religious leaders and laity, often reasoning and acting explicitly as people of faith, protested against the violence that often attended America's global involvements, and stood firmly against "Red" baiters and black-listers. Likewise, the civil rights movement, under the leadership of "Reverends," used religious and nonviolent impulses to counter violence. In fact, American fundamentalists and their counterparts on the radical left have rarely resorted to arms. The news will bring more accounts of violence associated with religion from most continents in any one day than are found in a half-century of American "culture wars." There has been plenty of rhetoric using religious symbols, and these do threaten civil peace. That said, it is important to keep in mind that, as a historian friend of mine told me years ago, "there are no machine-guns in the basement of Moody Bible Institute." In other words, extreme religious rhetoric in the United States is rarely accompanied by physical violence.

The debate in many people's minds is whether religion causes violence. Recent scholarly works such as William T. Cavanaugh's *The Myth of Religious Violence* further make clear that the terms *religion* and *violence* are themselves contested. Whatever we discuss as being "religion" is seldom isolated. It insinuates variegated topics such as tribalism, nationalism, militarism, terrorism, racism, economics, gender, "instinct," "original sin," political rhetoric, public symbols, shared myths, and more. All this raises questions about where religion ends and "the secular" begins. For such reasons, readers should be attuned to what I call the "religio-secular" nature of America's experience with violence, as discussed in this book under other names.

Except for those who dispute the existence of religion, it is almost universally perceived as an agent in world affairs. One need only recall the self-inflicted violence of Jim Jones's Peoples Temple, the deadly confrontation at the Branch Davidian compound in Waco, Texas, or the violence waged in Japan by Aum Shinrikyo to see that many religious groups can cultivate destructive impulses and cultures of violence that are based ostensibly upon holy books, prophetic teachings, religious practices, or apocalyptic visions. For a different example, Protestants and Catholics in Northern Ireland may have had economic and historical differences that kept them apart, but they made every effort to advance their cause through fundamentalist Protestant and militant Catholic traditions. Feuds between Muslims and Hindus in India and Kashmir follow similar patterns. In all these cases, it would be hard to understand why the participants were ready to kill and be killed without becoming familiar with the religious grounding and inspiration of the other. Phenomena associated with religion are real and observable but not overarching or all-defining. Humans are too complex to reduce their basis for commitments to one single, definable agent—even religion. Yet, even when people think they do not possess traditions, traditions still possess them. Evidence of religious traditions often shows up in language, accent, and taste—even among those trying to repudiate tradition, often under secular rubrics.

During my career, most scholars have treated religion more frequently as an epiphenomenon than as a primary, isolable, and independent phenomenon. That is, it tends to be a secondary or consequential element attached to something already there. This does not, however, diminish its power or importance when one is discussing motivations or sustenance of violence. Religion as epiphenomenon can lead cultural competitors to view each other as demons or heathens. Conceiving Jews as blasphemers and Christ-killers drew Klansmen in the 1920s to anti-Jewish violence. Because some religious revelations are so grounded in presumed absolutes, even religion as epiphenomenon can make compromise a sin and extremism a virtue. Religiously centered hopes—whether of heaven or an earthly paradise—can lead committed people to react with violence to the presence of a competing interest. Religious factors invite a different hermeneutic than when "ordinary" languages of territorial or economic interest are regarded as exclusive motivators. Politics by definition involves interest against interest, and interest groups contending with each other. Intense commitments often preclude compromise, as the history of persecution, resistance, and martyrdom makes clear. Remove that absolute religious commitment and replace it with economic and political outlooks, and there may be some opportunity for negotiation.

Violent religious movements can change over time. In their emergent state religions may be at their most uncompromising. In other words, when a movement is being formed, magnanimity, generosity, and openness to risky alliances are luxuries. At some stage many religions forged in fire begin to cool. Or, in Emile Durkheim's terms, those that erupt in effervescence can lose their alluring sparkle. Conversely, nonviolent religious movements may acquire religious symbols and doctrines that inflame violence or stoke its embers. Before World War I, most of the Anglican and Protestant clergy in England and the United States were pacifists or workers for peace. When war broke out, many of them suddenly provided religious motivations for war or issued murderous rhetoric against "the Hun." For reasons such as this, it is important that those seeking peace become informed about the religion of the other and the ways in which religious traditions can either promote violence or give warrant to those who seek reconciliation.

I conclude by turning to the philosopher George Santayana, who wrote:

[E]very living and healthy religion has a marked idiosyncrasy. Its power consists in its special and surprising message and in the bias which that revelation gives to life. The vistas it opens and the mysteries it propounds are another world to live in; and another world to live in—whether we expect ever to pass wholly over into it or no—is what we mean by having a religion.[1]

In the pages that follow, readers should assess for themselves the presence of religion in violence as well as the definitions of religion and violence understood and used by various voices in the book. As you read, consider Santayana's words, and ask the following: What does a religious person or group's attitude toward violence do to make a religion "living" and, in the eyes of its adherents, "healthy"? What "marked idiosyncrasies" of a faith define violence—or show its "bias" for life? What is the nature of a religion's "power" to engender or reinforce violent impulses and actions? What are the "surprising messages" particularly with regard to violence and nonviolence that a community's "revelation gives to [its] life"? What are the "vistas it opens" and the "mysteries it propounds" especially when violence is promoted or enacted in its name? For in the end, even a scholarly examination of this sober topic must have in its sights the hope of transcending violence.

NOTE

1. George Santayana, *Reason in Religion* (1905; reprint, New York: Scribners, 1922), 6.

Fifteen years ago, as we were entering graduate school in the fall of 1997, there was no field of study of religion and violence comparable to what exists today. At that time, scholarship examining the intersections of religion and violence or religion and war reflected scholars' individual research interests and disciplinary approaches—as historians, ethicists, anthropologists, or Americanists, and so on. Professors who engaged such themes in the classroom did so through specialized seminars within their fields—historiographical surveys of the medieval Crusades, anthropological studies of sacrifice and religious ritual, ethical analyses and applications of just war thought—in ways that understandably promoted disciplinary precision over interdisciplinary understanding. As graduate students at the University of Chicago—one a budding ethicist, the other a historian—we availed ourselves of such offerings, where we traded ideas, shared research questions, and discovered a great deal of unplowed ground.

Back then there were few if any research centers, encyclopedic handbooks, or conferences devoted to the study of religion and conflict. There was little market for popular books or media coverage raising urgent questions about religion's putatively violent tendencies. And television specials or prominent personalities calling out religious individuals and faith traditions were rare. The attacks of September 11, 2001, changed this landscape very quickly. In the past decade we have seen a flood of new academic hires in Islam, as well as a number of religion scholars arguing that this "problem of religion and violence" is neither new nor confined to any particular religion or region. Religion and violence, it is now well understood, is not limited to September 11, the ensuing declaration of a "war on terror," or the religiously inflected military invasions of Afghanistan and Iraq.

The phenomenon of 9/11 and its aftermath surely accelerated interest in religion and violence and brought many scholars to an emerging field. So, too, with this book, the conceptual beginnings of which took form during those shadowy times. One of our earliest goals was to show that September 11 was not the United States' first experience with religion and violence. It is one but by no means the only relevant chapter in America's five-hundred-year history. Thus we set out to tell this story by drawing on the expertise of scholars who, for much of their careers, have been thinking about religion and violence or religion and America from within their own disciplines. Along the way, though, we also discovered that this multidisciplinary approach to religion and violence in the American context offered new and compelling insights into the complex historical and moral legacy of the United States—observations, interpretations, and powerful insights about American identity that, presumably, no one author could have conceived alone. By examining prominent figures, beliefs, and events from the early colonial period down to our present day, this volume illuminates the continuities as well as discontinuities that contribute to a fuller, more nuanced, and more meaningful understanding of the United States and its history and place in the world.

This book goes to press at a more hopeful time than when it began. Recent events in the world—the Arab Spring of 2011, significant advances against al Qaeda leadership, the U.S. military withdrawal from Iraq and the relative stability taking hold there, and, one hopes, a sequel moment that will follow in Afghanistan—all point to the possibilities of a new dawn in which violence does not get the last word. We leave to the reader's judgment whether violence, force, revolution, or war has sometimes been vital or necessary to bring forth that new dawn. The pages that follow are instructive but offer no simple answer. We only suggest that peering deeply into the darkness should not blind us to the light but rather stoke our yearning for it.

· · ·

We would like to thank our home institutions, Arizona State University and the University of Illinois, for the excellent support they provided for this project. We are especially grateful for the financial and logistical help from the following programs that helped launch and sustain it: at Arizona State University, the Center for the Study of Religion and Conflict (CSRC) and the Department of Religious Studies; and at the University of Illinois, the Department of Religion, the School of Literatures, Cultures, and Linguistics, and the Illinois Program for Research in the Humanities. Several individuals at these institutions—Linell Cady, Joel Gereboff, Robert McKim, David Price, and Mark VonHagen—warrant special mention for their strong leadership, friendship, and support. Without the crucial administrative support of Carolyn Forbes and Laurie Perko at CSRC, this project could not have been accomplished. We also would like to thank Catherine Brekus, Tracy Fessenden, Jennifer Graber, Valerie Hoffman, Lynn Neal, and John Witte, who at various stages of the project took time from their busy schedules to read and comment on sections of the manuscript and to lend excellent advice that shaped the final direction of the project as a whole. Reed Malcolm, our editor at the University of California Press, showed tremendous faith and patience as we moved from concept to manuscript to book, and we are thankful for his friendship and support seeing this through. We would also like to thank two anonymous readers for their close readings and helpful comments. Additionally, we are deeply grateful for the often tedious but always indispensable efforts of the many research assistants who worked on this project: Jodie Baird, Rachel Bishop, Jessica Clemmons, Seth Clippard, Sarah Jackman, Paul Jackson, Jordan Johnson, Darren Kleinberg, William LeMaire, and Christopher Palfi. Finally, Barbara Goodhouse and Ann Hawthorne provided exceptional editorial support.

This project is the product of a friendship that has grown between us over many years and owes much to the University of Chicago Divinity School: first, for providing the intellectual setting in which we first met following our similarly circuitous career paths; second, for offering a first-rate graduate education and exceptional advisers who nurtured our academic interests; and even for the excellent fare served up at the at the Divinity School coffee shop in the basement of Swift Hall, where we consumed disturbing amounts of coffee. Most importantly, we both met our wives, Meredith and Ginger, in graduate school. They have supported us through thick and thin, through exams, dissertations, conference papers, job markets, cross-country moves, and the continuing challenges of our work. We love you, and we can never thank you enough for your tireless support.

We dedicate this book to our children, Sophia, Charlotte, and Beatrice Ebel and James and Christopher Carlson, in the hope that, as the young learn of the darker, violent episodes of our nation's history, they will lead us to a brighter place.

Ad astra per aspera.

Introduction

John Brown, Jeremiad, and Jihad

Reflections on Religion, Violence, and America

John D. Carlson and Jonathan H. Ebel

Following his infamous raid and dramatic capture at Harper's Ferry on October 16, 1859, the militant abolitionist John Brown was asked, during one of the more memorable interrogations in U.S. history, how he justified his actions. Brown had led a band of twenty-one men, including three of his sons, in a wildly conceived and shoddily executed effort to seize the federal armory in what was then the state of Virginia. His plan was to use the arms and munitions—and, for slaves unable to use guns, a thousand pikes prestaged in a nearby school—to lead a revolt for manumission in the state. In addition to enlisting several unwilling slaves (who knew well that their complicity would bring death), Brown's plan entailed making hostages of prominent citizens from the proslavery town, including a direct descendant of George Washington. The plan backfired when local officials and citizens—followed by a U.S. Marine contingent under Colonel Robert E. Lee's command—surrounded the arsenal. A two-day standoff and shootout ensued. When the dust settled, seventeen were dead, including two of the slaves Brown had "liberated" to fight with him, a black train porter (shot mistakenly), eight of Brown's men, and two of his sons. Brown himself was wounded and captured when the Marines invaded the arsenal.

How did Brown account for this far-fetched scheme? Rather easily, it seems. It could be justified, he attested to the audience thronging his jail cell, by "the Golden Rule": "I pity the poor in bondage that have none to help them: that is why I am here; not to gratify any personal animosity, revenge, or vindictive spirit. It is my sympathy with the oppressed and wronged, that are as good as you and as precious in the sight of God." When asked if he viewed his cause in religious terms, Brown answered, "It is, in my opinion, the greatest service man can render to God." And when prodded whether he conceived himself "an instrument in the hands of Providence," the stern Calvinist replied simply, "I do."[1]

For the short remainder of his life, Brown assumed a confident demeanor, neither fearing death nor repenting the violence that hastened it.[2] Justice for John Brown was swift. Convicted of treason in a fortnight, he ascended the scaffold on December 2, 1859, six weeks after the initial raid. Before he was hanged, Brown proleptically announced that America's crimes of slavery could be purged only through blood. His hope had been that he might end the national scourge by shedding only small amounts of blood at Harper's Ferry. But this hope had proved vain, and, realizing this, Brown prophesied that God would make his death "a thousand times more valuable to his cause" than all the "miserable service" he had ever achieved while alive.[3] It would take a Civil War—a war that would sacrifice 600,000 lives "upon the altar of the nation"—to complete the abolitionist work for which John Brown had been willing to kill and die.[4]

The story of John Brown and American slavery offers one window onto a far-ranging and thoroughly ambivalent relationship between religion and violence in the making of America. In this way, it raises overarching questions that pertain to other episodes of the nation's history:

- How should observers appraise the actions and justifications of those who have resorted to violence? Do moral ends justify violent means? If so, are there limits to such means? How should we distinguish—if we should—between the violent episodes of private groups and the government's use of force, including the collective violence of wars waged on behalf of the nation?
- What is the relationship between "extreme" episodes of violence in American society—committed by or against minority or "fringe" groups—and the broader social issues or violent struggles to which they call attention?
- Finally, how does understanding various forms of religious belief, identity, and rhetoric help us to interpret the violent episodes in America's past and, in all likelihood, its future as well?

This volume examines episodes from American history in which religion and violence converge and asks what they tell us about the United States and its vexing history. The book's organizing thesis is that the complex intersections of religion and violence afford crucial insight into the meaning behind "America"—its history, ideals, character, identity, sense of purpose, and place in the world. In particular, noble promises and ensuing successes and failures tell a story of America's ongoing effort to reconcile conflicting claims between majority and minority populations. While such conflicts are found in many nations, they are particularly acute for a "nation of immigrants" whose people, government, and founding principles are committed explicitly to religious liberty, pluralism, and diversity in many forms.

The story of John Brown—and the cultural, religious, and ethical issues it raises—serves as an entry point to the study of religion and violence in the American context. We begin by unpacking key terms—*religion* and *violence*—and their range of meanings, associations, and connections. The insights and limitations of recent scholarship in the growing field of religion and violence provide an important backdrop to the U.S. context. We then discuss the framing idioms of this work—*jeremiad* and *jihad*—as a way of investigating the American experience of religion and violence. Finally, after a brief summary of the diverse and discordant history of religion in America, we outline the volume's structure and present a preview of its contents.

DEFINING RELIGION AND VIOLENCE

John Brown's haunting legacy can be glimpsed by visitors to the Kansas state capitol in Topeka. There, on the second floor, a massive mural of Brown by the renowned regionalist painter John Steuart Curry depicts Kansas's troubled past. Curry's work, *Tragic Prelude*, which appears on this volume's cover, vividly portrays John Brown's fraught relationship to Kansas—if not to the entire nation. Before the raid at Harper's Ferry, Brown had been a "free-stater"—someone who moved to Kansas to help prevent the spread of slavery there. In the 1856 massacre at Pottawatomie Creek, he led a tiny war party to avenge the killing of several free-staters. By the end of a long evening in May, Brown and his "Northern Army" had broken into three homes and hacked five people to death using broadswords and Bowie knives. That none of the victims seem to have owned slaves was irrelevant, since they had all desired that Kansas become a slave state. "Bleeding Kansas" became the well-suited moniker for the civil strife that plagued the state, and, when conceiving his mural masterpiece, Curry painted John Brown as its personification writ large.

In Curry's mural an oversized Brown towers over the Kansas heartland, his fiery and tempestuous spirit engraved on his face, as if connected to, yet also holding at bay, the natural disasters in the background: one side is overtaken by prairie fire while a tornado threatens the other. The smoke and tornado converge at the top, separated by the turbulent Brown, whose outstretched arms create a clearing in the air—a thin swath of clarity that hovers above the discord and slaughter of the Civil War depicted below him. With outstretched arms, Brown stands between Union and Confederate fighters half his size; Brown appears literally larger than life. At his enormous feet are two dead soldiers, one from each side. In one of his powerful bloodstained hands, Brown grasps a Bible, in the other a Beecher Bible (as the rifle named after evangelist and passionate Civil War advocate Henry Ward Beecher would be called). A sheathed cutlass and holstered revolver hang about the warrior's waist. Brown's long white beard whips in the wind while the shock of upright hair on his head seems to resist it, imparting an air of deliverance. (Were his rifle replaced with a staff and the Bible with stone tablets, Brown's physical likeness to Moses, à la Charlton Heston, would be uncanny.) Blacks are portrayed both courageously and compassionately, either fighting for the North or suffering under the South. Elsewhere in the painting, settlers in the backdrop wearily make their way across the windswept prairie. Lofty aspirations, unbidden by nature and history, shine through in the state's motto *ad astra per aspera*: roughly translated, "to the stars through difficulties." Bleeding Kansas was but a prelude to the national "difficulties" surrounding slavery, secession, and war that would tear the nation apart.[5]

When Curry completed *Tragic Prelude* in 1940, many Kansans were displeased. The Kansas Council of Women protested Curry's obsession with "freaks"—freaks of history like Brown, freaks of nature like tornadoes and fires. "The murals do not portray the true Kansas," they complained. The state legislature ordered Curry to discontinue his work on several other murals commissioned for the capitol. In disgust, Curry refused to sign any of them. The unappreciated artist died a few years later, having never recovered from the rejection.[6]

Artists like Curry are not the only ones challenged by thorny problems of representation and interpretation. Worries over how to depict the "true Kansas" resemble in many ways current worries about how religion (or "true religion") should be represented. The problem is particularly acute in an age in which terrorism, war, and violence so dominate both popular and scholarly imaginations. If John Brown were catapulted into the present, people today might question whether he "hijacked" Christianity to justify his actions, much as some Kansans accused him (and Curry) of hijacking their state's identity. Many would observe how Brown's apparently sincere religious motives seem inextricably linked to his violence. Others, though, might point out how few people, Christian or otherwise, acted as extremely as Brown did. Still another approach would be to scrutinize whether there is such a thing as "true Christianity" (or a "true Kansas") that Brown's actions besmirched. In light of such problems of representation and implicit assumptions about religion and violence, it is prudent not to treat these terms as self-evident. In puzzling over their connections, one must be cautious about essentialization: defining terms so as to accent a particular essence—as if religion inherently possesses violent (or nonviolent) tendencies.

It is both practically difficult and heuristically unhelpful to offer simple definitions of religion and violence—especially for a multiauthored volume in which diverse contributors work with different presumptions, approaches, and viewpoints. Rather than defining these contested terms and their interconnections, then, this section proposes a range of associated meanings, cautions, and considerations to guide readers' encounters with the chapters ahead.

Violence, on its surface, would seem to require no thorough explication. Colloquially, the term characterizes a range of occurrences involving physical force (*vis*) that cause destruction or harm. While storms and collisions may be violent, this is a book about human violence, involving individual physical attacks as well as political violence such as rebellion, oppression, and war. Most contributors to this volume presume at least this expansive meaning. Some focus especially on the normative dimensions, noting that the word is often loaded with judgment and carries presumptive negative connotations. Consider that one must attach adjectives such as "justified" or, perhaps, "righteous" to correct this presumption or to legitimate a violent act. In this sense, violence, like aggression, connotes a different valence from terms like *self-defense* and *force*. States regularly distinguish violence from legal coercion and the threat of force that upholds the law. This does not mean that states do not resort to violence, of course. Clearly, they do. Moreover, when states are accused of being violent, implying etymologically a violation (from Latin *violare*), an ethical and political critique is usually implicit.[7] Disentanglement and discernment about such terminology is no simple task. Violence involves subjects and objects the experiences and perceptions of which are conditioned by culture and history. Violence is committed and justified either as a response to this history or in order to shape a new one.

Violence often connotes passion (from *violentus*, meaning vehement), as Curry's mural depicts in the face of John Brown. Yet violence can also be argued in rational terms, as Brown himself did (and "just war" claims seek to do). As well, John Brown's charges against slavery remind us that laws violating basic ethical and political principles do their own kind of violence. As such, legal forms of coercion and threats of enforcement may entail violence short of the actual use of force. The chapters in this book present no single account of violence. The range of denotations and connotations of violence draws attention to the variety of ways that events, institutions, actors, and communities can be interpreted: from the state's coercive use of force, to destructive acts carried out by individuals and groups, to imagined violence, vitriolic rhetoric, and the powerful ideologies that underwrite or encourage them. Various authors take up not simply wars, rebellions, and attacks but also what Mark Juergensmeyer has termed "cultures of violence"—the legal, social, and political contexts surrounding them.[8] As readers puzzle over varying accounts of violence in the pages ahead, it is worth keeping in mind the complex interplay among its many dimensions.

The task of defining religion, particularly in its relationship to violence, is both challenging and significant. For many scholars, religion entails those discourses, beliefs, institutions, and practices (and their associated rituals, myths, symbols, and creeds) through which individuals and communities understand and order their lives around an ultimate, sacred, or transcendent reality (often conceived in relation to God or other divinities). Much scholarship in the twenty-first century has foregrounded religion's apparent connection to or propensity for violence, with considerable attention to "evil" religion or terror emanating from the mind of or in the name of God.[9] Much religion and violence literature reinforces—albeit in more nuanced scholarly ways—presumptions found in many public sectors. For many people, events such as the Crusades, the European "wars of religion," and the attacks of September 11, 2001, are stark symbols of the violence that can be expected when religion "goes public," collides with politics, or unleashes its violent undercurrents.

More recently, other scholars have sought to deconstruct the "myth of religious violence" to show how modern societies have invented and used the category "religion" to shroud or justify violence, particularly as committed by putatively secular states.[10] These critiques often reflect the influence of anthropologist Talal Asad, who has argued that definitions of religion themselves have performed a kind of violence by injecting normative assumptions about religion into social and political discourses; the result has been to incline cultures and legal authorities to marginalize or persecute groups that do not conform to a prescribed Western vision of "religion" usually understood as rational, privatistic, even universal.[11]

If a shortcoming of much religion and violence scholarship has been to focus on extreme elements either beyond the United States or at the "fringes" of American society—thereby overlooking the role that mainstream forms of religion and violence have played in U.S. society—then myth-breaking scholars in the latter group are prone to understate the quite real connections between religion and violence as more than humanly constructed categories. The observation also can be stated affirmatively: there is some truth to both of these approaches. For these reasons, when studying violence in the American context it is vital to understand the different forms, both explicit and subtle, that religion has taken in authorizing or containing violence.

In the United States, definitions of religion have long reflected a Protestant—or at least a Christian—influence and, throughout much of its history, have favored what Bruce Lincoln calls "religious minimalism."[12] Religious minimalism suits secular societies that distinguish religion along public-private lines. The term does not necessarily mean *less* religious; it simply refers to an outlook that presupposes a narrow range of questions on which religion exercises influence: matters of ultimate meaning, expectations about life after death, and issues of social interaction—but generally not (or not ostensibly) major social, economic, political, or foreign policy issues.[13] However minimalistic, this form of religion has operated in the background of many prominent instances of violence, coercion, and war in American life.

American history also is full of individual men and women and entire communities—frequently labeled as "extreme"—who have either practiced or attempted to practice more "maximalist" strains of religion: explicit, public displays of religious belief (or actions informed by religious belief) that challenge or appear to challenge the premises of secular or religiously minimalist societies. John Brown is one such example; the Amish, the Oneida Perfectionists, and the Shakers are others. There have been many minority groups, the early Mormon movement being a famous example, that have been religiously maximalist while also committed to demonstrating their "American-ness." In other cases, religious maximalists such as the Branch Davidians and the Heaven's Gate movement have directly challenged the compatibility between their religious beliefs and American identity (or at least the U.S. government). Religious minimalists, for their part, often have questioned the "American-ness" of both these kinds of minority movements, by subjecting them to coercion or state-sanctioned violence. In the process, so-called religious minimalists—usually speaking on behalf of a Protestant majority—may not observe the boundaries between "religion" and "the secular" that they wish to enforce on others. In fact, as we will see, those struggling to "contain" a particular maximalist religion or to define strictly the boundaries of legitimate religious influence often have been driven by visions of "proper" religion more powerful, normative, and expansive than those they oppose. This book presumes that it is vital to examine the violence carried out by religious actors in both their minimalist and maximalist forms; and it shows how the broader cultural and historical lessons to be drawn about American violence often emerge from the interplay between those with religiously minimalist and maximalist affinities.

Several contributors, working with such insights, examine acts of violence fueled by conflicts over what constitutes "religion" and what legitimate or legally permissible religious behavior entails. Many authors also work with a conception of religion that extends beyond rituals, sacred texts, and doctrine to ideas and images from the popular press, literature, film, and political speeches. In American society and culture, religion is found every bit as much in the tropes that shape speech, the interpretive lenses through which people see the world, and intellectual frameworks that shape their judgments, as it is in the pews of churches, the sermons of imams, or the fasts and rites of holy days.

This book also devotes a great deal of space to the consideration of Christianity (often Protestant Christianity) and its influences in the United States. Christians are not the sole actors in most of the chapters that follow, but they are among the actors in every chapter. Given the longstanding religious diversity of North America and the fact that Christians have no monopoly on religion and violence, one might expect greater attention to acts of religion and violence perpetrated by Native Americans, Jews, and other religious minorities. The lesser focus on these groups as perpetrators of violence (though not as imagined enemies and as victims) reflects a feature of religious violence as committed and as considered. When we study religious violence we tend to focus on public rather than private episodes. Wars and cross burnings draw more attention than violence in the home, and with few exceptions in American history, most moments of violence or war have been authored by Christians against other Christians or against religious "others." Quite simply, for reasons of demographics, political power, and history, the study of religion and violence in America requires devoting a large amount of space to Christianity. At the same time, one must remain alert to diversity within and beyond American Christianity and to the normative power of the term *religion,* the boundaries of which were established in the United States by religious minimalists of many faiths, but which are regularly contested culturally, theologically, and legally.

This book does not seek to put a halo on American history and policies, especially the violent aspects of either. But neither is its primary task to find "imperial violence" and "blessed brutalities" in every corner of American history and culture.[14] The story is more complicated than either approach permits. In some cases, violence, or responses to it, foreground noble elements in America's past, even when imperfectly implemented or realized. In other cases, the most reprehensible episodes in America's past clearly are stained with blood. But whether for good or for ill, the character and sensibilities of such violence, or reactions to it, often have been religiously informed or can be religiously explained to yield a picture that defies oversimplification. As a whole, this book neither partakes in America-bashing nor takes on those who do. Rather, it seeks to raise deeper questions and concerns that anyone interested in earnestly understanding America's past can ill afford to ignore.

In exploring the intersections of religion and violence, this volume generally avoids talk of "religious violence," which too easily overlooks the religiously minimalist character of secular societies and too readily essentializes religion for its violent propensities. In determining what episodes qualify as a convergence of religion and violence, certain recurring criteria have been helpful: (1) A moment in which men or women fought or killed each other, openly claiming divine sanction or explanation for their actions. Where historical actors have conceived their violence in religious terms, we have taken them at their word. (2) A struggle between groups or parties differentiated importantly by religious identity. This might include struggles between a state or federal government, ostensibly secular yet shaped and led by Protestant figures and ideas, against some "other" religion or "cult," whether Mormon, Muslim, or Native American. (3) Violence framed by or described in terms of clearly religious idioms or frameworks. For example, from wars of the colonial era to World War I and the Cold War, the concept of covenant has played an important role. Although these and other struggles were arguably not *about* religion at the core, understanding the force of the religious

concepts on which they rely is an important part of understanding how participants conceived the conflicts and responded to them.

THE FOREIGN AND THE FAMILIAR:
JEREMIAD AND JIHAD

Controversy over how to remember—or even to depict or describe—John Brown
and his legacy vexed American culture at the time of his death and continues to
do so today. Representative of some of Brown's contemporary abolitionists, William Lloyd Garrison eulogized the "martyr" and used his death to beseech others
to follow his rigorous Christian stand—not through violent revolt but through
Northern secession.[15] Henry David Thoreau hallowed Brown as "an angel of light."
Victor Hugo called him a "fighter for Christ," while Ralph Waldo Emerson lik-
ened Brown to Christ himself, remarking that Brown would make the gallows
"as glorious as the cross." But such views were far from the norm. Even throughout the North and among many abolitionists, Brown was roundly condemned.
However noble his antislavery commitments, his rebellious actions outweighed
the cause. In addition to condemnations from many of the leading newspapers,
both the Great Emancipator Abraham Lincoln and the great novelist of American Puritanism Nathaniel Hawthorne labeled Brown a "fanatic" (according to
Hawthorne a "bloodstained fanatic," for Lincoln, simply a "misguided" one).[16]
Hawthorne added that no man was ever more justly hanged than John Brown.

Poets taking to their pens after Brown's execution portrayed him in various
ways, as suggested in the title of William Keeney's essay "Hero, Martyr, Madman." Keeney observes that to the extent that early Brown poets "fail to address
the subject of violence, they also fail by misrepresenting Brown . . . [including]
the facts, his motives, and his state of mind; and in doing this they misrepresent
his importance."[17] Keeney attributes this omission to the Brown poets' own ambivalence about the institutionalized violence of slavery. History textbooks, for
their part, have alternated between questioning Brown's sanity and emphasizing
his "religious fanaticism," on one hand, and labeling him, as in one 1995 text, a
"martyr to the cause of freedom and justice."[18] The difficulty of reconciling the
discordant representations of Brown stems directly from Americans' much
deeper ambivalence about violence itself.

Debates over how to remember John Brown and his legacy continue. In 2009
the United States commemorated—or at least recognized—the 150th anniversary
of John Brown's death. Major museum exhibitions, significant media coverage,
and national reflection about Brown's life were on display.[19] Biographer David
Reynolds called for the president and governor of Virginia to pardon Brown.[20]
The *New York Times* published Reynolds's editorial on December 2, the date Brown

was executed—opposite an editorial by another Brown chronicler who reminded readers that Brown "sought not only to free slaves in Virginia but to terrorize the South and incite broad conflict." In this regard, Tony Horwitz averred, Brown's aims were the same as those of the September 11 terrorists.[21] Meanwhile, everyday people continue to disagree. While some still consider Brown a madman, religious zealot, or an instigator of the Civil War, others take Brown at his own word. According to the caretaker for the Brown homestead, who shows the grounds to hundreds of pilgrims each year, "I personally believe that he was chosen to do this great work. He did exactly what he was instructed by a much higher power than you or I."[22] Brown's legacy and the lessons about violence he leaves for Americans are far from resolved.

As a way of exploring further such ambivalence surrounding religion and violence, two tropes, *jeremiad* and *jihad*, figure prominently throughout this book. At a basic level, these terms establish its chronological framework: from early American colonists' violent encounters with Native Americans to the "war against terrorism" in the twenty-first century. The *jeremiad* has been a feature of American public discourse since the founding of the Massachusetts Bay Colony in 1630, as sermons, essays, and political speeches of the time demonstrate. Taking its name from the prophet Jeremiah, the jeremiad is a biblically rooted, sustained lament about a nation or people and their failure to live up to divinely ordained ideals. Sacvan Bercovitch describes three main features of the seventeenth-century Puritan jeremiad: "first, a precedent from Scripture that sets out the communal norms; then a series of condemnations that details the actual state of the community (at the same time insinuating the covenantal promises that ensure success); and finally a prophetic vision that unveils the promises, announces the good things to come, and explains away the gap between fact and ideal."[23] Many chapters of this book look to the heyday of the American jeremiad, when Puritan divines in Massachusetts interpreted victory and defeat as signs of divine favor and wrath. They were followed by leaders of the Revolution (and later generations of Americans) who adapted the Puritan jeremiad and transformed it into a vital strand of what became an enduring American political and cultural creed.

Jihad, the Arabic word meaning "effort" or "exertion" to follow the path of God, has only recently become part of the common American lexicon. Jihad refers to a struggle that can involve (and has involved) violence or resistance against perceived enemies of Islam.[24] The terrorist attacks of September 11, 2001—waged by self-declared Muslim jihadists who viewed the United States as their greatest threat—made jihad an indelible part of the American experience. As well, on that day jihad converged with jeremiad as elements on America's left and right both interpreted al Qaeda's attack as the United States' bitter harvest for its various acts of immorality. This convergence serves as a crystallizing moment of recognition, inviting reflection upon a much longer history of religion and violence involving the United States.

In addition to the historical arc extending from Puritan jeremiad to anti-American jihad, these multivalent tropes offer useful conceptual tools for discerning, distinguishing, and comparing various modes and episodes of violence committed by and against Americans. Objective scholarly analysis benefits from making the seemingly familiar strange.[25] Placing these tropes together—combining the foreign with the familiar—invites a fresh reconsideration and evaluation of their meanings and significance for our global age. For the reality is that jeremiad and jihad have more in common than first meets the eye. Indeed, one may very well find that twenty-first-century American Muslims, like seventeenth-century Puritans, easily become stereotypes when a simplistic understanding of these terms is embraced. Scholars of Islam note that jihad is a command that pertains to all Muslims (not simply to militants) and that only the "lesser jihad" actually entails violence or force.[26] The "greater jihad" entails the internal struggle to live a righteous life and follow God's will, in accordance with one's faith. Surely, in this sense, Puritans sought similar goals—as do many people of faith today.

Consider, further, the fragility of community acknowledged and implied in jeremiadic rhetoric. Puritans began their "errand into the wilderness" as a religious minority, eager to create a "new world" that conformed to their faith. As Sacvan Bercovitch relates, "The purpose of their jeremiads was to direct an imperiled people of God toward the fulfillment of their destiny, to guide them individually toward salvation, and collectively toward the American city of God."[27] Similarly, from Sayyid Qutb in the 1950s to Muslim militants today, one finds concerns to protect a faith imperiled by corruption and the impure advances of Islam's enemies.

While the American jeremiad may have emerged out of a uniquely Puritan heritage, Bercovitch also details the gradual transformation of the jeremiad into a trope of consensus and renewal that has continually expanded the American mythos beyond its exclusivist origins. Bercovitch points to the "unswerving faith in the errand" among figures as diverse as Jefferson, Thoreau, Lincoln, Whitman, and King.[28] Through the rhetoric of promise, condemnation, and renewal, Americans of diverse backgrounds and persuasions have turned the jeremiad into a rhetorical device that has created consensus around aims such as technological progress and modernization, economic expansion, and increased individual liberty. Momentous struggles to achieve consensus also have involved the fulfillment of foundational U.S. principles and commitments such as the extension of natural and civil rights to all citizens. Jeremiads have warned of the costs of failure to live up to such ideals even while promising that devotion to these ideals would bring about renewal. In this sense, the jeremiad has been a recurring motif used in the effort to integrate minorities into the ongoing project of defining and expanding American identity.

Few founding ideals have been as important to the United States as the promise of religious freedom. Of course, this promise has been kept imperfectly. Many Muslim Americans in the early twenty-first century have found themselves the most recent victims of the American tendency to question religious minorities' qualifications for citizenship. Throughout U.S. history, religious minorities have been compelled to show that they are capable of being "good Americans." Since September 11, 2001—and peaking again nearly a decade later during congressional hearings on Muslim radicalization and amidst a controversy over building an Islamic center and mosque near the former site of the World Trade Center— Muslim Americans have struggled with how to be recognized as part of the American consensus. They may be waging an inner jihad to live according to their faith, but when they appeal to the American promise of religious freedom, they stand in a long, distinctly American tradition of the jeremiad.

Viewed these ways, neither jeremiad nor jihad by definition promotes violence. Yet both have been implicated in violence. The jeremiad has served as a way for Puritans and other religious Americans (especially Protestant majorities) to vocalize fears about declining faith or to issue "prophecies of Godlessness."[29] Concerns about non-Protestant immigrants and the adulteration of a "Christian nation" have been a recurrent feature of U.S. history. Some have looked upon such religious "impurity" as a call to action—and have acted with laws and extralegal violence against Catholics, Quakers, Jews, Buddhists, Hindus, Muslims, and Sikhs. Indeed, Protestant hegemony, some contend, is central to the myth of religious freedom. Challenges to this hegemony and moments of its forceful assertion have elicited jeremiadic rhetoric from those seeking to "protect America" or its Protestant establishment. Similarly, challenges to the rights of non-Protestant or non-Christian practitioners have generated jeremiads focused on America's failure to fulfill noble promises of religious freedom. Even efforts by modern U.S. courts to define religion, ostensibly to uphold religious freedom, have undermined those whose religion did not meet certain legal definitions established by those who belonged to a religious majority.[30] When the U.S. government has used coercive force to back such interpretations of legitimate or illegitimate religion, it has been accused of waging violence—even while simultaneously defending its commitment to religious freedom. Jihad also has served violent ends, most famously in the rhetoric of Islamic terrorists. But whether defined as a struggle against one's religious enemies or against immoral impulses within, efforts to purge or purify have been found not only in Muslim cultures but also in predominantly Christian and even secular ones.

Violence has been a critical fault line in America's struggles between majority and minority populations. Jeremiad and jihad serve as tropological devices for examining such struggles and evaluating their causes, complexities, and potential resolutions. Recall the case of John Brown. Should we remember him as a jeremiadic figure? A jihadist? Perhaps as both? The religious grounding of Brown's abolitionism is well known, but Brown was a radical in more ways than one. Biographer Stephen Oates observes that Brown was known to have been influenced by *Liberator* editor William Lloyd Garrison, whose "ringing pronouncements that slave owners were unregenerate sinners and that slavery itself violated both the Higher Law of God and the principles of the Declaration of Independence" provided "a splendid antislavery argument which Brown himself adopted."[31] Indeed, Brown had drafted his own "Declaration of Liberty by the Representatives of the Slave Populations of the United States of America." The striking similarity in language to the original U.S. Declaration makes clear how pivotal America's founding ideals were to Brown's abolitionist cause and call for renewal:

> When in the course of Human events, it becomes necessary for an oppressed People to Rise, and assert their Natural Rights, as Human Beings, as Native and Mutual Citizens of a free Republic, and break that odious yoke of oppression, which is so unjustly laid upon them by their fellow countrymen, and to assume among the powers of Earth the same equal privileges to which the Laws of Nature, and nature's God entitle, them; A moderate respect for the opinions of Mankind, requires that they should declare the causes which incite them to this just & worthy action.[32]

Brown may have been radical, but he spoke the rationalist vernacular of natural rights and the distinctly American language of consensus. He invoked America's founding principles—"eternal and self-evident truths"—and the failure to live up to them. On what basis, then, could Brown be called a traitor, when he clearly championed American ideals? Moreover, he extolled a form of "civil religion" that would be rearticulated by many greats of American history, including Martin Luther King Jr.

Brown also was very much on the fringe of society, giving voice to a minority view and speaking out on behalf of other minorities. Moved within by deep Calvinist stirrings, he rejected Garrison's religious "perfectionism," which sought to transform society through the power of words not violence.[33] Brown's piety—along with his conviction that Satan was not simply lurking in the "hellish system" of slavery but actively administering it—led him down a very different path. If slavery was the "most barbarous, unprovoked, and unjustifiable war of one portion of its citizens upon another portion," as Brown's constitution had stated, then one who waged battle against such a system must surely be a righteous warrior.[34] Is it too much to say that Brown's pious cause simultaneously embodied both a greater and lesser jihad?

It should be no surprise that Brown's violence emerged as he straddled the ambiguous terrain between consensus and fringe, between majority and minority, between patriot and traitor. Violence, coercion, and war often signal the struggle to define consensus, as the Civil War attests. This insight should be kept in mind as one encounters the stories in the pages that follow. For it is all too easy to dismiss violence or even war as aberrational: the antics of the irrational, the extreme, or the fanatical—or moments of collective crisis and destruction that are separated from the peaceful side of America's "true" character.[35] Indeed, the term *violence* is often used to discount individuals and groups who fail to conform just as it shuts down serious consideration of the connection between war and peace. But sometimes what is most revealing is not the actions of the "fringe" but the *reactions* of the "mainstream." Similarly, extreme moments of violence and war offer a window onto American identity and consciousness, inviting reflection and interpretation, appreciation and critique, justification and condemnation— in other words, ambivalence. This is where the craft of scholarly reflection on religion and the disciplinary tools of the trade perform their work.

A BRIEF OVERVIEW OF RELIGION AND VIOLENCE IN THE UNITED STATES

The convergence of religion and violence in the United States has been fueled by the diverse and discordant nature of its religious life. Americans embody a staggering array of religious beliefs and styles, from atheism to Zoroastrianism, from the Assemblies of God to Zen Buddhism. There are faithful of most of the world's religions living and practicing in the United States. While globalization and immigration have added (and continue to add) new layers of diversity, religious diversity is nothing new to the Americas. Prior to European contact and conquest of the so-called New World, Native Americans from the Caribbean to the Puget Sound lived and worshipped in hundreds if not thousands of different ways. Spanish and French Catholics—and, later, Protestants from England, Holland, Germany, and France—brought distinct and often divergent understandings of Christian faith to the Americas. This significant intra- and interfaith diversity grew with the mid-seventeenth-century addition of enslaved Africans (some of whom practiced tribal religions, some of whom were Muslim) and Sephardic Jews. By the time the United States had achieved independence, it was a picture of religious diversity relative to its time. Significant communities of Catholics, Lutherans, Quakers, Jews, Baptists, Congregationalists, Presbyterians, Episcopalians, Enlightenment Rationalists, and the nonaffiliated and nonreligious shaped the early national religious landscape. Throughout the nineteenth century, American Protestantism added new movements and submovements at breathtaking speed. America's Catholic churches incorporated first Irish and German immigrants and, eventually, millions more from Europe (primarily Italy and Poland) and from the Americas (primarily Mexico). In spite of intermittent efforts to eliminate or at least to contain this diversity, it grew and proliferated. At no time has America been anything but religiously diverse.

Given such religious diversity, it may surprise some that religious violence has not held as prominent a place in American history as, say, "wars of religion" have for modern Europe. Nevertheless, revealing points of contact between religion and violence go back to America's beginnings. For discord within and among religious communities in North America is as old as religious diversity itself. Native American tribes struggled against each other over resources, pitting cosmology against cosmology, sanctified warrior against sanctified warrior. European conquerors, often rapacious, nearly always condescending, killed, enslaved, and raped individual natives and eradicated or radically suppressed entire indigenous cultures. The actions of these men (rarely women) often were justified by citing the power of Christianity to "civilize" and save souls. As European powers and their colonists worried about and sometimes waged wars against enemies whom they strategically cast as "Catholic" or "Protestant," they also used coercive or violent means within their societies to punish error, purge difference, or enforce a particular moral vision. The Massachusetts Bay Colony's penchant for violent intolerance—manifested famously in the 1638 trial and expulsion of Anne Hutchinson, the 1660 hanging of Quaker Mary Dyer, and the Salem witch trials of 1692—was extreme but not unique. Peter Stuyvesant, governor of New Amsterdam, famously banned (and publicly tortured) Quakers and attempted to ban Jews from the colony; meanwhile Maryland's liberal-minded Act Concerning Religion (1649), authored by its Catholic governor, promised to enforce a ban on incendiary religious language with fines, imprisonment, whipping, and, for those who denied the divinity of Christ, death. In the 1760s itinerant evangelists who violated Virginia's licensing laws for preachers were jailed, placed in stocks, beaten, and urinated upon by taunting mobs.

Far more frequently than it has served as the overt cause of violent interactions, religion has been operative in the background culture of American violence. Familiar moments of war or state-sanctioned violence—such as the Revolutionary War, the War of 1812, the Mexican-American War, the Civil War, the so-called Indian Wars, the Spanish-American War, and the Great War—have been infused with religious rhetoric and faith-based "othering." These memorable wars often united Americans as memories of "shared sacrifice" fueled an emerging "civil religion." In other cases, though, violence divided religiously diverse Americans, pitting an ostensibly secular state against religious minorities: Protestant discrimination against (and occasional physical attacks on) Catholics;

state and sectarian violence against the Mormon movement; and the steady drumbeats of racism and anti-Semitism that accompanied both legalized repression and extralegal violence against African Americans and Jews.

In spite of apparent increasing secularization, the twentieth century witnessed violence at home and abroad in which religion played an important role. From the racial violence and ever-percolating Red scares of the 1900s and 1910s to the violent crackdowns on the civil rights movement of the 1950s and 1960s and a full-fledged Cold War fought at home and abroad, Christian men and women drew upon scripture and cited the words of their clergy to justify the struggles both for and against a host of causes such as segregation and capitalism. In 1935 Carey McWilliams reported from the agricultural valleys of California that Christian ministers were lending their voices to both sides of shockingly violent labor disputes. Some clergy goaded local vigilantes to deadly confrontations with organized labor and communist and socialist sympathizers; others provided comfort and encouragement to striking migrant farm workers from Mexico, the Philippines, Japan, Portugal, and America's own drought-ravaged plains, some of whom did not turn the other cheek.[36]

From the outset, the twenty-first century has renewed concern about religion's linkages to violence. More than any other event, the attacks of September 11, 2001, reminded the world of the cover and comfort violence can find in religion. Yet many also worried about the reliance of the George W. Bush administration upon a worrisome "foreign policy pietism."[37] Some went further to accuse President Bush of construing the entire "war on terror" through religious lenses, the Manichean nature of which increased the violence in his campaign to defeat "evildoers."[38] Needless to say, U.S. wars in Afghanistan and Iraq as well as more covert military actions in other nations make clear that U.S. reliance upon force or violence (depending upon one's view) remains central to the effort to defeat terrorists who often find inspiration in their religion. All of this is to say nothing of the even more controversial tactics that have been sanctioned by the U.S. government such as coercive interrogations that, say many, amount to torture. In an open letter to President Bush denouncing the measures he authorized, Andrew Sullivan observed the techniques' inescapably religious dimensions, which "depended for their effectiveness on the specific religious and cultural beliefs of Muslims. So to wage a war designed to expose the evil of the Taliban's religious intolerance, we deliberately manipulated Islam into a means of abuse. In a war designed to prove that the West was not Islam's enemy, we used Islam and Muslim culture as tools to break down the psyches of prisoners suspected of terrorism. To save religious freedom, we abused it."[39]

Upon taking office, President Barack Obama renounced harsh interrogation tactics, rearticulated his campaign promise to withdraw U.S. troops from Iraq, and pledged to close the Guantánamo Bay detention facility. Three years into his presidency, however, the facility was still open. As well, the president committed an additional 30,000 U.S. troops to support a surge in Afghanistan, authorized an ambitious covert mission in Pakistan to assassinate Osama bin-Laden, and significantly increased the use of unmanned aerial drone strikes in Afghanistan and Pakistan, well surpassing his predecessor's record. Additionally, other controversial instruments of power, including indefinite detentions and military tribunals for terrorists, have remained in place. Even as President Obama accepted the Nobel Peace Prize and recalled Martin Luther King Jr.'s renunciation of violence, he reminded his audience that "evil does exist in the world"; that the duties of his office included use of the instruments of force, which "have a role to play in preserving peace"; and that just war thinking could be a useful guide in this effort—a view shared by many Americans.[40] While condemning holy war and religious violence, he made no mention of how crucial religious ideas have been to the formation of the just war tradition; the point simply illustrates how easily Americans can overlook the religious dimensions of their wars. It seems that until the day that religiously inflected ideas and rhetoric no longer inform American policies, or until religious diversity no longer characterizes American society and the wider world of which it is part, religion, violence, and America will remain fascinatingly, if sometimes disturbingly, intertwined.

THEMES AND CONTENTS

Tracing the many faces of religion, force, violence, and war in America's domestic record and history of foreign affairs requires methodological breadth and diversity. A comprehensive account calls for multiple authors and the various disciplinary approaches—historical, ethical, political, cultural, theological, and rhetorical—they bring to the problem. Scholars who study religion—from either within or outside the field of religious studies—are well positioned to frame and engage the complex historical, cultural, and ethical questions that mark intersections of religion and violence in American history. They bring to this task not only expertise in the religious traditions involved and invoked, but also knowledge afforded by the wide range of methodological approaches that the study of religion entails. At their best, these approaches include deep and responsible engagement with the past, careful comparison of religious traditions and practices, critical analysis of the reciprocal influences between religious traditions and the broader culture, and normative evaluation of the ethical principles, reasoning, and justifications for the resort to violence. This book seeks to bring such approaches together by combining historical analysis, critical reflection, and ethical discernment. While not every chapter seeks to do all of those things equally—or equally well—collectively, the following chapters show that all these approaches are necessary to understand violence, religion, and how the relationship between them has informed the American experience. This work prods readers to ask thorny questions about the cultural and ideological influences that contributed to and were reflected in specific violent episodes. It also models a range of responses to the deep moral questions and issues that, coursing through every essay, are never far removed from intersections of religion and violence.

When religion and violence converge, at least in the American experience, several persistent questions and themes often emerge. Bearing these in mind will enhance the ability to analyze, synthesize, or contrast the vast array of subjects discussed in the following pages. The multivalent religious dimensions of the motivations, explanations, and repercussions of various violent actions raise a variety of questions worth pondering: Specifically, how have different parties understood religion as an acceptable (or unacceptable) resource for justifying, interpreting, or responding to violence? What were the goals or outcomes at stake—religious or otherwise—for perpetrators and for victims of violence? When and where has religion proved to be a valuable resource for providing clarity or a sensitive moral compass? How have some found in religion comfort for false certainty, arrogance, or rash actions? Finally, but perhaps most importantly, what do such queries and attendant responses suggest about the United States' history, identity, and global status?

The three parts of this book bring together chapters on the basis of the common phenomena they examine and the questions they ask. Part I features chapters on religious justifications for and explanations of violence; Part II examines American constructions of the religious "other"; Part III focuses on ethical questions about war and violence.

Religious origins and tropes of violence. The chapters in Part I explore how religious idioms and theological beliefs—jeremiad, covenant, providence—give meaning to various interpretations of America's history, purpose, or place in the world. These religious tropes have served to explain America's failures as well as it successes, often showing how violence, war, and suffering have been indispensable symbols of both. Political scientist Andrew Murphy and colleague Elizabeth Hanson begin the book by displaying the long pedigree of Americans' tendency to understand violence against them as divine punishment for their sinfulness. In turn, Americans have often portrayed their violence as divine retribution against God's enemies. After examining the jeremiads preached in response to King Philip's War, the American Civil War, and the attacks of September 11, 2001, the authors question whether belief in covenantal chosenness must necessarily be linked to violence. S. Brent Rodriguez-Plate, a scholar of religion and film studies, shows how religious tropes and symbols are projected onto the silver screen. Examining D. W. Griffith's *Birth of a Nation* and Paul Thomas Anderson's *There Will Be Blood*, Rodriguez-Plate shows how films create narratives about America's origins. In particular, he points to the violence embedded in such "cosmogonies," including how religious symbols and meanings pervade the broader landscape and scenery of American culture, connecting the nation's origins to its present.

Chapters 3 and 4 give particular attention to the motif of covenant that has been so influential in the United States. Historian Jonathan Ebel examines how shifts in America's understanding of this trope unfolded in the experience of World War I and, in particular, the postwar activities of the American Legion. Wartime covenantal rhetoric reveals a consciousness, at least in Woodrow Wilson and American soldiers, of the covenant's vertical reach, which binds a people to a judging God. He shows how the American Legion worked to eliminate this vertical and divine reach, flattening covenantal idioms into purely horizontal—nationalistic, uncritically pro-American—rhetoric. In his study of former Secretary of State John Foster Dulles, Ned O'Gorman describes the enduring power of covenantal themes in the era following World War II. A scholar of rhetoric, O'Gorman examines Dulles's notion of a new international covenant—a controversial contribution to the American diplomatic and military lexicon—and how it sought to bring nations together into a new world order. The consequences for threatening this new international covenant, though, were anything but consistent with "pacific universal goodwill."

Finally, Stephen Webb, a scholar of religion and philosophy, surveys how notions of providence and judgment have been bound up in American nationhood, focusing especially upon the more violent episodes of U.S. wars and expansion. Though Webb provides no uncritical embrace of all things explained by providence, he laments the politicization of providence spawned during the Vietnam War. Webb's essay is itself something of a jeremiad, as he argues that providential thinking and openness to judgment once unified Americans in a way that no longer seems possible in the post-9/11 world.

Religion and America's "others." Part II explores the second key theme of the book, the role of religion in designating or lifting up America's "others." Often this designation of members of certain groups has been a precursor to the use of violence or force against them. Several chapters in Part II examine how the study of rhetoric helps us understand recurring features and justifications of otherwise disparate acts of prejudice, war, or even mass murder. Although many of these chapters take up issues or individuals on the so-called fringes of American society, they say a great deal about mainstream American society and efforts to preserve a particular vision of American identity. In Chapter 6, historian John Corrigan takes the reader into the dark heart of Anglo-American relationships with Native Americans, Catholics, and Mormons to demonstrate the power of sacred scripture to shape perceptions of, and actions against, the religious and cultural "other." Examining the biblical story of the Amalekites (whom, according to the Hebrew scriptures, God twice commanded the Israelites to destroy),

Corrigan shows how those carrying out brutal—indeed genocidal—U.S. government policies conceived them as divinely ordained.

Eddie Glaude Jr., a scholar of African American religion and thought, examines the ways in which religion and violence were woven together during a particularly fraught period in the development of African American national consciousness. He shows how the antebellum speeches of two important black leaders, David Walker and Henry Highland Garnet, drew upon religious language to call for resistance and revolt; their approaches are emblematic of recurring tensions exhibited in African Americans' attempts to confront racism, transcend their status as "other," and achieve full equality as Americans.

In Chapter 8, Todd Kerstetter focuses on violence in the American West in the nineteenth and twentieth centuries. Taking up adversarial and violent relationships between the federal government and Mormons, then Native American Ghost Dancers, and, finally, the Branch Davidians, he shows that these groups (sometimes labeled "cults") have shared more than the same mythic frontier space. Kerstetter argues that they have been "othered" because, as "maximalist" religious movements, they have challenged or threatened the assumptions of a federal government that insists upon and coercively enforces "minimalist" religious practices. Lynn Neal recovers the Ku Klux Klan's anti-Catholic fervor in Chapter 9 by exploring the story of Alma White, founder and bishop of the Pillar of Fire Church. White was hardly a marginalized "other" herself; rather, she was a true trailblazer among early twentieth-century women. Neal shows how White's involvement with the Ku Klux Klan, and her tireless promotion of their Protestant vision of the United States, were part of an effort to fight back against the perceived menace of the Catholic "other." Although White spilled only ink—not blood—her full-throated apologia for the Klan provided written and oral support to the racist and religious bigots who wielded the weapons and burned the crosses.

Finally, Grace Kao examines in Chapter 10 how themes of the religious "other" surrounded the 2007 murder of thirty-two people and its aftermath at Virginia Tech University. As a professor there at the time, Kao combines her firsthand experiences with her insights as a scholar of religion and ethics to examine beliefs about religious terrorism and divine punishment that figured powerfully into popular explanations of this horrific event.

The ethics of violence and war. Part III explores and evaluates religious and ethical justifications of collective violence, including whether and how violence and force (or war) should be distinguished. Situating this discussion within the American context, these chapters tease out religious threads that connect elements of America's founding principles or defining character with the many wars fought on American soil and abroad. Ethicist John Carlson, in exploring the moral and religious arguments for the Revolutionary War, considers whether just war or holy war thinking provides a better ethical frame for understanding the nation's founding conflict. Recovering sermons of Revolutionary-era preacher Josiah Stearns, Carlson proposes how just war thinking in America today might reclaim insights from its earlier days. He then shows how this legacy of the Revolution bears upon contemporary formulations of civil religion and American exceptionalism. Theological ethicist Stanley Hauerwas reaches quite different conclusions about the United States in his study of the Civil War. Discussing the work of historian Harry Stout and analyzing Civil War–era sermons, Hauerwas critiques realist and just war approaches to war. On both Union and Confederate sides, he argues, clerical justifications for war and their fiery sermons helped turn the Civil War into a total war, no matter how just or moral its defenders said it was. The experience forever changed America's relationship to warmaking, Hauerwas claims, and turned the Civil War into a blood sacrifice to the nation: a sacrament in and of itself. This prospect should strike Christians in America as a moral impossibility.

In Chapter 13, just war historian James Turner Johnson examines how U.S. contributions to just war principles concerning war's conduct (*jus in bello*) have sought to limit violence, particularly against noncombatants and civilian populations. He charts important contributions from the U.S. Civil War to those witnessed during humanitarian interventions of the 1990s and various campaigns associated with the "war on terror." Johnson observes that the U.S. commitment to the laws of war contrasts starkly with moral and legal restraints collapsing in other parts of the world. Johnson's chapter considers why so few American just war thinkers from the 1960s to the 1980s—with the crucial exception of the influential ethicist Paul Ramsey—contributed to what has become a significant hallmark of American military action.

This same period, claims Sohail Hashmi, was also formative in the development of militant Islamic thinking about the United States. Hashmi, a political scientist, considers how U.S. foreign policy and involvement in the Middle East shaped Islamist understandings of legitimate violence, reconfigured longstanding assumptions within jihadist discourse about "far enemies" such as the United States, and inspired violent attacks against Americans and American interests, both overseas and on U.S. soil. Casual observers may doubt that al Qaeda's internal disputes over strategy and tactics have much religious content. The reality, though, is that al Qaeda's violence must be understood within Islamists' larger efforts to interpret centuries of qur'anic teachings about jihad, including how and against whom it should be waged. To illuminate fully the nature of al Qaeda's religious violence, Hashmi shows how U.S. foreign policy has shaped the sociopolitical context in which Islamists have read, interpreted, and debated key religious texts, tropes, and traditions.

Political philosopher and ethicist Jean Bethke Elshtain ends the book by pondering and evaluating from an ethical standpoint various construals of violence, coercion, and force associated with the "war on terror." Elshtain describes and discusses three categories of coercive force: "the forbidden" (abuses like those occurring at Abu Ghraib); "the permissible" (justifiable use of force as associated with "just war" principles); and the "morally ambiguous" (coercive interrogation under certain conditions). Only through careful and disciplined reflection on what is meant by violence, she insists, can one begin to gain moral clarity about the justifiability (or unjustifiability) of various facets of the U.S.-led fight against religious extremism and terrorism.

CONCLUSION

During the sesquicentennial of John Brown's death, the state of Kansas witnessed firsthand another "freak" incident. Scott Roeder walked into the Wichita church where Dr. George Tiller worshipped, pointed a pistol at his forehead, and pulled the trigger as Tiller's wife and children looked on. Tiller was the only doctor in Wichita who performed abortions and one of the few in the country who performed late-term abortions. Once apprehended, Roeder was called a religious fanatic, and his sanity was questioned. Yet he defended his actions by invoking a higher power and a higher cause. "From conception forward, it is murder," Roeder said of abortion during his trial. He continued, with no sense of irony, "It is not man's job to take life . . . it is our heavenly father's. He is our creator. He gives and takes life. It is never up to man to take life, only in cases of self-defense or defense of others."[41] Roeder, who had been influenced by televangelist Pat Robertson and was "born again" after watching *The 700 Club*, said his religion and views on abortion went "hand in hand."[42] When asked about the clinic's closure following Tiller's death, the unrepentant Roeder expressed relief: "Good. . . . no more slicing and dicing of the unborn child in the mother's womb and no more needles of poison into the baby's heart to stop the heart from beating, and no more partial-birth abortions."[43] He clearly viewed abortion much as Brown had viewed slavery: an instance of legalized violence.

Some, understandably, will object to mentioning Roeder in the same paragraph with Brown. But as historian David Blight probingly inquires, "Can John Brown remain an authentic American hero in an age of Timothy McVeigh, Usama bin Laden, and the bombers of abortion clinics?"[44] The fact that both Brown and Roeder committed murder, appealed to a higher law, and justified their actions on religious grounds invites at least a superficial comparison, however unsettling that may be. And while many pro-life groups have condemned Roeder's actions, others have tried to keep the focus on the cause animating him. Roeder's lawyers even disputed that he committed murder, arguing that his "unreasonable but honest belief that circumstances existed that justified his actions" warranted the lesser charge of manslaughter.[45] As in the case of John Brown, Roeder's trial was expeditious. It took only thirty-seven minutes for Roeder's jury to reach its guilty verdict: a mere blink of the eye compared to the time it will take for Americans to reach settled consensus about the moral causes fueling these men's actions. The story of John Brown offers a window onto the broad, complex, and thoroughly ambivalent relationship between religion and violence in the making of the United States. Scott Roeder's actions and his trial offer a grim reminder that such issues are not merely history. Moreover, the controversies surrounding each man point to important questions about how such troubling stories will be told in the future. How are they conceived, interpreted, and narrated? What words are chosen or omitted? And what meanings are attached to terms such as *violence* and *religion* that critically define them?

As its themes and contents suggest, this volume takes the reader into the heart of the American experience via some excruciating moments in the history of the American colonies and the United States. It also seeks to draw readers into normative reflections on these events—into discussions of right and wrong, just and unjust, moral clarity and moral perversion. Many of these moments in America's distant and not-so-distant past demand such discussion. This book by no means offers a comprehensive treatment of these topics, nor does it pretend to be flawless in what it does offer. Students, teachers, and citizens, however, may find this a helpful way to begin or continue conversations about religion, violence, and America. Scholars of many stripes, too, will benefit from its accounts of discrete moments and broad patterns of religion and violence. Indeed, any who seek a more just order in and beyond America—whether citizens of the United States or of other nations—would do well to reflect carefully about the violent side of American religion and the religious dimensions of American violence. Yet in all of this, readers should not forget the myriad ways in which religion in the United States and elsewhere has helped to build and rebuild communities, has inspired acts of courage and selflessness, and has emboldened women and men in their brave struggles against forces of oppression.

NOTES

1. Stephen B. Oates, *To Purge This Land with Blood: A Biography of John Brown* (Amherst: University of Massachusetts Press, 1954), 305.

2. Brown's demeanor was very similar to that of Nat Turner, who on August 21, 1831, led a small army of fellow slaves in a revolt in Virginia's Tidewater region. He and his followers killed fifty-five men, women, and children before encountering the overwhelming force of local white militias. In his confession Turner detailed his belief that God had called for the uprising and that he and his followers were acting righteously in carrying it out. See the "Confessions of Nat Turner" as recorded by Thomas Gray, http://www.pbs.org/wgbh/aia/part3/3h500t.html.

3. Quoted in Oates, *To Purge This Land with Blood*, 343.

4. Harry S. Stout, *Upon the Altar of the Nation: A Moral History of the Civil War* (New York: Viking, 2006). Stanley Hauerwas's chapter in this volume also engages this theme.

5. Information about the Curry mural is furnished by the Kansas Historical Society, www.kshs .org/cool2/curry.htm.

6. In 1992, over fifty years after the state ordered Curry to stop his work, the Kansas legislature issued a posthumous apology.

7. For a detailed discussion of violence and its connotations see John D. Carlson, "Religion and Violence: Coming to Terms with Terms," in *The Blackwell Companion to Religion and Violence*, ed. Andrew R. Murphy (Oxford: Wiley-Blackwell, 2011), 7–22.

8. Mark Juergensmeyer, *Terror in the Mind of God: The Global Rise of Religious Violence*, 3d ed. (Berkeley: University of California Press, 200, 2003), 10–14.

9. Ibid. See also Charles Kimball, *When Religion Becomes Evil: Five Warning Signs* (New York: HarperCollins, 2002); Charles Selengut, *Sacred Fury: Understanding Religious Violence*, 2d ed. (2004; reprint, Lanham, MD: Rowman and Littlefield, 2008).

10. William T. Cavanaugh's *The Myth of Religious Violence: Secular Ideology and the Roots of Modern Conflict* (Oxford: Oxford University Press, 2009) is essential reading for those interested in these issues.

11. Talal Asad, *Genealogies of Religion: Discipline and Reasons of Power in Christianity and Islam* (Baltimore: Johns Hopkins University Press, 1993).

12. Bruce Lincoln, *Holy Terrors: Thinking about Religion after September 11*, 2d ed. (Chicago: University of Chicago Press, 2006).

13. For extended discussion of just how religious the putatively secular can be, see Tracy Fessenden, *Culture and Redemption: Religion, the Secular, and American Literature* (Princeton: Princeton University Press, 2007).

14. John Pahl, *Empire of Sacrifice: The Religious Origins of American Violence* (New York: New York University Press, 2010); Rosemary Radford Reuther, *America, Amerikkka: Elect Nation and Imperial Violence* (London: Equinox, 2007).

15. William Lloyd Garrison, "On the Death of John Brown," http://www.historyplace.com/ speeches/garrison.htm.

16. Edward Rothstein, "One Man's Crusade against Slavery, Seen from Two Angles," *New York Times*, Oct. 28, 2009, C1.

17. William Keeney, "Hero, Martyr, Madman: Representations of John Brown in the Poetry of the John Brown Year, 1859–1960," in *Terrible Swift Sword: The Legacy of John Brown*, ed. Peggy A. Russo and Paul Finkelman (Athens: Ohio University Press, 2005), 142.

18. Kyle Ward, *History in the Making: An Absorbing Look at How American History Has Changed in the Telling over the Last 200 Years* (New York: New Press, 2006), 182.

19. For a review of exhibits at the Virginia Historical Society and the New York Historical Society, see Rothstein, "One Man's Crusade against Slavery."

20. David S. Reynolds, "Freedom's Martyr," *New York Times*, Dec. 2, 2009, A33.

21. Tony Horwitz, "The 9/11 of 1859," ibid.

22. Dennis B. Roddy, "John Brown's Legacy Divides: 150 Years after His Death, Abolitionist to Some, Lunatic to Others," *Pittsburgh Post-Gazette*, Oct. 18, 2009.

23. Sacvan Bercovitch, *The American Jeremiad* (Madison: University of Wisconsin Press, 1978), 16. For a classic explanation of the Puritan jeremiad, see Perry Miller, *Errand into the Wilderness* (Cambridge: Harvard University Press, 1956).

24. See Majid Khadduri, *The Islamic Conception of Justice* (Baltimore: Johns Hopkins University Press, 1984), chap. 7.

25. See Jonathan Z. Smith, *Imagining Religion: From Babylon to Jonestown* (Chicago: University of Chicago Press, 1982), xi–xiii.

26. For a detailed discussion of this distinction, see Sohail H. Hashmi, "Interpreting the Islamic Ethics of War and Peace," in *Islamic Political Ethics: Civil Society, Pluralism, and Conflict*, ed. Sohail

H. Hashmi (Princeton: Princeton University Press, 2002), 198–216; Michael Bonner, *Jihad in Islamic History: Doctrines and Practice* (Princeton: Princeton University Press, 2006); and David Cook, *Understanding Jihad* (Berkeley: University of California Press, 2005), chap. 2.

27. Bercovitch, *The American Jeremiad*, 9.

28. Ibid., 6.

29. See Charles Mathewes and Christopher McNight Nichols, eds., *Prophecies of Godlessness: Predictions of America's Imminent Secularization from the Puritans to the Present Day* (Oxford: Oxford University Press, 2008).

30. Winnifred Fallers Sullivan, *The Impossibility of Religious Freedom* (Princeton: Princeton University Press, 2007).

31. Oates, *To Purge This Land with Blood*, 30.

32. The document continues with the famous words "We hold these truths to be Self Evident; That all men are created Equal; That they are endowed by the Creator with certain unalienable rights. That among these are Life, Liberty; & pursuit of happiness. . . ." See http://www.digitalhis tory.uh.edu/learning_history/brown/planning3.cfm.

33. Garrison, like many other abolitionists, preferred the strategy of *Northern* secession: as the saying went, "If thy right hand offend thee, cut it off."

34. Brown's constitution also was modeled on the U.S. Constitution. His defense attorney, Samuel Chilton, introduced it during his trial as evidence of Brown's insanity in an unsuccessful effort to undermine the state's charge of treason. See http://www.law.umkc.edu/faculty/projects/Ftrials/johnbrown/brownconstitution.html.

35. See Harry Stout, "Religion, War, and the Meaning of America," *Religion and American Culture* 19, no. 2 (Summer 2009). Stout opens his review essay with the statement "The norm of American national life is war."

36. Carey McWilliams, *Factories in the Field: The Story of Migratory Farm Labor in California* (1935; reprint, Berkeley: University of California Press, 1999), 215, 221, 235.

37. John D. Carlson, "The Morality, Politics, and Irony of War: Recovering Reinhold Niebuhr's Ethical Realism," *Journal of Religious Ethics* 36, no. 4: 619–651.

38. Lincoln, *Holy Terrors.*

39. Andrew Sullivan, "Dear President Bush," An Open Letter to the President, *Atlantic Monthly,* October 2009, 84.

40. Barack Obama, "Remarks by the President at the Acceptance of the Nobel Peace Prize," Dec. 10, 2009, http://www.whitehouse.gov/the-press-office/remarks-president-acceptance-nobel -peace-prize.

41. "News Wrap," *PBS News Hour,* Jan. 28, 2010, http://www.pbs.org/newshour/bb/business/jan -june10/newswrap_01-28.html. Judy L. Thomas, "Roeder Jury Can't Consider Manslaughter in Til- ler Killing," *Kansas City Star,* Jan. 28, 2010.

42. Monica Davey, "Doctor's Killer Puts Abortion on Stand," *New York Times,* Jan. 29, 2009, A11.

43. "Suspect Claims 'Victory' in Closing of Slain Doctor's Clinic," CNN.com, June 9, 2009, http://articles.cnn.com/2009-06-09/justice/kansas.tiller.clinic_1_scott-roeder-dr-tiller-george-tiller? _s=PM:CRIME.

44. David W. Blight, "John Brown: Triumphant Failure," *American Prospect,* Nov. 30, 2002, http://www.prospect.org/cs/articles?article=john_brown_triumphant_failure.

45. Davey, "Doctor's Killer Puts Abortion on Stand," A11.

PART ONE

Religious Origins and Tropes of American Violence

1

From King Philip's War
to September 11

Religion, Violence, and the American Way

Andrew R. Murphy and Elizabeth Hanson

As a religious problem, the problem of suffering is, paradoxically, not how to avoid suffering but how to suffer, how to make of physical pain, personal loss, worldly defeat, or the helpless contemplation of others' agony something bearable, supportable—something, as we say, sufferable.
—CLIFFORD GEERTZ, "RELIGION AS A CULTURAL SYSTEM"

Clifford Geertz suggests an intimate connection between religion and suffering, a problem of interpretation central to any consideration of the relationship between religion and violence more generally.[1] This chapter examines key episodes in America's nearly 400-year history of turning to the jeremiad to explain violence endured and sometimes to justify violence inflicted.[2] The jeremiad is part of a longstanding American rhetorical tradition, one that understands the nation as existing in a special, covenanted relationship with God, with special purposes to accomplish in the world. Although the jeremiad did not originate in America, and is not unique to the American experience—other peoples, in many different times and places, have proven all too eager to claim sacred status for their own communities[3]—it has played a key role in Americans' self-understandings since the early days of colonization. The jeremiad draws its inspiration from the Hebrew prophets, who frequently lamented Israel's violation of its covenant with God. Through the jeremiad, prophets called Israelites to repent of their sins and rededicate themselves to their covenant with God; they predicted blessings if the people reformed, and catastrophes if they did not.[4] In like manner, many Americans, from the earliest days of colonial settlement down to the twenty-first century, have understood their nation as chosen to carry out God's purposes in human history. Thus Americans have often interpreted their nation's successes

29

(including the successful exercise of violence against other peoples) as signs that God approves of the nation's spiritual state. But a special relationship and special purposes imply special responsibilities; and thus Americans have also often interpreted episodes of violence and other misfortunes as punishment sent by God in order to chastise this chosen people for failing to live up to the terms of their covenant.

The jeremiad (and the view of history that undergirds it[5]) is based on two crucial claims. First, the *epistemological* aspect of the jeremiad involves a claim that humans, with some degree of certainty, can read God's purposes in earthly events; these events, properly interpreted, provide a way to assess the spiritual health of a given community. Second, the *ethical-theological* component of the jeremiad presumes that God's purposes encompass the use of violence in the pursuit of religious and divinely ordained political ends. Somewhere in the convergence of these two assumptions lies the power of the jeremiad to accomplish what Geertz saw as religion's central power, that of making suffering sufferable. At the same time, it can become deeply problematic when such certainty about God's will is combined with exhortation about the moral and religious dimensions of violence. Decoupling the epistemological from the ethical-theological claims makes possible important variations on the standard jeremiadic formula, as becomes evident through a consideration of Abraham Lincoln (who questioned the jeremiad's epistemological pillar) and Martin Luther King Jr. (who questioned its ethical-theological one). These latter variations suggest novel and creative ways of reframing how the jeremiad relates religion and violence in the American tradition.

WINTHROP'S *MODEL* AND THE CITY ON A HILL

Notions of a chosen America go back to the earliest days of colonization. John Winthrop's sermon *A Model of Christian Charity*, delivered on board the *Arbella* in 1630, provides the most famous reference to the American settlement as a "city on a hill."[6] But Winthrop's sermon did not simply proclaim that New England was a city on a hill. Rather, it laid out two possible scenarios for the unfolding of New England's future. Having entered into a covenant with God, Winthrop reports, the colonists of the Massachusetts Bay Company must decide whether or not to honor that covenant: "[I]f we shall neglect the observation of these articles . . . and, dissembling with our God, shall fall to embrace this present world and prosecute our carnal intentions, seeking great things for ourselves and our posterity, the Lord will surely break out in wrath against us, and be revenged of such a people, and make us know the price of the breach of such a covenant."[7] Failure to observe the covenant would put the community on the receiving end of holy violence, the wrath of God "break[ing] out against us." Winthrop's goal was to avoid this outcome, and the *Model* continues with a striking evocation of the social harmony and mutual forbearance that God expected of his saints in New England. In this scenario, the community will be able to overcome the violence of its enemies and to earn the praise and envy of surrounding lands: "We shall find that the God of Israel is among us, when ten of us shall be able to resist a thousand of our enemies; when He shall make us a praise and glory that men shall say of succeeding plantations, 'May the Lord make it like that of New England.' For we must consider that we shall be as a city upon a hill. The eyes of all people are upon us."[8] These settlements about which Winthrop was so concerned grew and flourished over the subsequent decades. But the covenant was always on the minds of the colony's ruling elite, and, given their providentialist worldview, New Englanders often interpreted their misfortunes—crop failures, Indian attacks, diseases, and epidemics—as signs of God's wrath at their failure to live up to the godly standards set by the founding generation. Thus was born the American jeremiad, an American variant on the long-standing rhetorical form that the Puritans brought with them from England.

In New England, the jeremiad most often appeared in the form of an occasional sermon. Authorized by the civil government, occasional sermons were delivered during significant public events. They were "solidarity rituals" that cemented religious piety and politics in one public event.[9] Occasional sermons delivered on days of thanksgiving or of fasting and humiliation sought to express either the community's gratitude to God for blessings, or contrition in hopes of regaining God's favor through public acts of penitence. According to Harry S. Stout, the speaker's goals were "not to be innovative or entertaining, but to recall for his audience the vision that first impelled New England's mission."[10] During election-day sermons, another variety of the occasional sermon, New Englanders were called upon to reflect on their collective past, to rededicate themselves as a community based on a common faith, and to choose godly leaders.[11] On more somber occasions, clergy inveighed against a society that had fallen away from its religious roots and was reaping the consequences in faction, pride, and vanity, in Indian wars and natural disasters. By restricting public oration on such important occasions to the clergy, New England civil magistrates ensured that the sermon would occupy a prominent, virtually unchallenged, status on that day.[12]

KING PHILIP'S WAR: RELIGION AND VIOLENCE IN EARLY NEW ENGLAND

Of the clergy likely to be called on to deliver occasional sermons in the generation following Winthrop, none played a more significant role in the colonies' public life than Increase Mather. Mather, the son of Richard Mather and son-in-law of John Cotton, both celebrated figures of early Massachusetts Bay, was a towering figure in New England society. And though he spoke in the style of a prophet, it is unlikely that Mather knew how prophetic his 1674 sermon *The Day of Trouble Is Near* would turn out to be.[13] For December of that year would see the beginning of King Philip's War, a series of catastrophic conflicts with the natives. This war, so named for the chief of the Wampanoag tribe who spearheaded the native tribes' armed resistance to the English colonists in 1675 and 1676, has been called "the great crisis of the early period of New England history."[14] By war's end fully half of the towns in New England were damaged severely, and twelve were completely laid waste; the economy was in shambles, with the colonial treasuries near bankruptcy. Hundreds of English colonists (and far more Native Americans) were dead, wounded, or in captivity.

These grim details were in the future on the day that Mather preached in Boston. What Mather saw all around him were the sins of a once-godly people and their breach of the covenant into which the colony's founders had entered. Mather called attention to "a great decay as to the power of godliness amongst us"; spiritual and carnal pride "in apparel, fashions, and the like"; disobedience within families, churches, and the commonwealth; insensitivity to the poor; and growing contentiousness and disunity.[15] Not only did Mather see his own generation falling short of the godliness of its parents; he feared that such a pattern was getting worse among the colony's youth. "Churches have not so performed covenant-duties towards their children, as should have been, and especially, the rising generation have many of them broken the covenant themselves, in that they do not endeavour to come up to that which their solemn vow in baptism doth engage them to before the Lord."[16]

Mather took his sermon text from Ezekiel and noted that, although in scripture the Chaldeans had inflicted judgment on Israel, the ultimate source of their punishment was God, who sent the Chaldeans as punishment for the Israelites' sins.[17] God's punishment was intended for a specific purpose: "that which the Lord intends by bringing his people into the furnace of affliction, is that he may make pure metal of them, yea, that they may be purged and sanctified, and become vessels meet for the master's use."[18] The reason for such a spiritual declension, in Mather's view, was clear: what was once a religiously based settlement had become infected with the poison of worldliness. "Alas! We have changed our interest. The interest of New England was religion, which did distinguish us from other English plantations; they were built upon a worldly design, but we upon a religious design, whereas now we begin to espouse a worldly interest, and so to chase a new God, therefore no wonder that war is like to be in the gates."[19] And yet, amidst the signs of trouble all around, Mather drew on his faith in God's promises and his reverence for the founding generation as he voiced hope for the colony's relationship with its God: "Our fathers have built sanctuaries for his name therein, and therefore he will not destroy us."[20] Not destroy, perhaps, but Mather felt sure that God was preparing to afflict New England.

Affliction came when armed hostilities began in 1675. By the spring of 1676, the Wampanoags and their allies were within ten miles of Boston. Although the jeremiadic emphasis on divine punishment had been a staple of New England public life for decades, the experience of King Philip's War pointed out just how terrible God's punishments could be. Between the spring of 1675 and the summer of 1676 scores of New England towns were burned, their inhabitants attacked and killed. When King Philip himself was killed in August 1676, hostilities came to a rapid conclusion. Shortly thereafter New Englanders began to produce histories of the war, trying to understand what had happened and why. One of the first came from the pen of Increase Mather. Mather's account painted a portrait of the violence unleashed on both sides: for Mather, New England had been both a recipient of God's violence, delivered by the Wampanoags, and an agent of divinely sanctioned violence inflicted upon the natives.

In such a providential framework, God rewarded righteousness with military victory, peace, and prosperity—and punished pride and disobedience with violence at the hands of the Indians.[21] New Englanders ascribed any victory they enjoyed to God's favor, rather than to their own military prowess, as when one author reported that "God (whose tender mercies are over all his works) in compassion to the English Nation in this Wildernesse, [did] wonderfully appear for our deliverance. . . . great numbers have surrendered themselves when by our own strength or outward Circumstances we could least expect it."[22] To claim success for one's good fortune or well-being was the height of pride. All good things flowed from God. Even in the midst of the war, they lived in the hope "that (if our sins obstruct not so great a blessing) we may shortly once again see peace and safety restored to our (lately disconsolate) habitations in this Wildernesse."[23] The rhetorical connections between New England's righteousness, God's will, and the outcome of the conflict played out more concretely after a Day of Public Thanksgiving in Massachusetts on June 29, 1676, when one author noted that "God himself hath sent from Heaven and saved us (for we see nothing of man, but God to be all in all) by Wasting [the Indians] with Sickness, Starving them through want of Provisions, Leaving them to their own Divisions, Taking away their Spirits, putting the Dread of us upon them, Cutting off their Principal men, Sachems and others. Blessed be his Great and Glorious Name."[24]

When New Englanders found themselves on the receiving end of violence, they sought to understand it by way of the same providential framework. At times God seemed to be punishing New Englanders for their waywardness by inflicting violence upon them at the hands of King Philip's warriors. In one incident, a settler named Wright refused to seek shelter at the garrison with the other inhabitants of his town when the Indians arrived; instead, "he had a strange confidence or rather conceit, that whilest he held his Bible in his hand, he looked upon himself as secure from all kinde of violence; and that the Enemy finding him in that posture, deriding his groundlesse apprehension or folly therein, ript him open, and put his Bible in his belly."[25] Wright's prideful approach to scripture provoked God's wrath against him, making him the object of divine violence, and a cautionary example to others.

Although the example of Wright's disembowelment made for sensational moral instruction, more typically, and in keeping with the social emphasis of the jeremiad tradition, chastening violence was interpreted by the entire community as punishment for collective sins. Even as they endeavored to mend their ways, their misfortunes at the hands of the Indians served as a yardstick by which to measure God's anger with them. Mather noted that a "day of prayer and humiliation was observed Dec. 2, when also something happened intimating as if the Lord were still angry with our prayers, for this day all the houses in Quonsickamuck were burnt by the Indians."[26] Similarly, on April 20, 1676, as the churches in Boston prayed for God's mercy in a day of humiliation, colonists in nearby Sudbury faced a grim judgment. Indians captured a number of them, "stripped them naked, and caused them to run the gauntlet, whipping them after a cruel and bloody manner, and then threw hot ashes upon them, cut out the flesh of their legs, and put fire into their wounds, delighting to see the miserable torments of wretched creatures."[27]

In some cases, New Englanders found themselves simultaneously the agents and the recipients of divine violence, a situation that required a more nuanced explanation. After a victory at Hadley and Northampton, the New Englanders destroyed the Indians' forges and lead supply, thus preventing the natives from making weapons, only to see their fortunes quickly reversed: "This great Successe was not altogether without its allay, as if Providence had designed to checquer our joys and sorrows; and lest we should sacrifice to our own Nets, and say, Our own Arms or prowesse hath done this, to permit the Enemy presently after to take an advantage against us; For as our men were returning to Hadly [sic] in a dangerous Passe, which they were not sufficiently aware of, the skulking Indians ... killed, at one Volley, the said Captain, and Eight and Thirty of his men."[28] On another occasion, fighting Philip's forces in a swamp, the English colonists were having considerable success but did not realize it and, in the heat of battle, called a retreat. As Mather interpreted it, "God saw that we were not yet fit for deliverance, nor could health be restored unto us except a great deal more blood be first taken from us."[29] The failure of this expedition later served to embolden the enemy and precipitated several murders by the Indians at Mendham. Even in the midst of apparent success, New Englanders were enjoined not to forget the source of their help. God might punish pride at any time.

New Englanders commonly regarded Indians not simply as a military enemy, but as the agent of divine violence, the instrument by which God punished their sins and urged them back toward righteousness. God's choice to use Indians as agents of violence was not arbitrary. A crucial feature of New England's punishment was that it was enacted by the people they had promised to convert, but had in fact led further into sin. Increase Mather reprinted a letter from Plymouth governor Josiah Winslow, which reminded his readers that "God is just and hath punished us far less than our iniquities have deserved; yea just in using as a rod, whose enlightening and conversion we have not endeavored as we might and should have done, but on the contrary have taught them new sins that they knew not."[30] The setbacks and tragedies of war were part of a broader cosmic framework of divine justice.

The New England jeremiad did not vanish after its heyday in the second half of the seventeenth century. Fast-day and election-day sermons continued, and clergy continued to lament perceived spiritual decline. "There was once a very distinguishing work of God's grace in the midst of us," preached John Webb in 1734, but "[t]his work of divine grace . . . is fallen into a languishing state for the present."[31] In 1740 Joseph Sewall took the example of the Ninevites in Jonah 3:10 as a fast-day sermon text, listing a familiar litany of sins (disrespect of the Sabbath, oppression, the abuse of taverns) and calling on his compatriots to "seek . . . God with prayer and fasting . . . with true repentance, and sincere endeavours after reformation." "[I]f we refuse to repent and reform," he continued, "we shall be condemned out of our own mouths."[32] The title of Samuel Wales's 1785 *The Dangers of Our National Prosperity; and the Ways to Avoid Them* illustrates how concerns over worldliness and wealth gave way to ongoing calls for repentance.

Clergy in early New England possessed, if not a monopoly on religious speech, a near monopoly on institutional resources to promote that speech, as well as control over educational and social institutions. Having such speakers selected and invited by the civil magistrates—and having their sermons reprinted and distributed by order of the General Court—was an effective way to shape public discourse and to present a unified set of guidelines for acceptable public behavior. Social critique, when it arose, came largely from within the colony's ruling elite.

The idea of America as the New Israel echoed down through the Great Awakening and into the Revolutionary period, providing powerful rhetorical support for the struggle for independence and providing preachers numerous opportunities to frame crises in jeremiadic terms. In 1777 Nicholas Street compared George III with Pharaoh, but reminded his listeners that God humbled the Israelites in the wilderness as punishment for their sins. True to the jeremiadic tradition, Street pointed to Americans' greed, selfishness, disregard for the Sabbath, profaneness, and corruption, and assured them that such judgments would increase "till we are brought to a repentance and reformation."[33] As in prophetic warnings to the ancient Israelites, America's Jeremiahs would continue to lament the inability or unwillingness of American Israelites to live up to their covenantal obligations. We can follow this distinction between suffering sacred violence and inflicting it down through one of the most traumatic episodes of American history: the American Civil War.

CARNAGE AND CHOSENNESS IN CIVIL WAR AMERICA

As in colonial New England, antebellum and Civil War–era jeremiads often appeared first in the form of fast, thanksgiving, or election sermons, and were then republished and circulated to a wider audience. But the United States, now a sovereign nation, had disestablished churches and ensured freedom of the press, association, and peaceful assembly. State establishments of religion, though not outlawed, were clearly declining in influence. There is no denying, of course, that many Protestant leaders occupied powerful public positions during the antebellum period, but they were leading players in a lively religious marketplace rather than an elite marked off from the people by distinctions of education and literacy. Religious discourse during the early national period came from increasingly diverse corners: revivals, lecture tours, newspapers, and a host of other opportunities for religious and political leaders to weigh in on public issues.[34]

Despite the radical transformations of American society from the early eighteenth through the mid-nineteenth centuries, the United States remained in many important ways a deeply Christian nation throughout the Civil War years. With the outbreak of the Civil War, many Northern thinkers and critics came to see the Union army as the instrument of God's holy vengeance—and purging justice—on the South, for the sin of slavery and rebellion. In 1864, looking back over three years of war and carnage, clergyman S. A. Hodgman explained the tragedy of the war by linking the suffering of God's chosen people with God's judgments: "It was not because the Lord abhorred us as a people, but because of his great favor towards us, that he hath purged us, as gold is purified in a furnace. We have a great mission to perform, and there is a bright destiny before us, in the future; and it was necessary that we should receive a discipline to prepare us for both. . . . It is to be our destiny, to teach all tyrants and oppressors, that their days are numbered. We are to be a city set on a hill, whose light can not be hid."[35]

As in early New England, jeremiadic thinking—chosen people, covenanted with God, with a special mission to fulfill, judged by God and found to be wanting—provided a meaningful guide for interpreting battlefield results. Victory proved God's favor. Defeat represented a sign of lingering sin in need of purgation. In their efforts to understand the reasons for the triumphs and terrible sufferings of the war, Southerners, too, drew on jeremiadic language. Preaching in 1862, Confederate supporter J. W. Tucker argued that "God is on our side—is with us in this conflict—because we have had reverses. 'Whom the Lord loveth he chasteneth, and scourgeth every son whom he receiveth.' . . . God sent our reverses for our good. They were necessary to humble our pride; to stop our foolish and absurd boasting, and to make us feel the importance of the conflict in which we are engaged."[36]

Jeremiahs on both sides alternated between elation and deflation depending on news from the battlefield. But common to all were two fairly straightforward assumptions, shared with New Englanders such as Increase Mather and John Winthrop: (1) the outcomes of battles provided a relatively clear window onto the will of God, and the spiritual health of the communities involved; and (2) God used the violence of human agents to achieve God's ultimate purposes. Perhaps the most vivid example of these two concepts came from Henry Ward Beecher, who delivered an oration on the occasion of the raising of the Stars and Stripes over Fort Sumter as the war wound down in April 1865. Looking across Charleston Harbor, Beecher observed: "Desolation broods in yonder sad city: solemn retribution hath avenged our dishonoured banner. . . . [The wreckage is a sign that] God hath set such a mark upon treason that all ages shall dread and abhor it. . . . We exult . . . not that *our* will is done, but that God's will hath been done!"[37]

Jeremiadic interpretations of violence in early New England were undergirded by twin epistemological and ethical-theological pillars, which claimed certainty about God's intentions and understood the moral appropriateness of violence in carrying out those intentions. Abraham Lincoln's reflections on the war's meaning and its connection with God's purposes provided an eloquent contrast to the Puritan "model" as well as to the Unionist triumphalism epitomized by his contemporary Beecher. Lincoln thus marks an important moment in the history of the American jeremiad. Given his unconventional religious life, his lifelong skepticism toward creeds and dogmas, it is unsurprising that his approach to the American jeremiad would involve modifications of its basic premises.[38] Lincoln illustrates one way of decoupling the jeremiad's epistemological and ethical-theological foundations. He did not dissent from a theological outlook that perceived violence as a part of God's judgment and government of the world. Lincoln departed from so many of his contemporaries by rejecting the epistemological claim that earthly events provided unambiguous evidence of God's purposes.[39] A few examples make this clear.

In September 1862 Lincoln entertained a delegation of Chicago Christians who urged him to issue an emancipation proclamation. Lincoln's response speaks directly to these issues of epistemological foundations of the jeremiad:

I am approached with the most opposite opinions and advice, and that by religious men, who are equally certain that they represent the Divine will. I am sure that either the one or the other class is mistaken in that belief, and perhaps in some respects both. I hope it will not be irreverent for me to say that if it is probable that God would reveal his will to others, on a point so connected with my duty, it might be supposed he would reveal it directly to me; for, unless I am more deceived in myself than I often am, it is my earnest desire to know the will of Providence in this matter. And if I can learn what it is I will do it! These are not, however, the days of miracles, and I suppose it will be granted that I am not to expect a direct revelation. I must study the plain physical facts of the case, ascertain what is possible and learn what appears to be wise and right. The subject is difficult, and good men do not agree. . . . the rebel soldiers are praying with a great deal more earnestness, I fear, than our own troops, and expecting God to favor their side.[40]

But Lincoln's position was more complicated than this passage suggests. In the same month Lincoln penned (apparently for private purposes) a document that has come to be known as the "Meditation on the Divine Will." It is worth quoting in its entirety:

The will of God prevails. In great contests each party claims to act in accordance with the will of God. Both may be, and one must be wrong. God can not be for, and against the same thing at the same time. In the present civil war it is quite possible that God's purpose is something different from the purpose of either party—and yet the human instrumentalities, working just as they do, are of the best adaptation to effect His purpose. I am almost ready to say this is probably true—that God wills this contest, and wills that it shall not end yet. By his mere quiet power, on the minds of the now contestants, He could have either saved or destroyed the Union without a human contest. Yet the contest began. And having begun He could give the final victory to either side any day. Yet the contest proceeds.[41]

Note the tentative and ambivalent nature of Lincoln's analysis: he proposes that it is "quite possible that God's purpose is something different from the purposes of either party" and pronounces himself "almost ready" to say that it is "probably" the case that God's will differs from that of the combatants. If God was speaking through earthly events, Lincoln suggests, God was doing so in a way that frustrated the efforts of partisans on both sides to claim God's unequivocal favor.

In his Second Inaugural, Lincoln further developed the reflections he had begun in the "Meditation." Distinctive in its lack of triumphalism, in its charity for the foe, in its intertwining of Lincoln's fatalism with a grander notion of the mysteries of God's providence, the Second Inaugural shows Lincoln "propound[ing] a thick, complex view of God's rule over the world and a morally nuanced picture of America's destiny."[42] Of course, Lincoln did suggest in the Second Inaugural that the war might be God's punishment for American slavery, and he certainly did not shrink from sanctioning violence in pursuit of his own war aims. Yet he did so hypothetically: "*If* we shall suppose that American slavery is one of those offenses which, in the providence of God, must needs come, but which, having continued through his appointed time, he now wills to remove . . . shall we discern therein any departure from those divine attributes which the believers in a living God ascribe to Him?"[43] Such a theologically tentative formulation mirrors that of the "Meditation on the Divine Will," and reinforces Mark Noll's view of Lincoln as a "holdout" from the more popular understandings of providential certainty common among his contemporaries.[44] In other words, compared with his more triumphalist fellow Americans—Northerners eager to see divine blessing in the Union's military triumph and Southerners consoled by a "Lost Cause" mythology, in which God allowed the Confederacy to be defeated in order to humble it for its own sins—"Lincoln . . . bowed to a different God."[45]

Lincoln's jeremiad took issue with the epistemological claims of its more traditional formulation. He made few claims that he could know God's will sufficiently to declare that the violence of Union forces against the South was somehow an enactment of that will. Yet Lincoln did affirm the theological-ethical component of jeremiad, which perceived that the violence of the Civil War was indeed an instrument of God's providence or even punishment for which the nation *as a whole* bore responsibility. In spite of differences from Puritan jeremiads, there were enduring continuities as well. For in both periods, violence and war created occasions for reflection, contrition, and, ultimately, rededication to the community's founding ideals, whether those of a budding colony drifting from its covenantal origins or a fractured body of states consolidating its identity as a nation around founding principles of inalienable rights to life and liberty.

THE POST-SEPTEMBER 11 JEREMIAD AND BEYOND

The success of a concerted political (and military) effort to purge the nation of the "national sin" of slavery was followed in the nineteenth and twentieth centuries by other American "prophets" and reformers who employed jeremiadic discourse to target other sources of moral decline or to initiate moral renewal.[46] Social movements associated with temperance, suffrage, civil rights, and desegregation come most immediately to mind. The reemergence of conservative Protestants in American civic life during the 1970s and 1980s was driven by a backlash against the social protests and counterculture of the 1960s and 1970s, Supreme Court decisions on school prayer and abortion, and an increasingly powerful federal government with a long reach into areas previously left to local institutions. Many conservative Christians saw these developments as proof of a deep-seated corruption in American culture. Given their past reservations about engaging in politics, fundamentalist leaders framed their reentry into political life as a defensive one—a response to a hostile mainstream culture increasingly dominated by secularism and liberalism. James Findlay points out that the "tactics of the liberal churches were a double-edged sword, which could be used to advance conservative as well as liberal ends. It was not long before exactly that happened. Perhaps ironically, then, the political successes of the mainline churches in the 1960s served as a precondition for the emergence of Jerry Falwell, Pat Robertson, and the Moral Majority in the 1980s."[47]

Clergy played a key role in convincing skeptical evangelical and fundamentalist congregations that political engagement need not come at the expense of their spiritual health. Jerry Falwell was perhaps the most influential of those clergy. Falwell built bridges between fundamentalist and evangelical Protestant communities by crafting a public language of American moral decline to which both groups could subscribe. Besides preaching sermons at countless conservative churches around the country, Falwell spearheaded the formation of the Moral Majority in 1979, building that organization into a formidable public voice in American politics. In 1980, disappointed with the presidency of Jimmy Carter (especially given the high hopes with which many born-again Christians had welcomed him, one of their own, to the White House), many Christian Right leaders supported Ronald Reagan. His personal religiosity was far more ambiguous than Carter's (and his personal life included a divorce), but Reagan was skilled at evoking the imagery of American chosenness. Although scholars have long pointed to the Christian Right's lack of concrete policy successes, this amorphous and increasingly diverse movement proved enormously effective in mobilizing traditionalist Americans concerned with the secularization of public life. The internal politics of the Republican Party have been transformed by this mobilization, and the presidency of George W. Bush made abundantly clear how evangelical ideas and rhetoric continue to influence the highest levels of American government.

Appearing on Pat Robertson's television program *The 700 Club* just days after the September 11 attacks, Jerry Falwell uttered the following memorable words:

> [W]hat we saw on [September 11], as terrible as it is, could be minuscule if, in fact—if, in fact—God continues to lift the curtain and allow the enemies of America to give us probably what we deserve. . . . The ACLU's got to take a lot of blame for this. . . . throwing God out successfully with the help of the federal court system, throwing God out of the public square, out of the schools. The abortionists have got to bear some burden for this because God will not be mocked. . . . [along with] the pagans . . . and the feminists, and the gays and the lesbians who are actively trying to make that an alternative lifestyle, the ACLU, People for the American Way.[48]

Falwell's remarks made clear that the United States was on the receiving end of divinely ordained violence and destruction because, through its moral decline, it had failed to honor its covenant with God.

These remarks were highly controversial, and public outrage led Falwell to retract them, though less than convincingly. But his interpretation of the events of September 11 are not nearly as far out of the American mainstream, historically speaking, as one might think. (Many on the political left, too, saw the terrorist attacks as fitting punishment for the U.S. government's foreign policy failures—an instance of "chickens coming home to roost" or the necessity for the United States to be taken down a peg or two.) Falwell's jeremiad follows directly from the epistemological claim that we can know God's will by reading earthly events. The call for national repentance accompanying Falwell's remarks about September 11 also suggests an embrace of God's use of sacred violence. Moreover, the strong (initial) support among American evangelicals for the Bush administration's "war on terror" and military campaigns in Afghanistan and Iraq often drew on the ethical-theological foundations of the jeremiad. In earlier jeremiads, this dimension was an occasion for interpreting military victory or defeat as a sign of God's blessing or punishment. In the war on terror, though, some on the religious right asserted the appropriateness of instrumental violence in pursuit of God's causes.

Among many other responses to Falwell's remarks, those of President George W. Bush warrant special note. Bush rejected Falwell's particular interpretation of the events of September 11 (the first pillar) without denying its underlying premise, namely that earthly events reflect God's assessment of a community's spiritual health. In fact, Bush actually inverted Falwell's logic and claimed that the United States had been attacked not because of its moral decadence and decline, but because of its virtue. Furthermore, Bush connected America's goodness to the nation's relationship with God: "In every generation, the world has produced enemies of human freedom. They have attacked America because we are freedom's home and defender. . . . The advance of human freedom . . . now depends on us. . . . Freedom and fear . . . have always been at war, and we know that God is not neutral between them. . . . [America's] responsibility to history is already clear: to answer these attacks and rid the world of evil."[49]

The president made clear that God was central to any interpretation of the events surrounding 9/11. He saw an opportunity for a chosen America, through the use of force in Afghanistan, to inflict divinely sanctioned violence on those who had attacked God's favored nation and, by extension, God's defender of freedom. In other words, God is not neutral between freedom and fear. Note how Bush's Second Inaugural Address, which beckons toward a post–September 11 world and was delivered as American forces were being deployed in Iraq, declines the mantle of chosen nation in one sentence, yet in the next lines reclaims the idea of America as indispensable to following the direction and will of the divine "Author of Liberty":

> We go forward with complete confidence in the eventual triumph of freedom. Not because history runs on the wheels of inevitability; it is human choices that move events. Not because we consider ourselves a chosen nation; God moves and chooses as He wills. We have confidence because freedom is the permanent hope of mankind, the hunger in dark places, the longing of the soul. When our Founders declared a new order of the ages; when soldiers died in wave upon wave for a union based on liberty; when citizens marched in peaceful outrage under the banner "Freedom Now"—they were acting on an ancient hope that is meant to be fulfilled. History has an ebb and flow of justice, but history also has a visible direction, set by liberty and the Author of Liberty.[50]

Four hundred years after the Puritans first invoked what would become the American jeremiad as their way of interpreting the intersections of religion and violence, much of their call for humility and contrition seemed to have been lost along the way.

CONCLUSION: A JEREMIAD BEYOND VIOLENCE?

The covenant theory behind the jeremiad holds that, as God's chosen people, covenanted with God, Americans have a responsibility to behave in certain ways, to honor certain religious principles, and to affirm publicly certain religious behaviors. The failure to do so can lead God to use violence—carried out by proxies, surrogates, and agents—to chastise the nation and restore it to righteousness. We have seen examples of this in colonists' responses to King Philip's War, the Civil War, and the September 11 attacks. Conversely, the triumph over one's foes has often been used—from Winthrop, to Mather, to Hodgman and Tucker, to Falwell—to provide evidence of the right ordering of the national soul. But are there other ways of conceiving the jeremiad or understanding the connections between religion and conflict in American history that reject the legitimacy of violence? If Abraham Lincoln provided an example of a jeremiad deeply skeptical about the ability of humans to discern God's will and intentions through precise and partisan interpretations of historical events, Martin Luther King Jr. provides a different example, one coming from deep within the Christian tradition that nonetheless rejects the moral-theological legitimacy of violence.

Like Lincoln, King complicates the tendency of other American prophets who simultaneously claimed epistemological privilege (knowing the mind of God, as read from historical events) and situated these claims about God's intentions in a theology of instrumental violence. King's approach, however, differs from that of Lincoln in that he showed little epistemological skepticism; he grounded his civil

rights activism in a claim that he and God were on the same side in seeking justice for the excluded and marginalized. "The arc of the moral universe is long,
but it bends toward justice," King pronounced.[51] One's obligations to God demand disobedience to unjust laws, which can be identified (rather unproblematically, it seems) by comparing them with God's just laws. As he put it in his "Letter
from Birmingham Jail," "A just law is a man-made code that squares with the
moral law or the law of God. An unjust law is a code that is out of harmony with
the moral law."[52] Yet King, unlike Lincoln, eschewed the second pillar of the jeremiadic tradition, the sacralization of violence. At the Lincoln Memorial in 1963,
King did suggest the possibility of future violence: "Those who hope that the
Negro needed to blow off steam and will now be content will have a rude awakening if the nation returns to business as usual. There will be neither rest nor
tranquility in America until the Negro is granted his citizenship rights. The
whirlwinds of revolt will continue to shake the foundations of our nation until
the bright day of justice emerges."[53] But rather than reinforce any justification
for violence, King then turned to his supporters and offered a different message.
King linked the civil rights movement—grounded deeply in the American tradition, the African American tradition, and the Christian tradition—to the overcoming of violence. "We must not allow our creative protest to degenerate into
physical violence. Again and again we must rise to the majestic heights of meeting physical force with soul force. . . . You have been the veterans of creative suffering. Continue to work with the faith that unearned suffering is redemptive."[54]
King's call, then, was to break the cycle of violence—"to overcome oppression
and violence without resorting to violence and oppression."[55] Indeed, part of
breaking the cycle of violence, King's writings make clear, entails a willingness to
suffer violence and to reciprocate such violence with love.

King's 1963 "I Have a Dream" speech is familiar to Americans and remains
instructive in the context of this exploration of religion and violence in America.
Recall the contents of his dream, the images he evokes:

[T]he sons of former slaves and the sons of former slave owners will . . . sit down
together.

[L]ittle black boys and black girls will . . . join hands with little white boys and
white girls.

[A]ll of God's children will . . . sing with a new meaning, "My country, 'tis of thee."

[A]ll of God's children, black men and white men, Jews and Gentiles, Protestants
and Catholics, will . . . join hands and sing "Free at last!"[56]

King offered a vision of the American future, as he put it, "deeply rooted in the
American dream," but deeply rooted in quite a different notion of America from
the one we have encountered above. It is a vision in which religion offers a way of

knowing God's will with a reasonable degree of certainty but a way out of the cycle of violence, between winners and losers, between conquerors and conquered. After all, those who are sitting down together, joining hands, and singing are members of two communities locked in a deep struggle over their individual identities and the identity of the nation they share. King's vision sanctifies "unearned" or "creative" suffering: not the violence unleashed by God in punishment for sin, not the victorious triumph of a godly people over a defeated foe. King offered a vision of a future in which Americans neither suffer divine violence at the hands of others, nor inflict it upon less powerful populations, but ultimately transcend it through a soul force deeply rooted in religion. The role of religion in this framework is one of transcendence and of redemption: King sought to make suffering not merely sufferable, but redemptive.

NOTES

1. Clifford Geertz, "Religion as a Cultural System," in *The Interpretation of Cultures* (New York: Basic, 1973), 104.

2. The historical material for this chapter is presented in greater depth in Andrew R. Murphy, *Prodigal Nation: Moral Decline and Divine Punishment from New England to 9/11* (New York: Oxford University Press, 2008), chaps. 2–4.

3. There is nothing uniquely American about a group of people claiming to be chosen by and in covenant with God. See, for example, the work of Anthony Smith, especially his *Chosen Peoples* (Oxford: Oxford University Press, 2003). See also William R. Hutchinson and Hartmut Lehmann, eds., *Many Are Chosen: Divine Election and Western Nationalism* (Minneapolis: Fortress Press, 1994).

4. See Walter Bruegemann, *Old Testament Theology: The Theology of the Book of Jeremiah* (Cambridge: Cambridge University Press, 2006); and John van Seters, "Historiography in Ancient Israel," in *A Companion to Western Historical Thought*, ed. Lloyd Kramer and Sarah Maza (Oxford: Blackwell, 2002).

5. See Winthrop S. Hudson, "Fast Days and Civil Religion," in *Theology in Sixteenth- and Seventeenth-Century England. Papers Read at a Clark Library Seminar, February 6, 1971* (Los Angeles: William Andrews Clark Memorial Library, 1971).

6. The image of America as a "city on a hill" has been employed repeatedly from early Puritan writings through the Civil War (see the example of S. A. Hodgman, discussed later) and beyond. It was invoked repeatedly by President Ronald Reagan.

7. Winthrop's *Model* has been extensively anthologized, originally appearing in *The Winthrop Papers*, vol. 2 (Boston: Massachusetts Historical Society, 1931), 282; and, more recently, Matthew S. Holland, *Bonds of Affection: Civic Charity and the Making of America—Winthrop, Jefferson, Lincoln* (Washington, DC: Georgetown University Press, 2007), appendix A; quotations at p. 274.

8. Ibid.

9. Richard P. Gildrie, "The Ceremonial Puritan: Days of Humiliation and Thanksgiving," *New England Historical and Genealogical Review* 136 (1982): 4.

10. Harry S. Stout, *The New England Soul: Preaching and Religious Culture in Colonial New England* (New York: Oxford University Press, 1986), 29.

11. T. H. Breen, *Character of a Good Ruler: A Study of Puritan Political Ideas in New England, 1630–1730* (New Haven: Yale University Press, 1980), chap. 3.

12. Darren Staloff, *The Making of an American Thinking Class: Intellectuals and Intelligentsia in Puritan Massachusetts* (New York: Oxford University Press, 1997).

13. Mather's sermon was delivered on the occasion of a day of humiliation, 12 mo 11 1673 (that is, February 11, 1674, under the Julian calendar used throughout colonial America before 1751), and published the following year.

14. Richard Slotkin and James K. Folsom, *So Dreadful a Judgment: Puritan Responses to King Philip's War, 1676–1677* (Middletown, CT: Wesleyan University Press, 1978), 3.

15. Increase Mather, *The Day of Trouble Is Near* (Cambridge, MA, 1674), 22.

16. Ibid., 24.

17. Ibid., 1, 15–17.

18. Ibid., 17.

19. Ibid., 23.

20. Ibid., 27.

21. See Nicholas Guyatt, *Providence and the Invention of the United States, 1607–1686* (New York: Cambridge University Press, 2007); Michael P. Winship, *Seers of God: Puritan Providentialism in the Restoration and Early Enlightenment* (Baltimore: Johns Hopkins University Press, 1996); and Alexandra Walsham, *Providence in Early Modern England* (Oxford: Oxford University Press, 1999.

22. *A new and further narrative of the state of New-England being a continued account of the bloody Indian war* (1676), in *King Philip's War Narratives*. March of America Facsimile Series, no. 29 (Ann Arbor: University Microfilms, 1966), 2–3.

23. Ibid., 14.

24. *A true account of the most considerable occurrences that have hapned in the warre between the English and the Indians in New-England* (1676), in *King Philip's War Narratives*, 5.

25. *New and further narrative*, 7.

26. Increase Mather, *A Brief History of the Warr with the Indians in New-England* (Boston, 1676), 19.

27. Ibid., 27.

28. *New and further narrative*, 12.

29. Mather, *Brief History*, 5.

30. Ibid., Postscript, 3.

31. John Webb, *The Duty of a Degenerate People to Pray for the Reviving of God's Work* (Boston, 1734), 5–6.

32. Joseph Sewall, *Nineveh's Repentance and Deliverance* (Boston, 1740), 13, 17; also 18, 29–33.

33. Nicholas Street, *The American States Acting Over the Part of the Children of Israel in the Wilderness* (New Haven, 1777), 31.

34. See George M. Fredrickson, "The Coming of the Lord: The Northern Protestant Clergy and the Civil War Crisis," in *Religion and the American Civil War*, ed. Randall M. Miller, Harry S. Stout, and Charles Reagan Wilson (New York: Oxford University Press, 1998); Phillip Shaw Paludan, "Religion and the American Civil War," also in *Religion and the American Civil War*; Mark Y. Hanley, *Beyond a Christian Commonwealth: The Protestant Quarrel with the American Republic, 1830–1860* (Chapel Hill: University of North Carolina Press, 1994); and Terrie Dopp Aamodt, *Righteous Armies, Holy Cause: Apocalyptic Imagery and the Civil War* (Macon, GA: Mercer University Press, 2002), H 53.

35. S. A. Hodgman, *The Great Republic Judged, but Not Destroyed*, 2d ed. (New York, 1865).

36. J. W. Tucker, "God's Providence in War" (1862). In *"God Ordained this War": Sermons on the Sectional Crisis, 1830–1865*, ed. David B. Chesebrough (Columbia: University of South Carolina Press, 1991), 229, 233–234

37. Henry Ward Beecher, *Oration at the Raising of the 'Old Flag' at Sumter; and Sermon on the Death of Abraham Lincoln, President of the United States* (Manchester: Alexander Ireland, 1865), 12–13.

38. See Andrew R. Murphy, "Religion and the Presidency of Abraham Lincoln," in *Religion and the American Presidency*, ed. Gaston Espinosa (New York: Columbia University Press, 2008).

39. One important exception is worth noting. When Lincoln announced to his Cabinet his intention to issue the Emancipation Proclamation, he claimed that, on the basis of a vow he had made to himself and to God, he interpreted the Union victory at Antietam as indicative of a divine will in favor of emancipation. The Cabinet's response to Lincoln's announcement was, predictably, one of surprise and confusion. See Allen Guelzo, *Lincoln's Emancipation Proclamation: The End of Slavery in America* (New York: Simon and Schuster, 2004), 153; see also Allen Guelzo, *Abraham Lincoln: Redeemer President* (Grand Rapids, MI: Eerdmans, 1999), 341; David Herbert Donald, *Lincoln* (New York: Simon and Schuster, 1995), 374–375; William J. Wolf, *The Almost Chosen People: A Study of the Religion of Abraham Lincoln* (Garden City, NY: Doubleday, 1959), 17.

40. Abraham Lincoln, *The Collected Works of Abraham Lincoln*, ed. Roy P. Basler (New Brunswick, NJ: Rutgers University Press, 1953), 5: 419–420.

41. Ibid., 403–404.

42. Mark A. Noll, *America's God: From Jonathan Edwards to Abraham Lincoln* (New York: Oxford University Press, 2002), 434.

43. Abraham Lincoln, "Second Inaugural Address" (March 4, 1865), in *Collected Works*, 8: 333 (emphasis added). On the scale of violence, see Harry S. Stout, *Upon the Altar of the Nation: A Moral History of the Civil War* (New York: Viking, 2006).

44. Stout, *Upon the Altar of the Nation*, 86.

45. Ibid., 426; also 145–146.

46. Gaines M. Foster, *Moral Reconstruction: Christian Lobbyists and the Federal Legislation of Morality, 1865–1920* (Chapel Hill: University of North Carolina Press, 2002), 223.

47. James F. Findlay, "Religion and Politics in the Sixties: The Churches and the Civil Rights Act of 1964," *Journal of American History* 77 (1990): 90; Carl F. Henry, *Twilight of a Great Civilization: The Drift toward Neo-paganism* (Westchester, IL: Crossway Books, 1988), 172. Richard John Neuhaus draws on Seymour Martin Lipset's notion of "aggressive defense": "Their defense is against what they perceive as governmental actions dictated by 'secular humanists' in control of American public life"; see Neuhaus, "What the Fundamentalists Want," in *Piety and Politics: Evangelicals and Fundamentalists Confront the World*, ed. Richard John Neuhaus and Michael Cromartie (Washington, DC: Ethics and Public Policy Center, 1987), 16.

48. Jerry Falwell, *The 700 Club*, Sept. 13, 2001.

49. George W. Bush, Remarks at National Day of Prayer and Remembrance for the Victims of the Terrorist Attacks on September 11, 2001, Sept. 14, 2001, http://www.opm.gov/guidance/09-14-01gwb.htm (accessed 29 December 2011).

50. George W. Bush, "Second Inaugural Address, http://www.nytimes.com/2005/01/20/politics/20BUSH-TEXT.htm.

51. Martin Luther King Jr., "Where Do We Go from Here?" Address to the 11th Annual Southern Christian Leadership Conference, 16 August 1967, Atlanta, Georgia, http://mlk-kpp01.stanford.edu/index.php/encyclopedia/documentsentry/where_do_we_go_from_here_delivered_at_the_11th_annual_sclc_convention./.

52. Martin Luther King Jr., "Letter from Birmingham Jail," in *Why We Can't Wait* (reissue; Boston: Beacon Press, 2011), 93.

53. Martin Luther King Jr., Speech at the Lincoln Memorial (1963), http://www.americanrheto ric.com/speeches/mlkihaveadream.htm.

54. Ibid.

55. Martin Luther King Jr., Nobel Prize Acceptance Speech (1964), http://www.nobelprize.org/ nobel_prizes/peace/laureates/1964/king-acceptance.html.

56. King, Speech at the Lincoln Memorial.

2

A Nation Birthed in Blood

Violent Cosmogonies and American Film

S. Brent Rodriguez-Plate

Toward the end of D. W. Griffith's 1915 film *The Birth of a Nation*, about the U.S. Civil War and its aftermath, an oversized, ethereal Jesus appears to a group of people from upon a hill—a heavenly declaration of coming harmony between North and South, black and white. The Christ figure is a unifier, bringing together divisive factions, attempting to prove that in spite of its racist history, its violent warring over political, racial, and religious issues, the United States will be born again. In its day, Griffith's film served as a cinematic cosmogonic myth—an accounting of national origins—for a nation asking, with increasing urgency, "Who are we?" "Where do we come from?" and "How did we become the America we are?" The nation's impulse to ask questions about its identity and origins is not hard to fathom considering its short remove from the recently ended Spanish-American War, Europe's rapid descent into war, and the ongoing traumas of historic immigration and society-changing industrialization and urbanization at home. Through sophisticated cinematic techniques, Griffith provided answers. Echoing the sentiments expressed by John Winthrop in his *Model of Christian Charity*, Griffith declared that God would smile on this chosen nation once unity, harmony, and hierarchy were reestablished. In Griffith's film, that would occur when nonwhite peoples returned to their "proper" place.[1]

Griffith's creation story functions as a precursor among precursors to Paul Thomas Anderson's 2007 film *There Will Be Blood*, which played to a United States again beset by turmoil and seeking answers to questions about its identity. Anderson's film describes the "birth" of the nation we know today through a mythologized take on the late nineteenth-century emergence of petroleum extraction, juxtaposed against a peculiar form of revivalist, charismatic Christianity. *Blood* is by no means the only cosmogonic film of the last century, but it does offer a cosmogony particularly relevant to American foreign policy and its wars against Iraq. It argues that central to American identity are oil, the self-made man, and religion, all of which depend, to varying degrees, on violence. The film points up some of the moral problems born of the convergence of these three American institutions. By reflecting on *There Will Be Blood*, we can see how film reflects and helps shape contemporary historical consciousness and how filmic displays of violence function to develop and sustain a national mythology.

This chapter considers the mythologies of films in general and *There Will Be Blood* in particular, situating Anderson's film within a history of other national cosmogonies. After outlining some of the ways in which film contributes to the study of history, religion, and mythology, I survey the ways in which violence is reconfigured in audiovisual media. I then discuss Anderson's film in relation to Upton Sinclair's 1927 novel, *Oil!*, on which *Blood* was loosely based. Like all cosmogonic myths, *Blood* speaks to and reflects the social, political, and economic interests of a particular historical moment. Film, I argue, has become critical to and even constitutive of the founding mythologies of U.S. history, expressing more clearly than any other medium the centrality of violence in the American character, consciousness, and cosmos. While narrating stories of origin, films such as *Blood* also offer penetrating critiques of American society and of its moral dimensions.

VIOLENCE IN FILM AND SOCIETY

In our attempt to understand the United States and its relation to violence in the world, it is necessary to come to terms with the violence the nation depicts and projects—both on the screen and on the psyche. Violent crime happens so regularly in the United States that we scarcely take note of it. War, too, has become an enduring reality of the American experience. Such violence also is represented on a massive scale every day in the United States through film, television, music, video games, and news analyses. Many studies point out the staggering number of violent depictions in video games, films, and television. Seldom do we stop to ponder how these violent projections become embedded in the mythic consciousness of Americans.[2] Among myriad others, film scholar Stephen Prince has written extensively on the role of violence within film, arguing that violent films, especially those beginning in the late 1960s like *Bonnie and Clyde* (Arthur Penn, 1967) have, against their makers' intents, actually desensitized people to violence on screen.[3] Arthur Penn and other directors believed that such depictions would reveal violence for what it is: ugly and mangling. They assumed their films would dissuade viewers from acting out violently themselves.

The debate over violence in the media is familiar. To some, depictions of violence in films are cathartic, safely releasing aggressive tendencies in the theater. To others, film depictions of violence insinuate themselves into the minds of their viewers, who then carry violent tendencies around in their bodies. The latter group can point to the 1995 film *Basketball Diaries*, in which the protagonist, Jim Carroll, played by Leonardo DiCaprio, fantasizes about a scenario in which, wearing a trenchcoat, he enters a school and begins to shoot fellow students. This film was released four years before the Columbine High School massacre in Colorado, in which, as was widely reported, the killers wore trenchcoats as they shot students and teachers in the hallways and classrooms. Were those who wrought such horrific destruction at Columbine consciously bringing to life a cinematic vision? Would their actions have been different or less violent without the stimulus of film violence? Whatever the answer, the fact remains that the vast majority of people who saw *Basketball Diaries* and who see violent movies do not go on killing sprees or commit acts of violence.

We will not soon resolve this debate over causality, but we can think in other, broader ways about violence in film and what it tells us about the violence in U.S. society. Americans draw on a storehouse of mythical images created in and through cinema, establishing a kind of collective unconscious. In cinema, violence—forces of destruction—often become intertwined with forces of creation. The creation myths at the heart of the world's religions are rife with violence. Human society is often understood to be founded upon murder: Cain kills Abel, in Hindu stories Purusha is dismembered and sacrificed, the ancient Babylonian god Marduk slays Tiamat, and so on. This is true also of national creation myths: "The Revolution" is a crucial starting point for foundational stories of the United States; "The Terror" stands at the origins of democratic France; "The Partition" is central to the formation of an independent India and Pakistan (and later also Bangladesh) and to the war that followed. And the Spanish-American War gave rise to the founding political identities of Puerto Rico, Cuba, the Philippines, and Guam, at the same time that it marked, as *There Will Be Blood* surmises, a new stage in the emergence of the imperial United States. Violence is an undeniably central and frequently glorified aspect of American "origins" and identities. Anderson's *There Will Be Blood* expresses this national and mythological tradition in powerful ways. It also, ultimately, provides viewers in the United States and abroad with an interpretive framework—a countermythology—with which to recognize and challenge the violence of America's cosmogonic mythologies.

CREATING WORLDS ON SCREEN

Film and religion are analogous. As Ian McEwan recently wrote, they are "two grand designs, conjuring light out of darkness."[4] They bring viewers or adherents before the screen or altar to offer them glimpses of another world. Religions work through their myths, rituals, and texts to enable adherents to imagine worlds. They describe the contours of past and future worlds, describing carefully points of origin and ultimate destinations, glorious and hellish, that await those who accept or challenge the cosmic order. Religions create mythic worlds in which the sick can be healed, rivers are goddesses, the dead are resurrected, animals prophesy to humans, and amulets ward off evil spirits. As they map these worlds, religions also serve as a base from which to critique and condemn, praise and glorify certain ways of being in the world. Through reenacted stories of creation, liberation, heroes, goddesses and gods, and apocalyptic endings, as well as everyday life, religions and their myths shape identities, origins, and moralities. They tell the faithful who they are, where they came from, and how they ought to be. Religious practitioners leave synagogues, temples, mosques, or churches contemplating these origins and identities and, sometimes, inspired to live according to them.

Film, too, creates alternative worlds and invites viewers to partake of the many delights and terrors of those worlds. Viewers experience these worlds through the screen and speakers before returning—enriched, enlivened, transformed—to their mundane lives in the "real" world. Films, like religions, often take their viewers back to the creation of a world or worlds. Film productions are quite self-conscious about this world creation: from the cosmically oriented production studio logos (note how many of them—whether it is Paramount, Columbia, Universal, or Dreamworks—orient themselves to the clouds, stars, moon, and high mountains), to the trailers for coming attractions (note how often the first line introducing a new film suggests, "In a world where . . ."), to the careful up-and-down camera tilts of the feature presentation ("up" is good, pure, a point of connection, while "down" is bad, chaotic, and disembodying), to the pulsing soundtrack that echoes in our heads. Film productions take the known or "real" world and recreate it, offering sometimes hopeful and sometimes dreadful glimpses into hypothetical alternative realities: *What if* the world were destroyed by global warming/an asteroid/a monster arising from the sea? *What if* a beautiful woman were hopelessly attracted to an oaf with no future? *What if* we could be young again? Film, like religion, asks us to contemplate possibilities, however impossible they may be, and what such possibilities tell us about ourselves, the United States, and its destiny.[5]

To be sure, religions and films possess their own purposes. World-creating, meaning-making activities are not central to all films or every religious consciousness. But we do well to recognize these points of connection between the cinematic and the religious registers. Such a recognition helps to situate the religion-film relation beyond the questions of whether a film features a Christ figure or concludes with a triumphant salvation scene. There are more important facets of film for the student of religious history. In recreating the possibilities of the known world, in proffering the question "What if?," films and religions each operate mythologically, proposing audiovisual narratives that have bearing, even if indirectly, on our lives. Moreover, the symbolic registers to which films appeal, while often informed by religion, are, equally powerfully, informed by the sacred narratives, symbols, and figures of the nation. Like religions, films tell stories, ask questions, and help form identities that reach beyond the individual to the collective. Religions and films speak from and to a society—whether a religious community or a nation. They purport to tell us—Americans, for example—who we are and how we should be or act. Like some forms of religion, certain films hope to tell a people where it has come from, where it is going, and where it should or should not go. These are foundational features of myth in general and national myths in particular. Many films act as myths or have mythic elements, but *There Will Be Blood* stands out for the vitality of such elements in the film's story and structure. Paul Thomas Anderson has provided an opportunity to tease out some of the interrelations of film, violence, and national mythology.

ANDERSON'S *BLOOD* AND SINCLAIR'S *OIL!*

We cannot take film seriously as a mythic medium without recognizing that adaptation is an inextricable part of the creative process. Like the creative forces that produce mythologies, filmic adaptation is a complex process that entails not only the creation of an audiovisual product, culled from the simply verbal-literary narratives of literature and spoken words; film also provides an updated way of retelling old stories. An audiovisualized story inevitably alters an already altered literary narrative, just as written and printed words alter oral stories. Thus, judging a film for not being "true to the book" misses the point.[6] Adaptation is inevitable and ongoing in myth and in film. There being neither a primordial medium, nor any strictly original myth that we can access, we should always ask: What are the characteristics of the world a film describes? Why has the director chosen to create this particular world? And, for our purposes, where do religion and violence figure in the creation of that world?

A look at Upton Sinclair's 1927 novel *Oil!* reveals a variety of specific instances adapted in Anderson's film. These adaptations give us a strong sense of Anderson's cosmogonic project and demonstrate the more general truths that myths are composed for an audience and are shaped by the worlds they address. Both *Oil!* and *There Will Be Blood* are morality tales. Both works dramatize how prioritizing the individual over the community—whether through the pursuit of oil and wealth or through the abuse of religious authority—corrupts the human psyche and disrupts social life. The differences between the novel and the film highlight for us how differently Sinclair and Anderson (and presumably their enthusiastic audiences) conceived of the relationship among oil, religion, and violence as defining features of America.

Some simple differences between the works require consideration. Sinclair's fictional work begins in 1911 in California, a time and place in which the rush for oil was already well under way. Anderson's film begins thirteen years earlier, in 1898, in New Mexico. Anderson's choice of setting is intriguing. Eighteen ninety-eight was, of course, the year in which the "splendid little war" between the United States and Spain broke out, the results of which made the United States into a transoceanic imperial power. Violence, war, and conquest hang invisibly in the background of *Blood*. Yet the canvas that Anderson allows us to see is oddly blank—it is arid New Mexico (territory also acquired by war), not lush California. The scramble to extract resources exists at the micro level, to be sure, but the emotional and violent trappings of that scramble are not yet evident. Impulses and energies exist, but they exist as potential, as unformed void. The film's opening symbolizes the creation of a new world, represented by Daniel Plainview (Daniel Day-Lewis), mining alone in a barren void. In suffering a debilitating fall and soldiering on in spite of it, Plainview foretells how a nation will be built—a new world created by self-made men willing to endure hardship and pain in the pursuit of wealth and greatness. *Blood* also operates as cosmogonic mythology as it moves forcefully, even violently, from chaos to order. Creation myths often depict chaos that exists at the origins of the world, placing that chaos underground or surrounding it with water (Genesis 1 is full of such language). At the beginning of *Blood* we find a claustrophobic cosmology, with a yet unnamed Daniel digging deep in a dark well for silver. A few years later, when he is digging again, this time in California, he stumbles on oil. As the film progresses, Daniel becomes a violent demiurge, imposing cosmic order on the chaotic reserves of oil lying below the California landscape, remaking the natural world and structuring and creating a new world according to his vision of order.

Anderson's naming of his characters also incorporates mythic and cosmogonic elements. The two families at the center of the story are named Plainview and Sunday (Sinclair had named them Ross and Watkins). These changes cry out for interpretation. Sunday, the Christian Sabbath when many Americans worship, invites reflection on the nature of the American "god" and the true teachings of its "church." The name Plainview suggests clear vision, but vision of a simple, limited, and qualified sort. One might think of "realism" (an apt descriptor of Daniel Plainview's worldview) or an inability to perceive subtlety and nuance. And what of Plainview's first name, Daniel? Did Anderson rename Sinclair's J. Arnold Ross, whose name echoed the names of contemporary captains of industry, to call forth the apocalyptic prophecies of the book of Daniel? Are we to see in Anderson's oil-soaked and blood-stained Daniel a man who can survive among lions, foretell the destruction of kingdoms, and read the writing on the wall? Surrounding Daniel with characters named Paul, Eli, and Abel (names Anderson retained from Sinclair's book) lends even greater biblical and mythic weight to the film. These alterations alert us that Anderson wants to do more than just tell a story. His goal, it seems, is to imagine a scene that tells an American creation story by investing the lives and decisions of its men (women are noticeably absent) with cosmic and cosmogonic significance.

The lifeblood of Upton Sinclair's novel and Paul Thomas Anderson's film is oil. Both men agree, though in different tones and with different bodies of evidence, that oil is the most crucial substance of the American cosmos. Formless and pulsing, it rages with unrealized potential beneath the ground, waiting to gush forth its creative energy. For the United States of the twentieth and twenty-first centuries, oil stands as one of the key creative elements in the shaping of the contemporary nation and its place vis-à-vis the rest of the world. Environmental studies scholar Brian Black has written extensively on the impact of petroleum production and consumption on the formation of the American national character and discusses it in terms of an ethic of extraction, including the psychological and often damaging lure of oil. Petroleum extractors in America took advantage of local communities, creating and eventually abandoning "boom towns" in the wake of oil extraction. This lust for oil—which drove the formation of communities as well as the willingness to abandon them—he argues, reshaped the individual and communal character of the people.[7] Today one can see myriad manifestations of this ethic and of the violence to which it can lead and has led. This violence, often draped in religion, emerges clearly in the film (more so than in the novel), as when Plainview exploits families and communities that sit atop great untapped reservoirs of oil. Religion is a tool of exploitation. Oil is precious—more precious than people. Oil is sacred.

A striking scene shared by the novel and the film points toward the sanctification of oil itself. It is the inauguration of the first oil derrick on the Watkins/Sunday property. In Sinclair's novel, Eli Watkins, the "Prophet of the Third Revelation," arrives at the event in a "big shiny limousine," "transfigured and glorified in a stiff white collar and black tie and black broadcloth suit." After J. Arnold Ross says a few words, he invites Eli to give a blessing of the well, to which the crowd responds "Amen!" Sinclair then makes the holy nature of the oil explicit: "All the lies that [Ross] had told to the Watkins family and to others, the bribes that he had paid . . . all these were abrogated, nullified and remitted, and the [well] was from that time forth a sanctified well."[8] Drilling for oil becomes a redemptive activity, absolution for one's sins.

There Will Be Blood affirms the holiness of oil but depicts the scene differently by showing a cosmic struggle between oil and the competing deity "religion." The acting and the characters emphasize the self-made men that Plainview and Sunday eventually become, and that the mythology of *Oil!* and *Blood* seek to highlight. Naked ambition drives the oilman and preacher man alike, making commerce and religion competing products of showmanship. In the film, Eli wishes to bless the rig upon its opening, but Daniel shrewdly bypasses him, departing from the religious message and undermining Eli's authority. Here holy oil displaces the traditional God of Christianity. Eli Sunday learns this lesson again through a violent "baptism" administered by Plainview. In the scene Plainview is in the oilfield talking to his associates when Sunday walks up, asking for some of the money that Plainview has promised. Plainview slaps him around, throws him down, and then smears his face with oil. In a later scene, though, Eli gains the upper hand in the struggle, this time on his turf and using the more familiar baptismal substance, water. A member of Eli's congregation demands that Plainview be baptized before extracting the oil from his property. Plainview consents—the pocket of oil is substantial—and thus submits to Eli's authority. As Eli is about to pour water over Daniel's head, Eli yells, "Do you want the blood?!" Daniel calmly but insincerely accepts: "Just give me the blood, Eli." Thus is the original, violent, humiliating "baptism" of Eli by Daniel reciprocated by the baptism and momentary humiliation of Daniel by Eli. The film portrays and ultimately resolves this cosmic struggle between oil and religion. The liquid elements may swirl and mix, exchanging symbolic properties: oil becomes water, water becomes blood. But oil, sacred substance that it has become to the United States, emerges supreme, with the mythic power to create. The film shows capitalism trumping and appropriating religion's properties to bless and curse, to coax and reward, to judge and redeem—and even, finally, to condemn.

The mythic signals of the film call us to take especially seriously the relationship between capitalism and religion in the world Anderson creates. It is here, after all, that we see a major departure from Sinclair's novel, revealing each artist's understanding of the American cosmos vis-à-vis oil and religion. Eighty years before Anderson, Sinclair concluded his story of American faith and American capitalism with the two in close allegiance. At the end of *Oil!*, J. Arnold Ross has disappeared and "Bunny," his adopted son, takes his inherited wealth and puts it toward social-political causes. Eli Watkins, the revivalist preacher, remains successful—"Eli's tabernacle was packed day and night . . . all California heard Eli's voice"[9]—and is an ardent supporter of capitalism. In Sinclair's socialist vision, revivalist-charismatic religion and capitalism work hand in hand to limit the aspirations of common folk. Anderson's story, however, ends with a shocking, violent assertion of "capitalist" domination over "religion." Sunday too becomes a self-made man whose quest for wealth and power, mirroring the efforts of Plainview, overshadows the sincerity of his faith. Alas, Eli Sunday, preaching star, has risen and fallen, and near the end of the film we find him begging the rich, irascible and misanthropic mogul Plainview first for money and then for his life. In Anderson's myth, capitalism and religion may at times coexist, but capitalism always sets the terms of the relationship. The film ends with Daniel shouting, "I'm finished!" Perhaps. But the capitalist forces he symbolizes and the world he creates endure.

These different tellings of a similar story about the origins, energies, and ambitions of the American character diverge in other places and, in those moments, reveal much about their creators. One is not more important than the other. *Oil!* and *Blood* are different stories, speaking in different media, to different audiences in different times. But the differences and similarities help to show the ways in which *Blood* is deeply entrenched in a mythological tradition of United States history, a tradition in which the nation's creation story must be retold, updated, and recreated as the nation itself is reborn, updated, and recreated.

THE MEANING OF MYTHIC ELEMENTS
AND STRUCTURES IN *THERE WILL BE BLOOD*

Cosmogonies, like other myths, rely upon certain recurring symbols and features. *There Will Be Blood* operates in a traditional mythic mode through its chronological and geographical setting, its narrative arc, and its portrayals of struggles between "brothers" representing forces competing for ultimate authority. Like all good stories, myths begin by specifying the time and space in which the forthcoming action will take place. With myths, however, original settings tend toward ambiguity: "In the beginning . . ." sets a time, yet what kind of time is it? When, exactly, is "the beginning"? While the opening minute of *Blood* fixes the year as 1898, the viewer is quickly thrown off by two additional bits of information. First, the date, like the title of the film itself, is scripted in a Gothic typeface, an antiquated script, that evokes the King James Version of the Bible and was no longer in use in the late nineteenth century (at least, outside Germany).[10] Is this 1898 or 1598? A second destabilizing datum is the searing music by Jonny Greenwood. Greenwood's score borrows much from contemporary avant-garde/classical groups providing at least a late twentieth-century sound, yet the music is performed on instruments available earlier in the century, and thus could have been heard at the time the film takes place. Again, is this really 1898—or 1998? Time-space discrepancies continue through the film's sights and sounds, culminating in the final devastating shot of the film, as Brahms's sublime Violin Concerto in D Major strikes up over a scene of barbarity made surreal by the civilized surroundings—a bowling alley in a mansion—in which it takes place.

The 1898 setting also seems odd since the action that occurs at this time involves a man in a mine looking for silver. The first fifteen minutes of nonverbal, almost silent, action could have taken place at any moment since the Iron Age. There is nothing precise about a man in a well looking for metal. In this timeless setting the quite specific historical events that inform the picture—the Spanish-American War and the theopolitics of manifest destiny, the ruthless economies of oil extraction and production,[11] and the efflorescence of charismatic forms of Christianity—become timeless themselves. They tell a history, yes, but they also foretell a future.

Cosmogonic mythologies often emerge from the natural environment: the narratives unfold on continents and in constellations, making use of trees, seas, and stars. Stories of creation begin, and end, with the natural world and show the human and cosmic dependence upon, and sometimes independence from, material realities. There Will Be Blood, as myth, constantly points toward the physical liquid elements of oil, blood, and water, as well as toward firmer substances like stone and sand, wood and steel. Some elements help create, others help destroy, and all are deeply enmeshed in the making and remaking of the American world or the world that America helped make. This cosmic landscape is imitated through filmic means as well. Blood portrays a horizontal view of the cosmos, punctuated by glances downward. (Blood's cinematographer, Robert Elswit, won the Academy Award for his achievement here.) The earth and sky are severed from each other. The film is shot in "big sky" country, but we are not shown the sun, moon, or stars, suggesting an immanent world cut off from the heavens or other transcendent features. When the sky can be seen, it is compressed into only the upper third of any shot, high on the horizon, and seemingly out of reach. We get the effects of the sun—human sweat, bleached landscapes—but never the sun itself. All light sources shown are human made, the most powerful example being the burning oil derrick at dusk, the result of an accidental explosion.

Like many prominent myths from religions around the world, There Will Be Blood features brothers/twins and relies on the forging and breaking of social and familial bonds: fathers sacrificing sons, brothers out for revenge, and men trying to subdue each other. Twins and brothers, false and true, shadows and doppelgangers, are spread across the world's great myths: Cain and Abel, Jacob and Esau, Gilgamesh and Enkidu, Heracles and Iphicles, Romulus and Remus, Thomas and Jesus. In Blood, brothers Paul and Eli Sunday (both parts played by Paul Dano) are antagonistic toward each other but are also instrumental in shaping Daniel Plainview's world. Daniel, loner that he is, desires familial connection. He readily takes in H.W. ("Bunny" in Sinclair's novel) as a son when H.W.'s father is killed in a mining accident. At another point in the film he eagerly believes that a stranger who finds his way to Daniel's house is his lost brother,

Henry. Henry quickly replaces Daniel's loyal right-hand man, Fletcher Hamilton, until Plainview realizes that this "brother" is an impostor. Plainview murders him.

By film's end, we see that it is Daniel and Eli, representing oil and religion, who are brothers. Functionally and allegorically they are twins. Daniel extracts oil from the earth as Eli extracts evil spirits from the bodies of people. Daniel is a murderous Cain. Eli, whose father is named Abel, dies by Cain's hand. Or, shifting the fraternal reference to Jacob and Esau, the heir to the nation's birthright is, in the end, the thoroughly violent and despicable Plainview. Plainview is the true prophet who compels Eli to confess that he is a false prophet. The real revelation, the true extraction from the hidden recesses of the cosmos, is not God above but oil below. The story that began with something like the first chapter of Genesis, with the divine formation of cosmic order out of chaos, has moved quickly to Genesis 4, in which Cain takes Abel into the field and kills him. In Jewish and Christian scripture, God responds to Cain's question "Am I my brother's keeper?" by asking "What have you done?" and then proclaiming, "Your brother's blood is crying out to me from the ground. Now you are accursed and will be banished from the very ground which has opened its mouth to receive the blood you have shed" (Gen. 4:10–11). Anderson's cosmos functions differently, showing the subversion of divine judgment to capitalist dominance. Prophets of God come and go, but the oil industry and capitalism endure.[12]

In *Blood*, we see the corrupting influence of these forces as Daniel Plainview is transformed from an eager, hard-nosed and hard-working silver prospector into a crazed, drunken, violent, lonely old man who grows more diabolical by the minute. He begins as a man capable of caring for and adopting as his own the orphaned son of one of his workers, but he eventually curses and turns his back on the boy. This film, like many cosmogonic myths, is not simply about individual morality but about the larger social structures and narratives that the film's personal ethics shape and symbolize. *Blood* cautions against individual greed, to be sure, but it also subtly tells a tale of the United States and the temptations to which it succumbed as it became a world power at the dawn of the twentieth century. The film shows how the confused and confusing moralities of the late twentieth and early twenty-first centuries were woven into the American cosmos "in the beginning." The deeply solitary moments of the film speak to a nation whose loneliness results from its capitalist excesses and lust for glory.

There Will Be Blood is certainly not an apology for the state of the nation in the twentieth or twenty-first century. It is, rather, an explanation: *This is who we are. This is our origin and our cosmos. Thus have we made the world. The United States we know today was born in the unnamed void of the late nineteenth century. Religion has been part of the national fabric, but America's god is oil and oilmen its high priests. The creation of this cosmos required that blood be shed, and so does the ongoing narration and unfolding of the American story. Moreover, when the story of the American cosmos is challenged—from without or from within—"there will be blood."*

Anderson's film operates within a genre of violent and ultraviolent films, like many of those directed by Penn, Scorsese, Peckinpah, and Tarantino. But in contrast to the plentitude of violent death that characterizes Tarantino's *Pulp Fiction*, Spielberg's *Saving Private Ryan*, and Gibson's *The Patriot*, the deaths in *Blood* are pedestrian and low-tech, brought about by fists, loose machine bits, and bowling pins. All but two are accidental. It is surprising, as Greenwood's overwhelmingly oppressive music meets the harsh southwestern landscape, that more blood hasn't been spent. The most graphically violent scene is the final one, one the title has promised. But like many films, *Blood* reaches well beyond its own narrative frame and, one could argue, shows so little of the anticipated violence precisely because the audience knows so well where the story is going and the extent of the bloodshed associated with it. The relative absence of bloody interpersonal violence in the film points to a powerful presence in the world Anderson is addressing. He doesn't need to hit us over the head, as Daniel does Eli, because U.S. and international audiences in 2007 already know the violent story of the American-ruled cosmos. There will be oil. There will be wealth. There will be empire. There will be blood.

REBIRTH OF A NATION: WHAT KIND OF CITY SHALL WE BE?

I close by returning to the concluding scene in Griffith's *Birth of a Nation*: Christ stands on a hill, ethereal and copious, evoking John Winthrop's striking rendition of Matthew: "For we must consider that we shall be as a city upon a hill. The eyes of all people are upon us." In his 1630 sermon, Winthrop invoked Jesus' Sermon on the Mount (Matthew 5: "You are the light of the world. A city set on a hill cannot be hid.") Today, the eyes of the world remain upon that city, the United States. The world is watching movies, many of them produced in the United States and shot through with American ideas and ideologies. And through this American projection, the United States must come to grips with its mythical and projected identity and also with its violent warrings, whether between black and white, between north and south, between oil and religion, or even between good and evil.

The medium of film projects a collective understanding of a nation's origins, identity, and the hopes of its people at a particular point in history, from a particular director's view. But film can also, ultimately, subvert or critique the mythologies it propagates. D.W. Griffith did not intend to upend the racist hegemony of his era, and he did not; but ninety years after his film depicted a Christ figure sanctifying a racist unity, *Birth of a Nation* is used in film classes everywhere to alert students to the phenomenon of racial stereotyping in media and to implicate film in its propagation. Here is the use of mythology as a critique of mythology, a turning of cosmology back onto itself—to recreate flawed earlier cosmogonies. This is another reason why Anderson's film is so valuable. It shows how mythological structures and elements can be used against other, perhaps more oppressive stories. With *Blood*, and with film more generally, we find another, more subtle, and I would suggest altogether more powerful, way to approach myth: violent myths retelling violent myths as a cautionary tale of American violence.

NOTES

1. Extensive study of Griffith's film is beyond the scope of this chapter. See Melvyn Stokes, *D. W. Griffith's The Birth of a Nation: A History of the Most Controversial Motion Picture of All Time* (New York: Oxford University Press, 2008). Many suggestions about Griffith's film were initially made in Kris Jozajtiz, "'The Eyes of All People Are upon Us': American Civil Religion and the Birth of Hollywood," in *Representing Religion in World Cinema*, ed. S. Brent Plate (New York: Palgrave Macmillan, 2003), 239–261.

2. Important works on violence and film from a film studies perspective include J. David Slocum, ed., *Violence in American Cinema* (New York: Routledge, 2000); and Christopher Sharrett, ed., *Mythologies of Violence in Postmodern Media* (Detroit: Wayne State University Press, 1999).

3. See Stephen Prince, *Screening Violence* (New Brunswick, NJ: Rutgers University Press, 2000) and *Savage Cinema* (Austin: University of Texas Press, 1998). *Bonnie and Clyde* is generally regarded as a watershed in violent film in the United States, particularly for the climactic scene in which the eponymous couple (played by Warren Beatty and Faye Dunaway) is riddled with bullets as their bodies writhe, twist, and turn. Never before in a prominent motion picture was death by shooting so extravagantly displayed: until that point, film characters were killed with a single shot that had little bodily impact and little more than a trickle of blood. As such, the late 1960s exploration of the body is roughly parallel to the late fourteenth-century renaissance of the body in European painting: before that time the crucifixion of Jesus was represented as a two-dimensional, relatively acorporeal stick figure, while the rebirth of classical culture gave rise to the challenging depictions of a truly suffering, bodily Jesus as seen in works by Mantegna, Grunewald, and Caravaggio.

4. Ian McEwan, "On John Updike," *New York Review of Books*, March 12, 2009.

5. The idea of film and religion as "recreated worlds" is argued further in my book *Religion and Film: Cinema and the Re-Creation of the World* (London: Wallflower Press, 2008).

6. In this light, the audiovisual nature of film often comes closer to the essential re-presentation of older, oral mythologies, told in close-knit communities, with an abundance of sensual triggers that reconstitute the world the book creates. Several reviews of *There Will Be Blood* criticized it for its failure to be "true" to Sinclair's original story, particularly because of a perceived neglect of Sinclair's socialist aspirations. See, for example, David Bacon at "Truthout," www.truthout.org/article/david-bacon-bad-capitalists-or-a-bad-system (accessed July 15, 2008); Spencer Dew at "Sightings," http://marty-center.uchicago.edu/sightings/archive_2008/0403.shtml (accessed July 15, 2008); as well as a response by Stephen Carter to an interview between me and Claire Hoffman at the *Washington Post*'s "Under God" blog: http://newsweek.washingtonpost.com/onfaith/undergod/2008/02/there_will_be_religion.html (accessed May 15, 2008).

7. See Brian C. Black, *Petrolia: The Landscape of America's First Oil Boom* (Baltimore: Johns Hopkins University Press, 2000) and *Nature in Everyday American Life*, 2 vols. (Westport, CT: Greenwood, 2006).

8. *Oil!* (New York: A. & C. Boni, 1927), 146–147.

9. Ibid., 497.

10. This style is revived in the DVD release of the film: the DVD package itself is made to look like a well-worn, leather-bound Bible.

11. See especially Ida Tarbell, *The History of the Standard Oil Company* (New York: McClure, Phillips, 1904).

12. See Fortune 500's website, http://money.cnn.com/magazines/fortune/fortune500/2007/index.html (accessed June 23, 2008).

3

From Covenant to Crusade and Back

American Christianity and the Late Great War

Jonathan H. Ebel

World War I is a vexing chapter in American history. In retrospect it stands awkwardly in the shadow of World War II, its more compelling, supposedly less morally complex sequel. Taken on its own terms, the Great War appears profoundly discontinuous from the historical currents surrounding it. How does one account for American involvement in such a devastating conflict during an era of optimism and faith in progress? What vital national interest could have drawn four million American men and tens of thousands of American women to serve in a war against European powers when the U.S. homeland was not directly threatened? What forces and dynamics could have impelled the U.S. government to forgo George Washington's famous caution against "permanent alliances" and to maintain the coalition it joined in the Great War through much of the subsequent century?

This chapter approaches these questions by way of wartime invocations of covenant and covenantal rhetoric. My argument has two parts. First, covenantal rhetoric played a significant role in bringing the United States into the war, explaining wartime experiences, and ordering the postwar world. Second, the Great War brought to the surface a tension inherent in Judeo-Christian covenantalism between two aspects of covenant: the vertical, which forges an alliance between parties of unequal power; and the horizontal, which forges a collective out of smaller parties or individuals. These two axes provided important interpretive frameworks for those who took America into the war. Covenantal thinking also shaped American self-reflection after the war ended. In a postwar world characterized by division and danger those who spoke in covenantal tones reconsidered the terms of prewar covenants and directed Americans' allegiances toward more immanent, knowable deities. The Great War and its aftermath paradoxically demonstrate both the appeal of covenantal rhetoric and, especially in the post-war period, discomfort with the judging, punishing, demanding supranational power so prominent in scriptural presentations of covenant. The attendant flattening of the covenant's vertical axis had the effect of making America its own deity.

ANCIENT COVENANTS AND AMERICAN HISTORY

To appreciate America's covenantal character, it is helpful to recall earlier influences and precursors. Scholars of ancient Near Eastern religions have shown that the sovereign-vassal treaty, common among political entities throughout that region, provided the template for the biblical covenant between Yahweh and the Israelites. Sovereign-vassal treaties in their raw political form established relationships between political leaders of unequal power and worked, albeit unevenly, to the benefit of both. The terms of such treaties generally stated that the sovereign, the more powerful of the two parties, would protect the vassal from attack and that the vassal would swear allegiance to the sovereign and provide him with resources and soldiers when needed. These treaties frequently spelled out dire consequences for the unfaithful or inattentive vassal, whose survival in the rough-and-tumble ancient Near East depended upon a powerful defender.

Exodus 19–24 is one moment in Jewish and Christian scripture when the connection between covenant and the sovereign-vassal treaty is especially apparent. In Exodus 19 the vassal Israelites, represented by Moses, receive a promise from Yahweh that they will have a special status before Him: "Now therefore, if you obey my voice and keep my covenant, you shall be my treasured possession out of all peoples. Indeed, the whole earth is mine, but you shall be for me a priestly kingdom and a holy nation." Yahweh then describes the terms of the treaty/covenant—the things the Israelites must do to maintain His favor. The most familiar conditions of the covenant appear in Exodus 20 as the Ten Commandments, but there are many other conditions as well. On the more violent side are Exodus 22:18, which requires the Israelites to kill female sorceresses; and Exodus 22:29, which asks for the sacrifice of a family's first-born son. Elsewhere in Exodus, a more benevolent Yahweh requires kind treatment of resident aliens (22:21; 23:9) and commands the Israelites to return their enemies' stray donkeys (23:4). Exodus 24:3–8 makes clear the Israelites' acceptance of these terms. Moses presents the covenant to "the people," who respond twice, "All the words that the Lord has spoken we will do."

Thinking of this covenant as a treaty allows us to see it not simply as an expression of religious devotion, but also as a political arrangement. Yahweh sought out and secured devotees by demonstrating his power against the Egyptians. The

Israelites took Yahweh as their sovereign and agreed to follow His rules because He promised to increase *their* power and to grant them security. In Exodus 23:20–33, Yahweh promised to improve the lot of His "priestly kingdom" by "send[ing] an angel in front of you on the way . . . to the place that I have prepared." He would ensure that they arrived safely, but the Israelites were bound not to waver in their faithfulness. "When my angel goes in front of you, and brings you to the Amorites, the Hittites, the Perizzites, the Canaanites, the Hivites, and the Jebusites and I blot them out, you shall not bow down to their gods, worship them, or follow their practices, but you shall utterly demolish them and break their pillars in pieces. . . . I will send my terror in front of you, and will throw into confusion all the people against whom you shall come, and I will make all your enemies turn their backs to you." The promise of military victory is woven together with a demand to worship Yahweh without the taint of foreign gods, religions, rituals, or altars.

The political and legal roots of covenant are apparent throughout Jewish and Christian scripture. We see time and again the power of covenant to bind a people together and to bind them to their god. Equally apparent is the role of covenant in interpreting violent encounters with other peoples or forces of nature. Prophetic literature provides many examples of Israelite voices recalling the terms of the covenant both to warn of impending catastrophe and to explain disasters already under way. Amos 2–3 is a particularly forceful statement directed at the Israelite kingdoms of Judah and Israel, each of which has transgressed against "the law of the Lord." Amos proclaims to Judah that an incensed Yahweh "will send a fire . . . and it shall devour the strongholds of Jerusalem." To Israel Amos promises, "An adversary shall surround the land, and strip you of your defense; and your strongholds shall be plundered." Acting as heralds of a divine sovereign, Amos, Jeremiah, Micah, and Joel among others narrate Israelite history through the lens of covenant, reminding audiences that triumph was never theirs alone and that tragedy came from division, transgression, or plain inattention to the terms of their covenant. The prophets' words offset Israelite chosenness with strong doses of humility, fallibility, and precariousness. When the Israelites accepted the terms of Yahweh's covenant, they placed faith in a being other than themselves, something directing but also judging. They bound themselves together through God in the task of being righteous and of rejoicing or suffering together.

The biblical covenant, so central to the stories of the Israelites, shaped American identity from colonial times forward. Puritan federal covenants, in which God was the sovereign and colonial collectives the vassal, asserted chosenness and served as the lens through which ministers and their faithful interpreted victory and defeat, prosperity and famine. Biblical covenants also provided a yardstick for righteousness, especially in times of unrighteousness and decline. The vertical and horizontal treaties reminded self-styled "Israelites" of who they ought to be as a people even when others in their midst embraced earthly measures. John Winthrop's "A Model of Christian Charity" (1630) is exemplary. The lawyer and future governor of the Massachusetts Bay Colony embraced the covenantal form and used it to remind fellow colonists of the importance of harmonious unity and of devotion to God. By connecting events in their world to the colonists' spirit of charity and love of God, Winthrop tempered chosenness with humility and mitigated suffering with meaning.

There is no covenantal moment like Winthrop's to serve as the starting point for a consideration of covenant and the Great War. There are, however, speeches, sermons, editorials, letters, and diaries that mention covenant or speak in covenantal tones as they lament decline or thrill at awakening. There is talk in newspapers and in poems of keeping and maintaining God's favor and provoking God's wrath. These materials show President Woodrow Wilson, son of a proslavery Presbyterian minister, deftly using the concept of covenant to unite the nation and the world, conceiving covenants and the act of covenanting as critical elements of a future peace. The letters and diaries of soldiers and war workers show a soldiery concerned that in peace America had violated its own covenant, but hopeful that the nation could renew this covenant in war. These sources show veterans struggling in war's aftermath to unite a nation divided by many forces, including the forces of faith. They show a movement toward a covenant with a robust horizontal reach. They also show a problematic departure from ancient and colonial precursors in the radical attenuation of the covenant's vertical reach, which, in postwar America, extended no higher than the nation itself.

FROM DIVISION, UNITY; FROM PEACE, WAR

Through the first seventeen years of the twentieth century, the United States suffered from a kind of schizophrenia that could have been born only of the distinctive developments of the era. The trend in intellectual, theological, and cultural circles toward a modernist progressivism was influenced by Darwin's insights and by German higher criticism of scripture. Darwin explained the development and diversification of species through natural means while German and German-trained scholars argued for more naturalistic understandings of the origins of the Bible. Theologians in Europe and the United States who embraced this set of perspectives worked through their faith and found a God whose revelation was ongoing and evolutionary, whose Truth was found in history rather than apart from and untouched by it. From this point of view, the rapid and disorienting changes affecting American society—industrialization, urbanization, immigration—could appear either as positive developments ordained by God or as challenges to be faced and overcome on progressivism's road to the Kingdom of God.[1]

But not all were convinced that history was progressive and that God was revealing new truths. Catholics, Jews, and Protestants alike were deeply affected by heated debates over the relationship between "the faith" and "the spirit of the age." The rise of Protestant fundamentalism and Pentecostalism, the quashing of American Catholic modernism, and the appeal of traditionalist Judaism serve as reminders that progressivism was contested in prewar America, and that there was much about the country and its course that raised concern.[2] Henry May has described the age's progressive optimism as a thin crust under which the seeds of future tension and conflict can be found.[3] This metaphor fails to capture the extent to which progressives, President Wilson among them, were engaged with and arguing against already resonant countervailing voices. One can see that engagement in Wilson's use of covenantal rhetoric in the early stages of American involvement in the Great War. In 1917, the year the United States entered the Great War, Wilson spent a great deal of rhetorical energy reminding Americans that they were a covenanted people, noting that there were noncovenanted people in the world, and arguing that the time had come for the chosen to join the war against the unchosen.

President Wilson invoked the notion of covenant repeatedly in his public pronouncements on war, using it to establish in-group and out-group identities at home and abroad, and to shape understandings of how victory would be achieved and peace maintained. As he used covenant to unite and to pacify, he used it also to divide and to incite. Wilson saw little room in the world and less in the nation for those unwilling, in Puritan terms, to "own the covenant." At the national level, Wilson's assertions of America's status as a covenanted nation functioned both horizontally and vertically. In his Second Inaugural Address, delivered on March 5, 1917, less than a month before the United States entered the war, Wilson spoke of war's covenantal benefits: "We are being forged into a new unity amidst the fires that now blaze throughout the world. In their ardent heat we shall, in God's providence, let us hope, be purged of faction and division, purified of the errant humors of party and private interest, and shall stand forth in the days to come with a new dignity of national pride and spirit."[4] With God as guide and war as a purging fire, the nation would be bound together for the war and beyond. For those whose "errant humors" resisted purgation, Wilson had little tolerance. On the occasion of his inauguration he warned Americans, as Yahweh had warned the Israelites, to guard against division, corruption, and the worship of mammon: "Beware of all men who would turn the tasks and the necessities of the nation to their own private profit . . . beware that no faction or disloyal intrigue break the harmony or embarrass the spirit of our people; beware that our Government be kept pure and incorrupt in all its parts."[5] Eight months later, as the first American combat troops joined the fight in France, Wilson addressed a convention of the American Federation of Labor and spoke directly about the consequences facing those who undermined covenantal unity. "The horses that kick over the traces will have to be put in corral."[6]

Deliberately or not, Wilson projected the voice of John Winthrop. On the edge of the wilderness of war, he reminded Americans that success in the Great War—an errand into a violent wilderness—depended on covenanted unity and harmony. His fears of factions and profit-seeking are clear echoes of Winthrop's pronouncement that "we must be knit together in this work as one man" and his warning against worshipping "other Gods, our pleasures, and profits."[7] The title of Wilson's November 12, 1917, speech to the American Federation of Labor Convention—"The American People Must Stand Together"—states clearly his deeprunning concern that "cooperation" and "self-control" would be undermined by "lawlessness," "mob action," and "anarchy." (The words *cooperate* and *cooperation* appear four times in the final three paragraphs of the address.) Also like Winthrop, Wilson let Americans know that a just God was watching and guiding them. He made reference in his Second Inaugural to his refusal to enter the war after the *Lusitania* sinking, and treated his reaction as emblematic of the American people. "We have . . . retained throughout [this affair] the consciousness of standing in some sort apart, intent upon an interest that transcended the immediate issues of the war itself."[8] Those who thought America a nation of cowards or blind to the nature of the war were thus made aware that what was really going on was something profound and transcendent: a godly, chosen, peace-loving people were wrestling with the world situation and their role in it.

Wilson's internationalization of the concept of covenant followed closely his application of covenant on the home front. The horizontal dimension divided the world community into righteous and rapacious, justifying violence by the former against the latter. The vertical dimension reminded nations that a judging God was watching—closely. The horizontal covenant emerged most frequently when Wilson spoke of the basis for peace. In a May 26, 1917 communiqué to the provisional Russian government, he wrote: "the free peoples of the world must draw together in some common covenant, some genuine and practical cooperation that will in effect combine their force."[9] On January 8, 1918, nine months after committing the United States to war against Germany, Wilson told Congress of his program for peace and noted that such horizontal covenants were the very goal of war: "For such arrangements and covenants we are willing to fight until they are achieved . . . we wish the right to prevail, and desire a just and stable peace."[10] And because Germany (like the Israelites' enemies before) was beyond the covenant of righteous nations, Germans deserved the violence directed at them. The German way, Wilson noted, favored "secret covenants" and "separate and selfish compacts," not the "open covenants of peace, openly arrived at" that were the righteous way of governing.[11] Germany's taste for secret dealings and intrigue, he told Congress in December 1917, made its very existence a threat: "this intolerable

Thing of which the masters of Germany have shown us the ugly face, this menace of combined intrigue and force, which we see so clearly as the German power, a Thing without conscience or honor or capacity for covenanted peace, must be crushed."[12] But even in crushing Germany, the covenanted community of righteous nations had to be mindful of the divine. "The hand of God is laid upon nations. He will show them favor, I devoutly believe, only if they rise to the clear heights of His own justice and mercy."[13] Blessings awaited righteous warriors fighting with an eye toward divine justice and mercy; curses would be the lot of all others.

Woodrow Wilson's national and international covenantalism featured a balance between the horizontal and the vertical elements. Some among the soldiery maintained this balance, but many imagined a covenant less with a divine being and more with the history and the heroes of America. Regardless of the deity to which they felt most covenanted, soldiers' words and sentiments shared understandings of America's breaches of the covenant and the path to redemption. America had breached a covenant by remaining neutral in the war. Only violent struggle could restore the nation to its chosen status and divine mission.[14]

SOLDIERS AND COVENANTS IN WAR AND PEACE

As early as 1914, some American men and women concluded that American neutrality was wrong—"immoral," in the words of soldier Edwin Abbey—and bound themselves to serve other nations.[15] One such man was the quintessential American poet of the Great War, Alan Seeger. While soldiering with the French Foreign Legion in 1916, he penned "A Message to America," a covenantal indictment of the United States. The character of the American people was suited to war, he wrote, but leaders and citizens were not fully aware of their covenantal duty.

> You have the grit and the guts, I know
> You are ready to answer blow for blow
> You are virile, combative, stubborn, hard
> But your honor ends in your own backyard.

In language infused with biblical allusion, Seeger called from the trenches for a new American Moses.

> You have a leader who knows—the man
> Most fit to be called American,
> A prophet that once in generations
> Is given to point to erring nations
> Brighter ideals toward which to press
> And lead them out of the wilderness.

Will you turn your back on him once again?
Will you give the tiller once more to men
Who have made your country the laughing-stock
For the older peoples to scorn and mock,
Who would make you servile, despised, and weak,
A country that turns the other cheek. . . . [16]

Only a new leader could return the once-proud United States to the promised land of honor violently asserted and defended. The manly activist Theodore Roosevelt, whom Seeger generously wove into the biblical narrative, was far more righteous, far more American than the professorial Wilson, who seemed to follow the teachings of an effeminate Jesus. Where the rugged, rough-riding Roosevelt could revive and redeem the nation, Wilson would only invite more shame. Before joining the army in May 1917, Quincy Mills used his job as an editorial writer for the *New York Evening Sun* to accuse American politicians (and others) of breaking faith with past warriors. In the months between the United States' entry into the war and the approval of plans for organizing and funding a substantial fighting force, he wrote numerous pieces condemning both America's lack of preparedness and the indecision that prevented a swift solution. Two weeks after Wilson declared war, Mills noted in an editorial, "Wake Up America Day," that the nation was slower to arm than righteous American warriors once had been. "It is time for them to comprehend that they must play men's parts as did their predecessors at the summons of Paul Revere. What would have happened had the patriots who fired at Lexington 142 years ago to-day 'the shot heard round the world' decided to discuss for a fortnight the advisability of lining up on the field of battle?"[17] In the face of such a threat, hesitation was unconscionable not to mention un-American.

Thomas A. Slusser, a first lieutenant in the U.S. Army's Thirty-Second Division, had a more robust sense of the vertical reach of covenant. He wrote to his wife in May 1918 that he was glad to see the nation awakened but that God was certainly displeased with America's dawdling. "If it shall be that all of our chatter . . . and folly must be paid for with blood and tears, we as a people can only bow our heads and say to the God who leads us through, 'Just and righteous are Thy Judgments altogether.' American citizenship must mean something. It has come too easy. Perhaps the American people will only be brought to a realization of their blessings when they have gone through the Valley of the Shadow of Death." Americans' sufferings in war came, in other words, from a God displeased with the nation. But by fighting and bleeding and dying, soldiers could revitalize the covenant. Later Slusser described his understanding of the new global role to which God was calling America. "It was the great truth of the Civil War that the Nation could not exist half-slave and half-free. As I see it now, the great truth in this War is that the World cannot, as a free world, exist half government by Autocracy [and half by democracy]. . . . The only salvation of free peoples, therefore, is to make all peoples in the world free. . . . And there is the end of our aloofness from the rest of the World and the beginning of the universal application of the great truth written in The Book by implication that We are our Brother's keeper."[18] On Slusser's account, God offered and honored only one covenant, the covenant of democracy, and called the United States, God's chosen nation, to establish such covenants worldwide—as a religious duty. No more could America, following Cain, deny responsibility for the blood of brother nations.[19]

The immediate aftermath of the war brought two trends regarding the war's covenantal significance to the pages of the soldier-authored *Stars and Stripes*. The first was defined by continuing assertions of the war's ability to unite the nation (and nations) in peace and of the divine's approval of this outcome. Two weeks after the Armistice, the *Stars and Stripes* affirmed that war had worked as a covenantal experience. An editorial pronounced America's regional, ethnic, and class differences resolved; the nation's unity was preserved and renewed. War had given American soldiers the chance to prove their worth. In the process, they had reforged the nation and ratified a new covenant. America, the editorialist wrote, "has seen her sons, fresh to the game of war, go forward and prove themselves worthy scions of the Minute Men that brought her to birth. She has seen her people, drawn from many races, united, welded together in pursuit of the common purpose as never before. She has awakened to the significance of her mission in the world. She has found her soul."[20] A December 20 editorial stated that the war generation—a generation that had walked in darkness—finally had seen a great light: "We of this generation had come to take our country for granted. We had come to take our liberty as a matter of course. . . . It was not so with the generation that wrung the first homesteads from the wilderness . . . But we—we of the easy spring of 1917—were like idle sons of some rich man, inheritors of a fortune which only he could value who by toil and sacrifice had amassed it. Now we have done more than inherit the treasure. We have earned it."[21]

In contemplating "Christmas, 1919," the *Stars and Stripes* editors turned their thoughts to the Christianity of soldiers' accomplishments. "The festival celebrating the coming of the Prince of Peace will take on a new significance, because the Prince of Peace has at last come into His own, and the mighty edifice of civilization that bears His name, after four long years, proved that it can and will endure and that 'the gates of hell shall not prevail against it.' "[22] Wilson's proposal for the League of Nations was treated by the *Stars and Stripes* as proof positive that the war really had been the covenantal event imagined, as a late January 1919 editorial made clear: "The plan of a League of Nations, laid this week at the door of the world, is the greatest gift that has been offered humanity since Cain spilled the first blood outside the fields of Eden."[23] The whole history of violence initiated with the first murder was coming to an end. Long ago the blood of Christ had atoned for Adam's sin and established a new covenant. Now the blood of American soldiers washed away the sin of Cain's fratricide and established a covenant of peace among nations.

A second cluster of voices offered a less sanguine tone than the more certain champions of covenant. They reminded American soldiers of the viciousness of the Russian Revolution and told them that peace was not yet perfect. They were concerned that the wartime covenanted unity might not hold. As the *Stars and Stripes* argued, perhaps the memories of battle could be both a unifying force and a barrier against violent strife. "Even those who are no disciples of the established order must hope in their more lucid moments, that America's coming progress toward greater social justice will be made without violence." The author acknowledged that alternate visions of the world and America existed, even that the "established order" was less than just—no small admission in the context! But violence toward that order could have no place at home. Violence would mean "hungry children, desolate wives, sorrowing mothers. . . . as is unhappy Russia's portion today." A better alternative was for the soldier to take back to civilian life "what he learned in France."[24] "Here was a democratic army. The family that came over on the *Mayflower* and the more recent immigrants met at last in the same company. The university products and the unlettered few rubbed elbows. . . . All classes were scrambled together, and it will be the salvation of America if they never again become completely unscrambled." In contrast to prior certitude regarding a new covenant forged in war, this author could only muster a guarded, "Here's hoping."[25]

America's diverse soldiery certainly conceived of the Great War in different ways. Many who described it in covenantal terms could balance the vertical and the horizontal axes in Wilsonian fashion. An equally common tendency, though, was to think exclusively along the horizontal axis in ways that conflated God with America. This also involved hoping, praying, and striving to create an idealized form of national unity from a postwar America that was increasingly diverse, diffuse, and difficult to comprehend.

FROM CRUSADE TO COVENANT

As postwar America celebrated victory, mourned losses, and grappled with labor and racial unrest, commentators and veterans continued to reflect on the covenantal significance of the war. Three different strands of covenantal logic, each revisiting and adapting Wilson's covenantal proclamations, are evident in the following: an essay by the former chief of chaplains of the American Expeditionary Force, Bishop Charles Brent, a poem by literary critic Mary Siegrist, and a meeting orchestrated by the American Legion. These strands persist in America today and evidence a reconsideration of vertical covenants described before and during the conflict. Subtly but surely the sovereign and judging Yahweh invoked by Wilson, the *Stars and Stripes*, and at least some American soldiers was impeached and replaced by a trinity consisting of deified principles, the war dead, and the nation itself.

An early stage of the postwar covenantal conversation featured the voice of Bishop Charles Brent. In July 1919 he contributed an article to the *American Legion Weekly*, titled "The Spiritual Spoils of War," in which he praised the lofty ideals of the Legion, founded that March by veterans of the Great War. Brent also argued that the war had reinvigorated America's covenant. He saw the war experience as both powerfully unitive and powerfully religious. "Those who fought and those who backed the fighters alike rose to a high spiritual plane where things seen, whether bodies of men or treasures of wealth, were laid on the altar of the unseen and things near were sacrificed for the benefit of things far off." Now was not the time, Brent continued, to return to selfish thought and action. To do so would undo all that war had done. "America, having found her soul, will have found it only to lose it."[26]

Having laid out the possibility of a fall from this exalted postwar situation, Brent expressed optimism that the nation would remain in a state of grace. Unlike the veterans of past wars, the veterans of the Great War had a "larger vision and one of longer range." Covenanted to a new sovereign and sacrificing themselves "for a cause a hundredfold bigger than nationalism," these soldiers had "enthroned *the spiritual* as the controlling force of national and international life." Brent continued: "The spiritual remains unchanged, is in command now and will not fail us if we are true to it and not led off by side issues. I heard General Pershing tell his soldiers that they had won a spiritual victory. By becoming part of the fighting body, they have identified themselves with a spiritual cause which shows its gratitude by enlarging and vitalizing the deepest part of man. Justice and honor and righteousness and liberty have laid a beneficent hand on every soldier and every citizen and claimed him for their own."[27] Brent believed that this "spiritual"—consisting at least of the principles of "Justice and honor and righteousness and liberty"—would motivate soldiers and war workers, unify them and their vision, and call them to act under wise leadership. Sensitive to the religiously diverse nature of the A.E.F. and to the country it represented, Brent did not name the spiritual or specify its traits, but it retained some of the qualities of the biblical Yahweh. "The spiritual" was bigger than the nation and capable of judging it. It demanded faithful following and focused worship. It offered exaltation and chosenness, but held out the possibility for decline, waywardness, and forsakenness—the traditional features of biblical forms of covenant and jeremiad.

Mary Siegrist, a 1912 graduate of the Teachers College of Columbia University, wrote, taught, translated, and occasionally reviewed works of poetry for the *New York Times*.[28] When she took up her pen to reflect on the recently ended Great War, she thought of death, suffering, relief, and covenant. Her poem "The New Covenant" mixes romantic and realist voices. She describes the war dead first in a romantic register.

> These Dead with their glad dying into light
> Who went with strange wild singing at the heart
> And laughter to the exalted sacrifice
>
> ....
>
> These of the great filled hungers of the heart.[29]

According to Siegrist, soldiers who lost their lives in the war had died gladly, singing and laughing. Resting now "at the holy Crossroad of the Dead," their hungry hearts were filled. But when she turned her gaze to "the mothers crying in their dreams" and the "lovers" "destined" now to "cloistral loneliness," her tone grew somber. As well, her description of those who survived the war is not only of a happy few, but also of those who returned with broken bodies and troubled minds. Her tone is appropriately melancholy.

> And lo, how these came stumbling back to us
> In darkness deep, with terrible shut eyes!
> And these, slow sons, who never more shall know
> The old sweet freedom of the limbs, but bear
> Alway [*sic*] the twisted hallmark of the brave!

"The New Covenant" leads the reader to reflect on the suffering of war while also resolutely directing the reader to think of compensation, of "Life . . . giv[ing] fully back" that which war took away, and of a new American unity, a "great good Covenant / Bought deep with death" that binds the people together in their reverence of the dead, their sympathy for the suffering caused by war, and a love of freedom. (Such covenantal aspirations have appeared in other U.S. wars before and since, especially in encomia and monuments to the fallen.) The "sovereign" in this covenant, however, is not a transcendent divine but a collective of the dead—in Siegrist's words, "Sleepers in some unguessed loveliness." Their demands of the vassal nation are respect, reflection on their sacrifices, and, perhaps, sympathy and aid for their loved ones.

A third covenantal moment came in June 1923, when the American Legion convened a small conference at its offices in Washington, D.C. Legion leaders had summoned representatives from a range of "Religious and Fraternal Organizations," including the Federal Council of Churches of Christ, the Salvation Army, the Young Men's Christian Association, the Knights of Columbus, and the

National Catholic Welfare Council, to a conference run by the Legion's national adjutant, Lemuel Bolles, and its national chaplain, Father William O'Connor.[30] When O'Connor rose to welcome the group, he emphasized the importance of unity and vigorous patriotism. He suggested that attendees should "take counsel together as God-fearing Americans to the end that from our deliberations come a rededication of Americans—of all creeds and beliefs—to the fundamental doctrines of patriotism, strengthened by mutual confidence and respect between those who join in such service."[31] The men and women were gathered, in other words, to covenant among themselves (horizontally) and to the nation (vertically); to pledge before Legion leaders and their God that religious differences would not interfere with the duties of citizenship. The terms of this covenant were set forward by Adjutant Bolles in a Creed of Citizenship, which all in attendance were asked to review and endorse. It read, in part: "We . . . do solemnly affirm our faith in the government and established institutions of the United States of America. . . . We feel that unity of sentiment for a better America must be developed among all classes of citizens and that difference of opinions on subjects which cannot be decided by the finite mind must be subordinated to love of our fellow man and for the country in which we live."[32] What the Legion wanted was not unity of faith per se, but unity of willingness to subordinate faith in God (including one's own religious tradition) to a common faith in the United States. They wanted to render irrelevant to civic life the many religious differences that existed among Americans.

This document and the moment that produced it reflect three concerns common in postwar America and especially common among Great War veterans. These concerns and their connections to Brent's vision and Siegrist's poem help us to understand not only how covenantal rhetoric helped explain the Great War but also how it was used in the aftermath of the war to create a "New Covenant" with new parties and new terms. The first concern, articulated forcefully by the American Legion, is that the war they had waged in Europe continued in America. Many veterans believed that a hydra-headed evil—represented usually by Bolsheviks, anarchists, and "alien slackers"—was working to undermine the United States. This was, therefore, a wartime covenant for a postwar nation still at risk of succumbing to enemies old and new. Like the Israelites, they expected conflict with those beyond the covenant and hoped to blot them out and thus to bring security to their promised land. The second concern, national cohesiveness, is evident in the horizontal dimension of covenant which is implied by the form and explicit in the text of Bolles's Creed. We see it also in Bishop Brent's invocation of "the spiritual," whose core principles were coterminous with the professed principles of "Americanism." Legionnaires and other war veterans knew the importance of unity in the face of the enemy. They had been part of a unified, covenanted military body, and had experienced the multileveled thrill of confronting and besting the foe. Men and women of many faiths had put their differences aside, struggled, and prevailed. There had been problems and divisions in the American Expeditionary Force to be sure, but few were explicitly religious in nature. One problem that veterans faced in postwar America was that religious differences mattered and mattered greatly. A resurgent Ku Klux Klan was beating the drum of anti-Semitism and anti-Catholicism. The modernist-fundamentalist controversy was at its most acrimonious, as the hyperdivisive rhetoric of Texas fundamentalist J. Frank Norris demonstrated. The Creed of Citizenship and Charles Brent's invocation of "the spiritual" were, thus, intended to bind people of different faiths together in a spirit of tolerance and shared commitment to a stable society.[33]

The third and most submerged concern has to do with the power of religious critique and, albeit less directly, the power of a hidden God. Legionnaires, though familiar with religiously informed criticism of the nation and its soldiers, wanted none of it. They felt that a God who stood above the nation and called the righteous to resist the nation's course could divide, damage, and bring about defeat. On the Western Front, soldiers and their weekly *Stars and Stripes* had railed against those whose God led them to question the righteousness of the war and the holiness of those who fought it. But the aftermath of the war brought a return of religiously informed reconsideration of war in general and of the Great War in particular. The public Christian pacifism of Sherwood Eddy, a former YMCA secretary on the Western Front and head of the Y during much of the 1920s, was particularly galling to the Legion; so, too, were the claims of moralist voices in the nation that drinking, gambling, and dancing were sinful in the eyes of God. The notion that virtue had something to do with turning from vice and that the sacrifices of veterans might not cover their sins was anathema to many.

Quite clearly, a Yahweh whose will and workings remained open to interpretation was something of a menace to a society that perceived grave threats to its existence. The Legion's new covenant argued that the will of the hidden God was coterminous with the will of the nation. Mary Siegrist's "New Covenant" accepted that those buried in war cemeteries were a unified chorus who favored the war aims and demanded silent reflection on the sacrifices of the dead. For America's covenantal custodians, Yahweh's will would, henceforth, be circumscribed by the Constitution, the nation's interest, the principles of capitalism, and the necessity of military service. All Americans—all but anarchists, atheists, communists, and aliens—were to demonstrate their acceptance of the covenant by worshipping in their faith tradition and supporting their government, especially in times of crisis. All Americans who refused, be they liberal or conservative, bigot or cosmopolitan, fundamentalist or modernist, Catholic or Jew, could expect harassment from the priests of this new nationalist faith.

It is unclear whether the men and women attending the Legion's conference approved the Creed unanimously. But the Legion subsequently succeeded in cultivating a civil religion that embraced the symbols, texts, and saints of American history, preached the gospel of one-hundred-percent Americanism, and worked to turn the nation away from a sovereign God. In short, the Legion succeeded in making Yahweh a vassal to the sovereign America.

From where we stand today, we can lament postwar efforts to demote Yahweh and to replace God with an American faith that worships at the altar of the nation, that venerates its soldiers martyred in the Great War, and that absorbs God's grace into a national spirit. We must, though, understand these efforts for what they were: a reworking and not a rejection of the covenantal form. The logic behind them is very similar to the logic that bound the Israelites to Yahweh in the book of Exodus and bound vassals to sovereigns throughout the ancient Near East. The spiritual, the fallen soldier, and the nation had all, according to their proponents, earned the people's reverence by bringing vision, victory, and security. Americans of all stripes could unite around these deified entities and could fathom their power. Most welcomed limiting religious critiques of the nation and its course; resisting the claim that America stood before a judging God. The social benefits and the moral consequences of this covenant remain with us to this day.

NOTES

1. William Hutchison, *The Modernist Impulse in American Protestantism* (Oxford: Oxford University Press, 1976).

2. See T. J. Lears, *No Place of Grace: Antimodernism and the Transformation of American Culture, 1880–1920* (Chicago: University of Chicago Press, 1981); George Marsden, *Fundamentalism and American Culture: The Shaping of American Evangelicalism* (Oxford: Oxford University Press, 1980); Henry May, *The End of American Innocence: A Study of the First Years of Our Own Time, 1912–1917* (New York: Columbia University Press, 1992); Grant Wacker, *Heaven Below: Early Pentecostals and American Culture* (Cambridge, MA: Harvard University Press, 2001).

3. May, *The End of American Innocence*, xxiv.

4. Arthur R. Leonard, ed., *The War Addresses of Woodrow Wilson* (Boston: Athenaeum Press, 1918), 30.

5. Ibid., 31.

6. Ibid., 72.

7. Conrad Cherry, ed., *God's New Israel: Religious Interpretations of American Destiny* (Chapel Hill: University of North Carolina Press, 1998), 40–41.

8. Leonard, *War Addresses of Wilson*, 27.

9. Ibid., 49.

10. Ibid., 100.

11. Ibid., 96, 97, 108.

12. Ibid., 79.

13. Ibid., 91.

14. Jonathan H. Ebel, *Faith in the Fight: Religion and the American Soldier in the Great War* (Princeton: Princeton University Press, 2010).

15. Edwin Austin Abbey, *An American Soldier: Letters of Edwin Austin Abbey, 2d* (Boston: Houghton Mifflin, 1918), 12.

16. Alan Seeger, *Poems* (New York: Charles Scribner's Sons, 1916), 162–166.

17. Quincy Sharpe Mills, *Editorials, Sketches, and Stories* (New York: G. P. Putnam's Sons, 1930), 733.

18. Thomas Slusser, *Letters to Her, 1917–19* (Chicago: Privately printed, 1937), 86–87, 125.

19. Edwin Abbey, *An American Soldier*, 96.

20. *Stars and Stripes*, Nov. 22, 1918, 4.

21. Ibid., Dec. 20, 1918, 4.

22. Ibid., Dec. 6, 1918, 4.

23. Ibid., Jan. 31, 1919, 4.

24. Ibid., May 2, 1919, 4.

25. Ibid.

26. Charles Brent, "The Spiritual Spoils of War," *American Legion Weekly*, July 18, 1919, 8.

27. Ibid.

28. "Miss Mary Siegrist, Poet and Translator," *New York Times*, March 17, 1953. Siegrist died at the age of seventy-one. She lived in New York City, in a Carnegie Hall studio.

29. Mary Siegrist, "The New Covenant;" Wanamaker Collection, World War I, WW-74-16, Indiana University.

30. Ebel, *Faith in the Fight*, 186–190.

31. Meeting notes, June 1923, "Religion," Archives of the American Legion, Indianapolis.

32. Ibid.; emphasis added.

33. This concern was also evident in the Legion national commander's defense of New York governor Al Smith, a Catholic, in the face of a steady stream of attack and innuendo from Protestant politicians, especially during his presidential campaign in 1928.

4

From Jeremiad to Manifesto

The Rhetorical Evolution of John Foster Dulles's "Massive Retaliation"

Ned O'Gorman

On December 8, 1953, as he stood before the General Assembly of the United Nations to give his "Atoms for Peace" speech, President Eisenhower declared, "I have a sense of exhilaration as I look upon this Assembly. Never before in history has so much hope for so many people been gathered together in a single organization."[1] It is in hindsight a remarkable statement of confidence in the potential of the United Nations by a U.S. president, connected to a peculiar postwar faith in the possibilities of a worldwide federation of nations. More than the residue of Wilsonian idealism, in the aftermath of World War II and the atomic bomb many felt that only a form of worldwide communion could save humanity from catastrophe. Eisenhower himself may or may not have genuinely possessed this faith, but his secretary of state, John Foster Dulles, clearly did. As early as 1941, Dulles proclaimed: "The fundamental fact is that the nationalist system of the wholly independent, fully sovereign state has completed its cycle of usefulness."[2] Needed in its place, he argued, were an international federalist system and, just as importantly, a spiritual awakening among people everywhere that would bring them to recognize both their fundamental kinship as humans and an objective moral law to which all should submit.

Those who remember John Foster Dulles as a Cold War militant, an advocate for "rolling back" Soviet expansion, a proponent of nuclear brinkmanship, and, above all, the sponsor of "massive retaliation"—the threat to strike back with overwhelming nuclear force in response to Soviet military aggression—may find his interest in world communion surprising. Indeed, a number of scholars have tried to account for the so-called conversion of Dulles from a progressive world federalist to an ardent cold warrior. What rupture, what demon, what trauma wrought such a dramatic transformation? Scholars offer differing answers, focusing on Dulles's Protestant piety, his sense of nationalism, or the hyperbolic and performative nature of his speeches.[3]

In this chapter, I suggest that a fundamental religio-political continuity, not a discontinuity, in Dulles's outlook explains his invocation of massive retaliation and the overwhelming violence it authorized. Massive retaliation was the product not of a real trauma to Dulles, but rather of a sense of moral and political outrage at the Soviet Union. The continuity in Dulles's outlook was a covenantal view of world affairs. He adopted from Protestant thought the perspective that human community was bound to a moral law both objectively and subjectively: objectively, in that there was a set of moral principles that all were obliged to accept; and subjectively, in that he believed that one should feel reverence for the law, not merely know and adhere to it. This moral law constituted for him a kind of universal spiritual covenant to which all were bound. That not everyone acknowledged this same universal spiritual covenant meant not that it was limited or conditioned, but rather that work remained to achieve universal subscription.

If my argument is correct, then it can help explain how the political culture of the United States has, throughout its history, moved so seamlessly between a rhetoric of pacific universal goodwill and one of militant national righteousness. Dulles's outlook, I propose, drew from the political wellspring of Protestant America. His virtues were several: he took the rule of law seriously; he assumed the moral agency of others, even the foreign and distant "other"; he was willing to consider radical alternatives to the status quo, including the abolition of the nation-state; and he was possessed by a sense of responsibility to the world. The problematic aspects of his outlook, however, are instructive: before seemingly insurmountable hostility to his vision, Dulles adopted a language of extreme violence; this language was legitimate for him in part because he assumed people should submit to a universal moral law even if it had not been explained or enumerated to them. This language in its moral outrage ended up colluding with Eisenhower's fundamentally amoral *realpolitik* that, in putting power up against power, force against force, threatened the extinction of humanity.

To illuminate the religious roots of rhetoric in the atomic age, I first take up discourses of the covenant by looking at the relationship of covenantal thinking to the jeremiad and the manifesto. Next, I look at Dulles's jeremiadic public discourse in the 1940s. I conclude by looking at the speech in which Dulles declared a strategy of massive retaliation, arguing that this doctrine should be understood not so much as foreign policy, nor even primarily as a national attitude, but as a manifesto—a speech act in response to a covenantal breach. In this way, I hope to show how the evolution of particular historical forms of discourse tie religion and violence together.

COVENANTAL DISCOURSES

To see the covenantal framework in Dulles's thought, we must first look more broadly at forms of public rhetoric that have enjoyed a distinct relationship to the covenantal outlook. Indeed, covenantal politics enjoy an acute relationship to public discourse, for it is in public, in the presence and, hence, participation of the people, and through speech that the covenant is founded and renewed. Covenants constitute communities, but not just any community. Covenants constitute moral communities, bound by solemn promises of fidelity, long-suffering, and the persistence of hope. Covenants mitigate risk and uncertainty by casting a vision of a future that is bound by the same principles and promises that hold the community together in the present. Thus, covenants guarantee community members a place, a standing among others that is visible, free, and responsible, both in the present and in the future.

Because covenantal communities rest on a solemn promise and agreement, they also develop specialized forms of public discourse that address promise-breaking. Most notable among these is the jeremiad, a critical form of American public discourse explored widely in this volume. As Sacvan Bercovitch has shown, the jeremiad was a New England Puritan ritual that presented communal norms from scripture, condemned the breaking of those norms, called for repentance, and offered covenantal promises to ensure the ultimate success of the community if repentance was pursued.[4] The jeremiad, in other words, is a rhetoric of memory, judgment, and promise: memory, because it recalls for the people the communal norms of the covenant; judgment, because it calls the people to account for violating those communal norms; and promise, because it pledges future well-being if the people repent of their violations and recommit themselves to the communal norms.

However, there is a second form of discourse strongly tied to the covenantal outlook but often overlooked or neglected in discussions of the rhetoric of covenantal communities. This is the manifesto, a genre that dominated the religiously infused English Civil Wars of 1638–1660. The manifesto was a rhetoric of judgment that decried an irreparable breach of a promise. The manifesto was what happened beyond the jeremiad, when communal norms were seen as having been upended so grievously that the possibility of their restoration among a people had evaporated. Instead, either an exodus or a revolutionary confrontation was called for. In the manifesto, the oppressed presented themselves as having been the objects of covenantal violations; they divided the community into "us" and "them," covenant-keepers and covenant-breakers, respectively. The manifesto reconfigured the memory of a people to cultivate strong identification with their resistance to oppression.

A possible etymology of *manifesto* is instructive: David Graham Burnett has suggested that the Latin *manus* (hand) together with a form of *facio, factus* (to do, to act), create the image of the fist striking, the hostile hand. Thus, in seventeenth-century Italy, a manifesto was a text that made public the purpose of a military unit or the will of a sovereign. It was a speech act entailing force, and the authority to which it appealed needed only to be a temporal one.[5] However, by the eighteenth century the manifesto came to represent a different range of speech acts: those that confronted power in the name of universals. The manifesto developed into a recognizable and widely used rhetorical form that chronicled oppressions in light of universal principles or commitments and declared a political and historical rupture, a new way of collective being in the world. This new way of being hung upon an us/them dichotomy which placed distance between the people and their oppressors. Furthermore, as the manifesto proliferated as a rhetorical form, writing a manifesto came to mean writing the grievances of one's own group into the history of resistance. As Janet Lyon writes, the manifesto is a "multiaccentual ideological sign, one that can be evoked in any number of struggles, on any number of sides." To write a manifesto is "to participate symbolically in a history of struggle against dominant forces; it is to link one's voice to the countless voices of previous revolutionary conflicts."[6] The manifesto not only creates a distance between oppressors and oppressed, but allies the latter with the larger historical struggle of truth and justice against falsehood and domination.

Lyon argues that the proliferation of manifestoes in the modern era is due to the scope of the promises of modernity itself. "The promises held out by the developmental narratives of modernity—promises of universal freedom, autonomy, equality, and inclusion—are reiterated and recast in political manifestoes in the eighteenth and nineteenth centuries as the broken promises of modernity."[7] In this way, the emergence of the "ideology of a universal subject with universal rights and sensibilities" found a counterpart in "a public genre geared to contesting or recalibrating the assumptions underlying a 'universal subject,'" whether that subject was envisioned as all rational persons, all property owners, all the children of Adam and Eve, or in some other way.[8] One way to make sense of the manifesto is to see in modernity an attempt to apply universally a covenantal (or contractual) framework. Indeed, once a Lockean social-contract approach is fused with a Judeo-Christian imaginary (even more than in Locke's writings themselves), it is hard not to see social contract as covenant, binding all humans to universal norms of polity. It is precisely such a fusion on which the American founders capitalized in writing the quintessential American manifesto, the Declaration of Independence. In the thinking of many American Protestants like John Foster Dulles, the universal promises of modernity could not be separated from a covenantal framework. Indeed, Dulles found in a modernist Protestantism a means by which to spiritualize the covenant and to align a Judeo-Christian message with the modern Enlightenment view of a universal subject with universal rights and sensibilities.

JOHN FOSTER DULLES'S JEREMIADS

Six months after the signing of the Charter of the United Nations in 1945, Dulles praised the document as the successor to the Magna Carta and the U.S. Constitution. Speaking at Princeton University on George Washington's birthday in 1946, he declared: "The Charter gives the Assembly enormous possibilities of developing an active principle. It can seek to advance human welfare in all of its phases—spiritual, cultural, and material. It can promote basic human rights and fundamental freedoms. It can fight diseases. It can help solve the vast colonial problems. It can develop world trade. It is given almost unlimited opportunity to advance the welfare of the member peoples."[9]

Dulles's glowing appraisal of the Charter was not made from afar. He had been appointed by Truman as a delegate to the formative 1945 UN Conference on International Organization in San Francisco, and he felt that many of his ideas had been written into the Charter. It was not just Dulles's political connections that earned him the post under Truman, but his ecclesiastical ones as well.

Since the late 1930s, Dulles, a Presbyterian of the "liberal" or "modern" school, had been chairman of the Federal Council of Churches Committee for a Just and Durable Peace. In that role, he was the chief architect of the committee's widely publicized "Six Pillars of Peace," which entailed a bold call for universal rights, international economic and diplomatic cooperation, and the liberation of subjected peoples. These principles, Dulles claimed, were the bases of the UN Charter. For Dulles, religion and political principles of international life were intertwined. Of the UN conference in San Francisco, Dulles exhorted: "To Christians this Conference is not merely one more diplomatic conference. This Conference has been an item in their program. They have helped to bring it about. This Conference is, in a very real sense, their Conference."[10] As Dulles further wrote in a draft speech, his sense of exhilaration before the UN Charter was an evangelical one. "Basically the task is to assure that God's will be done on earth as it is in heaven. That is first of all an evangelical task. Also, however, there is the task of developing political institutions which will make it easier for men to live together in harmony and fellowship. The first and paramount task of the Christian churches remains that of bringing more persons to subject their lives to the will of God as revealed in Jesus Christ. For us He is the source of the moral law of which we speak."[11]

The Jewish theologian Neil Gillman has argued that, in Jewish thought, the concept of resurrection has been displaced by that of immortality. Resurrection is a historical and bodily event, whereas immortality involves spiritualized assurance of the perdurance of the soul beyond history and body.[12] Dulles's covenantal thought represents a similar transformation. Dulles spiritualized the covenant in presenting Christ as the source of the moral law, in suggesting that the evangelical mission was bringing more and more people to submit themselves to that law, and in blurring the boundaries between contingent political associations and the Kingdom of God. Dulles transformed the notion of covenant from historical document ratified in public performances to an eternal law to which all are, by virtue of being human, subject.[13]

We see this spiritualization in Dulles's speeches in the 1940s, especially in his jeremiadic condemnations of America's apathy before the great problems of the world and in his rejection of mechanistic, formal, or procedural solutions to such problems. Indeed, although Dulles's 1946 speech at Princeton University extolled the potential of the United Nations, most of the speech was aimed at condemning the people of the United States for their lack of faith in the UN's potential. "For the last six weeks, I have been taking part in the first meetings of the United Nations. Now, on my return trip, I could speak merely as a bearer of good tidings. I could tell you of a difficult job of organization done by the Assembly and of the proceedings of the Security Council which brought even great powers to alter their position in deference to public opinion. But I prefer, on this occasion, to talk of what remains to be done, for that is the heart of the matter."

This passage foregrounds Dulles's tone, which was consistent with what I see as his central message: the future of the world depends ultimately on the spirit, mood, and attitude that its people possess. The love of great purposes and a spirit of fellowship are essential to world transformation. Fear, materialistic motives, and "apathy and cheap emotionalism" are great hindrances to such progress.

In focusing on the affections, Dulles also presented the discursive dimensions of politics as penultimate. Very early in the speech, he suggested the secondary status of words over and against deeper, more heartfelt devotion. "The United Nations will not achieve peace and security merely because those words are written into its Charter or because the Charter is now implemented by a personnel. These were necessary preliminaries, and they have been well done. But what remains is the essential, that is, to assure that our new world organization will be dedicated to some great purpose."

In Dulles's view, a developed and realized world society would gain its unity ultimately from a common purpose rather than from a common charter. The people of the world, he claimed, borrowing a phrase used by both Alexander Hamilton and Henri Bergson, needed an "active principle" for any charter to be effective. In this regard he argued that America was potentially catastrophically at fault. Though the nation had spiritual resources, he warned, it had failed to generate the vital "spiritual power" needed for world organization. "Unhappily,"

Dulles told his audience at Princeton, "the fact is that at this critical juncture the people of the United States have no great faith which moves them. We are in no mood to seize on the United Nations as an agency for accomplishing some great purpose in the world." This weakening of will, he explained, would not have happened among previous generations of Americans. "Then the American people were imbued with a great faith," he explained. "We acted under a moral compulsion, as a people who had a mission to perform in the world. Our conduct was largely determined by a religious belief that every human being had a God-given possibility of spiritual development and that to realize this was man's chief earthly aim." He went on: "That mood has passed, with the result that at this critical time we may fail the world." America was doing its part in the world materially and intellectually, but spiritually it was lacking, and thus was "incapable of breathing into that organization the spirit needed to make it a living body."

In a letter to Walter Lippmann later in 1946, Dulles wrote that the great unanswered question with respect to America's role in the new world order was "whether the American people can see the truth and not react foolishly." "If," he concluded, "as a people, we do not have self-restraint, then we are not entitled to freedom and in fact cannot keep it long."[14] Throughout the 1940s, Dulles felt that if America was to fulfill its global mission, it would do so because of its moral and spiritual discipline and courage. Thus, he traveled about the country urging his audiences to recall sacred norms like freedom and dignity, condemning American failures to achieve those vital national norms, and recalling the people to, in his words, a "spiritual" way of life that would not only help them keep their freedom, but usher in a new epoch of world peace.

These speeches were for Dulles often explicitly Christian in character. As a representative of the Federal Council of Churches, he spoke as a churchman. However, the Christian framework he adopted was at least modestly skeptical of the historical and textual roots of the Christian faith despite being enthusiastic about the potential of the spirit of Christianity for humankind. Indeed, in the 1920s Dulles had played pivotal roles in the successes of the Protestant "modernists" over the "fundamentalists" in the Presbyterian Church, arguing against the likes of William Jennings Bryan and on behalf of Harry Emerson Fosdick.[15] Inasmuch as Dulles adopted a creed, it was a creed focused on the moral and spiritual principles of the Christian religion, rather than on its historical and doctrinal claims. It was this dehistoricized and universalized Christianity that provided the framework for Dulles's 1940s jeremiads. Quoting Dulles's Committee for a Just and Durable Peace, a statement written by sixty-one Protestant leaders in July 1943 read: "The Christian Church believes and declares to the world that 'there is a moral order which is fundamental and eternal,' and that, 'if mankind is to escape chaos and recurrent war, social and political institutions must be brought into conformity with moral order.' This moral order is the will of God, the creator of mankind. Basic in it are the law of justice, and [the] principle that man should love his neighbor as himself."[16] Christianity here represented an essential, eternal, and universal "moral order." It was a Christianity realized in basic precepts and principles of universal morality and a political order to which it should conform, over and against any particular religious doctrine or faith claims. And it was a form of Christianity that lent itself to a vision of an expansive, universal covenant, applicable to all humankind.

Shortly before his speech at Princeton in 1946, Dulles addressed an audience at Union Theological Seminary in New York on "The Atomic Bomb and Moral Law." The central argument of the speech anticipated his theme at Princeton. While covenants among nations might be the product of admirable efforts, their power, he argued, would be limited until the moral sentiments of nations became commensurate with their legal and diplomatic statements. The Hague Peace Conferences and League of Nations had failed, Dulles insisted, because they were "artificial in that they did not reflect the moral judgment of the world." The "ultimate fallacy" in international relations, Dulles argued, was the view that "great reforms can be wrought by paper agreements." In light of the atomic bomb, he continued, the central problem was to develop a common world law rooted in common moral judgments and general trust and fellowship among peoples from all nations. The UN, he hoped, would represent an evolution from "mechanistic solutions" in international covenants to ones grounded in the moral law.[17]

The logic of Dulles's messages implied that a covenant among nations was already in place before any conventions or charters. Inasmuch as the moral law was present and knowable to them, the peoples of the nations should—in a strongly normative sense—subscribe to it. If so, then world peace and stability would follow. If they refused, then disaster, including use of atomic weapons, would be imminent. Within this vision, America had a special role to play, but only in a contingent and historical sense: because America was, for Dulles, the strongest, most prosperous nation on earth, and because in its history it had demonstrated fidelity to the universal moral and spiritual principles, it was obliged to extend its spiritual resources to a war-weary world. However, America, Dulles believed, enjoyed no unique or exceptional status. It, too, was one nation among many obliged to evolve creatively toward the universal spiritual and moral ways expressed broadly in the Christian gospel. When and where it failed to do this, jeremiadic chastisement and a call to renewal was needed. But where renewal could not be achieved within the existing framework, a manifesto was required.

It was this new universal moral and spiritual framework to which Dulles aspired in his infamous 1954 declaration of massive retaliation as Eisenhower's secretary of state. Massive retaliation was less a developed strategic doctrine and more a manifestic statement of a covenant irreparably broken. Akin to the Declaration of Independence's announcement of the states' power to levy war and a people's right to separate from tyranny, it was the announcement of a struggle against a dominant and oppressive force in light of that force's violation of universal covenantal norms. Manifestic protest was integral to the covenantal vision Dulles espoused and provided the basis for a new covenant.

DULLES'S MASSIVE RETALIATION

Dulles threatened massive retaliation in a speech before the Council on Foreign Relations in New York in January 1954. "The way to deter aggression," he declared, "is for the free community to be willing and able to respond vigorously at places and with means of its own choosing"; "massive retaliatory power" would let an aggressor "know that he cannot always prescribe battle conditions that suit him."[18] Immediately a firestorm erupted in the press because it was assumed that Dulles was driving the world toward nuclear war. However, because the threat of U.S. counterattack in response to Soviet provocation was so disquieting, little attention was or has been paid to the fact that Dulles's speech was not meant to be about nuclear retaliation per se, but about "an over-all view" of American foreign policy vis-à-vis security. This overall framework was thoroughly internationalist in orientation and moral in tone.

The speech began with a series of commendations of the Truman administration for its loyalty to the United Nations, its recognition that America's "own safety was tied up with that of others," and its support for "Congressional bipartisanship which puts the nation above politics." Thus, the first part of the speech put special emphasis on the principle of national and international interdependence, and on the need for such global concerns to transcend mere party or national politics. Secondly, the speech stressed America's moral commitment in the Cold War—that the United States sought to act honorably in the cause of advancing human welfare. In fact, Dulles's commitment to the United States' maintaining its right to act at the time and place of its own choosing was presented as a prerequisite for moral as well as strategic initiative in the Cold War. The Soviets, he claimed, had no moral scruples; therefore it was crucial that the United States maintain its prerogative so that some semblance of moral agency might endure during the Cold War.

Within this context, Dulles's language of massive retaliation was not simply about deterrence, but about the preservation of moral agency. Tellingly, Dulles used a community analogy to explain the principle: "We keep locks on our doors; but we do not have an armed guard in every home. We rely principally on a community security system so well equipped to punish any who break in and steal that, in fact, would-be-aggressors are generally deterred." Thus massive retaliation was presented as the expression of a communal ethic; in threatening severe punishment for attack, he suggested, the U.S.-led international community was merely enlarging the practices of local communities to publicize the consequences of violating communal norms in order to discourage their violation.

Massive retaliation, however, clearly also entailed something more than the extension of a communal ethic. It was a claim—a claim to a right "to retaliate, instantly, and by means and at places of our own choosing" including, albeit implicitly, attacks against civilian targets. It is here that the manifestic nature of Dulles's words is most apparent. In claiming an absolute right to absolute retaliation, Dulles was claiming the right to initiate the ultimate end to the remaining solidarity of the international community *in the name of the norms of that community*. In other words, like the manifesto, the moral force of Dulles's "massive retaliation" position was presented as residing within the communal norms rather than outside it. It was a stance, he claimed, intended to guarantee "the long-term defense of freedom," to "leave unimpaired those free world assets which in the long run will prevail," and indeed "to advance the cause of human welfare." Massive retaliation as a stance would in the long run "let time and fundamentals work for us." "The fundamental, on our side, is the richness—spiritual, intellectual, and material—that freedom can produce and the irresistible attraction it then sets up. That is why we do not plan ourselves to shackle freedom to preserve freedom. We intend that our conduct and example shall continue, as in the past, to show all men how good can be the fruits of freedom." Dulles's massive retaliation was thus presented as both the expression and protector of communal norms, norms assumed to have global reach.

It was only after Dulles explained the doctrine of massive retaliation that he specifically invoked the Soviets. Importantly, they were addressed as a "dictatorship," a repressive power. Indeed, the conclusion to Dulles's "massive retaliation" speech entailed a list of grievances against the Soviets—for denying the worship of God, the dictates of reason, and freedom of speech, and for establishing a society premised on a police state and forced labor. Dulles argued that in no society could such practices long be maintained, and that the hope of the free world was that the Soviet leaders might "be dimly perceiving a basic fact, that is that there are limits to the power of any rulers indefinitely to suppress the human spirit. In that God-given fact lies our greatest hope. It is a hope that can sustain us. For even if the path ahead be long and hard, it need not be a warlike path; and we can know that at the end may be found the blessedness of peace." Thus Dulles's "massive retaliation" speech ended on a strongly universalistic, and even benevolent, note.

CONCLUSION

In Dulles's "massive retaliation" speech the Soviets appeared as covenant-breakers. America, at least when compared to the Soviet Union, emerged as a covenant-keeper. More than that, before apparent Soviet intransigence, Dulles moved from a jeremiadic to a manifestic mode, which sought not simply to preserve a covenant but to restore, even recreate, a new covenant in place of one that had been irredeemably broken. Massive retaliation was a claim to moral prerogative and a declaration of resolute opposition to an oppressive dictatorship. Far more than a military strategy, it was a moral stance, one that made sense only in light of a history of radical opposition to covenant-breakers. For, one could protest, as Oliver O'Donovan has in his theological reflections on the theory of deterrence (with reference to Dulles), "when someone thinks that it would be better for there to be *no* conditions for individual fulfillment than for the present satisfactory ones to be replaced with others less satisfactory, then he has categorically left the liberal tradition behind him, embracing a form of political totalitarianism."[19] O'Donovan thus presents the logic of massive retaliation as a departure from classical liberalism, as its choice for human annihilation over political subservience abandons a scale of relative values in favor of absolute ones. Although I agree with O'Donovan in principle, he has misunderstood Dulles's position vis-à-vis American political traditions. Dulles's massive retaliation was a form of radical protest, not an expression of intent to choose annihilation over subservience. It was articulated as part of a covenantal rhetorical repertoire that has been integral to classical liberalism in American political culture. To be sure, while the social contract notion of classical liberalism entails limited commitments among the parties involved and insists on reciprocity as a condition of obligation or duty, in the United States *contract* has been fused (even *con*fused) with *covenant*, which presumes that a universal absolute bond conjoins all humans to each other and to their Creator. As an act of covenantal protest, massive retaliation cannot be said to be a departure from American political liberalism, but rather an outgrowth of one of its principal traditions: covenantal politics. Working within this tradition, Dulles was trying with massive retaliation to maintain a place for a moral stance in a world that seemed to him to be growing more and more immoral, unspiritual, violent, and self-destructive. Language—moral, radical, and absolute in nature—was the means by which he sought to preserve this moral stance.

The prudence of this language can certainly be questioned, as can the worldview beneath it. But to question this language and worldview is to question America's political history. American progressive liberalism has been deeply moral, urging principles of individual rights, equality, and the diffusion of power. This moral dimension has played an integral role in American uses of force abroad. After all, it was progressive liberals who championed American intervention in World War I, a progressive liberal president who led America into World War II, and progressive liberals who helped lead the way into the Cold War. American liberals of the twentieth century, far more than extreme conservatives, took upon themselves the national moral burdens first carried by the Puritans in the early colonies, and then by Protestant evangelicals of various stripes in nineteenth-century America. And it has been American liberalism—more than any other political ideology in modern America—that has sanctioned the use of national violence in the name of universal norms of justice.

However, liberalism's challenge, as O'Donovan suggests, has been not to undermine its moral commitments in the name of those same commitments. The paradox of massive retaliation—the purported right to initiate the ultimate end to the remaining solidarity of the international community in the name of the norms of that community—is an extreme example of a basic problem that inheres in many progressive political visions (the preponderance of which in the West are significantly indebted to Protestantism). Implicit in such visions is a desire to move beyond corruption, intransigence, and abuses of power—thus, the call of the jeremiad. However, the persistence of political vices can drive adherents of liberalism either to despair or to violent confrontation. In both cases, the moral commitments of liberalism are themselves put in jeopardy. The abandonment of liberal moral commitments out of despair ends in a cynical concession to power politics, while the defiance of such principles descends into amoral *realpolitik*. Therefore, the challenge before liberalism and other morally informed social and political visions is one of fidelity, endurance, and introspection. The challenge, in other words, is to resist the move from the jeremiad to the manifesto, and to remain jeremiadic even in moments that, seemingly, call out for manifesto.

NOTES

A longer version of this essay appears in Ned O'Gorman, *Spirits of the Cold War: Contesting Worldviews in the Classical Age of American Security Strategy* (East Lansing: Michigan State University Press, 2011).

1. Dwight D. Eisenhower, "Address before the General Assembly of the United Nations on Peaceful Uses of Atomic Energy," New York City, December 8, 1953; available at John T. Woolley and Gerhard Peters, The American Presidency Project, Santa Barbara: University of California at Santa Barbara Gerhard Peters (database), http://www.presidency.ucsb.edu/ws/?pid=9774.

2. John Foster Dulles, "Speech: Second Presbyterian Church," Philadelphia, March 12, 1941, Papers of John Foster Dulles, Princeton University (hereafter JFD Papers), box 289; Dulles, "Speech: United Nations—Its Challenges to America," Speech at Princeton University, Feb. 22, 1946, JFD Papers, box 293.

3. See, for example, Townsend Hoopes, *The Devil and* John Foster Dulles (Boston: Little, Brown, 1973); Mark Toulouse, *The Transformation of* John Foster Dulles (Macon, GA: Mercer University Press, 1986); H. W. Brands, *Cold Warriors: Eisenhower's Generation and American Foreign Policy* (New York: Columbia University Press, 1988).

4. Sacvan Bercovitch, *The American Jeremiad* (Madison: University of Wisconsin Press, 1978), 16.

5. See Janet Lyon, *Manifestoes: Provocations of the Modern* (Ithaca, NY: Cornell University Press, 1999), 14.

6. Ibid., 3-4.

7. Ibid., 30.

8. Ibid., 32.

9. Dulles, "Speech: United Nations—Its Challenges to America."

10. John Foster Dulles, "The Beginning of World Order," San Francisco, April 22, 1945, JFD Papers, box 291.

11. John Foster Dulles, "Speech [Draft]: San Francisco Conference," March 29, 1945, JFD Papers, box 292.

12. Neil Gillman, *The Death of Death: Resurrection and Immortality in Jewish Thought* (Woodstock, VT: Jewish Light, 1997).

13. Behind this spiritualization was a general movement in American liberalism beginning in the late nineteenth century away from Lockean political theory and a Newtonian "mechanistic" view of the world toward an "organic" and evolutionary perspective influenced by Darwinism and continental philosophy. Dulles spent time before World War I studying with the French philosopher Henri Bergson, author of *Creative Evolution* (New York: Modern Library, 1944).

14. John Foster Dulles to Walter Lippmann, June 4, 1946, JFD Papers, box 29.

15. Toulouse, *The Transformation of* John Foster Dulles, 17–26.

16. Federal Council of Churches Committee for a Just and Durable Peace, "A Christian Message on World Order," International Round Table of Christian Leaders, Princeton, New Jersey, Federal Council of the Churches of Christ in America [FCCCA], July 1943, JFD Papers, box 283 (see also box 291). The quotations in the statement were from the "Guiding Principles" of the Dulles-led National Study Conference of the FCCCA.

17. John Foster Dulles, "The Atomic Bomb and Moral Law," published in *Christian News-Letter*, January 9, 1946, JFD Papers, box 284.

18. This and all following references to the speech are from John Foster Dulles, "Evolution of Foreign Policy," Council on Foreign Relations, New York, January 12, 1954, JFD Papers, box 322.

19. Oliver O'Donovan, *Peace and Certainty: A Theological Essay on Deterrence* (Oxford: Clarendon Press, 1989), 95.

5

American Providence, American Violence

Stephen H. Webb

One cultural constant throughout American history has been the popular but controversial contention that God has chosen America to play a special role on the global stage. Whatever the theological merits of this claim, most historians agree that the doctrine of providence has played a crucial role in the formation of American identity.[1] From the Great Seal, with its Latin inscriptions *annuit coeptis* (God has favored our undertakings) and *novus ordo seclorum* (a new order of the ages), to President George W. Bush's many evocations of God's guiding hand, Americans have sought their identity not so much in what they are but in what they hope and believe their country is destined to be. That is, Americans are brought together by shared aspirations rather than a common cultural tradition or specific geographical location. Even President Obama resides in the mainstream of providential rhetoric when he says that our shared dignity "should give us faith that through our collective labor, and God's providence, and our willingness to shoulder each other's burdens, America will continue on its precious journey towards that more perfect union."[2] America is less a place than an idea, and what has held Americans together, across religious, ethnic, and political lines, is the idea that America has a special role in the world: upholding ideals that represent the greatest political aspirations of all the peoples of the Earth. In this sense, many Americans have conceived their nation as a gift to their descendants and the world.

A gift, however, entails a giver. Or, to shift the metaphor, a script entails an author. Many Americans insist that God is the giver who authorizes America's unique role in history. The idea that God determines, shapes, and guides human history falls under the category of what Christians call the doctrine of providence, and, regardless of its theological technicalities and complexities, many Americans adeptly use its rhetoric to frame the American story. Providential rhetoric is especially useful in times of political and moral crisis involving violence and war, though these crises also have challenged the explanatory power of the doctrine of providence and undermined its ability to unite Americans around a shared national history. The idea that God created in America a land bound only by freedom and opportunity consolidated America's diverse ethnicities, but that same idea has also inspired Americans to exclude and persecute others, to expand boundaries at the expense of other peoples, and to intervene in the affairs of other nations and communities. As such, the theology of providence has been mired in partisan politics and the tragic consequences of collective national pride. This chapter takes up these and other episodes of violence and war as they have been informed by beliefs about providence.

Just as theologians rarely agree about what providence means in theory, Americans have rarely agreed about what this doctrine means in practice. Both liberals and conservatives use providentialism to justify their idealistic visions of what America has been or should yet become. The doctrine is as elastic as America is pluralistic. It is a doctrine made for America as much as America was made by it. The critical question I undertake here is whether Americans have lost the cultural coherence—and the resulting confidence in America's purposes—that render meaningful the idea that God is intimately involved in guiding American history. I do so by giving special attention to how violence and war have impacted providence's hold on Americans. After offering a short history of American providentialism, I consider how the Vietnam War provided the occasion for challenging and undermining Americans' confidence in providential thought. I close by considering what recent presidential rhetoric bodes for the future of providential thought.

My argument overall is that providentialism properly understood, is necessarily implicated in both the responsible exercise of American power in a complex world and full-throated discussions of whether and how to apply that power, including the resort to force or war. Moreover, the relatively recent thinning of providentialist discourses in political rhetoric is not only theologically incoherent but also politically misguided. From the left, right, or the middle, America simply cannot—and should not seek to—escape the deep grammar of providence. A theologically robust version of this doctrine is central to America's most ethically coherent understanding of its place in the world.

THE ASCENT OF PROVIDENTIAL THOUGHT
IN AMERICAN HISTORY

Some historians argue that it is nature and geography, not history and providence, that give America its character and cohesion. For these historians, the trope of the wilderness is central to American identity because it symbolizes the open frontier that allowed America to expand both physically and spiritually throughout the nineteenth century.[3] What these historians often miss, however, is the way in which biblical narratives have provided the foundation for the wilderness myth. The wilderness had such power over the American imagination because Americans were so powerfully shaped by the Bible, with its story of paradise lost, exodus from bondage, and paradise regained. Within this biblical framework, nature is the site of God's work in and through history, including through times of war.

There are also historians who reject the significance of theology in understanding American history. They speak of "American exceptionalism" or "manifest destiny" in political and sociological terms, with little or no reference to how deeply religion pervades those concepts or penetrates the American psyche.[4] When the idea of exceptionalism is stripped of its theological roots, however, it looks quite unexceptional, since every country thinks it is special.[5] Of course, many countries, especially those in the Western tradition influenced by Judaism and Christianity, have a strong sense of providential election and purpose. Even before Christianity came onto the scene, Roman poets like Virgil were writing about Rome's special relationship to the gods. Providential theology reached new levels of both theoretical elaboration and practical application in the English-speaking world after the Protestant Reformation, which set loose a hunger for a new configuration of religious and political freedom. Through the European settlement in America—where it was hoped that the restoration and purification of the church would bring about political transformation that would guarantee religious freedom—the American version of providentialism was on its way.

Puritan Roots

American interpretations of providence reflect the shaping hand of Puritanism, an especially influential form of Calvinism that always and happily has combined two apparently contradictory notions: a strong doctrine of God's sovereignty over history and a robust view of human responsibility and freedom.[6] Together, these views often underwrote a strong concern for moral order. Calvinist Puritans, after their failure in England, turned Calvin's idea of a holy city into a vision for an entire continent. Indeed, the Puritans interpreted the discovery of the New World as itself a kind of revelation. They understood their migration from England in terms of Israel's escape from Egypt. Through this interpretive grid, the wilderness of America became a new land of promise. The Puritans came to North America bearing on their backs the burden and the gift of providence. It was not simply a rhetorical weapon in a geopolitical war of words but paradoxically a source of ambition as well as national humility.

No theologian today would argue that the Puritan interpretation of history was very objective according to academic standards. Early Americans debated what providence really meant. Roger Williams, for example, rejected Calvinism by restricting the idea of God's election to the Israelites of the Old Testament. The Puritans, meanwhile, insisted that biblical history was ongoing, and they were creative in using figurative and typological language to demonstrate how God worked through nations to achieve the divine plan. Even Williams drew from their providential logic in restoring the simplicity of the primitive church in his new colony of Rhode Island. After all, he also thought God was using America to develop freedom (including religious freedom) for the world, as demonstrated by the name he chose for his new city: Providence.

For all of their faults, the Puritans did not limit the doctrine of providence to self-congratulatory interpretations of their own accomplishments. Belief in providence presupposed rigorous standards of piety and moral conduct. They understood that Americans were not literally the new Israelites, but that if America was a chosen nation, it would be held up to the high moral demands that God set for the Israelites. After all, God's covenant with Israel involved judgments and punishments as well as blessings and promises. God gives every nation what it needs to flourish, and thus each nation is held accountable for its use of God's bounty. God does not choose or bless nations because they are good. No nation (or individual) actually *deserves* God's grace. Rather, God gives various goods to the nations on the basis of God's own divine plan. God's ways are mysterious, so it is best not to be too presumptuous about what God has done and for whom. Puritans often saw in their wars against American Indians signs of God's judgment, whether divine approval when they were victorious or punishment when they were defeated. Discerning providence was a delicate matter and something of an art for the Puritans. History had to be read carefully, much as they read the Bible.[7] As much as they thought—or hoped—they knew how history would come to an end, they were quick to confess that they did not know precisely how God would use the events of their lives to get there.

The Early Republic

While debates about the piety of the founding fathers abound, no one can question their indebtedness to providential reasoning. Even deists such as George Washington, Thomas Jefferson, and Benjamin Franklin, who were the least orthodox founders in terms of their theological beliefs, had internalized Calvin's understanding of history. Washington's belief that the hand of heaven was in everything he did—as citizen, statesman, Revolutionary War general, and first president of the new republic—was an important source of the modesty that guided not only his personal conduct but also his understanding of politics. During a low point during the war, Washington wrote a minister, "We have abundant reason to thank providence for its many favorable interpositions in our behalf. It has, at times, been my only dependence for all other resources seemed to have fail'd us." After the war, commenting on the spread of democratic ideas in Europe, he observed that only "the great ruler of events" could know how the political future would be resolved, but that we should trust "in his wisdom and goodness" and "safely trust the issue to him."[8] For Washington and his contemporaries, *providence* was a synonym for God. He took great comfort from the idea that God was directing the course of history, asking only that he, Washington, play his assigned role.

Deism was the theology of choice of many of the cultural elite during and following the Revolutionary War. Deists could downplay the divinity of Jesus Christ because they trusted so firmly in the sovereignty of God the Father. For deists, the Newtonian regularity of the natural world, matched by the rational orderliness of human affairs, dovetailed with the order and regularity found in Calvinism and Puritanism. The divinity of Christ was not essential for deists, since God was in charge of history. Reason could be trusted over faith, since history could be read providentially as a story that climaxes in enlightenment and freedom. Nevertheless, the new independent nation retained a unique ability to synthesize faith and reason as well as religion and politics. While Europe experienced democratic revolutions that opposed the unity of altar and throne, the American Revolution united the altar of religion with the political will of the people. Where the French Revolution was fueled by antireligious sentiment, the American Revolution had been augmented by religion. The American experiment required a strong national government to ensure its survival, and that strong government required and made use of religion to bring the people together. Indeed, separation of church and state revealed just how much the political and the religious depended on each other. Religion was more the source of America's yearning for freedom than an obstacle to the establishment of national independence, since many colonists and early Americans derived their yearnings for freedom and their hopes for the new republic from common religious sources. Thus, political developments in America were more amenable to providential interpretations.

The period following the Revolutionary War was a time of relative religious calm, when politics replaced theology as the subject of public debate. Providentially, God had guided America through the war as a blessing to the world, but how could the new country take on such an immense task if it was growing so terribly divided along political lines? Federalists and Republicans each appealed to interpretations of providence to pit their political enemies against God. The polemics came to a climax with the War of 1812. As John Berens has shown,

Federalists took the war to be a chastising of America for the sin of departing from Washington's virtuous policies. Federalists thought Madison was unduly influenced by the nation's "unnatural" alliance with the infidel France and thus defended their dissent and opposition to the war as the best expression of God's will. Republicans defended the war with equally intense providential rhetoric.[9]

When battles were lost, Federalists claimed that God was punishing America for embarking on an unjust war in the first place. When battles were won, Republicans invoked a holy crusade. In the summer of 1814, a British expedition seized and burned Washington. Federalists believed the Madison administration courted this judgment of God, while Madison and his supporters saw their successful escape from the burning capital as a stroke of divine favor. Besides, the destruction of Washington was just what the nation needed to provoke it into decisive action. The War of 1812 was an early test of whether the rhetoric of providence could survive bitter political partisanship. In short, it took a war to demonstrate that it could.

The Second Great Awakening put more robust forms of religion back on the map. The revivals of the nineteenth century returned the doctrine of providence to its biblical foundations. History was again understood on the basis of patterns found in scripture, not nature's laws analogous to the natural sciences. Revivalists also made providence a more optimistic affair. For them, politics was not only about restraining human avarice but a means of implementing the kingdom of God. Many Christians thought that the millennial rule of Jesus could begin in their lifetime if they only worked hard enough to make America worthy.[10] For providential revivalists, the Constitution had provided the conditions that made the spread of Christianity possible, because only a free people could preach the Gospel to the whole world.

Though American providential thinking emerged out of covenantal theology, it became flexible enough to extend its influence well beyond the Puritans and their heirs. Eighteenth-century deists wholeheartedly internalized providential thought even if they transformed the Puritan face of God into "Nature's God." Catholics and Jews, for their part, later embraced those aspects of providential thinking that emphasized religious freedom as the essence of American identity. Today it is easy to take such freedom for granted, when tolerance is the presumed goal of American history. But tolerance did not always excite or unify Americans in the period up to the Civil War. Perhaps it was providential that the doctrine of providence was so important to the Puritans, since it is hard to imagine how any other religious belief could have provided a strong sense of cultural cohesion that also affirmed religious and social diversity. The master plot of American history took shape around the proposition that America was a place where faith and freedom not only met but also joined forces. Providence supplied a foundation for patriotism because so many people believed not only that God was on the side of liberty but also that God used America as an example of how liberty is meant for everyone. This is not, however, to overlook how Americans tested and transgressed ideals of providence during darker, violent periods of their history.

Manifest Destiny and the Civil War

The idea that America was chosen to be a gift to the world has obvious dangers. It led to the arrogance of manifest destiny, which replaced the millennium of Christ's rule with the geographical expansion of America's boundaries, turning any impediment to that expansion into a cause for war. Manifest destiny had many roots and flourished in different kinds of ideological soil, including the putatively enlightened deism. Thomas Jefferson, for example, put his hope not in Alexander Hamilton's dream of a strong federal government but in agrarian growth that entailed westward expansion. Deist par excellence Benjamin Franklin expressed a consummate faith in providence's blessings upon great polities when he said, "And if a sparrow cannot fall to the ground without His notice, is it probable that an empire can rise without His aid?"[11] Centuries later, in a different context, this line reappeared on the 2003 family Christmas card of Vice President Dick Cheney. Many wondered whether the "empire" here referred to the United States and whether it was expanding through its invasion of Iraq, which some critics compared to the Spanish-American War and other militaristic expressions of manifest destiny.

Manifest destiny has often been depicted as the essence of providential logic, but it should be seen instead as one variation (if not an aberration) of providence—indeed one that departed significantly from its earlier Calvinist progenitors. The Puritans looked to the history of Rome as a moral lesson for would-be empires seeking to expand beyond their divinely mandated limits. Puritans believed that only a republic founded on virtue could withstand the temptations that come with wealth and power. They also taught, following the Old Testament, that God chastises God's chosen. When the Puritans called America a new Israel, this was as much a warning as a sign of blessing. Unfortunately, the ideologues who equated America's destiny with westward expansion at any cost took all the mystery out of the doctrine of providence. They turned the Puritan concept of covenant into a crass rationalization of acquisitiveness and the pursuit of glory—a celebration of opportunity for its own sake. The idea of God's special mission for America was reduced to a call to arms, without any accompanying call to repentance or humility that Puritans understood it to entail.

Manifest destiny is in no way a manifestation of everything Americans have ever thought about their destiny, and American providence is certainly broader and deeper than such jingoism. As a deviant form of American providence, manifest destiny lacked any covenantal dimension. In the covenantal theology of providence, there is no gift without responsibilities and obligations attached; the gift of freedom, like the grace of faith, can be received fully only if it is properly appreciated and passed along. Manifest destiny lamentably associated America with Rome, neglecting how Puritans associated Rome with the pride that goes before a fall. Manifest destiny turned the open invitation of the church into hateful intolerance and racism. Fusing faith with violent expansion rather than with freedom, it was more the heretical language of the elite than the sustaining creed of everyday Americans.

This is not to say that the doctrine of providence was otherwise innocent of racist implications. English versions of providence could easily slide into justifications of the racial superiority of Anglo-Saxons. Providence also was used to promote a nativist suspicion of Roman Catholics, since so many Americans merged their story of freedom with the Protestant Reformation's criticisms of Catholic tyranny. The Civil War caused most Americans to view providence through one of the two geographical blocs of North and South, obscuring for a time the gulf between Protestantism and Catholicism, but throughout the nineteenth century providence was typically thought to exclude a role for Roman Catholics in the progress of the nation, since they were suspected of hierarchical politics and foreign loyalty. As Philip Hamburger has shown, the phrase "separation of church and state" emerged in the 1840s as a means of imposing "an aggressively Protestant Americanism on an un-American Catholic minority."[12] The very elasticity that made the doctrine of providence promising to many different religious groups also made it susceptible to abuse. Nevertheless, at its best, it allowed many Americans, including eventually Catholics and other religious minorities, to see their country as a sanctuary for the deprived and the persecuted, where blessings and opportunities were coupled with duties and obligations.

Moreover, the very same Americans oppressed by providential doctrines could invoke providence for their own advancement. For example, providence helped blacks find meaning in and give purpose to their struggles.[13] African American slaves experienced God's presence as a force both intimately personal and deeply historical. As one former slave put it, "The God I serve is a time-God. He don't come before time; he don't come after time. He comes just on time."[14] Black ministers were drawn to the Old Testament story of Joseph, sold into slavery by his brothers. Like Joseph, blacks had been betrayed by their own kinspeople. The story of Joseph assured blacks that God had a reason for their suffering. Joseph, after all, rose to power and helped his brothers in their time of greatest need. Psalm 68:31 was a favorite passage of black ministers: "Princes shall come out of Egypt; Ethiopia shall soon stretch out her hands unto God." Against this backdrop, the rise to power and recent election of the first African American president is a reminder that providence is a doctrine for the patient and hopeful, for the faithful and steady of will.

Like Lincoln, many former slaves interpreted the Civil War as an act of punishment that also redeemed the nation for its sins of slavery. Black leaders later interpreted the civil rights movement as a way of redeeming the nation following the tribulations of segregation. Their sufferings had given them a unique understanding of the Bible and a unique collective experience of salvation. The Puritans had conceived America as the new Israel, but African Americans were the ones who literally experienced enslavement and exodus. Consequently, this collective experience of salvation was not a subjective feeling of release but a concrete historical event of liberation from every form of bondage—physical, moral, and spiritual. In this sense, the Civil War and the violence against the civil rights movement were crucial chapters in the story of how providence enables the cause of human liberty to prevail.

African Americans used the doctrine of providence to support a progressive view of history, but they did not separate the idea of progress from the demands of morality. They knew that the road from slavery to freedom was as straight and narrow as it was long and hard. They tapped deeply into the Puritan insistence that progress is moral before it is material. For both blacks and whites during the nineteenth century, providentialism was a severe doctrine. One of the favorite sayings during this period was that "man can appoint but God can disappoint." God's plans are not the same as human plans; indeed, God's plan usually involves a disruption of human beings' best preparations and efforts. God is jealous, not nice. Covenantal theology reinforced the belief that God was every bit as demanding as giving. Punishment, often meted out through violence and war, was sure to follow when people misused God's good gifts—especially when the gift of freedom was denied to others.

Surely no American leader was more indebted to Puritan understandings of providence's burdens than Abraham Lincoln. His Second Inaugural Address interpreted the Civil War as a judgment of God on the sins of both sides of the Mason-Dixon line. Yet, just as the excessive deaths of the Civil War caused some to doubt the doctrine of providence, providential reasoning also provided a bulwark against despair.[15] How else to find meaning in the deaths of over 600,000 citizens? Far from dispensing with the doctrine of providence, Lincoln interpreted the Civil War through its Puritan roots, chastening all Americans—South *and* North, each of which had claimed God was on their side—with a humbling recognition of the limits of theological knowledge. Yet, Lincoln remained convinced that providence was at work in the efforts to unify a divided nation. The Civil War raised fundamental and, to some, quite troubling questions about God's use of violence in history. These questions would return in the next century, challenging those who assumed that providence could explain meaningfully all instances of violence and war.

After the Civil War, the doctrine of providence was transformed further by the evolutionary theory of Charles Darwin. Contrary to stereotypes, many theologians responded to Darwinism both positively and creatively. They argued that Darwin had discovered how nature follows the laws of progress, just as history—including American history—followed an evolutionary teleology.[16] Rather than seeing evolution as the negation of religion, Darwin's theological allies believed that evolution made no sense without religion. God directs the progress of biology to the endpoint of human nature just as God directs history by leading the nations—sometimes through war, bloodshed, and violence—toward their goal of democratic forms of government. In this way, providential "uses" of human conflict to advance liberty mirrored the often harsh means by which natural selection gave way to evolution. For these theologians, Darwinism had the effect of lengthening and broadening the doctrine of creation, since creation was now seen as an incredibly gradual, if often violent, process. Providence, they thought, provided assurance that chance, competition, and violence led not to disaster and despair but, rather, to progress and the triumph of humanity.

Other theologians more in tune with Darwin's rejection of nature's purposiveness took a harder look at the doctrine of providence. They reasoned that where the sciences could not detect design or order in the evolution of life, God must not be involved. At best, God may have been concerned with nature as a whole, but not with its parts. For them, if nature was full of violent predation and ceaseless strife, perhaps it was best just to remove God from the scene. God might establish laws of nature, but God did not directly intervene. Much as violence was present in nature, so too in history; but one had to look to humanity—not providence—to explain human violence. This debate over providence and violence in the age of Darwin foreshadowed deeper differences about providence and war in the next century.

THE DECLINE OF PROVIDENTIAL THOUGHT
IN THE TWENTIETH CENTURY

Well into the twentieth century, providence offered a lens for interpreting wars and other national crises. Providential rhetoric fueled President Franklin Roosevelt's fight to save democracy against fascism and his offer of a New Deal for Americans hit hard by the Great Depression. The fact that Roosevelt was extremely private about his religious faith has led many historians to miss how much he drew from American providentialism. Nonetheless, as Gary Scott Smith writes, "He frequently asserted that God directed history, considered himself to be God's agent, and insisted that the United States would prosper only if its citizens sought divine guidance and followed biblical principles."[17] Roosevelt's May 27, 1941 radio address announcing an unlimited national emergency offered a providential frame even before U.S. entry into World War II. In it, FDR proclaimed, "Today the whole world is divided between human slavery and human freedom—between pagan brutality and the Christian ideal. We choose human freedom—which is the Christian ideal." Emphasizing the connection between Christianity and democracy, he further declared, "We reassert our abiding faith in the vitality of our constitutional Republic as a perpetual home of freedom, of tolerance, and of devotion to the word of God." He ended the speech repeating the words of the Declaration of Independence: "With a firm reliance on the protection of Divine Providence, we mutually pledge to each other our lives, our fortunes, and our sacred honor."[18] Whether FDR used these words out of personal conviction or to quiet critics who accused his administration of being sympathetic to communism, he was fluent in the language of American providence.

Following World War II, exceptionalism was in full force with pundits heralding "the American Century." By the time World War II ended and the Cold War began, most Americans perceived an overlap, continuity, and complementarity between tropes outlining God's salvific plan for humanity and God's providential action in history. How God would save humanity in the end was tied to how God was moving through history in the meantime.

In the second half of the twentieth century, America's power in the world would be checked, first by the external threat of the Soviet Union (and its associated threat of "godless communism") and, second, by the internal crisis of confidence brought about by the Vietnam War. Both figured centrally into the decline of the providential idea in America. By the 1960s the Korean War and the Vietnam War were beginning to tarnish the luster of providential thought and the purplish sheen of providential rhetoric. Amidst the cascading conditions and climbing casualty count in Vietnam, many Americans worried that God had turned his back on the nation. Although President Kennedy had stated in his 1961 inaugural address that the United States would "pay any price, bear any burden, meet any hardship, support any friend, oppose any foe to assure the survival and success of liberty,"[19] by 1965, with President Johnson's first major increase in the number of troops bound for Vietnam, that price struck many Americans as too high. When Norman Thomas, six-time Socialist presidential candidate, cajoled a crowd of protestors to wash, not burn the flag, he was drawing from the Puritan-revivalist strand of American providentialism. Americans needed to repent—to cleanse and purify their nation—because they had not lived up to their stated ideals. As George McKenna writes, "The [Vietnam] war stirred emotions not unlike those stirred by slavery more than a century earlier."[20] Many Americans became jaded with politics altogether, turning instead to experiments dramatizing extreme human subjectivity or exploring interpersonal relations, what Doug Rossinow calls "the politics of authenticity."[21] As James Reston wrote in the *New York Times* in 1975, in the aftermath of the disastrous consequences of

America's retreat from Vietnam, "What is fading is not America, but the illusions of America—the illusions that we could control events."[22] "We" had met the enemy, and for many, it was the United States. The Vietnam War eroded American self-confidence in making political judgments about good and evil. Vietnam was traumatic because it showed that the triumph of American virtue was not inevitable. (It never had been, of course, but the postwar years engendered a national crisis in confidence.) However good America's intentions may have been, God neither rewarded the United States with military victory nor expanded liberty in Southeast Asia. Indeed, what was most troubling was the question of whether the United States itself had misinterpreted its role as a force of liberty.

Vietnam was too politically complex, morally confusing, and seemingly unending to be amenable to providential interpretation. Whatever God was doing in Vietnam was incomprehensible to many Americans, and it was certainly not identical with American foreign policy. Some wondered whether divine blessing had become curse. Some claimed that Americans needed to repent of the idealism that had led to Vietnam; in doing so they showed that even criticisms of American exceptionalism rely on the covenantal logic of providentialism. To critics and partisan detractors, U.S. intervention in Vietnam's civil war and in other nations was a sign that America's mission of democratization was paternalistic at best and exploitative at worst. Many liberals began lumping—and jettisoning—providentialism alongside paternalism, neocolonialism, and exploitation.

Domestic political forces also gave way to the declining appeal of providential thought, contributing further to a growing partisan divide between those who embraced and those who lamented providential thinking. Before the 1960s, liberals and conservatives alike had relied on providential tropes to explicate, interpret, and further their agendas. Perhaps the turning point came with the collapse of the Cold War front that had united politicians from across the spectrum in their opposition to communism. Dominic Sandbrook traces this collapse to Democratic Senator Eugene McCarthy's decision to challenge President Johnson for the presidency in 1968. McCarthy spoke to those liberals who, stirred by controversy over the Vietnam War, were anxious about America's role in the world. McCarthy was influenced by Reinhold Niebuhr's arguments against the blinding pride of nationalism. McCarthy also was influenced by Roman Catholics who criticized Vietnam on just war grounds. Vietnam, McCarthy declared in a 1968 speech in San Francisco, was no accident. Rather, it was the sour culmination of a broad consensus dating back to the 1950s: "America in that period set for itself a moral mission in which we took it upon ourselves to judge the political systems of other nations and the right to alter those systems if we found them wanting."[23] McCarthy was the first major presidential candidate since 1948 to question the providential grounding of America's role in the Cold War. Indeed, McCarthy did not just question providence; he called for "a hard and harsh moral judgment on the United States position in Vietnam."[24] But why would America warrant such judgment if it was not in some way special—accountable by virtue of its moral calling, unique status, and providential history? It seems that even when the appeal of providentialism was on the wane or under attack, it was hard to expunge it altogether.

PROVIDENTIALISM AND THE WAR ON TERROR

Some wager that President George W. Bush's robust providential framing of the "war on terror" showed that providentialism was making a comeback.[25] Yet widespread criticisms of Bush's references to God's guiding of history indicate just how much this doctrine, which had once united the nation following the Civil War, still divided it following the Vietnam War.[26] President Bush's revival of providential rhetoric responded to a new kind of international conflict; the war against terror was more complex, both militarily and morally, than the fight against communism. Like the revivalists of the nineteenth century, Bush spoke a decidedly optimistic language of providentialism. For example, in his 2005 State of the Union Address, he proclaimed, "The road of Providence is uneven and unpredictable—yet we know where it leads: It leads to freedom."[27] This line would have fitted within mainstream political discourse a hundred years ago and would have escaped widespread scrutiny and criticism. However, articulated within a wartime framework, it sounded too certain and proud to many people's ears. Such words were even potentially dangerous.

By the midpoint of Bush's first term in office, critics (especially those influenced by the Vietnam years) worried that Bush's religious beliefs and references to God were being used to justify foreign interventions. Following the invasion of Afghanistan, the Iraq War became the chief example. The decision to overthrow Saddam Hussein's government was a world historical gamble with unknown repercussions for politics at home and abroad. Critics worried—as much as supporters hoped—that the Iraq War represented a new era in international relations and a sign that America was poised to reclaim its providential role in the world. Once again, as in the Vietnam era, the partisan divide over providential thinking deepened. Critics succeeded in framing the debate as a contest pitting American humility against American triumphalism. Polarizing rhetoric of this kind is unfortunate because it separates into opposite camps the very elements that providential logic should succeed in integrating. Indeed, a humbling, self-critical belief in providence is intended to correct triumphalist conceit. When God chooses to work through an individual or a nation, God should be identified as the source of any good that agent achieves, a belief that goes back to the Puritans. A providential reading of history should help a person or a nation to resist the temptation to become self-congratulatory. Providence asks Americans to identify what God has done for them—to acknowledge the blessing and the attendant burdens of their covenantal obligations. Providence does not give Americans license to identify whatever *they* do with the will of God.

In fact, President Bush was capable of sounding this more modest, Puritan tenor of providential talk, as when he claimed in the 2003 State of the Union, "The liberty we prize is not America's gift to the world; it is God's gift to humanity."[28] The line can be read as humbling in that America cannot take credit for the blessings of political freedom; such freedom is too precarious to have been brought to America's shores by forces other than providence. Moreover, such freedom is too important for providence not to extend it to the rest of the world. When Bush spoke at Warsaw University on June 15, 2001, he observed that the Polish people had spurned totalitarianism, "armed only with their conscience and their faith." He saw "the hand of God" in their history.[29] At the time, before the "war on terror," nobody complained about this rhetoric. Yet, even if one affirmed that God was the giver of freedom, a key question still hovered over the wars in Afghanistan and Iraq: Was it America's role to help others attain such freedom? And what were the limits to using military force to help others pursue this lofty goal?

"History has an ebb and flow of justice, but history also has a visible direction, set by liberty and the author of liberty."[30] These lines from Bush's Second Inaugural Address were penned by White House speechwriter Michael Gerson, who has articulated his own providential agenda. Gerson has advocated a "heroic conservatism" that seeks to unite Christians across the globe to fight poverty and stem the tide of AIDS.[31] Gerson's theology of providence rubbed off on President Bush. Where the president intoned his speeches with a Texan flatness, Gerson embossed them with biblical cadences. A prominent example from the 2003 State of the Union address: Bush declared that "there is power, wonder-working power" in the idealism of the American people.[32] When journalists complained that Gerson was planting religious messages in the president's speeches, Gerson patiently explained that "these are not code words, they are literary references understood by millions of Americans."[33]

What grates on the secular ear is the presumptuous, triumphalist tone Gerson put into Bush's mouth. Critics complained that, speaking Gerson's words, Bush sounded as if his policy decisions came straight out of the Bible. For both Gerson and Bush, this providential interpretation of American history stood in a long, worthy tradition exemplified by Puritan colonists, republican founders like George Washington, and Abraham Lincoln. Gerson has admitted, though, that Lincoln's doctrine of providence was more tragic than Bush's. "For Lincoln, this Providence was harsh and just, requiring blood spilled in war for blood spilled in slavery—a conception of God that led to resignation before his purposes. For President Bush, this Providence is ultimately loving and personal and concerned to vindicate the right—a conception of God that leads to trust and confidence."[34] Lincoln's doctrine of providence emphasized the mysterious and judgmental ways of God, while Bush's sunnier view of God idealized, even oversimplified, the doctrine of providence.

We should not ignore how the doctrine of providence, properly understood and applied, has pointed—and can still point—to the need for humility, including the realization that human understanding of the divine will is at best partial. Perhaps Bush's most creative and constructive appeal to providence came during a visit to Senegal's Goree Island in 2003 in which he spoke of slavery and American sinfulness. "In America, enslaved Africans learned the story of the exodus from Egypt and set their own hearts on a promised land of freedom. Enslaved Africans discovered a suffering savior and found he was more like themselves than their masters."[35] Without minimizing the horrors of slavery, Bush exposed the deeply and divinely ironic relationship between slavery and Christianity in American history. Not only were putatively Christian slave masters tragically limited in their faith, but those whom they saw as cursed and inferior found in the Christian narrative a moral vision that helped them critique, withstand, and ultimately defeat slavery. Regardless of what one thinks about America's providential role in the world, there is hope yet for a political use of the doctrine that might be self-reflective and humble; attuned to ironies and the limits of human knowledge; confident that God is working in history and that America has an important role to play, but also cautious when it comes to describing the twists and turns of an obviously complicated plot. Thus understood and applied, the doctrine of providence is an essential ingredient in the responsible exercise of power and the kind of national introspection that ought to precede the use of force by God-fearing (that is, humble) people.

A NEW ERA OF AMBIVALENT PROVIDENTIALISM?

In spite of President Obama's mention of providence, it is too soon to tell where he ultimately will stand in this rhetorical tradition and whether he can evoke it in new and creative ways that unite Americans. In his Notre Dame commencement address invoking providence, he also emphasized the irony of history, a concept he explicitly borrows from Reinhold Niebuhr: "But remember too that the ultimate irony of faith is that it necessarily admits doubt. It is the belief in things not seen. It is beyond our capacity as human beings to know with certainty what God has planned for us or what He asks of us, and those of us who believe must trust that His wisdom is greater than our own."[36] Obama acknowledges that God has plans for us, but he believes that we have little knowledge of what those plans are. Such providential modesty seems to be a direct response to Bush's more grandiose rhetoric and certitude.

Early signs suggest that Obama is pushing providential rhetoric in new directions. Obama began this ambitious theological task in his 2009 Cairo speech seeking to repair U.S.-Muslim relations damaged in the war on terror. Here he spoke from the heart, telling the story of his own humble beginnings and rise to political prominence. The moral of this story is that countries should provide freedom and opportunities for everyone. However, Obama did not say that Americans should take credit for defending and promoting this moral to other countries: "Any world order that elevates one nation or group of people over another will inevitably fail."[37] This speech declared that the age of what some have described as American arrogance or global imperialism would end with his presidency. But what exactly does this mean or foretell?

Consider how, when remarking upon the principle of democracy, Obama simultaneously both affirms and challenges the providential tradition. "Each nation gives life to this principle in its own way, grounded in the traditions of its own people. America does not presume to know what is best for everyone, just as we would not presume to pick the outcome of a peaceful election."[38] Providence for Obama is relative to national self-understanding and should not be judged according to universal (or American) interpretations of world history. Yet history does point toward certain moral universals that Obama clearly defends: "I do have an unyielding belief that all people yearn for certain things: the ability to speak your mind and have a say in how you are governed, confidence in the rule of law and the equal administration of justice, government that is transparent and doesn't steal from the people, the freedom to live as you choose."[39] Are both of these elements—respect for self-determination and belief in certain universal values that, he claims, America exemplifies—always compatible?

These words, uttered early in Obama's presidency, demonstrate an eagerness to distance himself from his predecessor's more controversial interpretation of providence (particularly as viewed through the lens of the Iraq War) while also embracing providential rhetoric to justify a quite ambitious vision of global peace, harmony, and unity. How Obama manages to balance these conflicting elements will no doubt determine much of the shape and success of his presidency. Interestingly, while seeking to replace the rhetoric of war and terror with the rhetoric of peace and mutual respect, Obama has escalated the use of military force in Afghanistan and Pakistan well beyond what his predecessor undertook. What observers might look for is whether Obama's providential rhetoric, for all his attempts to emphasize mutual respect and move beyond war rhetoric in achieving his vision, turns out to be even more idealistic—and more dependent upon the instruments of war—than his predecessor's. Such an ironic twist would indeed be surprising for a president so otherwise alert to the ironies of history.

NOTES

1. For my previous reflections on this topic, see Stephen H. Webb, *American Providence: A Nation with a Mission* (New York: Continuum, 2004).

2. Barack Obama, "Remarks by the President in Commencement Address at the University of Notre Dame," South Bend, Indiana, May 17, 2009, http://www.whitehouse.gov/the_press_office/Remarks-by-the-President-at-Notre-Dame-Commencement/.

3. See, for example, Catherine L. Albanese, *Nature Religion in America: From the Algonkian Indians to the New Age* (Chicago: University of Chicago Press, 1990).

4. See Anders Stephanson, *Manifest Destiny: American Expansion and the Empire of Right* (New York: Hill and Wang, 1995). On the theological background of exceptionalism, see John F. Berens, *Providence and Patriotism in Early America, 1640–1815* (Charlottesville: University Press of Virginia, 1978); Richard T. Hughes, *Myths America Lives By* (Chicago: University of Chicago Press, 2003); and Russel B. Nye, *This Almost Chosen People* (East Lansing: Michigan State University Press, 1966).

5. On the theology of the gift, see R. Kevin Seasoltz's excellent book *God's Gift Giving: In Christ and through the Spirit* (New York: Continuum, 2007). American exceptionalism stripped of religion can also look unnecessarily menacing and arrogant. At its best, exceptionalism trains the eye on God the giver (not the recipient) so as to lessen conceit, not raise it.

6. Andrew Pettegree nicely emphasizes how providence reinforces responsibility in "European Calvinism: History, Providence, and Martyrdom," in *The Church Retrospective*, ed. R. N. Swanson (Woodbridge, Suffolk, UK; Rochester, NY: Ecclesiastical History Society in association with the Boydell Press, 1997), 227–252. See also Richard Forrer, "The Puritan Religious Dilemma: The Ethical Dimensions of God's Sovereignty," *Journal of the American Academy of Religion* 44, no. 4 (December 1976): 613–628.

7. For an excellent reflection on how providence sustains a coherent reading of history, see Mike Higton, *Christ, Providence and History: Hans W. Frei's Public Theology* (New York: T & T Clark, 2004).

8. Quoted in Mary V. Thompson, *"In the Hands of a Good Providence": Religion in the Life of George Washington* (Charlottesville: University Press of Virginia, 2008), 111, 113.

9. Berens, *Providence and Patriotism in Early America*.

10. Stephen H. Webb, "Eschatology and Politics," in *The Oxford Handbook of Eschatology*, ed. Jerry L. Walls (New York: Oxford University Press, 2007), chap. 29.

11. From Benjamin Franklin's Request for Prayers at the Constitutional Convention, July 28, 1787, http://candst.tripod.com/franklin.htm.

12. Philip Hamburger, *Separation of Church and State* (Cambridge, MA: Harvard University Press, 2002), 36.

13. Sandy Dwayne Martin, "Providence and the Black Christian Consensus," in *The Courage to Hope: From Black Suffering to Human Redemption*, ed. Quinton Hosford Dixie and Cornel West (Boston: Beacon Press, 1999).

14. Clifton H. Johnson, ed., *God Struck Me Dead: Voices of Ex-Slaves* (Cleveland: Pilgrim Press, 1993), 170.

15. Mark A. Noll, *The Civil War as Theological Crisis* (Chapel Hill: University of North Carolina Press, 2006), 4–6; Harry S. Stout, *Upon the Altar of the Nation: A Moral History of the Civil War* (New York: Viking, 2006), 188–189.

16. James R. Moore, *The Post-Darwinian Controversies: A Study of the Protestant Struggle to Come to Terms with Darwin in Great Britain and America, 1870–1900* (Cambridge: Cambridge University Press, 1979).

17. Gary Scott Smith, *Faith and the Presidency: From George Washington to George W. Bush* (New York: Oxford University Press, 2006), 192.

18. Franklin Delano Roosevelt, "We Choose Freedom," Radio Address Announcing the Proclamation of an Unlimited National Emergency, May 27, 1941, http://www.usmm.org/fdr/emergency.html.

19. John F. Kennedy, "Inaugural Address," Jan. 20, 1961, http://www.americanrhetoric.com/speeches/jfkinaugural.htm

20. George McKenna, *The Puritan Origins of American Patriotism* (New Haven: Yale University Press, 2007), 305.

21. Doug Rossinow, *The Politics of Authenticity: Liberalism, Christianity, and the New Left in America* (New York: Columbia University Press, 1998).

22. Quoted in McKenna, *Puritan Origins of American Patriotism*, 316.

23. Dominick Sandbrook, *Eugene McCarthy: The Rise and Fall of Postwar American Liberalism* (New York: Alfred A. Knopf, 2004), 195.

24. Ibid., 148.

25. Kevin Coe and David Domke, "Think Religion Plays a Bigger Role in Politics Today? You're Right," Dec. 16, 2007, http://hnn.us/articles/45469. According to Coe and Domke, this revival can be traced to President Reagan's impromptu invocation of "Divine Providence" during his 1980 acceptance speech for the Republican nomination.

26. For the context of President Bush's religious rhetoric, see Smith, *Faith and the Presidency*.

27. George W. Bush, "State of the Union Address," Feb. 2, 2005, http://www.americanrhetoric.com/speeches/stateoftheunion2005.htm.

28. Ibid., "State of the Union Address," Jan. 28, 2003, http://www.washingtonpost.com/wp-srv/onpolitics/transcripts/bushtext_012803.html.

29. Ibid., "Address at Warsaw University," June 15, 2001.

30. Ibid., "Inaugural Address," Jan. 20, 2005, http://www.presidency.ucsb.edu/ws/index.php?pid=58745#axzz1k1rgTeWg.

31. Michael Gerson, *Heroic Conservativism: Why Republicans Need to Embrace America's Ideals* (New York: HarperOne, 2007).

32. Bush, "2003 State of the Union Address."

33. From a Pew Forum conference, "Religion, Rhetoric and the Presidency," held in Key West, Florida, December 2004.

34. Gerson, *Heroic Conservatism*, 74.

35. George W. Bush, "Remarks by the President on Goree Island, Senegal," Jul. 8, 2003, http://georgewbush-whitehouse.archives.gov/news/releases/ 2003/07/20030708-1.html.

36. Obama, "Notre Dame Commencement Address."

37. Ibid., "Remarks by the President on a New Beginning," Cairo University, Cairo, Egypt, June 4, 2009, http://www.whitehouse.gov/the-press-office/remarks-president-cairo-university-6-04-09.

38. Ibid.

39. Ibid.

PART TWO

Religion and America's "Others"

6

New Israel, New Amalek

Biblical Exhortations to Religious Violence

John Corrigan

In the West, the authorization of brutality against religious and political enemies often has been rooted in scriptural hermeneutics. Religiously derived logics that had directed violence through the European middle ages and Reformation—and were polished in the Thirty Years' War and other early modern catastrophes— were adapted to the circumstances of encounter in the French, Spanish, and English empires in the Americas. The anglophone writings relevant to that de- velopment, which would profoundly shape a pattern of thinking about religion and violence in the United States, relied heavily on the biblical account of Israel's annihilation of the Amalekites, and deployed it as legitimation for cruelty, and genocide, against religious opponents. The story of the Amalekites, ornamented with aggregate detail drawn from its deployment during political and religious hostilities, served as the basis for much subsequent theorizing about difference, extermination, secrecy, conspiracy, sectarian troublemaking, paranoid fantasy, forgetting, and other components of the history of conflict in America.

The Amalekites appear in the Old Testament as descendants of Esau, the grand- son of Abraham who married Canaanite women (Canaanites being depicted in the Old Testament as bitter religious opponents of the Israelites). The Amalekites stalked the Hebrews in their exodus from Egypt, attacking them in the desert, falling upon the sick and weak in the rear, killing them and claiming their pos- sessions. Moses miraculously aided Joshua in his victory over the Amalekites in the desert, but the victory, while complete, did not annihilate the Amalekites. A few centuries later the prophet Samuel informed Saul, Israel's first king, that God wished the Amalekites finally erased from history: "Thus says the Lord of hosts: 'I will punish Amalek for what he did to Israel, how he ambushed him on the

way, when he came up from Egypt. Now go and attack Amalek, and utterly destroy all that they have, and do not spare them. But kill both man and woman,
infant and nursing child, ox and sheep, camel and donkey.'" Saul, however,
spared the life of Agag, the Amalekite king, as well as the livestock, which he intended to sacrifice formally to God. Consequently Samuel reprimanded Saul that
"to obey is better than sacrifice," put Agag to the sword, and abandoned the king
to his regrets for his disobedience.[1] The earliest English settlers of Massachusetts
Bay were well versed in the story of the Amalekites. The iconic speech made by
John Winthrop aboard the *Arbella* in 1630, usually cited for its call to the nascent
New England community to be a "city on a hill," a model to the world of Christian faith and virtue, broached Amalek. The speech exhorted the men and
women on board the vessel to obey God, and to remember the example of Saul in
not carrying out to the letter the command of God.[2]

However, Old Testament references to the Amalekites had been, and were to
be, important less for their illustrating the necessity of obedience to God than for
their encouragement to genocide.[3] Genocide, as commanded by God of Saul, was
to be undertaken not only to "blot out" the Amalekites but, more specifically, to
"blot out the remembrance" of them.[4] Moreover, that erasure of memory was
linked in narrative to the righteous possession of the land awarded by God to the
Jews and to the clandestine, deceitful behavior of the Amalekites in raiding the
weakest of Israel as it made its escape from Egypt. "Remember what Amalek did
to you on the way as you were coming out of Egypt," God said to the Jews, "how
he met you on the way and attacked your rear ranks, all the stragglers at your
rear, when you were tired and weary; and he did not fear God. Therefore it shall
be, when the Lord your God has given you rest from your enemies all around, in
the land which the Lord your God is giving you to possess as an inheritance, that
you will blot out the remembrance of Amalek from under heaven. You shall not
forget."[5] In an interesting example of curved logic, the program of violence undertaken to annihilate a people and the memory of them is, in its constant oral
repetition, and eventually as written record, also a summons to remember. Over
time, the imagery of Amalek was imported into writing about Mormons, Jews,
Jehovah's Witnesses, Muslims, Catholics, and an assortment of other religious
groups. Extermination, blotting out, and annihilation were the linguistic lynch-
pins of a biblically driven glossary of religious vengeance that blossomed from
colonial experimentation with the Amalek story in polemics against Indians.

NATIVE AMERICAN AMALEKITES

English colonists came to the New World well prepared to see certain religious
others as Amalekites and, through such comparisons, to justify violence against

them. English writers in the seventeenth century deployed the Amalek trope in their anti-Catholic polemics. When Thomas Taylor offered a London audience *An everlasting record of the utter ruine of Romish Amalek* in 1624, he referenced the Book of Exodus in warning that "In our way to heaven we must make account of many Amalekites."[6] Why, asked Taylor, was God's punishment of the Amalekites so harsh? Why were they annihilated and memory of them blotted out? Noting their "underhand practices," which were "crafty and cowardly done," he stressed above all their "fraud." The Amalekites, he argued, were of Jewish ancestry, and accordingly they were a "neere relation" of Israel. All the worse that "it was unnaturall, for Amalek was of the same blood and neere kinred with Israel . . . so as they forgetting bloud and kinred, nourish an unnaturall wrath" against Israel. God accordingly punished them in a stark display of divine vengeance.[7] After that explication of scripture, Taylor progressed in typical Puritan fashion to an application of the lesson. Catholics, he said, were faith traitors in the same way that the Amalekites had been apostate in the Old Testament. It was Christian "dutie . . . to fight with God in blotting out their rememberance," to "utterly destroy the kingdom and the memory of Amalek," that is, Catholics.[8]

New England Puritans, building on the foundation provided them by English writers, condemned Indians as Amalekites, wrote and preached excitedly about blotting them out, and rhetorically presented the Indian-fighter in the figure of a biblical hero. Before the middle of the nineteenth century, a crucial linkage had formed among several component ideas, namely, the Indian as both distant other and as religious kindred, the desirability of exterminating one's enemies, of destroying their traces in collective memory, and of justifying such actions through appeal to a well-known, even ingrained, biblical narrative. Those ideas developed largely through incidences of contact between Native Americans and persons who had migrated to the Americas from Europe. The colonialist conceptualization of "the other" was grounded in the distinction that early English colonists made, like the French and Spanish before them, between Christian and heathen. Also influential was the theory that Indians were of the Ten Lost Tribes of Israel. Indians were the religious other at the same time that they were religious collaborators—distant brethren, but brethren nevertheless.

In America, interest in the story of Amalek, and its application to religious opponents, stood up to the passage of time and the exploration of space. George Whitefield reminded Philadelphians in 1746 how William, Duke of Cumberland, rescued England from "popish cruelty" in the form of Jacobites, whom he defeated at Culloden that year, "that Amalek might not prevail."[9] American writers added their own distinctive regional and political emphases. Cotton Mather, Increase Mather, Jonathan Edwards, Mary Rowlandson, Alexander Campbell, John Greenleaf Whittier, Ellen Gould White, and Charles Grandison Finney all found ways to express their thinking about God's vengeance by referencing Amalek.[10] Cotton Mather, an early leader in this enterprise, found a way to blend his rough-hewn ideas about "just war" with a call to destroy Indian opponents in the way that God had destroyed the Amalekites. "Turn not back till they are consumed," he exhorted New Englanders in 1689. "Tho' they Cry; Let there be none to Save them; But beat them small as the Dust before the Wind." We pray, he said, for "vengeance upon our murderers . . . against the Amalek that is now annoying this Israel in the Wilderness." In New England, Indian plots were easily enough equated with Catholic plots on the other side of the Atlantic (although Catholic plotting would soon inflame the New England imagination as well). Mather, in fact, explicitly linked the two: "The Papists," he declared, "contribute what help they can" to the Indians, "and say Mass with them (as of Late) after their Little Victories." The alliance of Catholics with some Indians was doubly unholy, and did "prognosticate their Approaching Ruine."[11]

Indians, like Catholics, were apostate. Consequently they were religiously and politically dangerous. English conceptualization of Indian apostasy, and the figuring of Indians as Amalekites, was advanced through the depiction of Indians as remnants of the Ten Lost Tribes of Israel, who had vanished from history after the Assyrian destruction of Israel. Such was the view of many Spanish colonial clergy and laypersons, as well as English such as Cotton Mather, William Penn, Samuel Sewall, Jonathan Edwards, and John Eliot. Accordingly they conceived Indians as distant kin. Moreover, as Jews who had not yet heard the Christian gospel, they were ripe for saving. Catholic and Protestant clergy in the New World approached them as such, armed with the mythology of *praeparatio evangelica*, a trust that American indigenes had been readied by history to receive word of Christian salvation. Some Europeans even believed that Native Americans were in fact lapsed Christians, and that the Christian responsibility was to reclaim them for Jesus. When encounters went sour, Indians as "neere kin" to Christians—as either lapsed Christians or descendants of Jews—were the subject of a religiously driven violence modeled on the extermination of the Amalekites. Captain Samuel Appleton's voice in this regard was typical, in his writing a friend regarding his role as commander of the colonial forces arrayed against the Narragansett tribe in 1675: "By the prayers of God's people, our Israel in his time may prevail over this cursed Amalek; against whom I believe the Lord will have war forever until he have destroyed him."[12]

The idea that Native Americans deserved the same punishment as Amalekites was carried forward into the nineteenth century by writers who claimed knowledge about the colonial period. The *North American Review* observed that New Englanders had harbored dangerous ideas about Native Americans from the earliest English settlement of North America: "Heathen they were in the eyes of the good people of Plymouth Colony, but nations of heathen, without question, as truly were the Amalekites." The late nineteenth-century Methodist minister from Indiana, Edward Eggleston, lamented the "scenes of savage cruelty" at Mystic, Connecticut, in 1637, when a colonial force that had trapped Pequot women and children systematically shot and burned them, a genocide, Eggleston added, that ministers rhetorically justified through "citation of Joshua's destruction of the Canaanites." The slaughter likewise was noticed by other nineteenth-century writers, such as the author of a story in the Saturday magazine *The Living Age*, which matter-of-factly reported of the event, "As the Israelites slew the Amalekites, so did the Pilgrims slay the Pequot." So also was the tone of Bostonian Frederick D. Huntington, who eventually became a bishop of the Protestant Episcopal Church, in commenting in 1859 that the military exercises against Native Americans in New England had been led by men who were "evidently of an energetic spirit and quite Old Testament cast of mind."[13]

Some spoke against the violence associated with the image of Amalek, but the scattered complaints only reinforced the fact of the widespread acceptance of the ruthless religious vengeance represented in the trope. The Rev. James M. Whiton, for example, published in the *New Englander and Yale Review* in 1884 an impassioned plea that Sunday school teachers tone down their presentation of the story of Amalek. Arguing that "it is one of the most unfortunate mistakes of ordinary Bible readers, which Sunday school teaching has done nothing to correct," and that the story of the Amalekites was presented in a "literally objective sense," Whiton explained that in Samuel's time, "this robber tribe of Amalek were [sic] hanging about the southern frontier of Judah very much as Indian tribes about our own western settlements." The Israelites had been forced to come to terms with the necessity of waging a war of annihilation against the Amalekites just as "in the case of white farmers against red savages—a clean sweep of the pests, men, women, and children, like so many wolves. It had to be done." Whiton's objection to this version of the story was not directed to the genocide itself. Rather, it had to do with God's role in it. "Not that God *actually* ordered it," he argued. "To Samuel, however, it was *as if* God had ordered it." And so it was done, and without remorse.[14]

While a few were looking back regretfully on the power of the trope in shaping religious ethical thought—especially as utilized in early New England's campaigns against the Indians—settlers out west were appealing to it. Exploration of the western frontier brought with it bloody contestations and a reinvigorated language advocating the extermination of the Indian. Speechmakers and writers who commented on these clashes still wrapped their remarks in Old Testament language, and especially images of Amalek. In the stripped-down ferocity of the battle for land and power in the West, however, the reference to biblical heroes that provided a shorthand for an ideology of genocide was often put to the side; it was well enough known already—like a *doxa* in the sense proposed by Pierre

Bourdieu[15]—to make unnecessary its ongoing rehearsal for an audience of migrants arriving from back east. What the West retained were specific wordings that were rooted in those Old Testament stories, linguistic codings that carried forward the frameworks for thought provided by biblical accounts. In 1856 Commissioner George W. Manypenny already had imagined in biblical terms the tragic ending of the Native American collision with westward expansion, and was "so sure will these poor denizens of the forest be blotted out of existence, and their dust be trampled under the foot."[16] In the Pacific Northwest, James Y. McDuffie, superintendent of Indian affairs for California, wrote to his boss A. B. Greenwood in 1860 about settlers' antipathy toward Indians, remarking on "the determination of a portion of the settlers to exterminate them from the face of the land."[17] A few years later the *Chico Courant* reinforced the religious framework for hatred of the Indian by arguing that "it is a mercy to the red devils to exterminate them."[18] Such pronouncements were built upon the assumption, thickly woven out of various bits of cultural fabric over three centuries, that as non-Christians Native Americans were religious opponents, that by their sneaky and duplicitous behavior they had earned a sentence of extermination, and that the land belonged to the Euro-American population.

The European encounter with Native Americans did not spontaneously generate the hate rhetoric we have examined, whatever the circumstances of those encounters. New Englanders adapted the anti-Catholic rhetoric of English polemicists to their own purpose of constructing the Indian as enemy. In so doing, they brought to the fore the notion of extermination, of blotting out memory, and, in its rudimentary forms, of secrecy as a trait of the other. Most importantly, Americans who commented on relations with Indians in these terms fully expected that their readers and auditors grasped the Old Testament framework for these ideas. As that rhetoric developed over the nineteenth century, it gradually shifted its primary reference from the story of Amalek per se to a more precise focus on the *modus operandi* of the other, to the secrecy, conspiracy, and cowardice of the other. Those who sought to stir up hatred still made explicit reference to Amalek in their discussion of Indians, and, increasingly, in complaints about Catholics and Mormons. But the emphasis was moving to certain characteristics of the religious other, to the other as a traitor and a coward and a conspirator in secret schemes against "real" Americans. All these character traits were rooted in American renderings of Amalek and the Amalekites.

CATHOLICS AND MORMONS AS AMALEKITES

The history of anti-Catholicism in America—from Protestant harassment of Catholics in colonial Maryland to the burning of Catholic buildings in Boston,

Philadelphia, and other cities in antebellum America, and hate-driven campaigns of the late nineteenth and early twentieth centuries—has been well documented.[19] These episodes of anti-Catholic violence and the attitudes that encouraged them were shot through with a biblically grounded rhetoric of hate that drew heavily on the imagery of Amalek. English writers cast Catholics as Amalekites from the sixteenth century onward. In the colonies and in the republic, rhetoric never lost its moorings to anti-Catholic projects.

The influence of English anti-Catholicism (eventually enriched through incorporation of anti-Catholic streams of intolerance brought to North America from nonanglophone countries) was felt in other ways besides the survival in New England and elsewhere of English anti-Catholic rhetoric. Protestant military actions against Catholics in Maryland overturned the vaunted Catholic order of that colony in the seventeenth century, and other colonies discouraged Catholic settlement by denying Catholics the right to worship and by banishing priests. In Boston in 1647 priests were threatened with execution. At street level, the regular enactment of anti-Catholic dramas in New England built anti-Catholic momentum in the eighteenth century. Puritans changed Guy Fawkes Day to Pope's Day, and the occasion was celebrated in America with burnings-in-effigy and, eventually, rioting. In Boston, Pope's Day riots resulted in anti-Catholic violence on November 5 in 1745, 1747, 1755, 1762, and 1764. People were killed and maimed in such rioting, and in some cases, such as the anti-impressment Knowles riot of November 1747, mob action in Boston spilled over into other causes. These incidents set the pattern for other and more lethal mob actions directed against Catholics in the nineteenth century.[20]

Criticism of Catholics as Amalekites developed further during the French and Indian War (1755–1763). New Englanders believed that Roman Catholicism was institutionally corrupt and that Catholics were spiritually lost.[21] Nathan Stone reminded his auditors in 1760 that the French were "Amalektish enemies" who deserved to be "blotted out."[22] He and other preachers drew heavily on the apocalyptic Revelation to John (also known as the Book of Revelation) in blending Old Testament accounts with New Testament messages so that religious publications such as the *Christian Monitor* could explain to their early nineteenth-century readerships that "the ten-horned beast therefore represents the Romish church."[23] The linking of apocalyptic imagery to rhetoric drawn from the story of the Amalekites was familiar to most readers by the middle of the nineteenth century and could be adapted to apply to any number of religious opponents. When in 1844 an editorial published in Tennessee opined, "Our opinion is, that there is to be no peace in this country, till the Mormons and Catholics are exterminated," the staff of the *Boston Investigator* could translate its meaning easily, remarking that it was about "blotting out Amalek," in view of the imminent "millennium."[24] By bringing an end to the existence of their religious opponents, some Christians presumed to bring an end to time itself. Identifying the final defeat of enemies with the dawning of the millennium, Christians imagined that salvation would be conjoined with forgetting on a massive scale.

American Protestants increasingly voiced their anxieties about Catholics with interlocking references to both testaments. Dr. Joseph F. Berg, who wrote animatedly about the perils of popery in antebellum America, asserted that "Rome is the Amalek with which God will never make peace. . . . Rome is that wicked one whom the Lord will destroy," linking that vision to Catholicism as "the system of popery. . . . the Master-piece of Satan. . . . the impudence of Anti-Christ."[25] The heart of the message remained a call to action, to blot out the other. Accordingly, the picturing of Catholics as Amalekites throughout the nineteenth century typically fueled calls for their extermination or pronouncements that they be "blotted out," memory and all. Looking back from the early twentieth century, an observer of anti-Catholic violence wrote that a previous generation of German Protestant immigrants "thought nothing of shooting at a window behind which they suspected a cardinal in Cincinnati, or of shying bricks in the direction of a priest in Milwaukee. . . . There could be no peace with Amalek." The anti-Catholic American Protective Association and the League for the Protection of American Institutions endeavored, as the *North American Review* observed, to "blot out from memory" Catholic figures from the American past. Toward the end of the nineteenth century, it was still the case, wrote the Reverend William Barry, that "Old Protestant hatred still breeds men, neither few nor feeble," who wanted to "abolish" Catholicism in America. The oath sworn by members of the American Protective Association, which was founded in Clinton, Iowa, in 1887, included the telltale promise to "erase the name on the ticket" in the voting booth if it identified a Catholic. And as was often the case, such claims were reinforced with reports that Catholics, in fact, were the ones who wished to destroy Protestants, not only in the United States but elsewhere in the Americas as well. This conceptual reversal of position, so important in the cultivation of hatred, was reported continuously by the Protestant press. The *Methodist Review*, for example, claimed that Catholic clergy in Mexico had inspired mobs with a "hatred of Protestantism" and had set out to "exterminate Protestant congregations in all that region."[26]

As the imagery associated with Amalek was enriched and focused in a Bible-conscious American society, it proved useful for dominant groups in picturing their religious enemies and for minority religions as well. Protestants could imagine Catholics seeking to blot out Protestantism at the same time that Catholics claimed that Protestants wished to blot out Catholicism. Moreover, in the dysfunctional attachment that is religious hatred, the sharing of rhetoric underscored the "kindredness" of the groups in conflict. Mormons and their largely Protestant opponents, for example, could see each other as Amalekites— cowardly, crafty, and covert—who must be destroyed. Mormons themselves knew about the Amalekites not only through their familiarity with the Old Testament, but through the *Book of Mormon*, which made reference to the Amalekites as a wicked and murderous people who inhabited pre-Columbian North America.[27] Those "Amalekites," also portrayed as "evil Lamanites" in Mormon scripture, made war on the righteous Nephites, another group that inhabited North America according to Mormon accounts.

After the founding of the Church of Jesus Christ of Latter-day Saints (Mormonism) by Joseph Smith in 1830, and on the heels of a series of run-ins with non-Mormon populations in several communities, a decade-long cycle of escalating threats between Mormons and non-Mormons in Missouri led to armed conflict with the Missouri militia. Mormon elder Sidney Rigdon, protesting the persecution of Mormons, delivered a Fourth of July speech in 1838 in which he declared that the "mob that comes on to disturb us, it shall be between us and them a war of extermination; for we will follow them until the last drop of their blood is spilled; or else they will have to exterminate us."[28] Joseph Smith shortly thereafter characterized the situation in Missouri: "The Governor is mob, the militia are mob, and the whole state is mob."[29] In the midst of an increasingly threatening war of words, and in the wake of skirmishes between Mormons and non-Mormons, Governor Lilburn Boggs eventually responded in kind, in late October, in a letter to General John B. Clark of the militia: "The Mormons must be treated as enemies and must be exterminated or driven from the state. . . . Their outrages are beyond all description."[30] The "mobbers," as Mormons called the militia, attacked and killed twenty Mormons (including children) at Haun's Hill, Missouri, on October 30, precipitating the mass exodus of Mormons across the Mississippi River to Nauvoo, Illinois.

The rhetoric of extermination traded in confrontations such as that in Missouri illustrates the manner in which religious minorities in some cases adopted the language of those who sought to destroy them. As part of an ongoing, reflexive, mimetic process of religious groups in conflict accusing each other of extermination schemes, the battles between Mormons and their enemies in Missouri and elsewhere, like the battles between Catholics and Protestants, evidenced the fluidity of hate rhetoric. Each side, by the nineteenth century, could adopt the position of victim, and each side criticized the other for similar offenses, including secrecy, conspiracy, and a plan to exterminate the other.

Anti-Mormons' perception of the kindredness of Mormonism to the Christianity of well-established denominations was crucial to the organization of resistance to Mormonism. Mormons called themselves Christians, but anti-Mormons considered the followers of Joseph Smith to have misinterpreted scripture and to have abandoned many of the fundamental precepts of Christianity as practiced by Protestants and Catholics. As historian of Mormonism Jan Shipps has pointed out, the opponents of Mormonism, beginning in the 1830s, made elaborate theological and historical arguments aimed at proving that Mormonism was not Christianity.[31] But underneath those polemics was a profound sense that Mormonism was a cancer that had somehow entered the body of Christianity and was corrupting it from the inside. Mormons accordingly were imagined as deceived and misled followers of a compromised Christianity at the same time that they were constructed as non-Christian, as fully other. Like the Amalekites, they were related to God's people, but acted in such a way as to indicate their clear difference from the truly faithful. "The doctrines of Mormonism," wrote one critic, "profess to be derived chiefly from the Old and New Testament Scriptures, and constitute a corrupt form of Christianity." Another, in discussing the need to "inoculate" people against the "viruses of superstition," protested that Mormonism was sickening the souls of God's children like "deadly poison," and was even more detrimental to spiritual life than "those forms of Christianity which are exceedingly corrupt."[32]

Who portrayed Mormons as Amalekites who must be exterminated? A resolution by civic leaders in Warsaw, Illinois, following Joseph Smith's murder by a mob in 1844, announced that "we hold ourselves at all times in readiness to cooperate with our fellow-citizens of this state, Missouri, and Iowa, to exterminate, utterly exterminate, the wicked and abominable Mormon leaders."[33] This Old Testament language of "abominations" and "wickedness" recurred frequently throughout the nineteenth century as frictions between Mormons and other religious groups cycled through periods of varying intensity. The evacuation of Mormons to Utah did little to slow the war of words—or the war of swords. The Mormon *Messenger and Advocate*, in Kirtland, Ohio, published in 1836 the prophecy of Elder Orson Hyde, who drew precisely on his Old Testament lexicon in lamenting the persecution of Mormons "in a republican government holding out the delusive, fallacious profession of equal rights. The arch fiend seems to have marshaled all his forces; every art is tried, every stratagem invented, every weapon put in requisition to destroy the influence of the saints [Mormons], and if it were possible to blot out their name from under heaven."[34] A few years later, as one of the many seeming confirmations of Hyde's prophecy that appeared in the form of hateful articles, *Atkinson's Saturday Evening Post* observed the troubles in Missouri and remarked that "there is no doubt that very strong measures must and will be adopted" there "to extirpate the whole fraternity of Mormons."[35] As the nation began its recovery from the Civil War and turned its attention westward, the polemics heated up. A Protestant clergyman in San Francisco could warm his audience with reports of his visit to Utah, where he saw "the most dreadful blasphemy in the face of heaven, and the most horrible insult to the Christian civilization that ever came out of hell."[36] In 1882 the *New York Times* reported a meeting of the Presbyterian Ministerial Association in Cincinnati, whose attendees planned another session at which "resolutions will be offered providing for the preparing of petitions asking Congress to take immediate and energetic means to blot out Mormonism.... It is thought that the Methodists will follow much the same plan that the Presbyterians are planning to adopt."[37]

Mormons resisted such rhetoric by turning it back upon their critics. As the Nauvoo *Times and Seasons* declared shortly after Joseph Smith's death in 1844, "prophets ... die for the sake of the truth ... and no man, no mob, no king, no potentate has been able to blot it out."[38] Such resistance included, said one turn-of-the-century writer, raising ten million dollars to arm a militia for the purpose of "resisting troops sent (as they supposed) to exterminate the Mormons."[39] More importantly, that resistance featured an escalating cycle of threats and rejoinders, leading to a state of affairs described by an anti-Mormon convert to Roman Catholicism, Orestes Brownson, in 1857: "'You must exterminate us,' said a Mormon elder to the writer, 'or we, as we become strong enough, shall exterminate you.'" Each side saw Amalek in the other.[40] When President Buchanan sent an army to Utah to enforce federal rule there, Brigham Young immediately surmised its purpose and announced it in a broadside issued in Salt Lake City in 1857: "We are evidently invaded by a hostile force who are assailing us to accomplish our overthrow and destruction." Said Mormon leader Isaac C. Haight: "they are sending an army to exterminate us."[41] The federal force arrived in Salt Lake City on June 26, 1858. The Mormons had gathered a 2,000-soldier militia, but there was no spilling of blood because Brigham Young and other Mormon leaders announced to the federal commander Albert Johnston their love of the Constitution and their agreement to live according to it (although the issue of polygamy would not be settled for many years).

The averted confrontation came on the heels of another encounter between Mormons and non-Mormons that had not ended so well. In 1857, near Enterprise, Utah, Mormon militia and Indian confederates massacred 120 unarmed men, women, and children, nearly an entire caravan of people on their way overland from Arkansas to California. Investigators, among them Judge John Cradelbaugh, who vigorously pursued responsibility for the case into the Mormon hierarchy, believed that the massacre had taken place in accord with an oath added to the temple ceremony (initiation liturgy) after the murder of Joseph Smith. Mormons vowed revenge upon Smith's murderers in these words spoken to the initiates: "You and each of you do covenant and promise that you will pray and never cease to pray to Almighty God to avenge the blood of the prophets upon this nation, and that you will teach the same to your children and to your children's children unto the third and fourth generation." (The language remained a part of the temple oath until 1927.)[42] Thorough press coverage of the massacre and its aftermath condemned Mormons for treason and human slaughter. Essayists, travel writers, and autoethnologists such as Mark Twain made certain over the years that it remained fresh in memory. Twain sympathetically recalled after his own trip out west in the 1860s the words of Cradelbaugh that "it was one of the most cruel, cowardly, and bloody murders known in our history."[43] Although many contemporaries as well as historians believed that the orders to murder the caravan came from the top of the Mormon organization, it was a Mormon bishop, John D. Lee, who was eventually executed for the crime. Lee employed the familiar language of Amalek in describing how he came to be involved in carrying out the commands of church superiors: "The substance of the orders [was] that the emigrants should be *decoyed* from their strong-hold, and all exterminated."[44]

The massive Protestant domestic missionary enterprise that was close to full stride by the mid-1870s held out little hope for the redemption of Utah. Protestant missionaries whose call to ministry led them into contact with groups whose beliefs and customs often seemed to them corrupt or immoral balked at the prospect of evangelizing Mormons. Thus the American Home Missionary Society, as it aimed itself westward in the mid-nineteenth century, planned evangelical forays to "the cities of Romanism, 'great and fenced up to heaven,' in New Mexico, Arizona and elsewhere," but seemed less confident of its goal of reaching "the Amalekites of Mormonism in Utah."[45] Mormons for their part continued to turn the tables on their critics, characterizing "Gentile" Americans as the Amalekites. A writer back east noted that Mormons expressed their religious views in a "long train of Hebraic similies: the Church was in bondage in Egypt,—it was in the wilderness of Zin,—it was to overthrow the Amalekites (Missourians) and repeat all the wonderful achievements in the fruitful annals of Israel."[46] Mormons likewise imagined defectors from their faith according to a "Hebraic simile." A visitor from New York reported on a Mormon sermon preached in Salt Lake City that was "of a denunciatory rather than a benevolent nature, and turned upon the wrath of God toward apostates, and the propriety of rooting out those who had gone astray after Amalek."[47] Some non-Mormon observers got the message, and noted that Mormons considered other religions to be idolatry, and that a Mormon embrace of "Gentile" Christianity was as unlikely "as it would have been for the children of Israel to have surrendered Moses or Joshua or the Decalogue for the idolatrous rule of Pharaoh or of Amalek."[48]

CONCLUSION: AMALEK, HERESY,
AND CONSPIRACY PARANOIA

As secretive and cowardly betrayers of their kindred relationship with the ancient Jews, Amalekites were seen as traitors of a particularly vile and dangerous sort: conspirators and heretics. English writers' characterizations of Catholics developed in America into a more complex profiling of French and Spanish Catholics, Native Americans, and eventually American Catholics and Mormons. Americans took from their colonial denigrations of Indians a sense of righteousness in exterminating their opponents, added specific concerns about covert scheming on the part of American Catholics, and topped it off with angry rhetoric about heresy and, especially, sectarianism that came to the fore in denunciations of Mormonism. A letter to the *New York Observer* just before the Fourth of July 1857 reflected the tendency of anti-Mormon and anti-Catholic writers to conflate the two religious groups in cataloguing their offense against Protestantism (and to toss into the story mention of Islam and "secret societies" as well):

> The fact is, Mormonism, (it is not denied,) is a modern form of Islamism, the former seeking to engraft itself upon Christianity. . . . Besides this, there is a large mixture of popery in the councils of the "Saints" and no little Freemasonry. On the one hand there is the adaptation of teaching and on the other the secrecy of carrying it out. The end sanctifying the means, is as much a principle in Mormonism as it is in Romanism, and the secrecy of the confessional is the safety valve of both. . . . The popish priesthood screen the assassin who murders for the good of the church, and the Mormon priest will do the very same thing. . . . In point of fact, there is no feature in the worst characteristics of Irish or Italian Popery, but that its type may be found in anti-Christian Mormonism.[49]

"What stratagems have been invented? What deep and artful plots have been laid?" asked the Rev. William Adams, referencing the plottings of the Catholic "Amalek" in a thanksgiving sermon in 1760. In an elaborately gendered nineteenth-century American culture in which secrecy increasingly was judged the equivalent of cowardice, the two flaws came to be intertwined in speechifying about Amalek. Presbyterian pastor John M. Lowrie, of Fort Wayne, Indiana, in his 1865 essay "War with Amalek," could easily enough boil it all down to the bone in typically economical Scots prose: "But theirs was not the bold and open defiance of a manly foe."[50]

Secrecy and conspiracy had for centuries been associated with heresy, and especially with sectarianism. Americans who believed themselves native defenders of a Protestant culture of Bible and democracy made certain to emphasize those associations in their warnings about Catholics, Mormons, and other religious groups with whom they clashed. As the nineteenth century wore on and turned the corner into the twentieth century, a widening assortment of religious or parareligious groups would inherit the scorn of critics whose thinking was grounded in the Amalek story. What historian Richard Hofstadter famously labeled the "paranoid style" in American political life is replete with pronouncements that secret, subversive, conspiratorial organizations are pursuing and preying upon righteous Americans. Not far beneath the surface is the desire to exterminate and blot out those predators. According to Hofstadter,[51] nativists and extreme right-wingers believed that a "'vast' or 'gigantic' conspiracy" was "the motive force in historical events," that "[h]istory is a conspiracy, set in motion by demonic forces." This fundamentally religious understanding of history has deep biblical roots. It was and is animated by the *doxa* of Amalek.

NOTES

1. Exodus 17:8, 14; Numbers 24:20; Deuteronomy 25:17–19; 1 Samuel 15:2–3.

2. John Winthrop, *A Modell of Christian Charity* (1630), Collections of the Massachusetts Historical Society, 3d series, vol. 7 (Boston, 1838), 46.

3. On this aspect of the Amalekite story as an example of the "ban" (*hērem*, the destruction of all life in Old Testament holy war), see Susan Niditch, *War in the Hebrew Bible: A Study in the Ethics of Violence* (New York: Oxford University Press, 1993); and Roland H. Bainton, *Christian Attitudes toward War and Peace: A Historical Survey and Critical Evaluation* (New York: Abingdon, 1960), 151ff., 168ff.

4. Judges 18:14.

5. Deuteronomy 25:17–19.

6. Exodus 17:14.

7. Thomas Taylor, *An everlasting record of the utter ruine of Romish Amalek* (London, 1624), 5, 7, 13.

8. Ibid., 18, 20–22, 24–25. See also John Geree, *Iudah's ioy at the oath* (London, 1641), sig. C4v; John Flavel, *Tydings from Rome, or England's alarm* (London, 1667), 18, 19, 15; Andrew Marvell, *An account of the growth of popery, and arbitrary government in England* (1677; reprint, London, 1678), 5, 11; Marvell, *A seasonable argument . . . for a new parliament* (Amsterdam, 1677), title page, and *An account of the growth of popery, and arbitrary government in England* (Amsterdam, 1677), 11; William Perse, *A sermon preached at Malton in Yorkshire. June 27ᵗʰ. 1706. Being the day of publick thanksgiving* (York, 1706), 1, 25, 21, 18, 23; Abraham Jobson, *The conduct of Moses when Israel fought with Amalek, compared with that of Admiral Lord Nelson, in the battle of the Nile* (Cambridge, 1798), 8, 1, 11; Horatio Nelson to the Right Honorable Sir William Hamilton, K.B., Aug. 8, 1798, in *Dispatches and Letters*, ed. Nicholas Nicolas (London, 1845), 93–94. See also Arthur F. Marotti, *Religious Ideology and Cultural Fantasy: Catholic and Anti-Catholic Discourses in Early Modern England* (Notre Dame: University of Notre Dame Press, 2005), 44; and Jonathan Scott, *England's Troubles: Seventeenth-Century English Political Instability in European Context* (Cambridge: Cambridge University Press, 2000).

9. George Whitefield, *Britain's mercies, and Britain's duties* (London, 1746), 14–15.

10. Jonathan Edwards, *A history of the work of redemption* (New York, 1786), 95. The project was based on a series of sermons that he preached in 1739; Charles G. Finney, "Attributes of Love," in *Lectures on Systematic Theology*, vol. 20 (London, 1851), 15; Alexander Campbell, *Popular Lectures and Addresses* (Philadelphia, 1863), 334, 335.

11. Cotton Mather, *A discourse delivered unto some part of the forces engaged in a just war of New England* (Boston, 1689), title page, 37, 28.

12. Quoted in ibid., *The Mystery of Israel's salvation opened* (London, 1669), 96. Mather seems to have had second thoughts about the theory, given the tone of his remarks about Eliot's embrace of the theory of Indians as the ten tribes; *Magnalia Christi Americana*, bk. 3, 192–193. Discussion of Williams, Penn, Samuel Sewall, and others is in Alden T. Vaughan, *Roots of American Racism: Essays on the Colonial Experience* (New York: Oxford University Press, 1995), 50ff. and 274nn58, 63, 67. Appleton quoted by Frederick D. Huntington, *Celebration of the Two Hundredth Anniversary of the Settlement of Hadley, Massachusetts* (Northampton, MA, 1859), 31; see also Mary White Rowlandson, *The sovereignty and goodness of God . . . being a narrative of the captivity and restauration of Mrs. Mary Rowlandson* (Cambridge, MA, 1682). Ellen Gould White, *The Story of Patriarchs and Prophets* (Washington, DC: Herald and Review Publishing Association, 1958), 453; John Greenleaf Whittier, *Old Portraits and Modern Sketches* (Boston, 1850), 294.

13. "History, as Expounded by the Supreme Court," *Putnam's Monthly Magazine of American Literature, Science, and Art* 9 (1857): 543; George Bancroft, *History of the United States*, vol. 3 of 10 vols. (Boston, 1837–1874), 408; F. A. Walker, "The Indian Question," *North American Review* 116 (1873): 330; Edward Eggleston, *Century Illustrated Magazine* 26 (1883): 717; *The Living Age* 111 (1871): 462; Frederick D. Huntington in *Celebration of the two hundredth anniversary of the settlement of Hadley, Massachusetts* (Northampton, 1859), 31.

14. Rev. James M. Whiton, "Moral Defects in Recent Sunday School Teaching," *New Englander and Yale Review* 43 (1884), 240–241. Italics in original.

15. "L'ensemble de croyances fondamentales qui n'ont même pas besoin de s'affirmer sous la forme d'un dogme explicite et conscient de lui-même"; Pierre Bourdieu, *Méditations pascaliennes* (Paris: Seuil, 1997), 26.

16. Quoted in George E. Tinker, *Missionary Conquest: The Gospel and Native American Cultural Genocide* (Minneapolis: Fortress Press, 1993), 98.

17. Quoted in Lynwood Carranco and Estle Beard, *Genocide and Vendetta: The Round Valley Wars of Northern California* (Norman: University of Oklahoma Press, 1981), 104.

18. *Chico Courant*, July 28, 1866, quoted in Clifford E. Trafzer and Joel R. Hyer, *Exterminate Them: Written Accounts of the Murder, Rape, and Slavery of Native Americans during the California Gold Rush, 1848–1868* (East Lansing: Michigan State University Press, 1999), 1.

19. Scholarship on English and American anti-Catholicism has grown in recent years. Most has developed out of the groundbreaking work by Ray Allen Billington, *The Protestant Crusade, 1800–1860: A Study of the Origins of American Nativism* (New York: Macmillan, 1952); and John Higham, *Strangers in the Land: Patterns of American Nativism, 1860–1925* (New Brusnwick, NJ: Rutgers University Press, 1955). Recent studies include Jenny Franchot, *Roads to Rome: The Antebellum Protestant Encounter with Catholicism* (Berkeley: University of California Press, 1994); Francis D. Cogliano, *No King, No Popery: Anti-Catholicism in Revolutionary New England* (Westport, CT: Greenwood Press, 1995); Jody Roy, *Rhetorical Campaigns of the 19th Century Anti-Catholics and Catholics in America* (Lewiston, NY: Edwin Mellen Press, 2000).

20. Jack Tager, *Boston Riots: Three Centuries of Social Violence* (Boston: Northeastern University Press, 2001), 15, 41–51; Dirk Hoerder, "Boston Leaders and Boston Crowds, 1765–1776," in *The American Revolution*, ed. Alfred Young (De Kalb: Northern Illinois University Press, 1976), 239–245; Alfred Young, "Pope's Day, Tar and Feathers, and 'Cornet Joyce, jun.': From Ritual to Rebellion in Boston, 1745–1775," paper cited in Gary Nash, *The Urban Crucible* (Cambridge, MA: Harvard University Press, 1986), 165.

21. James West Davidson, *The Logic of Millennial Thought: Eighteenth-Century New England* (New Haven: Yale University Press, 1977).

22. Nathan Stone, *Two discourses delivered at Southborough . . . October 9, 1760. Occasioned by the entire reduction of Canada* (Boston: S. Kneeland, 1761), 2.

23. *The Christian Monitor* (Boston, 1809). Pagination missing.

24. "Extermination," *Times and Seasons* 5 (1844): 624. The publication is Mormon.

25. Joseph F. Berg, *Farewell Words to the First German Reformed Church, Race Street, Philadelphia. Delivered March 14, 1852* ((Philadelphia, 1852), 21; and Berg, *Lectures on Romanism* (Philadelphia, 1840), 23, 24.

26. Heinrich H. Maurer, "The Problems of a National Church before 1860," *American Journal of Sociology* 30 (1925): 534; George Parsons Lathrop, "Hostility to Roman Catholics," *North American Review* 158 (1894): 569; William Barry, "'Americanism,' True and False," *North American Review* 169 (1899): 39; "The Secret Oath of the American Protective Association, October 31, 1893," in Michael Williams, *The Shadow of the Pope* (New York: McGraw-Hill, 1932), 103–104; *Methodist Review* 3 (1887): 939.

27. *Book of Mormon*, Alma 43:6; 21:2–3; 43:13.

28. B. H. Roberts, *A Comprehensive History of the Church of Jesus Christ of Latter-day Saints*, vol. 1 (Provo: Brigham Young University Press, 1965), 441.

29. Winn reconstructed this speech by Joseph Smith from several sources. See Kenneth H. Winn, *Exiles in a Land of Liberty: Mormons in America, 1830–1846* (Chapel Hill, NC, 1989), 140, 231nn35–36.

30. Joseph Smith, *History of the Church of Jesus Christ of Latter-day Saints*, vol. 3, 2d ed. (Salt Lake City: Deseret, 1973), 183–186.

31. Jan Shipps, *Mormonism: The Story of a New Religious Tradition* (Urbana: University of Illinois Press, 1987), x.

32. "The Mormons and Their Religion," *Scribner's Monthly* 3 (Feb. 1872): 401; "Christian Missions," *Charleston Gospel Messenger and Protestant Episcopal Register* 23 (March 1847): 370.

33. "Miscellany: Mormon War," *The Liberator*, July 5, 1844, 108.

34. *Messenger and Advocate*, July 1836, 347–348.

35. "The Mormon War," *Atkinson's Saturday Evening Post*, Nov. 24, 1838, 3.

36. A Traveler's Views," *New York Times*, June 26, 1871, 8.

37. "Steps to Blot Out Mormonism," *New York Times*, Jan. 22, 1882, 7.

38. "Truth Will Prevail," *Times and Seasons*, April 15, 1845.

39. Joel Shoemaker, "A Co-operative Commonwealth," *The Arena* 27 (Feb. 1902): 169.

40. Orestes A. Brownson, *Christianity and the Church Identical* (New York, 1857), 344.

41. "Proclamation by the Governor," broadside, Sept. 15, 1857, signed by Brigham Young; reproduced in Nels Anderson, *Desert Saints: The Mormon Frontier in Utah* (Chicago: University of Chicago Press, 1942), 173; Haight quoted in Juanita Brooks, *The Mountain Meadows Massacre* (Norman: University of Oklahoma, 1991), 52.

42. The "oath of vengeance" came even more visibly to the forefront of public debate about Mormonism during the crisis surrounding the seating of U. S. Senator Reed Smoot in 1903. See Kathleen Flake, *The Politics of American Religious Identity: The Seating of Senator Reed Smoot, Mormon Apostle* (Chapel Hill: University of North Carolina Press, 2004). On the oath (and its relation to Smoot), see David John Buergur, *Mysteries of Godliness: A History of Mormon Temple Worship* (San Francisco: Smith Research Associates, 1994), 133–136.

43. Mark Twain, *Roughing It*, vol. 2 (1871; reprint, New York: Harper Bros., 1904), 350; Will Bagley, *Blood of the Prophets : Brigham Young and the Massacre at Mountain Meadows* (Norman: University of Oklahoma Press, 2002).

44. John. D. Lee, *Mormonism Unveiled; or the Life and Confessions of the Late Mormon Bishop John D. Lee* (St. Louis, 1877), 234.

45. *Christian Pamphlet* 5 (1864–1882), 9.

46. J. H. Beadle, "The Mormon Theocracy," *Scribner's Monthly*, July 1877, 393.

47. Mrs. Frank Leslie, *California: A Pleasure Trip from Gotham to the Golden Gate* (New York, 1877), 73.

48. "A Way to End the Mormon War," *Littell's Living Age* 20 (Feb. 10, 1858), 494.

49. Edward Rigley, "The Aspects of Mormonism (Letter the Second)," in *New York Observer*, ed. Sidney E. Morse and Richard Morse, vol. 35 (New York, 1857), September 10, 1857, p. 209.

50. William Adams, *A discourse delivered at New-London, October 23d. A.D. 1760* (New London, CT, 1761), 8; John M. Lowrie, "War with Amalek" in *The Hebrew Lawgiver*, vol. 1 (Philadelphia, 1865), 276. Manly openness or boldness, a kind of manly "pluck," was crucial to male identity in the years when Lowrie was writing. See John Corrigan, *Business of the Heart: Religion and Emotion in the Nineteenth Century* (Berkeley: University of California Press, 2002), 128–162, 186–206.

51. Richard Hofstadter, *The Paranoid Style in American Politics and Other Essays* (New York: Vintage, 1967), 16.

7

Religion and Violence in Black and White

Eddie S. Glaude Jr.

During the "July Days" celebrations of 1834, a mob of angry merchants attacked a racially integrated Fourth of July gathering at the Chatham Street Church in New York City. Rumors that the church condoned "amalgamation" by not segregating its pews had made it an especially attractive target. The angry crowd set fire to the church, burning it to the ground. But the mob refused to stop there. They found another target in St. Philip's African Episcopal Church on Center Street, whose pastor, Reverend Peter Williams, had been accused of officiating an interracial marriage. The raucous crowd invaded his church, destroying everything in sight, and subsequently carried their violence into the streets of the Five Points neighborhood. In an odd allusion to Passover, the mob "demanded that white families illuminate their windows so that their race might be identified and their homes passed over; the mob would attack homes with darkened windows only."[1] Like the attacks carried out by a Protestant mob on a Catholic convent and girls school in Charlestown, Massachusetts later that summer, the violence directed against African American churches in New York can be interpreted in many ways. Both episodes can be read as straightforward expressions of hatred— attempts to purge a community of a despised other. But in the July Days attacks, the violence and the hatred were fueled by deeper concerns about who was fit to be an American and what it would mean to incorporate into the young nation racial and religious identities deemed incompatible with a racialized conception of citizenship. For those engaged in the violence and many others across the United States, only white Protestant men could be Americans.

From its very inception, America has considered itself a "redeemer nation," a city on a hill. This was the common vocabulary to describe the nation, its mission, and its people in the early nineteenth century. For some, this vision endures today. Ronald Reagan called America a "shining city on the hill." We also hear its echoes in the words of President Obama. Yet, for most of U.S. history, such language flowed less easily from black Americans. Slavery in the American South and the more subtle but still violent racism of the North constantly reminded African Americans of the deep flaws in the American experiment. These flaws engendered a profound ambivalence about the nation's commitment to democratic principles. American civil religion and its attendant rituals like the Fourth of July only served to cement this ambivalence. Free blacks were not allowed to participate in most of the celebrations of America's commitment to freedom and liberty. Their presence called into question the very meaning of America's past and present. The Fourth became one of the most menacing days of the year for free blacks in the North.

The violence of the 1834 celebration in New York illustrates one chapter in a larger story of how religion and race have clashed and converged in the formation of American national identity and how, in turn, this experience has shaped African Americans' relation to the United States. Such words as *We the People, freedom, liberty,* and *equality* have often served as thin cover for a deeply racist, violent society with little desire to extend its promises to African Americans, slave or free. Moreover, many aspects of the dominant forms of American Christianity—scriptural interpretation, theology, religious figures, and institutions—offered added justification for racist practices, giving them, in some terribly ironic sense, divine sanction. The very idea that black and white Americans might share the same pew in a church was enough to bring crowds to violence.

This chapter considers how central religion and violence have been to African American struggles for liberty and equality, both in the past and more recently. Religion and violence provide a revealing lens for the interpretation of racial injustice in America and efforts to correct it. Through a close reading of David Walker and Henry Highland Garnet, two African American leaders who called for armed slave revolt, one sees the importance of biblical stories and prophetic rhetoric to mobilize a subjugated people. Both figures appealed to racial solidarity grounded in concerted efforts to achieve freedom. Yet even as they did so, Walker and Garnet differed. Their rhetorics offered divergent understandings of the relationship between black slaves and white citizens—between what Martin Delaney described as a "nation within a nation" and a burgeoning nation-state committed to the idea that it was a white nation in the vein of Old Europe. In quite different ways, Walker and Garnet drew upon the scriptural and rhetorical traditions of American Christianity to make a case for African American freedom. Their words and their visions demonstrate the centrality of violence to the developing notion of America and to the formation of selfhood among its black "others." Walker's and Garnet's use of the rhetoric of the jeremiad, harkening back to a particular foundational narrative of the nation itself, also provided a powerful resource for finding meaning in the violence African Americans endured and for attributing sacredness to the violence that these abolitionists, at times, commended. The relationship represented by Walker and Garnet is a paradigmatic chapter in the larger African American story of the struggle for freedom in America.

RACIAL VIOLENCE AND EXODUS

The specter of violence and its relation to death and suffering are crucial to understanding distinctive tropes and metaphors in the political rhetoric of early nineteenth-century black Americans. The economies of violence surrounding black subjugation in the nineteenth century affected all persons marked as black, slave or free. Such violence, physical and epistemic (in the very ways African Americans understood themselves and the world around them), circumscribed the life chances of free blacks in the North, since traditional forms of political and legal redress remained, for the most part, unavailable. In the South, violence remained inextricably bound up with labor discipline; its presence policed the boundaries of the possible and secured the social and economic arrangements of southern communities; its markings could be found on the very bodies of slaves not only by way of physical wounds but also by the very ways in which they labored. Slaves had no choice but to work. Violence and its potentially deadly consequences were constitutive of the horizons within which all African Americans produced and reproduced political and social identities. No one could escape the potential threat: black skin linked one inextricably to modes of expression that drew on what Cornel West describes as the "ur text" of black cultural expression—guttural moans and cries for home and recognition based in the persistent violence of antebellum America.[2] Such a way of being in the world yielded structures of perception (such as conceptual schemes, common sense, and stereotypes) that colored how slave and master, black and white, actually saw the world and each other.

To live under the threat of violence, to be subjected daily to forms of humiliation, and to know that only those who look like you, regardless of class, experience this kind of humiliation and suffer this form of brutality creates feelings of terror and uncertainty that necessitate forms of solidarity grounded in the experience of a violent, racist culture. Moral identities constituted under such conditions of severe moral injury differentiate in real terms black America and white America. Moral injury places, minimally, distrust at the heart of social and political interactions among whites and blacks. And, perhaps more poignantly, this violence lends a sense of permanence to a "state of exception" as the lived experience of African Americans, where the principles that purportedly animate American democracy are suspended in relation to black folk. Under such conditions, ideas of duty and virtue, notions of the moral life and of democratic life, take shape over and against those who embody and enact their negation.

Biblical narrative, particularly the Exodus story, aided in efforts to make sense of an environment in which stated commitments to democracy stood alongside undemocratic practices. To be sure, Christian stories provided a large portion of the public vocabulary for African Americans of the period: the covenant, Egypt, the wilderness, and the promised land were tools in black public life that disclosed the violence, suffering, death, yet also the hope that was so indicative of African American experiences. The journey in the Exodus story also provided a crucial source for the construction of a national identity for African Americans. The story concerns not only heroic individuals who escaped the persecution of Pharaoh but also the people of Israel (a "nation" in its earliest form) as they journeyed toward moral renewal and self-determination. We should consider Exodus, then, not only for its historical relevance to any account of the emergence of a vocabulary of nationhood in the United States (Exodus figured prominently in many early Americans' understandings of the Revolution and the founding of the nation) but also as a metaphor for a particular style of imagining the nation in early nineteenth-century black America. Exodus is a metaphor for a conception of nation that begins with the common social heritage of slavery and the insult of discrimination—the psychic and physical violence of white supremacy in the United States—and evolves into a set of responses on the part of a people acting for themselves to alleviate their condition. Exodus drew on the persistence of violence (that of Pharaoh and Egypt) to shore up the importance of thanksgiving, remembrance, and duty, and to manage (or contain) the distrust that threatened an enveloping paranoia about white folk and their intentions. It also often provided the existential resources to answer the questions Why go on? What's the use? What is it all for?[3]

I call this a form of *Exodus politics* because the story, by direct or indirect reference, gave expression to what can be called the soul of the nation.[4] Its languages and images aided in the articulation of a tragicomic disposition toward life in that the invocation of the story announced an ongoing struggle, aided by a transcendent God active in history, against the realities of lived experience. Moreover, the story told of black America's sojourn, directing the consciousness of the group back to significant points in its common history, enabling, as it were, a constant renewal of community through social memory. Exodus politics, then, was based in a form of common complaint against oppression; a "hope against hope" for deliverance; a sense of obligation to and solidarity with those similarly situated; and the deep conviction that the true test of American democracy rested in the nation's darker sons and daughters. American democracy is embraced and imagined here in spite of its attenuation and arrest vis-à-vis black bodies.

By appropriating Exodus, African Americans articulated their own sense of peoplehood and secured for themselves a common history and destiny as they elevated their experiences to biblical drama.[5] This analogical reasoning provided many black activists with the vocabularies to condemn the practices of the United States and to talk of emancipation. In 1831 the young Boston-based abolitionist Maria Stewart cried out: "America, America, foul and indelible is thy stain! For the cruel wrongs and injuries to the fallen sons of Africa. The blood of her murdered ones cries to heaven for vengeance against Thee."[6] Because of its transgressions America did not symbolize—as it had for many whites—a promised land in the wilderness. Rather, America was Egypt, the enslaver of the black Israel, God's chosen people. Stewart continued: "You may kill, tyrannize, and oppress us as much as you choose, until our cry shall come up before the throne of God; for I am firmly persuaded, that he will not suffer you to quell the proud, fearless and undaunted spirits of the Africans forever; for in his own time, he is able to plead our case against you, and to pour out upon you the ten plagues of Egypt."[7] The appropriation of the Exodus story not only gave an account of the circumstances of black lives, offering a regulative ideal to guide action and to define the nation; it promised retribution for the continued suffering of God's people.

In the early decades of the nineteenth century, two northern black leaders declared that it was God's will that African American slaves should rise up violently against their oppressors. In their calls for resistance, David Walker and Henry Highland Garnet drew in different ways on the stories and themes of Exodus. Their deployments of the story reflect a vacillating hope among African Americans about whether or not genuine freedom was attainable in the United States. Walker saw a land that could be awakened and redeemed. Garnet harbored no such hope. The tension between these two understandings and those who shared them offers a window onto a centuries-long tension in how African Americans not only view the nation but also draw from religious wellsprings to correct America's shortcomings. And it is precisely in this modulating relation— at once an embrace and rejection—that the tension and tone of African American politics and its religious underpinnings can be felt and heard.

DAVID WALKER, EXODUS, AND THE BLACK JEREMIAD

David Walker was born in Wilmington, North Carolina, in 1785 to a free black mother. (His father, a slave, died before his birth.) Walker left the South and settled in Boston, where he opened a business and developed a reputation for generosity.[8] After many years of anger and frustration about the brutal injustices of slavery, Walker put pen to paper in the hope of bringing about radical change. His *Appeal to the Coloured Citizens of the World* (1829) stands as a critical indication of a new way of thinking and acting among antebellum northern blacks in the late 1820s. Not only the content of the document but its form heralded a dramatic change in the nature of black public engagement in the North. Walker explicitly called for armed black resistance against the sinful institution of slavery—resistance sanctified by the grace of God. He also prophesied America's fall and destruction unless the nation repented of this evil.

Walker's *Appeal*, then, was a black jeremiad—a rhetoric of indignation urgently challenging the nation to turn back to the ideals of its covenant. The black jeremiad grew out of an ambivalent relation with white evangelical Christianity in which African Americans simultaneously rejected white America yet participated in one of the nation's most sacred rhetorical traditions. The black jeremiad can thus be understood as a paradigm of the broader structure of ambivalence—of simultaneous eschewal and embrace—that constitutes African Americans' relation to American culture. Walker's words evoke the covenantal sermons of Puritan colonists such as John Winthrop and Increase and Cotton Mather. Winthrop's *Model of Christian Charity*, delivered aboard the *Arbella* in 1630, framed the significance of the journey from the Old World to the New in covenantal terms, enumerating the blessings God would bestow on a righteous settlement and the curses God would rain down upon those who carelessly broke faith:

> Beloved there is now sett before us life, and good, deathe and evil in that wee are Commaunded this day to the Lord our God and to love one another, to walke in his ways and to keepe his Commanundements and his Ordinance, and his lawes, and the Articles of our Covenant with him that wee may live and be multiplied, and that the Lord our God may blesse us in the land whither we goe to possesse it: But if our heartes shall turne away soe that wee will not obey, but shall be seduced and worship other Gods, our pleasures, and profits, and serve them; it is propounded unto this day, wee shall surely perishe out of the good Land whither wee passe over this vast Sea to possesse it.[9]

Walker echoed Winthrop's warning but with jeremiadic urgency. He wrote in his *Appeal*: "Oh Americans! Let me tell you, in the name of the Lord, it will be good for you, if you listen to the voice of the Holy Ghost, but if you do not; you are ruined!!! Some of you are good men; but the will of God must be done. . . . When God almighty commences his battle on the continent of America for the oppression of his people, tyrants will wish they never were born."[10]

Walker's *Appeal* not only prophesied God's wrath in order to arouse whites from their moral slumber; it also proposed to awaken a spirit of inquiry and investigation among antebellum blacks based in their experiences of severe moral injury. Walker appealed boldly to the moral responsibility of self-determination; African Americans had to strike the blow for freedom. His use of the jeremiad urged the entire nation to turn from sin, while specifically exhorting African Americans to act intelligently for themselves in pursuit of *their* freedom. The audience of the *Appeal* was multiple—white, black, and the entire nation—and his message functioned on a number of frequencies. He told whites that in order to save America they had to extend the benefits and burdens of freedom to African Americans. For blacks, Walker's words were clear: in order to be free, they must understand and intelligently articulate the nature of their situation, act for themselves in pursuit of freedom and, above all, do so in light of an obligation to each other.

A year before the publication of his *Appeal*, in December 1828 at the General Colored Association in Boston, David Walker called America to account for its racial sins. In so doing, he urged African Americans to organize and to engage in united action. He posed the question: "Do not two hundred and eight years of very intolerable sufferings teach us the actual necessity of a general union among us? Do we not know indeed, the horrid dilemma into which we are, and from which, we must exert ourselves, to be extricated?"[11] Enduring and overcoming the evil of racist violence, Walker believed, entailed faith in God and in other black individuals: "It is our duty to try every scheme that we think will have a tendency to facilitate our salvation, and leave the final result to that God, who holds the destinies of people in the hollow of his hand, and who ever has, and will, repay every nation according to its works."[12] Here Walker simultaneously warned white America of its impending judgment and urged black America to action, reminding the latter that God's judgment of nations extended not only to acts of evil but also to submissiveness in the face of evils. African Americans must extricate themselves from their oppression—no one else could. And they should do so together. A crass form of individualism must give way to a communitarian ethic: one's duty was not only to oneself, averred Walker, but to the entire community. Only with this orientation and the will of God, he claimed, would the "dejected, degraded, and now enslaved children of Africa ... take their stand among the nations of the earth."[13]

Walker counted American slavery as one of the most brutal forms of bondage in human history. What distinguished American slavery from all other historical examples was the ideological justification of the institution, which argued that African peoples were not a part of the human family—that these organisms stood somewhere between man and ape. Walker wrote, "I call upon the professing Christian, I call upon the philanthropist, I call upon the very tyrant himself to show me a page of history either sacred or profane, on which can be found ... that the Egyptians heaped the insupportable insult upon the children of Israel, by telling them they were not of the human family. Can whites deny this charge?"[14] Such claims circulated in the overall economy of violence that defined slavery and racial subordination more generally; its use value can be located in the very ways in which the ideological justifications framed how black bodies were perceived, classified, and imagined. Walker refused to accept the grounds on which Thomas Jefferson and others argued for black inferiority, for their appeal to science and rational deliberation emptied the issue of slavery of its moral significance and the felt sense of severe moral injury. For him, the psychic and physical horror of the consequences of such ideas required a response predicated on the pain and suffering of African Americans, an outpouring that called attention to the absurdity of the utterance. Such a response gave powerful voice to matters otherwise considered private and to the fact that African Americans were not dimwitted beasts of burden but rather human beings capable of genuine feeling, critical intelligence, and discernment of their own interests. As Walker wrote, here speaking directly to whites, "You are not astonished at my saying we hate you, for if we are men, we cannot but hate you while you are treating us like dogs."[15] In short, the logics of violence had to be directly challenged, but not on the terms set by the very economy of violence and certain attendant and pernicious notions of rationality that subjugated African Americans.

Just as Walker rejected the so-called rationalism of those who denied that he and other blacks were fully human, he empowered African Americans to use reason to draw on their experience when engaging in public deliberation. Walker believed that any discussion about race in the United States—and this insight remains true today—required that interlocutors confront the true terror the subject called forth, not only the physical pain but the psychic violence of slavery and racial discrimination. Walker's *Appeal*, then, gave voice to a range of emotions and impulses, habits and discoveries that characterized a people experiencing the violence of white proscription. He believed that one of the real tragedies of slavery and racial discrimination was the extent to which these practices cultivated habits of servility among African Americans. In some ways, the problem Walker confronted was not so much the failure of African Americans to strike the first blow for freedom but, rather, their submission to racial hierarchies and "their consequent belief that they owed all whites certain respectful duties, that they were prevented from perceiving themselves as entitled to freedom and personal empowerment, and thereby seizing it when it was before them."[16] He aimed to shift the center of gravity from that of abject servility to that of critical intelligence and action. African Americans could not begin to change their condition until "they could acknowledge and describe the conditions and system under which they existed." Such an effort, in Walker's view, did not "consist in protecting devils."[17]

Walker hoped through demonization of white slaveholders and racists to provoke blacks to think of freedom apart from white people and to define themselves not by whites' standards but by the laws of God. The conversion would begin only when blacks unleashed their anger, expressed in public rage. Walker wrote: "There is an unconquerable disposition in the breast of blacks which, when it is fully awakened and put in motion, will be subdued, only with the destruction of the animal existence."[18] If African Americans were not enraged about their conditions, he maintained, they obviously had failed to analyze and understand the problems of race and its consequences. Expressions of rage, then, began the process of purging blacks of the habit of servility and of clarifying the particulars of their miseries.

Public rage served only to jump-start action in light of the moral imperative to respond to the evil of white supremacy—an evil that often shook the foundations of Walker's faith: "I aver, that when I look over these United States of America, and the world, and see the ignorant deceptions and consequent wretchedness of my brethren, I am brought ofttimes solemnly to a stand, and in the midst of my reflections I exclaim to my God, 'Lord, didst thou make us to be slaves to our brethren, the whites?' "[19] Here Walker confronted head-on the particular problem of evil facing African Americans: how to reconcile their present circumstances with faith in a just God. His answer drew on the distinctive evangelical tradition of black America and his faith in the capacity of African Americans to confront their condition courageously: "When I reflect that God is just, and that millions of my wretched brethren would meet death with glory . . . in preference to a mean submission to the lash of tyrants, I am with streaming eyes, compelled to shrink back into nothingness before my Maker and exclaim again, thy will be done, O Lord God Almighty."[20] Yet African Americans could not wait for God to liberate them. They had to act for themselves.

The great sin of Walker's contemporaries, in his view, was their failure to act intelligently for themselves, and, insofar as they failed to do this, they failed to act on what God promised them. Walker stated the point quite directly: "If you commence, make sure you work—do not trifle, for they will not trifle with you—they want us for their slaves, and think nothing of murdering us in order to subject us to that wretched condition—therefore, if there is an attempt made by us, kill or be killed. . . . Look upon your mother, wife and children, and answer God Almighty! and believe this, that it is no more harm for you to kill a man, who is trying to kill you than it is for you to take a drink of water when thirsty; in fact, the man who will stand still and let another man murder him, is worse than an infidel."[21] It was the duty of every black Christian to fight, even if it meant death, against the scourge of slavery and racial discrimination. For submission to such evils was tantamount to a sin against God. Yet violent resistance remained a last resort; it was inevitable only if white America failed to live up to the principles of its covenant. In the form of a typical jeremiad, Walker wrote: "I speak Americans for your good. . . . And woe, woe to you if we have to obtain our freedom by fighting. Throw away your fears and prejudices then, and enlighten us and treat us like men, and we will like you more than we now hate you.... Treat us then like men, and we will be your friends. And there is no doubt in my mind, but that the whole of the past will be sunk into oblivion, and we yet, under God, will become a united and happy people."[22]

Walker's jeremiad called on white Americans to humble themselves before God and to live up to the nation's promise. He also exhorted African Americans to see their worth and dignity. Despite its venom, the *Appeal* was ambivalently tied to "the values and equality that actually formed the hope that was America."[23] The *Appeal's* rhetoric drew on tropes common in American discourse and extolled a vision of America that all races could understand and embrace. For Walker, African Americans, remade in the image of the Hebrew slaves crying for freedom in Egypt, called the nation back to its principles and, in the process, also defined themselves as a distinct people who were distinctly American—a claim that, in end, counseled violence against the economy of violence so central to white supremacy in the United States.

The publication of David Walker's *Appeal* sent waves of fear throughout the slaveholding South. Indeed, its most profound effects seem to have been on the psyche of white southerners. In defiance of laws banning the document, copies of the *Appeal* were smuggled onto plantations and disseminated clandestinely among free black communities in southern cities. Nat Turner, whose rebellion in August 1831 ended only after fifty-five white men, women, and children had been killed, did not connect his actions to Walker's call, but the violence of his actions and the violence extolled in Walker's words led to the imposition of even greater restrictions and even more repressive measures on both free and enslaved blacks.[24] Underlying America's economy of violence were deep-seated fears about black revenge and retribution. Distrust between black and white was growing and cut both ways.

HENRY HIGHLAND GARNET: ENGAGING AND REJECTING EXODUS

Henry Highland Garnet's "Address to the Slaves of the United States of America" broke like a tsunami over the National Negro Convention of 1843 in Buffalo, New York. Like Walker's *Appeal*, it indicated a shift in African American approaches to the race problem in America. It demonstrated an increasing maturation among black communities in the North and a more aggressive voice among an emerging black political class. Garnet's address is an early example of the pessimism that developed among blacks of the mid-nineteenth century, an outgrowth, as it were, of entrenched racism in the late 1830s. For lingering on the borders of the call for self-determination among the oppressed was the specter of violence:

the raging swell of despair in the face of repeated indifference and the demand "to strike the blow for freedom."[25]

Similar to Walker's *Appeal*, Garnet's call for a general slave rebellion took seriously the extent of moral injury that penetrated the lives of African Americans, slave or free. But unlike Walker and many African American leaders who were his contemporaries, Garnet both refused to frame his call with reference to the redemption of the United States and rejected Exodus as a model for political action. In his eyes, Exodus induced in slaves and freemen a passive gradualism in which the group, like the children of Israel, waited for providential deliverance. Instead, Garnet employed what Michael Walzer has called a "messianic" voice and called upon African Americans to force the End. The End simply denotes a people's refusal to suffer any longer. This desire to force the End—to actively bring about slavery's collapse—was the product less of a longing for the apocalypse of unconditional victory and more of a desire to arrest the psychic and physical scarring and bruising of repeated indifference.

Garnet met other African American leaders' demands for restraint with accusations of cowardice and explained the sense of urgency by pointing to the pain and suffering of slaves. No black person, he argued, should rest until the scourge of slavery and racial prejudice was destroyed. Garnet further grounded his call to revolt in Christian duty. There was, in other words, a short distance between the "sanctifying grace" of true Christianity and the "sanctified violence" of a slave revolt. Slaves, Garnet argued, were justified to use any means to end slavery, since slavery, a form of violence itself, rendered futile their attempts to live a Christian life. Prudential constraints ought to be cast aside. No danger was too great to confront. "Life was not worth having on some terms."[26]

Garnet understood that his call to action, to some extent, challenged the slave—or at least the black Christian—imagination. He turned then to the most important story of this people in bondage, Exodus, and decried its analogical use in the black American context. This rejection of Exodus was a direct attack against slaves' beliefs that God was acting in history and the promise that God would act on their behalf as he had acted for Israel. Providential gradualism stood in the way of Garnet's eagerness to force the end, and he attacked it head-on. Garnet enjoined his listeners:

> But you are a patient people. You act as though you were made for the special use of these devils. You act as though your daughters were born to pamper the lusts of your masters and overseers. And worse than all, you tamely submit while your lords tear your wives from your embraces and defile them before your eyes. In the name of God, we ask, are you men? Where is the blood of your fathers? Has it all run out of your veins? Awake, awake, millions of voices are calling you! Your dead fathers speak to you from their graves. Heaven, as with a voice of thunder, calls on you to arise from the dust.[27]

The paragraph evokes the seemingly endless succession of births and deaths in slavery. The only way to end this cycle was through a cathartic moment of violence, a once-and-for-all struggle that would clear the present burden of slavery from the future and relegate it to the past. A call for confrontation immediately followed. "Let your motto be resistance! Resistance! RESISTANCE! No oppressed people have ever secured their liberty without resistance." Garnet questioned the manliness of both the slave and black leaders, in effect articulating a form of muscular Christianity that replaced quietism with the call to awaken, rise up, and resist.

In the most stunning moment of his address, Garnet's rejection of Exodus became a model for the liberation of blacks in America. "You had far better all die—die immediately, than live like slaves, and entail your wretchedness upon your posterity. . . . Rather die freemen, than live to be the slaves. It is impossible, like the children of Israel, to make a grand exodus from the land of bondage. The Pharaohs are on both sides of the blood-red waters."[28]

Garnet's realism short-circuited any invitation to optimism predicated upon God's promised intervention. Instead he urged a violent challenge to state power and forced his audience to make a choice between identifying, however ambivalently, with this fragile experiment of democracy or defining themselves and their political aims over and against it. Exodus did not affirm the Americanness of black folk, as it had for Walker; it could not. Rather, it was violence that sealed black fate and, rightly deployed, would secure their freedom. Garnet confronted African Americans with a critical choice of national politics: moral suasion— which he cast as cowardly and un-Christian—or political militancy, which involved a violent rejection of the economy of violence of American racism and which he saw as the truest expression of God's will.

In 1848, Garnet reprinted the "Address" alongside the full text of David Walker's *Appeal*, but the rhetorical effect of his speech remained quite different from that of Walker's. The "Address," like the *Appeal*, called for slave insurrection and viewed the submission to slavery as sin. But unlike the *Appeal*, Garnet's speech was not a jeremiad directed at the United States. The call for violence was not couched in a prophetic language that warned the nation of the wages of sin or the failures to live up to divine ideals. In fact, Garnet explicitly rejected attempts to imagine African Americans as a chosen people who had a special role to remind America of its covenantal duty to deal justly with others (particularly blacks). Saving America's soul was not Garnet's errand.

Walker's *Appeal*, on the other hand, despite its call for violence, forced no such choice of native identification as Garnet did. Walker may have demonized slaveholders and their defenders, but, in the end, he claimed the country as his birthright and offered it a means for salvation. African Americans, in his view remade in the image of Hebrew slaves, called the nation back to its principles and made it possible that "we may yet, under God . . . become a united and happy people."[29] Nowhere in Garnet's address is this possibility mentioned. He simply ends obliquely, "Labor for the peace of the human race, and remember that you are FOUR MILLIONS."[30] Garnet's was a call that constituted what would become an enduring underside of African American struggle: a profound skepticism about the possibility of genuine freedom for African Americans in the United States and an insistence that the economy of American racial violence required in response a severing of ties altogether with this fragile experiment.

AMERICAN DEMOCRACY SINGS THE BLUES

We should not conclude from all of this that Garnet rejected America outright or that his political aims were the overthrow of the country and the formation of a black nation-state. Rather, Garnet's "Address" exposed the ambivalence at the heart of African American experiences: the way severe moral injury both colored any embrace of America and provided impetus to reject it. In this sense, the tension between Walker and Garnet is emblematic of a broader struggle within African American history. Juxtaposing these two figures forces an apparent choice. Garnet emphasized the plight of African Americans irrespective of the state, arguing as forcefully as he could that blacks must be their own saviors. Neither the "American ideology," nor the rhetoric of the jeremiad in which it was steeped, was reliable or instructive. A new trope of salvation, violent and revolutionary, must be found. Early nineteenth-century African American uses of Exodus politics, like those of David Walker, urged solidaristic efforts to resist suffering. They also proposed a future that consisted not in the violent subjugation of African Americans but in the extension of U.S. principles of democracy to all. With this view in mind, and with the more hopeful counterexample of Walker's *Appeal*, we should read Henry Highland Garnet's address as exposing the tragic sense of life at the heart of African American politics: the fact that African Americans are constantly having to choose either to identify with this fragile democracy, struggling for its soul, or to define themselves over and against it—and then to live with the consequences of such choices without yielding to despair. Pharaoh or some such evil is indeed on both sides of the blood-red water.

To choose America is not to efface the evil of white supremacy. No matter how you read the Exodus story, it begins with concrete evil, just as the American founding was steeped in racism. American racism remains in spite of the choice, and the brutality of bondage is kept alive in living memory to remind us from whence we came. To choose America, then, is not to choose the nation as it is or as it was but, rather, as we hope it to be. The choice is prospective; it is all about a risk-ridden future. But, as Garnet's reading of Exodus so incisively pointed out, the evil persists. This modulating relation—what I have called elsewhere a structure of ambivalence—continues to animate American political and religious life even in the so-called age of Obama, who has conceived himself at the forefront of the post-Exodus Joshua generation. For many, Obama's election ushers in a post-racial era, in which the burdens of the past are finally left aside and America can now step into its awaited future. Race no longer matters. For others, however, Obama's presidency only deepens the marginalization of the black poor and banishes from sight the racial inequalities that continue to frustrate the life chances of so many of our fellow citizens. Moral injury goes unacknowledged, and distrust festers. Under these conditions America's economy of violence continues. It no longer requires the whip or the language of biological inferiority to justify its ends; conspicuous consumption, a prosperity gospel, and accusations about "personal irresponsibility" suffice. And the prison industrial complex or violent death awaits many of those caught in its intricate web.

Walker's and Garnet's words thematize a particular dimension of African American political and religious life: How do we embrace—should we embrace—a country committed simultaneously to democracy and to the continued existence of racial inequalities? In offering an answer, the point is not to choose between Walker and Garnet, between Marcus Garvey and W.E.B. Du Bois, Martin Luther King Jr. and Malcolm X, Barack Obama and Jeremiah Wright. All of these figures have made crucial contributions to the African American experience. Rather, we should see that violence rests beneath practices that short-circuit the possibilities of so many of our fellow citizens. And this continues even today. What is required of all Americans (including those who use black Christian languages) is a concerted effort to expose the violence that undergirds so much of American life today. To do so is not to choose the path of violence as a form of political redress but to show how violence stands as a check on national hubris and a rejection of the illusion of American innocence.

NOTES

1. Linda Kerber, "Abolitionists and Amalgamation: The New York City Race Riots of 1834," *New York History* 48 (January 1967): 33.

2. See Henry Louis Gates Jr. and Cornel West, *The Future of the Race* (New York: Alfred A. Knopf, 1996), 81.

3. Questions asked by Clifford Geertz in *The Interpretation of Cultures* (New York: Basic, 1973), 253.

4. See Ralph Ellison, "What Would America Be Like without Blacks?," in *The Collected Essays of Ralph Ellison*, ed. John Callahan (New York: Modern Library, 1995).

5. Albert Raboteau, "Exodus and the American Israel," in *African-American Christianity: Essays in History*, ed. Paul E. Johnson (Berkeley: University of California Press, 1994).

6. Marilyn Richardson, ed., *Maria Stewart, America's First Black Woman Political Writer: Essays and Speeches* (Bloomington: Indiana University Press, 1987), 39.

7. Ibid.

8. "David Walker," in *Dictionary of North Carolina Biography*, ed. William S. Powell (Chapel Hill: University of North Carolina Press, 1996). See also http://docsouth.unc.edu/nc/walker/ bio.html.

9. John Winthrop, *A Modell of Christian Charity*, reprinted in *God's New Israel: Religious Interpretations of American Destiny*, ed. Conrad Cherry (Chapel Hill: University of North Carolina Press, 1998), 41.

10. *David Walker's Appeal to the Coloured Citizens of the World, but in Particular, and Very Expressly, to Those of the United States of America* (1829; reprint, New York: Hill and Wang, 1965), 13.

11. David Walker, "Address Delivered before the General Colored Association at Boston," *Freedom's Journal*, Dec. 19, 1828; reprinted in John Bracey Jr., August Meier, and Elliot Rudwick, eds., *Black Nationalism in America* (Indianapolis: Bobbs-Merrill, 1970), 31.

12. Ibid.

13. Ibid.

14. *Walker's Appeal*, 10.

15. Ibid., 70n.

16. Peter Hinks, *To Awaken My Afflicted Brethren: David Walker and the Problem of Antebellum Slave Resistance* (University Park: Pennsylvania University Press, 1997), 214–215.

17. Ibid., 224; *Walker's Appeal*, 25.

18. *Walker's Appeal*, 25.

19. Ibid., 28.

20. Ibid.

21. Ibid., 25–26.

22. Ibid., 69–70.

23. Hinks, *To Awaken My Afflicted Brethren*, 247.

24. "David Walker."

25. Here and in the following paragraphs I am drawing on Michael Walzer, *Exodus and Revolution* (New York: Basic Books, 1985).

26. See Sterling Stuckey, *Slave Culture: Nationalist Theory and the Foundations of Black America* (New York: Oxford University Press, 1988), 164.

27. Garnet, "Address," in Bracey, Meier, and Rudwick, *Black Nationalism in America*, 76.

28. Ibid., 73.

29. *Walker's Appeal*, 70.

30. Garnet, "Address," 76.

8

State Violence and the Un-American West

Mormons, American Indians, and Cults

Todd M. Kerstetter

It is a consistent feature of America's past and present that religion serves as a marker of individual and group legitimacy, by which the status of "good American" might be assigned. This chapter addresses four episodes occurring in the past century and a half in the American West in which federal and state authorities used rhetorical, legislative, and physical violence against religious groups it considered "un-American." This recurring pattern presupposes that a particular style of religion (namely, Protestant Christianity in secular trappings) is necessary to "good" Americanism. Collectively, these episodes point to an ongoing struggle between a government suspicious of "religious fanaticism" and those within its borders who pursue a different religion deemed threatening to secular society.

Bruce Lincoln provides useful categories for explaining the conflict between state governments and religious minorities. In his book *Holy Terrors: Thinking about Religion after September 11*, Lincoln notes that relations between colonizers and colonized peoples have often involved troublesome dichotomies vis-à-vis religion. Those in power often have thought in terms of binary categories—"moral/immoral, sacred/profane, modern/primitive . . . dominant/submissive"—that privilege the religion of colonial elites and denigrate the faiths of others. For Lincoln, colonial and secular governments react against a publicly and visibly prominent style of religiousness that he terms "maximalism," favoring instead a more privatistic style, "minimalism." Maximalism describes a condition in which religion permeates all corners of society and exercises powerful influence on diet, dress, family structures, leisure, politics, and economics. Religious minimalism, a child of the Enlightenment, is characterized by a far more restricted role for religion and, more to the point, the belief that religion *ought* to have such a restricted role. In religiously minimalist societies, religion is restricted to faith beliefs that have their place in the private sphere, while phenomena such as cultural preferences, political behavior, or economic markets are presumed to be governed by secular principles. Minimalists tend to view maximalists as either quaint throwbacks or dangerous, reactionary fanatics.[1]

Lincoln's categories help us to see continuities among otherwise disconnected confrontations in the American West. In clashes with Mormons, Ghost Dancers, Branch Davidians, and the Fundamentalist Church of Jesus Christ of Latter-day Saints (FLDS), a minimalist state confronted a maximalist religious minority and sought either to coerce the minority into minimalism or to eradicate it altogether. The nineteenth-century U.S. expansion westward was facilitated by the power of religious minimalism. In the course of this "colonization," state authorities encountered, coerced, and sometimes killed religious maximalists who stood in their way. Even today, national and state governments react violently against maximalist groups that threaten U.S. identity and hegemony.

That all four conflicts discussed below took place in the trans-Mississippi West makes them all the more interesting. The religious landscape of the United States clearly has been shaped by the First Amendment. Americans are wont to envision a land of liberty, where governments shall make no law restricting the free exercise of religion. But the restricting hand of the government has been noticeably rough in the West. Powerful myths of westward expansion, boosted by affiliated notions of manifest destiny, freedom, and opportunity, have long given events in the American West a special purchase on the American imagination. As a space and an imaginary, "the West" is fraught with ambivalence, simultaneously bearing the hopes for "America's" future while also corroding or, at least, threatening the institutions of civilization. I suggest that the indeterminacy of "the West," its imagined centrality to America's future, and the violent hand of the state all are connected. Religious differences that might otherwise be tolerated are more threatening when they appear on the frontier, calling forth uses of force to expand, and also to tame and Americanize maximalist religious minorities. Such violence makes sense when understood as blows struck by a minimalist state eager to extend religious minimalism into future territories of the republic.

LEGISLATIVE VIOLENCE: MORMONS AND THE STATE

In 1844, members of the Church of Jesus Christ of Latter-day Saints, commonly known as Mormons, fled a nation they believed lacked the will to protect them. After a dramatic flight from Nauvoo, Illinois, they settled in the remote basin of the Great Salt Lake. Though they built a home there, their refuge proved fleeting. Brigham Young and the Mormons soon found themselves back within the jurisdiction of the United States and engaged in a political and moral struggle for what Utah Territory and, ultimately, the nation would become. Mormons sought to establish a maximalist theocratic state that would codify and protect their vision of Zion within the United States, and the government took strong issue with this vision. In 1857, galvanized by reports of mistreatment of federal officials and nascent rebellion (and by the perceived threat to the nation's social fabric posed by plural marriage), the federal government dispatched roughly a third of the U.S. Army to Utah to install loyal, compliant territorial officials. This mostly bloodless "Utah War" marked the beginning of decades of rhetorical and legislative activity intended to shape the Mormon faith according to the minimalist standard if not to destroy Mormonism completely.

U.S. Senator Justin Morrill of Vermont fired a significant legislative shot in this battle with his sponsorship of the Morrill Anti-Bigamy Act of 1862. Morrill had charged Mormons with using religion as a cover to introduce polygamy, which he described as a "Mohammedan barbarism revolting to the civilized world." Morrill's initial legislation, which seems more an act of individual pique than part of a congressional struggle against an infidel population, missed its target, but his rhetoric cast Mormons as dangerous outsiders. He linked them explicitly with "exotic" and "uncivilized" Muslims and, implicitly, with American Indians, who were commonly described as barbaric, savage, and uncivilized. That Mormons had removed themselves to the heart of the West and lived in the midst of Native Americans may well have added to perceptions of the threat they posed to the expanding nation and national culture. Morrill's prejudices, though strong, were typical of public officials of his day. His legislation paved the way for antipolygamy legislation, and for the U.S. Supreme Court's eventual limitation of First Amendment guarantees of religious freedom.[2]

In the late 1870s a case designed to test the constitutionality of the Morrill Act found its way to the U.S. Supreme Court. In *Reynolds* v. *United States* (1879), the Court ruled that certain conduct, even if religiously inspired, could be controlled by civil authorities. Polygamy, which the court deemed a threat to public order, fitted the description of such conduct, highlighting what legal scholar Sarah Barringer Gordon has called "a democratically constructed yet indelibly Protestant public morality." Plural marriage, defined as a social evil, stood beyond First Amendment protection. Mormons found that the full practice of their faith would lead them into legal jeopardy.[3]

During the 1880s, Congress, urged on by the likes of journalist and reformer Kate Field, passed increasingly restrictive and punitive laws aimed at ending plural marriage and reforming Mormon society. Field, who wrote editorials advocating withholding statehood for Utah until plural marriage ended, drew sellout audiences to her "Mormon Monster" lectures during the mid-1880s. In language shot through with violent imagery, Field called plural marriage a monstrosity, a "rock that need[ed] blowing up with the dynamite of the law."[4] Congress supplied that dynamite in the Edmunds Act of 1882 and the Edmunds-Tucker Act of 1887. The Edmunds Act closed loopholes in the Morrill Act; provided penalties for cohabitation; allowed for potential jurors to be dismissed for simply approving of polygamy; marked children of polygamous marriages as illegitimate; and prohibited polygamists and illegal cohabitors from voting or holding public office. Congress subsequently created the Utah Commission to enforce the act by registering voters in Utah and supervising territorial elections.[5] The Edmunds-Tucker Act of 1887 extended the life of the Utah Commission and took action against the LDS Church. It ended the Perpetual Emigrating Company (an organization designed to promote emigration of poor Mormons to Utah), abolished the Nauvoo Legion, and dissolved the church as an incorporated body. Church assets went to a receiver. The government hired hundreds of officials to administer the act, essentially creating a bureaucracy to dismantle the Mormon Church.[6] These legislative acts represented the boldest strikes in the sustained campaign to shape Mormonism and Utah society to acceptably minimalist norms. Mormons at the time viewed this action as part of a campaign of legislative violence.

In September 1890, after waging a resistance campaign for decades, the church announced a manifesto indicating it would forbid plural marriages. The church also agreed to abandon other practices deemed at odds with republicanism. It promised not to dictate members' voting behavior and not to support linkages of church and state. The church changed, Utah society changed, and when Utah entered the union in 1896 it did so under a constitution that prohibited plural marriages.[7] Less than seventy years after its founding and after numerous episodes of physical violence between Mormons and non-Mormons, the force of federal law reigned in the LDS Church.

SIOUX GHOST DANCERS AND THE MINIMALIST STATE

As action on the Mormon front cooled, U.S. relations with American Indians, marked for decades by physical violence—as well as what some would describe as rhetorical and cultural violence—produced a new and bloody chapter. In this clash between Native American maximalism and U.S. government minimalism, policies and laws designed to shape the "religious" and cultural life of this minority gave way to massacre.

The first century of interactions between the U.S. government and Native American tribes was violent in many ways. The federal government took control of Indian lands and forced whole tribes to resettle. Government officials and churchmen tried to "civilize" Native Americans by forcing them into agricultural lifestyles and trying to convert them to Christianity. The U.S. Army and American settlers clashed with American Indians on grand and small scales. During his tenure as president, Ulysses S. Grant experimented with a "peace policy" that invited religious denominations to supply clergy and laymen to work as agents and Bureau of Indian Affairs officials. Grant's aim was to pursue policies of resettlement and conversion but in a kinder, gentler, less corrupt fashion. Richard Pratt, founder of the U.S. Training and Industrial School at Carlisle Barracks, Pennsylvania, and a leading advocate for using education to "civilize" former slaves and American Indians, demonstrated that even kindness could be marked by stunning brutality when he wrote, "Kill the Indian in him, and save the man." Likely saying more than he knew, Pratt stated further that the nation's work of civilization would not be done until every community across the country completely and unequivocally accepted U.S. doctrines, "both national and religious."[8]

At the same time that the government produced this violent "peace policy," it also began actively suppressing American Indian religion and persecuting indigenous religious leaders. Confrontations between a land-hungry nation and Native American tribes encouraged the growth of maximalist religions, the ritual expressions of which provoked violent reactions from government officials. In the 1850s, Smohalla, a Wanapum from the Columbia River region, prophesied the destruction of whites and the restoration of a golden age for Indians. Smohalla's visions became the foundation for the Dreamer religion. At its inception, General O. O. Howard of the U.S. Army feared the vision would produce a "craze" that could spread among tribes in the region and possibly incite a rebellion. Howard called Smohalla's teachings "fanaticism" and in 1877 tried to silence him. When the Nez Perce War broke out, a group of whites blamed Smohalla for sparking the conflict and organized a lynch mob to kill him. Squsachtun (also known as John Slocum), a Nisqually from the Puget Sound area, founded the "Indian Shaker" religion in 1881, which taught followers about God, Christ, heaven, and hell and instructed them to heed his prophesies. Squsachtun was harassed and imprisoned, but his religion took hold on the West Coast and was incorporated in 1910.[9] These incidents caused no small amount of concern among a minimalist American elite waging a struggle for uniformity of civic and religious values.

In 1878 the U.S. government provided funding for reservations to hire Indian police to enforce the "civilization" program and to assist in the eradication of Indian religious practices, specifically dances and ceremonies. Candidates for jobs as Indian police had to swear loyalty to the civilization programs. By 1880 two-thirds of agencies had Indian police forces; by 1890 nearly all did. Indian police had to practice civilized behavior in their own lives: they could marry only one wife and had to oppose ceremonial dancing and the work of medicine men. One officer who called a medicine man to treat his sick children lost his job.[10] Shortly after the Indian police forces appeared, Secretary of the Interior H. M. Teller established courts to handle cases stemming from the work of the Indian police. Hiram Price, commissioner of Indian affairs and an active Methodist, drafted the rules and regulations to be enforced by the courts. The most common cases brought against Indians included adultery, polygamy, cohabitation, licentiousness, and fornication. According to an agent at the Cheyenne River Agency in South Dakota, the American Indians who heard these cases were hand-picked by U.S. government agents because they came from "the civilized or Christian element." Two of these judges had converted to Episcopalianism and one to Roman Catholicism. In the Interior Department's 1883 annual report, Secretary Teller identified the continuation of the old "heathenish dances" as the greatest obstacle to assimilation and demanded they be stopped. In 1888 and 1889 government officials took aim at the Kiowa Sun Dance and, with the use of military pressure, ended it by the summer of 1890.[11] That year, in addition to hearing the types of cases described above, the judges heard cases—and convicted plaintiffs—for encouraging the Ghost Dance.[12]

In April 1890, Pine Ridge agent Hugh Gallagher jailed Ghost Dance leaders who refused to discuss the ceremony with him. After two days in jail, the organizers agreed to stop promoting the ceremony but still refused to answer the agent's questions. When the dancing began again in August, Gallagher dispatched Indian police to stop it. After they failed, Gallagher himself went to the dance ground accompanied by twenty Indian police. They met Ghost Dancers armed with rifles and prepared to fight to defend their faith. The two sides managed to avoid violence, and Gallagher reported religious fervor had subsided.[13] No blood had been shed yet over the Ghost Dance, but Gallagher was clearly willing to use force to stop the dancing. Agents at the Standing Rock and Rosebud reservations used similar tactics to discourage practice of the new ceremony. When Sitting Bull invited Kicking Bear, a leading Ghost Dance advocate, to visit him, agent James McLaughlin sent Indian police to arrest Kicking Bear and escort him from the reservation. The first contingent failed, but McLaughlin sent another group, which succeeded in removing Kicking Bear. The Rosebud agent asked Ghost Dancers under his jurisdiction to stop performing the ceremony. When they refused, he threatened to cut off their government rations until they ceased and went home.[14] Even when physical force was not used to shape religious belief, the threat of legal coercion served a similar function.

Lakotas practiced the Ghost Dance into November, and tensions mounted as reports of armed Ghost Dancers and rumors of an uprising spread through newspapers. The participation of Lakotas, well-known opponents of U.S. expansion, and of Sitting Bull, who had defeated Custer at Little Bighorn, contributed to outsiders' perceptions that the Ghost Dance was a growing threat to peace, property, and life. When in mid-November President Benjamin Harrison ordered the War Department to suppress the threat of an uprising, he paved the way for violent suppression of the religious ceremony.[15] At Standing Rock, agent McLaughlin tried to squelch the Ghost Dance with coercion. McLaughlin declared that all Ghost Dancers who renounced the ceremony and camped at the agency for a few weeks would receive the supplies promised in their treaty with the government. Those who continued to dance in violation of orders would receive nothing. When this tactic failed, McLaughlin ordered Standing Rock's Indian police to arrest Sitting Bull with explicit orders: "You must not let [Sitting Bull] escape under any circumstances." On the morning of December 15, 1890, the Indian police charged with arresting Sitting Bull gathered for a Christian prayer. Later that day, in a struggle to arrest an unarmed Sitting Bull, two Indian policemen shot and killed him.[16]

The most notorious, graphic, and indisputably violent chapter of the struggle over the Ghost Dance came at Wounded Knee Creek two weeks to the day after Sitting Bull's murder. Soldiers from the Seventh Cavalry surrounded a camp of Miniconjou Ghost Dancers whose ranks had been swollen by Hunkpapa Ghost Dance refugees from Sitting Bull's camp. The U.S. soldiers killed hundreds of the Ghost Dancers under circumstances that remain cloudy. Accounts conflict regarding the initiation of the rifle and artillery fire. Some point to one or more Lakotas opening fire at the exhortation of a Ghost Dance leader. Some point to a struggle between a Lakota and a soldier over a rifle that produced an accidental gunshot that, in turn, triggered the cavalry opening fire. However the shooting started, though, it resulted in the deaths of between 146 and 300 American Indian men, women, and children.

One might argue that the killings at Wounded Knee had little to do with religion, beyond the fact that misunderstandings of the Ghost Dance made a tense situation even more so. One might even argue that the murders were revenge for the lives of George Custer and his men. But from the viewpoint offered by the longer history described here, we see a concerted effort by federal officials to "civilize" and convert Native Americans, an effort that many Native Americans rejected. Their protests unfolded through apocalyptic theologies, associated ritual expressions, and the repeated assertion of traditionally maximalist understandings of religion vis-à-vis land, dress, language, and cultural expression. In the end, the Indians' religiously motivated rejections of a religiously informed civilization program, compounded by centuries of prejudices, were tremendously significant in creating the attitudes and the situation that led to the massacre. The Ghost Dancers killed at Wounded Knee may not have been victims of religious violence, yet they died because their widely maligned maximalist religion was seen by an activist state as incompatible with its minimalist, putatively Christian program for civilization.

MAXIMALISM IN THE NEW WEST

The United States moved on from Wounded Knee with little serious reflection on the moral problems it posed. The West was "won," and American religious minimalism prevailed. Small pockets of resistance remained, to be sure, but more as museum pieces than as noticeable countermovements. More than a century after the anti-Mormon crusade and the push to "civilize" American Indians, the West again became the site of marginalization and violence against a maximalist religious other. In February 1993, agents of the Bureau of Alcohol, Tobacco, and Firearms (BATF) stormed the residence of the Branch Davidians near Waco, Texas, to serve search and arrest warrants related to suspected weapons law violations. Four BATF agents and at least two Branch Davidians died in the raid, initiating a fifty-one-day standoff. Then, on April 19, agents from the Federal Bureau of Investigation (FBI) used armored vehicles to insert tear gas into the Branch Davidians' residence. Fires broke out during the gas insertion and quickly destroyed the building. By day's end, nearly all the Branch Davidians inside were dead. Most evidence suggests that the Branch Davidians set the fires that destroyed their structure; as well, a few members died of self-inflicted gunshots. In total seventy-six men, women, and children lost their lives in a tragedy that many believe was avoidable.

Branch Davidian leader David Koresh was no innocent. The rationale for the raid was that group members were practicing illegal and dangerous behavior within the compound (for example, FBI officials claimed that David Koresh had several wives and had fathered children with girls as young as twelve) and that the commune also threatened the wider community (for example, the FBI accused Koresh and his followers of amassing illegal weapons). This combination of illegal guns, alleged child abuse, and David Koresh's apparent deviancy (including his self-professed divinity) became the ostensible cause for government intervention. Nevertheless, to focus exclusively on Koresh is to overlook how such action could be justified on nonreligious grounds, since "real" (that is, minimalist) religions don't pose such threats. The state could act—indeed, it felt compelled to act—against this maximalist community precisely because it was not a true religion but, rather, a dangerous "cult."

Like the Ghost Dancers who died at Wounded Knee, the Branch Davidians perished at least in part because of their maximalist religion. Additionally, the anti-Davidian rhetoric of the press and of religiously minimalist state officials bore striking similarities to words used in the nineteenth century in confrontations with Mormons and American Indians. Again in 1993, these ways of representing a maximalist religious minority made them not just different or "weird" but also outsiders to the national community—un-American, threatening, and, thus, legitimate targets of state violence.

The forebears of the Branch Davidian community came to Texas from southern California in 1935. Victor Houteff, a Bulgarian immigrant and convert to Seventh-day Adventism, developed a movement to purify the church from within and to gather the 144,000 "servants of God" who would be saved at the Second Coming. After church officials removed him from their rolls, Houteff moved his followers to Texas and established a commune named Mount Carmel near Waco. Over the following decades, the group experienced leadership and name changes. During the late 1980s Vernon Howell, who changed his name in 1990 to David Koresh, joined the group and assumed control. Much of his power and influence depended on his interpretations of the Bible, especially the Revelation of St. John. He depicted himself as a Christ figure and claimed to speak the words of God.[17]

In reporting on the Branch Davidians, the press took a hostile stance toward the group and depicted them as aberrant and deluded. Two reporters from the *Waco Tribune-Herald* investigated the Branch Davidians for eight months preparing for a seven-part exposé titled "The Sinful Messiah." Many of the articles relied heavily on ex-members of the group and anticult activists. For many readers around Waco and for the massive press corps that descended on Waco as the siege unfolded, the series served as a primer on the Branch Davidians. The series vilified Koresh and reported on practices that put the community at odds with the laws and sensibilities of the land. The *Tribune-Herald* series alleged that the Branch Davidians were stockpiling illegally modified guns and that David Koresh had married his legal wife when she was only fourteen. In the series and other articles covering the siege, the *Waco Tribune-Herald* referred to Koresh as a "doomsday prophet," "a deranged, violent megalomaniac with a messiah complex," "a classic sociopath," and a "false prophet." Other publications followed suit. *Christian Century* described Koresh as having a "twisted notion of himself as a messiah" and as being a "religious fanatic." *Time* called him "the mad messiah of Waco."[18]

Several members of the academy added the weight of scholarly expertise to the conclusion that those who followed Koresh had been duped or were mentally defective. Scholars of "cults" and religious communities noted that the charismatic Koresh exerted nearly absolute control over the community and its followers. During the siege, the *Waco Tribune-Herald* ran a story about what life would be like for Branch Davidians after Koresh. A professor of religion at Baylor University claimed that Koresh interpreted Bible prophecies as if they applied directly to him. "How you psychologically deal with somebody like that I don't know," he said. An emeritus professor of psychology from the University of California at Berkeley observed, "The whole group of them really needs help in understanding how it was that they followed this guy . . . how they were duped, why they did not leave at any point." A psychiatrist and professor of psychiatry at the University of Texas Southwestern Medical School said the surviving Branch

Davidians would have to face the fact that "they have been wrong for a substantial period of time" and that they would need "intensive therapy" to lead normal lives. To deal with that fact, he suggested that survivors would need help from friends and family, mental health professionals, and mainstream religious leaders.[19]

The record of responses to the Branch Davidians by government officials indicates that they, too, saw group members as deluded. FBI officials studied Isaiah and Revelation for clues about how to handle Koresh and his followers, but they grew tired of Koresh's long discussions of his beliefs and interpretations during negotiations and dismissed them as "Bible babble." A sniper on the FBI's Hostage Rescue Team (who at one point during the siege had Koresh in the crosshairs of his high-powered rifle, which he called "The Truth") described Koresh as "a salesman" and "a bullshit artist" comparable to "a time-share pimp, selling chunks of salvation." In his mind, Koresh lured prospective converts to Mount Carmel to hear his sales pitch and convinced them to sign over their souls. President Bill Clinton called Koresh "dangerous, irrational, and probably insane" and charged that he had violated federal law and common standards of decency. Clinton also pointed to the tragic end of the siege as a lesson: "I hope very much that others who will be tempted to join cults and to become involved with people like David Koresh will be deterred by the horrible scenes they have seen over the last seven weeks."[20] Attorney General Janet Reno, in charge of both the FBI and the ATF, repeatedly raised concerns about the children in the community.

It is clear from these comments that the Branch Davidians stood outside the limits of acceptable religious belief and practice in the United States. They were members of a "cult," not a religion. The press, representatives of institutions of higher learning and mainstream religious groups, and government officials branded them as outsiders and thus implied that violence against them (and those like them) was legitimate—even necessary. My purpose here is not to defend the Branch Davidians but simply to show that their designation as religious outsiders and maximalists cannot be expunged from this episode of intense violence. Expanding the spectrum between these binary categories of minimalist state/maximalist cult might have helped to avoid this tragedy—especially given the fact that many now well-established American religious groups were branded sects or outsiders in their early formations.

In 2008 another conflict involving forces of a minimalist state and a maximalist outsider religious group, the Fundamentalist Church of Jesus Christ of Latter-day Saints, unfolded in the West. This final case study seems to continue an already familiar pattern of government coercion of maximalist religious minorities. Once again, the western United States has become a frontier for defining America by identifying outside groups.

The Fundamentalist Church of Jesus Christ of Latter-day Saints (FLDS), now headed by convicted felon Warren S. Jeffs, split from the Church of Jesus Christ of Latter-day Saints after the manifesto of 1890 renounced plural marriage. The splinter group continued to practice polygamy and established its central community on the Utah-Arizona border. State forces raided the community in 1953 to enforce antipolygamy laws, but over fifty years of peaceful coexistence followed between the group and state authorities, who chose to ignore the group's marriage practices. As of 2008 the group had an estimated 10,000 members, most located in the West.

In 2003 a company named YFZ L.L.C. bought land in Texas, ostensibly for a corporate retreat.[21] Ultimately, the FLDS used the land to establish a community called the Yearning For Zion (YFZ) Ranch. Through the spring of 2008 the Texas community coexisted with its neighbors, although when the land's true use became clear, the local newspaper reported that residents were surprised to learn that a "corporate hunting retreat" was "actually an FLDS compound."[22] Around midnight on April 3, 2008, Texas Child Protective Service (CPS) investigators accompanied by law enforcement agents raided the YFZ Ranch investigating charges of child abuse. The state removed more than 400 children from the ranch, first placing them and their mothers in shelters, then placing the children in foster care. According to a spokesman for the Texas Department of Family and Protective Services, the state believed that all children living at the YFZ Ranch had been abused or were at risk of abuse. Neither religion nor lifestyle, they claimed, had influenced the raid. But Representative Harvey Hilderbran, Eldorado's state representative, told a New York Times reporter that state authorities had been looking for a way to fight FLDS polygamy, especially the taking of underage wives. The state expanded its investigation to include DNA sampling of the children and adults from YFZ to determine family relationships and to aid its research into underage marriages and abuse.[23]

The state of Texas faced remarkable challenges in caring for the children, not only because there were so many, but also because of religious and cultural differences. A children's shelter in San Antonio removed red objects from its facility because some FLDS members believe that when Jesus returns he will wear red robes and that red is reserved for that occasion. FLDS children also had never eaten processed foods, attended public school, or watched television. Those issues only scratched the surface of the complexities involved in moving children isolated from modern culture into mainstream America. As investigators tried to understand FLDS family structure, they learned that women shared parenting duties, including breastfeeding. When asked to identify their mothers, FLDS children often named several women because they considered all women in their household mothers and all children siblings.[24]

Despite the sensitivity that some foster care facilities showed for FLDS mores, the seizure of children broke up families in ways atypical of the Texas system. State policy directs that geographic distance between seized children and their parents should be kept to a minimum to allow supervised visits. That proved a tall order in the FLDS case because of the number of children involved and the strain they placed on resources. One FLDS mother, Nora Jeffs, had eight children seized and placed throughout the state. Those placed closest to Eldorado were about 150 miles away; the farthest was more than nine hours away by car.[25]

The raid drew tremendous scrutiny as its origins came to light. It had been sparked by an anonymous phone caller who claimed to be the pregnant, abused sixteen-year-old wife of a fifty-year-old FLDS member. Even after the call was determined to be a hoax, Texas Governor Rick Perry expressed his support for the CPS action. "The governor is very proud of the work being done by CPS," a Perry spokeswoman said. About a week after Perry's endorsement, the Third Court of Appeals revoked the state's custody over the children of thirty-eight mothers, citing lack of evidence that they faced any immediate danger of abuse. The ruling eventually extended to virtually all the seized children. The unanimous ruling said that removing children from their home was "an extreme measure" and could be justified only in cases of immediate danger. (The state treated the entire YFZ Ranch as one home and took the position that the FLDS "belief system" condoned underage marriage and pregnancy.) The appeals court found no evidence of widespread abuse and said the district judge had approved the removal without sufficient evidence. The state appealed the ruling, but the Texas Supreme Court agreed with the appeals court's decision, paving the way for the children to go home, which most did by early June 2008.[26]

Criminal investigations into conduct at the YFZ Ranch continue, but the damage done to the YFZ children by their seizure, not to mention the alleged abuse some suffered at YFZ, may not appear for years. Child welfare experts note that a growing body of research indicates that forceful removal of children from their mothers can produce both short-term and long-term harm, especially in younger children, including anxiety, extreme distrust of strangers, and, eventually, higher rates of teenage pregnancy and juvenile incarceration. YFZ Ranch children abused by community members likely suffered additional trauma. This is the price of stopping child abuse, and it is a price that society generally accepts. But because of the government's blunt-instrument approach to an entire religiously maximalist outsider group, those children *not* subjected to abuse by YFZ members—and this constitutes the great majority of those removed—have now been wronged, as the Texas Supreme Court ruling admits. Many of these children were also needlessly harmed, for example, by being subjected to therapy treatment the effects of which can mimic child abuse.

In the end, the CPS raid produced a twenty-first-century reprise of the 1890 manifesto in which the Church of Jesus Christ of Latter-day Saints renounced polygamy. In early June, shortly after the children returned, an FLDS spokesman read a statement to clarify the group's position: "In the future, the church commits that it will not preside over the marriage of any woman under the age of legal consent in the jurisdiction in which the marriage takes place. The church will counsel families that they neither request nor consent to any under-age marriages. This policy will apply churchwide."[27] The minimalist state, once again, reshaped an American religion.

CONCLUSION

The FLDS raid presents troubling continuities with past state actions even as it offers reassuring signs of a gentler state in matters of child welfare. In all four cases discussed here, maximalist religious communities seeking to live apart from mainstream society came under attack for the perceived threat they presented to others within or beyond their community. Religious differences were important insofar as they informed lifestyle choices and decisions to withdraw from society, but these were not battles over theology. They were, instead, battles over how properly to configure the relationship between faith and society and, therefore, over how properly to configure society. Mormons fled westward pursuing the freedom to establish and live in a theocracy in which plural marriage was legal. Native Americans pushed back against Anglo-American "civilization" efforts and insisted that land, language, and dance were sacred. Branch Davidians and FLDS members separated themselves spatially by moving to compounds and, to an extent, morally, by tolerating or embracing sexual expressions and family structures that run counter to the law and, some argue, weaken the bedrock of American civilization. In all these cases, the space afforded by the American West would make western states not only frontiers of new freedom but places where the U.S. government would challenge and enforce the limits of American behavior, identity, and civilization.

Merrill E. Gates, educational reformer and eventual chairman of the U.S. Board of Indian Commissioners, wrote in 1885: "The family is God's unit of society.... On the integrity of the family depends that of the State. There is no civilization deserving of the name where the family is not the unit of civil government."[28] It is hard not to see the connection between the charges of "savagery" that hung in one form or another over each of these conflicts and Gates's view that "civilization" is not civilized without properly configured families—at least as defined by Christian minimalism. It is also hard not to see that today, as in 1890, the trans-Mississippi West is a uniquely troubling landscape for federal and state apparatuses. The future of the nation seemed precarious throughout the nineteenth century, and the West was imagined as the place where America's future—its destiny—would be won or lost. No reasonable voices today suggest that "bad religion" or "irreligion" in the West will drag America down, but federal and state governments have recently pursued aggressive (some would say reckless and violent) policies against religious maximalists. And while each case warrants individual analysis, by considering them together we can see that, although the nation has certainly become more tolerant of religious difference, there are limits to acceptable difference. Religiously maximalist groups often have found themselves at or beyond those limits, while the U.S. government stands ready to assert and coercively enforce those limits even—indeed especially—in the wide-open West.

NOTES

1. Bruce Lincoln, *Holy Terrors: Thinking about Religion after September 11* (Chicago: University of Chicago Press, 2003), 34; 59–60.

2. Quoted in Justin S. Morrill, "Speech of Hon. Justin S. Morrill, of Vermont, on Utah Territory and Its Laws—Polygamy and Its License; Delivered in the House of Representatives, February 23, 1857," in *Appendix to the Congressional Globe: Containing Speeches, Important State Papers, Laws, Etc. of the Third Session, Thirty-fourth Congress* (Washington, DC: Congressional Globe, 857), 287; for the national context of the Morrill Anti-Bigamy Act, see William P. MacKinnon, ed., *At Sword's Point, Part 1: A Documentary History of the Utah War to 1858*, vol. 10 of *Kingdom in the West: The Mormons and the American Frontier* (Norman, OK: Arthur H. Clark, 2008).

3. *Reynolds v. United States*, 98 U.S. 145 (1879); Edwin Firmage and Richard Mangrum, *Zion in the Courts: A Legal History of the Latter-day Saints, 1830–1900* (Urbana: University of Illinois Press, 1988), 151–156; Sarah Barringer Gordon, *The Mormon Question: Polygamy and Constitutional Conflict in Nineteenth- Century America* (Chapel Hill: University of North Carolina Press, 2002), 135.

4. Quoted in Sarah Barringer Gordon, "'The Liberty of Self-Degradation': Polygamy, Woman Suffrage, and Consent in Nineteenth-Century America," *Journal of American History* 83 (Dec. 1996): 815.

5. Firmage and Mangrum, *Zion in the Courts*, 161–162. See also U.S. Congress and Secretary of State, "Chapter 47," in *The Statutes at Large of the United States of America from December, 1881, to March, 1883 . . .* , vol. 22 (Washington, DC; Government Printing Office, 1883), 30–32.

6. Howard Lamar, *The Far Southwest, 1846–1912: A Territorial History* (New Haven: Yale University Press, 1966), 397–398; Firmage and Mangrum, *Zion in the Courts*, 198–204.

7. Lamar, *The Far Southwest*, 403–405; G. Homer Durham, "A Political Interpretation of Mormon History," *Pacific Historical Review* 13 (March 1984): 147–148; Jan Shipps, *Mormonism: The Story of a New Religious Tradition* (Urbana: University of Illinois Press, 1985), 126–129.

8. "'Kill the Indian, and Save the Man': Capt. Richard H. Pratt on the Education of Native Americans," http://historymatters.gmu.edu/d/4929 (accessed Sept. 5, 2008). For a thorough discussion of religion and violence with respect to the Ghost Dance, see Weston La Barre, *The Ghost Dance: Origins of Religion* (Garden City, NY: Doubleday, 1970).

9. Colin G. Calloway, *First Peoples: A Documentary History of American Indian History*, 3d ed. (Boston: Bedford/St. Martin's, 2008), 314; Howard quoted in Clifford E. Trafzer and Margery Ann Beach, "Smohalla, Washani, and Religion as a Factor in Northwest Indian History," *American Indian Quarterly* 9 (Summer 1985): 314–320.

10. William T. Hagan, *Indian Police and Judges: Experiments in Acculturation and Control* (New Haven: Yale University Press, 1966), 26–27, 42–43, 69–70, 73.

11. Ibid., 104, 107–109, 123; John R. Wunder, *"Retained by the People": A History of the American Indians and the Bill of Rights* (New York: Oxford University Press, 1994), 35–36; Joel W. Martin, *The Land Looks after Us: A History of Native American Religion* (New York: Oxford University Press, 1999), 91–92; Clyde Ellis, "'There Is No Doubt . . . the Dances Should Be Curtailed': Indian Dances and Federal Policy on the Southern Plains, 1880–1930," *Pacific Historical Review* 70(November 2001), 548, 561.

12. Commissioner of Indian Affairs (hereafter CIA), *Sixtieth Annual Report* (Washington, DC: Government Printing Office, 1891), 389–390. Many officers of the U.S. Army shared Teller's belief that Native American religions had to be suppressed in order for Indians to "advance." See "Captain Bourke's Suggestion," *Omaha Morning World-Herald*, Dec. 14, 1890.

13. Robert Utley, *The Last Days of the Sioux Nation* (New Haven: Yale University Press, 1963), 74–75; CIA, *Sixtieth Report*, 124.

14. James McLaughlin, *My Friend the Indian* (Boston: Houghton Mifflin, 1926), 21–65; CIA, *Sixtieth Report*, 126, 330, 411–412.

15. CIA, *Sixtieth Report*, 330; "Settlers Feeling Safer," *Omaha Bee*, Nov. 16, 1890.

16. "Last Visit to Sitting Bull," *Omaha Bee*, Dec. 16, 1890; Colin G. Calloway, ed., *Our Hearts Fell to the Ground: Plains Indian Views of How the West Was Lost* (Boston: Bedford Books, 1996), 193; Robert M. Utley, *The Lance and the Shield: The Life and Times of Sitting Bull* (New York: Henry Holt, 1993), 298, 300–301.

17. James D. Tabor and Eugene V. Gallagher, *Why Waco?: Cults and the Battle for Religious Freedom in America* (Berkeley: University of California Press, 1995), 33–35, 37–41; "Howell Said to Have Lived Double Life," *Waco* (Texas) *Tribune-Herald* (hereafter *WTH*), May 2, 1993; "The Sinful Messiah: Part One,", *WTH*, Feb. 28, 1993; U.S. House of Representatives, Committee on the Judiciary, *Activities of Federal Law Enforcement Agencies toward the Branch Davidians: Joint Hearings before the Subcommittee on Crime of the Committee on the Judiciary and the Subcommittee on National Security, International Affairs, and Criminal Justice of the Committee on Government Reform and Oversight (Part 2)*, 104th Cong., 1st sess., July 25, 26, and 27 (Washington, DC: Government Printing Office, 1996), 243–244.

18. "Sinful Messiah: Part One"; "Reporter Named in Lawsuit," *WTH*, April 7, 1993; "Sinful Messiah: Part Three"; "FBI: Howell Cares Only for His Own Life," *WTH*, March 28, 1993; "Making Koresh a Kind of Hero," *WTH*, April 4, 1993; "'Visitor' Leaves Cult Compound," *WTH*, April 18, 1993; "Family Uneasy about 'Flea Market,'" *WTH*, Aug. 1, 1993; James M. Wall, "Eager for the End," *Christian Century* 110 (May 5, 1993): 476; Sophronia Scott Gregory, "Children of Lesser God," *Time*, May 17, 1993, 54.

19. "Negotiators Taking Course in Revelation," *WTH* March 14, 1993; "Emerging from Cult Command," *WTH*, March 3, 1993.

20. "Negotiators Taking Course in Revelation," *WTH*, March 14, 1993; "New Talks Lend Hope of No Fight," *WTH*, March 31, 1993; "Feds Let Lawyer Run Ball," *WTH*, April 1, 1993; FBI agent quoted in Christopher Whitcomb, *Cold Zero: Inside the FBI Hostage Rescue Team* (Boston: Little, Brown, 2001), 201, 286; Clinton quoted in U.S. House of Representatives, Committee on the Judiciary, *Activities of Federal Law Enforcement Agencies toward the Branch Davidians: Joint Hearings before the Subcommittee on Crime of the Committee on the Judiciary and the Subcommittee on National Security, International Affairs, and Criminal Justice of the Committee on Government Reform and Oversight (Part 3)*, 104th Cong., 1st sess., July 28 and 31, Aug. 1, 1995 (Washington, DC: Government Printing Office, 1996), 288–289; "Not All Presidential Advisers Talk Politics," *New York Times*, March 18, 1997.

21. "Corporate Retreat or Prophet's Refuge?" *Eldorado* (Texas) *Success*, March 25, 2004; Ralph Blumenthal, "52 Girls Are Taken from Polygamist Sect's Ranch in Texas," *New York Times*, April 5, 2008.

22. "Prophet vs. President," *Eldorado Success*, July 15, 2004.

23. "52 Girls Taken from Sect's Ranch"; "Kirk Johnson, "Texas Polygamy Raid May Pose Risk," *New York Times*, April 12, 2008; Corrie MacLaggan, "Raid, Aftermath's Early Cost: $7.5 Million," *Austin* (Texas) *American-Statesman*, May 16, 2008; John Moritz, "Senate Panel Suggests Taking FLDS Sect's Assets to Cover Costs," *Star-Telegram*, May 21, 2008; Kirk Johnson, "DNA Is Taken from Sect's Children," *New York Times*, April 22, 2008. A DNA expert pointed out that the evidence would not reveal the age of any mother at the time she gave birth, a central issue in the allegations.

24. Kirk Johnson and Dan Frosch, "Sect Children Face Another World, But Still No TV," *New York Times*, April 26, 2008; Dan Frosch, "Texas Reports Added Signs of Abuse at Sect's Ranch," *New York Times*, May 1, 2008.

25. Kirk Johnson, "Far-Flung Placement of Children in Texas Raid Is Criticized," *New York Times*, May 20, 2008.

26. Bill Hanna and John Moritz, "Gov. Perry Praises CPS' Handling of Polygamist Sect Cases," *Fort Worth Star-Telegram*, May 15, 2008; Ralph Blumenthal, "Court Says Texas Illegally Seized Sect's Children," *New York Times*, May 23, 2008; Ralph Blumenthal, "Texas Loses Court Ruling over Taking of Children," *New York Times*, May 30, 2008.

27. Leslie Kaufman and Dan Frosch, "Sect Mothers Say Separation Endangers Children," *New York Times*, May 29, 2008; "Kirk Johnson and Gretel Kovach, "Daughter of Sect Leader Gets Additional Protection," *New York Times*, June 4, 2008.

28. Merrill E. Gates, *Seventeenth Annual Report of the Board of Indian Commissioners* (1885), quoted in Calloway, *First Peoples*, 408.

9

Alma White's Bloodless Warfare

Women and Violence in U.S. Religious History

Lynn S. Neal

"For the Christian life is a warfare. It does not consist merely in a profession of faith, joining a church, accepting certain truths, and conforming to certain rules and regulations. It is a conflict of forces."[1] As she encountered this warfare throughout her life, Bishop Alma White (1862–1946), author of these words, fashioned herself a warrior. Martial words, phrases, and imagery—warfare, soldiers, armor, blood—permeate her sermons, her hymns, and her autobiography. She understood her life and the Christian life as an unending battle "against the world, the flesh, and the devil."[2] Or, as she wrote, "the followers of Christ are continually on trial and the people are deciding for or against Him in their treatment of them."[3] There was no middle ground. One either embraced Christ or rejected him, and to embrace Christ meant to fight. White's contemporaries recognized her combative spirit. One observer described her as "a woman of forceful personality," and another called her "one of the foremost warriors in the battle between darkness and light."[4] Over the course of her life, Alma White fought for her Protestant faith by establishing a denomination, the Pillar of Fire, publishing over thirty books, starting colleges, operating two radio stations, preaching to thousands, and endorsing the second Ku Klux Klan.

Alma White's endorsement and defense of the Ku Klux Klan cannot be separated from her Protestant faith and her belief in a Christian America. For her, the Klan was God's heroic force poised to defend her sex, her faith, and her nation. "At this time," White explained, "the Lord has raised up the Invisible Empire to wage bloodless warfare against Rome's religio-political system."[5] In her three books—*The Ku Klux Klan in Prophecy* (1925), *Klansmen: Guardians of Liberty* (1926), and *Heroes of the Fiery Cross* (1928)—she described in detail the satanic threat facing America and proclaimed the Christianity of the Klan, America's foremost defenders. In these works, White used the Bible, history, and gender, as well as paranoia and prejudice, to enact "bloodless warfare" against her foes. She constructed heroes, villains, and victims; she assailed her enemies and called the righteous to action. By disseminating religious intolerance and justifying violence against religious others, she created conditions that encouraged people to move from bloodless to bloody conflict.

As scholars and as citizens, we often see women as the victims of violence. Very few of us analyze or acknowledge the role women play as perpetrators of violence. In some ways this approach makes sense. Studies reveal that young white men are responsible for the vast majority of contemporary hate crimes, and men, often in groups, have dominated the commission of physical violence throughout history.[6] However, as the example of Alma White reveals, male dominance of the category of violence does not mean women's absence. If we broaden our definition of and perspective on violence—if we "abandon formulaic conceptions" of violence "as simply social action," and view it "as relational and processual"[7] and understand violence in terms of a continuum involving hatred, intolerance, and physical action—we can see more clearly women's place in the history of religion and violence. Women have helped create and foster religiously intolerant worlds in which violence is an acceptable part of life.

The ministry of Alma White provides us with a way to study this phenomenon in a concrete and discrete way, "on a scale small enough to pin down and dissect."[8] In White, we find a woman of remarkable accomplishment and complexity. She was a fearless preacher and an early feminist, yet she believed in white supremacy and promulgated anti-Catholicism. Her Holiness church, the Pillar of Fire, was one of the few American denominations to support the Equal Rights Amendment of the National Women's Party, yet it also stands as the only one to publicly endorse the Klan.[9] She associated herself with the violence of the Klan, yet advocated "bloodless warfare." Her legacy defies the neat categories of history and points to the complexity of individual sympathies and agendas. The swirling debates and issues of early twentieth-century America coalesce in the figure of Alma White.

Throughout this chapter, three interrelated themes recur that speak to and beyond the specific case of Alma White. First, Alma White's life is testimony to the centrality of religion in provoking and justifying violence. Her legacy requires that we consider more fully the ways in which "religion may be a bandage for the wounded soul, but . . . also the weapon that inflicts the wound."[10] Second, White often used gender constructions—conceptions of manhood and womanhood—as powerful weapons in religious conflicts. Her career and her writings force us to grapple with the complex and sometimes harmful interactions among religion, gender, and power.[11] Third, Alma White focuses our attention on women as participants in and supporters of religious violence. She reminds us of the many ways in which women fight religious wars: through words both public and private, in their support for soldiers, and in the rearing of would-be warriors. In these and other meaning-making activities, women have played vital roles in the dissemination of religiously intolerant ideology and in the performance of religious violence in U.S. history.

"OH, WHAT HAVOC IS BEING WROUGHT!" THE CULTURAL CLIMATE AND CRISES

The issues confronting American citizens in the 1910s and 1920s were daunting for many—immigration, urbanization, industrialization, suffrage, evolution, Bolshevism, the Great Migration, fundamentalism, modernism, flappers, the Harlem Renaissance, the growth of modern film, labor disputes, Prohibition, World War I and its aftermath.[12] This welter of changes was shot through with intolerance and violence. The Espionage and Sedition Acts of 1917 and 1918 limited civil liberties; the Johnson-Reed Act of 1924, a legislative manifestation of widespread anti-immigrant sentiments, established restrictive immigration quotas that disproportionately affected non-Protestants; the Red Scare of 1919 and rampant racial prejudice claimed numerous victims; anti-Semitism and anti-Catholicism were on the rise.[13] Intolerance, hatred, and violence were not the province of a marginal few. They shaped the worlds of a great many Americans.

In 1915 the Ku Klux Klan was reborn under the light of a burning cross on Stone Mountain, Georgia. The revitalized Klan, like its predecessor, espoused a combination of white supremacy and conservative Protestantism, and by the early 1920s the Klan was a strong current in the mainstream.[14] Historian Robert Alan Goldberg writes, "Preaching a multifaceted program based upon '100 Per Cent Americanism' and militant Protestantism, it enlisted recruits in every section of the nation. Perhaps as many as six million Americans heeded its call to resist Catholics, Jews, lawbreakers, blacks, and immigrants."[15] Clergy and laity from a wide range of Protestant denominations joined the Klan and supported its diverse campaigns, which ranged from public parades and political propaganda to the commission of violent acts.[16] In the 1920s the Ku Klux Klan was a national organization.

Many historians who study the second Klan downplay the power and importance of Klanswomen and the Women's Auxiliary.[17] The tendency to minimize women's participation in the Klan and to ignore the ties between women and violence is puzzling and problematic. The Auxiliary included more than half a million white Protestant women. Historian Kathleen Blee writes, "Women constituted nearly half of the Klan membership in some states and were a significant minority of Klan members in many others."[18] Thus, although Alma White was one of the most visible exemplars of women's involvement with the Klan, she was by no means alone. In her pro-Klan writings, she gave literary voice to an ideology that other women spoke in more subtle ways. Such women "spread hatred through neighborhoods, family networks, and illusive webs of private relationships."[19] Rather than night riding or physical assaults, women used personal relationships and polemical writings to advance the Klan's agenda. These acts did not exist apart from the Klan's real violence. Klanswomen's words encouraged and shaped religious intolerance and violence.

The Klan, for White and many others, represented God's "white-robed army" sent to "meet the issues"—to protect and restore a besieged Protestant America. Indeed, in White's eyes, "Christianity" itself was in peril. Christians everywhere were falling away from the faith—many of White's Holiness brothers and sisters had embraced the "Tongues Heresy" (Pentecostalism), and theological modernists were surrendering to the forces of secular culture. Amidst this turmoil, White and her Pillar of Fire denomination embraced many of the "fundamentals"—the miracles of the Bible, the creation account of Genesis, and the necessity of salvation. Modernists questioned these criteria and, according to White, threatened the very foundations of Protestantism.[20] Employing the language of siege and warfare, White described the battle. "In religion the modernists are holding the fortresses in almost every Protestant denomination. Orthodoxy is being undermined to an alarming extent, while multitudes remain unconscious of the danger."[21] The enemy—Satan—was on the move.

While some fundamentalists focused their efforts on this internecine feud, others, including White, saw the modernist battle as one in a series of spiritual attacks. For them, the challenges of the 1920s went beyond movies and Model Ts. Not only was Protestantism facing decay from within; powerful forces—namely immigrant Catholics and Jews—threatened from without. The size and power of this "invading force" were overwhelming. "From 1900 to 1920," writes Wyn Craig Wade, "14.5 million immigrants arrived at American shores, averaging two thousand per day."[22] These immigrants changed the social, political, and economic climate of the United States and challenged Protestant dominance of the American religious landscape. Together these forces threatened Christianity and the nation's Christian identity. In White's estimation, only a powerful counteroffensive could repel them.

"AROUSE THE SLEEPING MULTITUDES":
THE POWER OF LITERATURE, HISTORY,
AND GENDER AS WEAPONS

True Christians—Protestants—needed to fight, according to White, but they remained ignorant of or indifferent to the dire reality. In response, she used literature to "awaken" people to the existence and scope of this religious conflict, and thereby move them from indifference to action.[23] White's wake-up calls, which she repeated in all three of her pro-Klan volumes, convey her sense of concern and crisis. "The sleeping multitudes," she wrote, "must be awakened to a full sense of their duty before disaster overtakes the nation."[24] In using literature to sound the alarm, White joined a long line of Protestants who responded to perceived spiritual threats and problems with the power of the printed word.[25] Through the printing of tracts and Bibles, newspapers and pamphlets, Protestants viewed "mass publication" as "a powerful way of effecting change."[26] Literature afforded White an accepted way to construct and advance her war.

The centrality and power of the "Word" in Protestantism also informed White's choice of literature as a weapon. If the Christian life was one of battle, then the Bible was the most powerful weapon in one's arsenal. "The Word of God is the 'Sword of the Spirit,' and no man can stand before it." It was "holy dynamite," and its truth defeated enemies.[27] The Bible infused White's pro-Klan books and enhanced their persuasive power. "The truth that is now being made manifest," White proclaimed, "is destined to bring about a transformation in the country, morally, socially, industrially, religiously, and politically."[28] Other members of the Klan agreed. As Wyn Craig Wade writes, "Imperial books, tracts, magazines, pamphlets, flyers, and placards overflowed with the Christian message, wedding the goals of fundamentalism to those of the Klan."[29] White's works joined a rising tide of Klan print culture that spread throughout the country in the early 1900s.

While White's use of literature draws on patterns common in both Protestantism and the Ku Klux Klan, it also reflects societal constraints placed on her as a woman. White American middle-class women often used literature to enact power and effect change. For women denied access to the pulpit and political office, literature was an important way to claim a public voice. It provided them with an accessible pathway to power and a safe vehicle for participating in public conflicts. Scholar Mary Kelley describes how nineteenth-century female writers negotiated power and argues that literature afforded women a measure of privacy—a sense that they remained in the domestic realm—while giving them a public voice.[30] Alma White knew the power of literature for women and for her cause. She was all too familiar with the constraints placed on women's rights and women's leadership. In a world where gender roles were being contested and redefined, White understood the power that men continued to wield. Literature provided her with a powerful and effective medium for change that was acceptable to men and women, Protestants and Klansmen.

Alma White used literature to awaken the sleeping multitudes from their deluded and optimistic dreams to the reality of the present nightmare. To persuade readers of this truth, White first labored to help readers identify the enemy and its threat. As a result, a dominant part of White's work involved "exposing" the nature of the enemy, making public its evils. "There is no time to lose in creating sentiment to offset the activities of the foes of our country at work within our own borders," she wrote.[31]

In White's war (and the Klan's), Catholics were the primary religious and national threat.[32] She urged readers not to be fooled. "They" might look like white Protestants and, like Protestants, claim to be Christian; but this claim was false. "Roman Catholicism," she wrote, "is paganism, and cannot be called Christian in any sense."[33] Echoing themes dominant in anti-Catholic literature, White decried the idolatry and superstition of Catholicism and added charges of sedition.[34] Catholics could not be good Americans because of their loyalty to a foreign power—the pope. In addition, she placed Catholicism's hierarchical structure in opposition to a democratic and Christian America. White explained, "The true Church is democratic, and is the very opposite of Rome with her autocracy and so-called infallibility."[35] This betrayal of the republic was further evidenced, she argued, by Catholicism's history of religious establishment, which demonstrated its inherently undemocratic, and therefore un-American, character. Be warned, White wrote, "Rome" worked "to unite church and state and make America Catholic."[36] Even worse, it sought to "rule the world" via the pope.[37]

Despite the continued dominance of Protestantism in the American religious landscape, White reiterated her belief that Catholics, not Protestant Klansmen, were the instigators of conflict and the perpetrators of religious intolerance. She explained, "Rome has always persecuted true Christians, or those who constituted the visible body of Christ."[38] Catholics wanted "to crush Protestantism," White explained, "and because of this the Invisible Empire has providentially arisen."[39] Throughout, White cast herself and other Protestants as the victims while she depicted the Klan as a divinely ordained force defending Protestant America. White and the Klan thus became heroic saviors, not aggressors or lawless vigilantes.

White framed the current war as Klansmen versus Catholics, Americans versus immigrants, but she used religious history to place this conflict within a grander narrative of good versus evil, and God versus Satan. "The whole system shows that the devil has never given up his program to rule the world through a demonized agency. The claim that the papal head has the keys of earth, hell, and heaven is a glaring example of Satanic audacity."[40] In another instance she explained: "Satan in all ages has had his myrmidons working to degrade and destroy the human race."[41] By framing the Klan's battle with Catholicism in terms of this larger continuing conflict, White emphasized the religious import of the current battles. Her use of religious history provided the Klan with a spiritual genealogy and transformed them from an aggressive violent order into a divine defensive force. Select versions of biblical, Christian, and American history unified her supporters, validated Klan activities, and helped people recognize the real heroes and the true villains.

White regularly framed contemporary Klansmen as the inheritors of a distinctly heroic biblical history. In all the "important" ways, she pointed out, Klansmen were like the biblical Shadrach, Meshach, and Abednego, who refused to submit to the idolatrous regime of Nebuchadnezzar.[42] White also compared members of the Klan to the biblical prophet Elijah. She cited how Elijah "slew Jezebel's false prophets" and urged Klan members to follow his lead.[43] Her selective biblical citation framed Klan members as inheritors of the biblical traditions of martyrdom and prophecy. They were warriors in an age-old battle.

White also placed Klansmen in the historical lineage of Protestant heroes such as Martin Luther. She highlighted how Luther stood up to the corruption of Rome and "proclaim[ed] spiritual liberty for enslaved millions."[44] This action incited a Catholic backlash then and now, but Protestant Americans had nothing to fear, she wrote: "the heroes of a new Reformation are here."[45] These Klan reformers, like Luther, endured persecution and misrepresentation as they fought against "an iniquitous system of corruption and graft."[46] The results, White noted, were miraculous. "Through the efforts of the Knights of the Ku Klux Klan," she praised, "the people have received greater enlightenment than at any other period since the Lutheran Reformation."[47] White's comparison of the Klan with Martin Luther allowed her to create a reputable lineage for the Klan and to portray current events as the latest in a series of battles with Satan and Rome.

This use of history continued in White's retellings of the American story. She explained, "Our heroes in white robes are the perpetuators of the work so nobly begun by the colonists and the Revolutionary fathers, and they will yet plant their banner on the heights of victory while the artillery of heaven and earth roars applause."[48] She framed pivotal patriotic figures in U.S. history as Klansmen, including the Puritans, Samuel Adams, Paul Revere, George Washington, and the members of the Boston Tea Party.[49] White wrote, "The parallel between the Klansmen of the Revolution and those of today is obvious to anyone who has eyes to see."[50] These forefathers fought and died for liberty. The Klan, White assured readers, would do no less. At this "crucial hour" the knights of the Klan "contend for the faith of our fathers who suffered and died in behalf of freedom."[51]

In White's hands history became a theater for a larger battle between good and evil—a backdrop for the battle against Satan. The settings and the actors changed, but the story line remained the same. White wrote, "I have endeavored to show that the principles for which the Ku Klux Klan is contending are not new, that the powers of evil have long fought against these principles all down the ages. But though the conflict at times is fierce we have the promise of the Almighty that right will finally triumph."[52] White constructed an elaborate apology for Klansmen; she depicted them as an army defending all that "real" Christian Americans held dear.

White's framing of Klan-Catholic conflict foregrounds four factors that inform our thinking about women and violence in American religious history. First, White's example demonstrates the important role played by literature in the dissemination of intolerant ideology and incitements to violence. Literature provided White with a powerful weapon that prompted others to see the conflict in a different way. Second, White's writings reveal the need to examine the religious motives and rationales of violent actors, both male and female. While many may want to write off White's Protestant faith as a mere guise for her hatred, her endorsement of the Klan grew out of her Protestant faith and her belief in a profound Catholic threat. Third, White's works force us to look at the power of history in religious conflicts. In "History as a Weapon," Brian Levin explores how contemporary extremist groups use Holocaust denial as a way to advance their cause and justify their actions.[53] While Levin's analysis focuses on the intolerant and violent consequences of historical denial, certain types of revisionist or proof-texted history can have equally dangerous effects. Historical narratives matter because they both reflect and construct our perceived realities. They include and exclude, commit sins of omission and commission, and, perhaps more importantly, negotiate power and construct identity.[54] Fourth, we cannot forget that a woman, Alma White, wielded these weapons. Her example directs us to examine more fully how women play and have played a seminal role in the commission of religious violence in the United States. She challenges the dichotomy that some construct between rhetorical violence and physical violence, and draws our attention to the ways in which these concepts work together. Violence, her works reveal, is a process that moves back and forth along a continuum, from intolerant ideology to social action, from rhetorical attacks to physical conflicts.

"WOMEN HAVE ALWAYS BEEN THE GREATER SUFFERERS"

To this point, we have seen how Alma White sought to awaken Protestants to the dangerous reality of Catholicism and the virtuous nature of the Klan.[55] She also raised the alarm and rallied the troops by invoking concepts of manhood and womanhood, femininity and masculinity, to discredit Catholicism and advance Protestantism. In the 1920s, debates about women's and men's roles raged, so much so that historian Dorothy Brown writes, "in no other decade of the twentieth century, until the 1970s, have women been so at the center of the major issues."[56] Muscular Christians were trying to take back their "feminized" Protestant churches, while many women were caught between divergent ideals—the attractive independence of the New Woman and the Victorian ideals of the Old Woman, the virtues of protective legislation and the possibilities of gender equality.

Alma White fought tirelessly for women's rights in all arenas of life and rooted that vision for equality in her Christian faith. "I felt that God makes no distinction between the sexes, whatever the verdict of man may be," she stated in her autobiography.[57] She endorsed women's ordination and began her own denomination. White's views of women were not, however, without contradiction. Even as she advocated for women's equality and power, she also saw women as victims and argued for protective measures, including Prohibition. And she used both viewpoints—equality and fragility—to expose how the Catholic Church oppressed white women and, ultimately, to promote an alliance between conservative Protestants, white women, and the Ku Klux Klan.

In many ways, White's use of gender echoes strains common in anti-Catholicism and in American history more broadly.[58] Women "figured prominently in the fevered imaginations of [anti-Catholicism's] apologists."[59] Historically, conceptions and idealizations of womanhood have also figured prominently as a weapon with which to combat other religions and other races. The defense of idealized white women was long part of the rationale for lynching African American men. It also played a pivotal role in the lynching of Leo Frank, a Jewish man accused of sexually assaulting and murdering Mary Phagan, a young girl who worked in his factory. The idea of woman as innocent and fragile—as a victim—also provided the foundation for the 1920s Klan-Catholic conflict. To expose readers further to the depravity of Catholicism, Alma White depicted white women as its victims. Employing the language of involuntary confinement, she described how Catholicism "enslaved" and "imprisoned" women in convents, or, as she called them, "slave-pens."[60] She delineated how these institutions denied white women their freedom, exploited their labor, and controlled their minds. She did not go into the salacious details, but, like her anti-Catholic predecessors—Maria Monk and Rebecca Reed—she clearly hinted at the possibility that Catholic priests wielded sexual power over nuns and novices. She explained the conditions for abuse: "The moment a young woman crosses the threshold of a convent . . . is she then not body, soul, and spirit the property of the Roman clergy who may do with her as they please and the outside world be none the wiser?"[61] White's emphasis on the isolation of convent life, the power of Catholic clergy, the disruption of "normal" family life, and the passive bodies of white women raised the specter of sexual abuse and exploitation. She concluded that Catholicism reduced white women to the status of property and then proceeded to abuse them physically, mentally, and spiritually.

Convents represented just one more way in which Rome oppressed women and denied them religious and political rights. And, White emphasized, Catholics were doing this right here in the democratic United States. If Rome continued to gain power, she implied, all white women would be vulnerable to its oppressive regime. In this gender-based attack, her writings exposed how the innocent suffered and would continue to suffer under Catholicism. Her books rallied supporters to end this injustice. "It is time," White implored, that "blinded eyes were opened and deaf ears unstopped."[62]

To cast white women as the victims of Catholicism meant the construction of two other gendered roles, the hero and the enemy. Protestant girls clearly required a protector, someone to defend them and their rights. God had "raised up" the white knights of the Ku Klux Klan for the very purpose of rescuing white women and the Protestant nation. White's depiction of the innocent's victimization highlighted the Klan's masculinity. She stated, "We are looking to the Knights of the Ku Klux Klan to champion the cause of woman and to protect her rights."[63] This sense of the Klan as a protector was reinforced by her consistent reference to Klansmen as "Knights," evoking chivalry and honor, and images of heroes rescuing damsels in distress. The message was clear. The Catholic Church oppressed women; the Protestant Klan liberated them.

This emphasis on the Klan's masculinity also chastised Protestant men who had not yet joined the Klan. "There is too much passive indifference," White wrote, "on the part of Protestants today when the knife is at the throat of liberty."[64] She urged her readers not to be "weak and unsophisticated" or "spineless" Protestants who refused to join the fight and do what was right.[65] She cast aspersions on the manliness and steadfastness of Protestants who either remained apathetic about the present spiritual crisis or were opposed to the Klan's mission.[66] This language and desire for "real" men resembles the urgings of Muscular Christianity in the early twentieth century.[67] Both the Klan and Muscular Christianity "used . . . sexualized language because they understood power and religion in terms of gender."[68] We can see this linking of power, religion, and gender throughout Alma White's works. Protestant women were innocent victims, Klansmen were masculine Protestant heroes, and the indifferent were effeminate Protestant wimps.

In contrast to the masculine Klan, Catholicism was the embodiment of fallen womanhood. White constructed this binary, in part, through her naming of the two groups. She referred to the Klan as a "white-robed army" and a "star of hope," emphasizing its purity and virtue; the Catholic Church was the "Scarlet Mother," connected to blood, violence, and sin.[69] In this depiction, White drew upon "the Woman" of Revelation 17 to paint the picture of Catholicism's corruption: "Her lust for power is everywhere manifest."[70] "She has added," White explained, "one strange and unscriptural tenet after another to her gigantic system of greed and graft."[71] The threat was both seductive and sly. "The 'Scarlet Mother,' with her cunning and deceit, sets her incubators and hatches the brood that will finance her schemes and help to carry out her well-laid plans to grasp the reins of government and make America Catholic."[72] White's feminization and sexualization of the Catholic Church emphasized the enormity of the threat it posed. At the same time, by casting Catholicism as a fallen woman, White also showed that "she" was vulnerable. A fallen woman was no match for the Klan's godly men.

White's emphasis on Rome's corrupt motherhood demonstrated the importance of Protestant women and mothers in this war with evil. Women, too, were soldiers in the fight. Catholic mothers reared their children in a foreign faith. Catholic nuns had forsaken motherhood altogether. These choices threatened the family and menaced the nation. For White and proponents of Republican motherhood and true womanhood before her, mothers played a pivotal role in Christian America: "Women have given birth to our legislators, governors, and presidents. . . . . Study the family trees of our great men, and in their lives you will find reflected the character of their parents, especially of their mother."[73] Using the image of corrupt motherhood heightened Catholicism's betrayal of white womanhood, and simultaneously highlighted the white Protestant mother as the producer of both America and Christianity. Practically, this tactic functioned to appease both of her constituencies: it upheld the ideals of white Protestant masculinity and white Protestant motherhood. Moreover, it made women vital to her war effort.

White's constructions of gender reveal the category's importance in the religious and cultural debates of the 1920s. Even more, her example challenges us to consider more fully the relationship between women and violence in the United States. Scholars have often considered how people have employed gender to advance or hinder causes such as women's rights or women's ordination. White's example focuses our attentions on the ways women have employed gender ideology to disseminate religiously intolerant visions of the world. Her case forces us to ask: Have others done the same? We cannot only listen to the voices of "nice" women and examine the practices of "nice" religion. We also need to recover the history of the women as well as the men who created and committed religious violence. White's tactics draw our attention to the ways victimization, masculinization, feminization, and sexualization shaped people's perceptions of the crisis and encouraged them to join the war against Catholicism.

THE MORAL AUTHORITY OF WOMEN'S LITERATURE

It matters that Alma White—a woman—constructed pro-Klan arguments and wrote such an extensive literature. Gender was a weapon employed within her literature, but her sex also proved pivotal. Writing of connections between victimhood and moral authority, Diane Lipstadt observes, "If you devictimize a people you strip them of their moral authority, and if you can in turn claim to be a victim . . . that moral authority is conferred on or restored to you."[74] Applying these thoughts to Alma White, we see that by portraying women as the victims of the Catholic threat, she claimed the moral high ground. She knew what it was like to be the victim of male religious, domestic, and political power. Methodists had refused to ordain her, her husband had mistreated her, and Catholic policemen had persecuted her and her Pillar of Fire Church. It gave her the moral authority, the power, to denounce the villains, in a way that Protestant and Klan men could not. Men were not the victims. They could be heroes, protectors, wimps, or villains, but they did not have the same moral authority as a victimized and innocent woman. Many other women have used this understanding of white middle-class women as pure and moral to advance causes both noble and odious. Some promoted women's suffrage on moral grounds. "Accepting the notion that women belonged in the home, some advocates believed that women were more moral than men and would vote to protect the home against evils."[75] This moral authority also allowed women to pick up the pen, denounce the evils they saw and experienced, and be taken very seriously.

White was not a completely isolated figure of her day. She belonged to a broader culture that used tropes of female innocence and virtue to justify bigotry and intolerance. Helen Jackson's *Convent Cruelties* (1919) tells the sordid and sad tale of Jackson's early life. At an early age, she joined a convent out of spiritual desire, only to find herself the victim of the most awful tortures. Denied an education, forced to work, cut off from her family, Jackson described the ways she was trapped in the convent and denied the freedoms of American life. Even more disturbing were the inhumane acts committed upon her and other girls— beatings, coldwater baths, confinement in small spaces, being tied up, and a host of other atrocities. Jackson's book, like those of White and nineteenth-century authors Maria Monk and Rebecca Reed, cast her and other women as victims. If the reader had not been convinced by the end, *Convent Cruelties* features "indorsements" and "testimonials," as well as a photo of a "victim weighing only 86 pounds," to witness to the alleged truth of Jackson's claims.[76]

These women used literature to establish, as Alma White put it, that "women have always been the greater sufferers."[77] Their portrayals of women as victims of unjust systems granted them the moral authority to denounce the villains and effect social transformation. The truth demanded action. White reminded readers of their responsibility. "To be indifferent to the part that we as individuals have to play in the world's great drama is a crime against humanity. We cannot shirk our responsibility, or lay it upon the shoulders of others."[78] Jackson's urgings were similar. "Remember, that only one word to the wise is sufficient, so do your duty and profit by the experience of others and thus begin at once to give assistance for destroying the seed of iniquity which is taking root in private institutions."[79] These women hoped that by revealing their vision of the truth, violent change would occur in the world—convents would be invaded, and Catholicism would be defeated.

CONCLUSION: THE VIOLENCE
OF BLOODLESS WARFARE

Women like Alma White and Helen Jackson expected their books to do something. Literature was their weapon of choice, and they used religious history and gender constructions as tactics in their "bloodless warfare." Through this, they hoped that Protestants would wake up and join the battle against Satan. Thus, their literature was not simply intolerant rhetoric. It wielded power in the world—the power to move people to action. White wrote, "It behooves every lover of liberty to see that his own part is faithfully performed."[80] And, women, as much as men, would play an important role in this battle.

Interestingly, though, Alma White emphasized the need for women to take advantage of the democratic weapon at their disposal—suffrage. The moral purity and authority of Protestant women combined with their new voting power offered unparalleled possibilities in White's eyes. She urged women to act and help their oppressed sisters. "Women with the ballot will help to vote down the walls of the convents and liberate the victims of their sex held here in galling bondage."[81] The woman's vote could defeat the forces who opposed Prohibition; it could agitate for convent inspections, and it could crush the Catholic threat.[82] "If woman's new place in religion and politics is not to make the world better," White explained, "then the Bible scheme of redemption is a failure and the story of creation in the Book of Genesis a myth."[83] White Protestant women, like Klansmen, were soldiers in the battle, and the vote was a "mighty weapon" that could defeat the enemy without shedding blood.[84]

"Bloodless warfare," however, did not preclude violence. According to White, the female vote might not be enough. "It is evident that if the country is saved it will have to be done by the Bible and the ballot, or by bullets. The latter by all means should be the last resort."[85] Physical violence was a last resort, but a resort nonetheless. From her perspective, wickedness and evil might reach a level where "forbearance may no longer be a virtue."[86] She justified this position through her view of the law and interpretation of the Bible. If laws were passed, but not enforced, then "revolution," White assured readers, was "as sure to follow as night follows day."[87] She also emphasized scriptural support for violence and told readers that "God never fails to punish the wicked."[88] At some point, the battle with Catholicism would shift from "bloodless" to bloody. "We must now look to unexpected sources for true men and women who, like Elijah, will take the heads off the false prophets and bring an end to selfish interests and corruption in both church and state. According to the Scriptures it will take another war to do it."[89]

White prepared many soldiers in her day. Her books were extremely popular, and she gave sermons and lectures across the country advancing the Klan's cause. One advertisement boasted that the first edition of *The Ku Klux Klan in Prophecy* sold 11,000 copies in just three weeks and assured readers that the second edition was now available, as "orders for hundreds more" had been made.[90] Local newspapers also commented on the popularity of White's work. One described her 1924 campaign in Jacksonville, Florida. "The revivalist draws freely from the rich storehouse of faith experiences, which with her healing accounts and keen knowledge of political affairs, hold the rapt attention of her hearers, old and young."[91] Likewise, a 1926 account from Colorado reported that "a large and enthusiastic audience heard Bishop Alma White discuss the principles of Americanism and the 'dangers' that are threatening the nation."[92] People responded to her call for "bloodless warfare," but what was the result?

By broadening our understanding of violence, we can more fully assess and appreciate the impact of White's words. For example, existing evidence does not provide us with examples of men and women reading White's works and then storming a convent or lynching a man; however, the Klan in Colorado and in New Jersey, White's two main centers of power, was not known for its violent physical actions. Rather, in these areas, the Klan sought power through the existing political system and social reform causes.[93] That does not mean they were not violent. These tactics, combined with public displays of power, made the Klan an intimidating force in both areas. Whether or not someone was physically attacked, people felt threatened by the Klan. They understood the potential for violent acts to occur because intolerance, discrimination, and bigotry infused this culture of hate.

In this context, some Catholics and anti-Klan activists viewed White's attacks, literary and verbal, as "violent." In 1923 a *Denver Catholic Register* staff writer raised the alarm in an article titled "Self-Named Bishop Violent in Anti-Catholicity." It stated, "Mrs. Alma White . . . has advertised herself widely as 'the only woman Bishop,' having as much right to the title of Emperor of Mars and Neptune, has been making violent attacks at Longmont against the priests and nuns of the Catholic Church and the Knights of Columbus." The article then protested the renting out of a city auditorium to White and accused her of creating "animosities" and "religious fights." A local priest, quoted in the article, feared that White's "asinine mouthings" would lead "some unbalanced mind to an unpremeditated act and serious harm and disgrace to our city might result."[94] The article used the word *violent* more than once and pointed to the real consequences of White's words: "religious fights." This writer and others interpreted her "bloodless warfare" as a violent attack.

To dismiss this language and these fears as rhetoric or "not actual violence" obscures the effects of White's work. Is her "bloodless war" the same as a physical assault? Certainly not, but neither are they unrelated. Language can be violent. It can have real consequences in our world; as Simon Wiesenthal stated, "Genocide does not begin with ovens; it begins with words."[95] The example of Alma White demands that we conceive of the relationship between literature and violence, between rhetoric and reality, in more complicated ways. Looking for single causes or easy answers belies the complexity of religious violence. We must examine "the complex, interactive nature of movement—societal violence" and work toward a "sophisticated, multidimensional understanding" of violence.[96] A more expansive understanding can illuminate the variety of ways violence is disseminated and enacted; it can highlight the symbiotic relationship between symbolic and social violence and focus our attention on the movement from one to the other.

If we adopt this expanded perspective, it appears that the violence of Alma White's pro-Klan writings lies in their contribution to a larger culture of hate in the United States in the 1920s. Her works helped sustain an environment that already endorsed intolerance and violence against those defined as "other." In that way, her writing represents one factor among many that encouraged the commission of religiously violent acts. White's literature reconciled religion and violence as well as Christianity and the Klan, in its Protestant readers' minds. Her writings, in addition to other forces and factors, fostered the creation of a world in which numerous Protestants accepted the intolerant ideology and violent action of the Klan. Perhaps, then, the violence of White's pro-Klan writings emerged not primarily in their ability to foment violent acts by a minority of people, but rather in their ability to reconcile a majority of people to accept religious violence and social injustice—in other words, to do nothing. In this way, we must acknowledge that Alma White's "bloodless warfare" was not so bloodless after all.

NOTES

1. Alma White, *Short Sermons* (Zarephath, NJ: Pillar of Fire, 1932), 254.

2. Alma White, *Radio Sermons and Lectures* (Denver: Pillar of Fire, 1936), 14. See also Susie Cunningham Stanley, *Feminist Pillar of Fire: The Life of Alma White* (Cleveland: Pilgrim Press, 1993).

3. White, *Short Sermons*, 55.

4. C. R. Paige and C. K. Ingler, *Alma White's Evangelism: Press Reports*, vol. 1 (Zarephath, NJ: Pillar of Fire, 1939), 205; Alma White, *The Ku Klux Klan in Prophecy* (Zarephath, NJ: Good Citizen, 1925), 3.

5. White, *The Ku Klux Klan in Prophecy*, 55.

6. Phyllis B. Gerstenfeld, *Hate Crimes: Causes, Controls, and Controversies* (Thousand Oaks, CA: Sage Publications, 2004), 72; Kathleen M. Blee, *Women of the Klan: Racism and Gender in the 1920s* (Berkeley: University of California Press, 1991), 40.

7. J. Gordon Melton and David G. Bromley, "Challenging Misconceptions about the New Religions—Violence Connection" and "Violence and Religion in Perspective," in *Cults, Religion, and Violence*, ed. J. Gordon Melton and David G. Bromley (Cambridge: Cambridge University Press, 2002), 54, 1–2.

8. Grant A. Wacker, "Travail of a Broken Family: Radical Evangelical Responses to the Emergence of Pentecostalism in America, 1906–1916," in *Pentecostal Currents in American Protestantism*, ed. Edith L. Blumhofer, Russell P. Spittler, and Grant A. Wacker (Urbana: University of Illinois Press, 1999), 24.

9. Larry Eskridge, "White, Alma Bridwell," in *American National Biography Online*, http://www.anb.org/articles/08/08-01640.html (accessed April 23, 2007).

10. Wacker, "Travail of a Broken Family," 36.

11. Gail Bederman, "'The Women Have Had Charge of the Church Work Long Enough': The Men and Religion Forward Movement of 1911–1912 and the Masculinization of Middle-Class Protestantism," *American Quarterly* 41, no. 3 (Sept. 1989): 435.

12. See Lynn Dumenil, *The Modern Temper: American Culture and Society in the 1920s* (New York: Hill and Wang, 1995); and David J. Goldberg, *Discontented America: The United States in the 1920s* (Baltimore: Johns Hopkins University Press, 1999). The quotation in the section title is from Alma White, *Heroes of the Fiery Cross* (Zarephath, NJ: Good Citizen, 1928), 36.

13. Paul L. Murphy, "Sources and Nature of Intolerance in the 1920s," *Journal of American History* 51, no. 1 (June 1964): 60–76.

14. Dumenil, *The Modern Temper*, 8, 235–244.

15. Robert Alan Goldberg, *Hooded Empire: The Ku Klux Klan in Colorado* (Urbana: University of Illinois Press, 1981), vii; David M. Chalmers, *Hooded Americanism: The History of the Ku Klux Klan* (Durham, NC: Duke University Press, 1987), 109.

16. Chalmers, *Hooded Americanism*, 245, 247; Wyn Craig Wade, *The Fiery Cross: The Ku Klux Klan in America* (New York: Simon and Schuster, 1987), 169.

17. David H. Bennett, "Women and the Nativist Movement," in *"Remember the Ladies": New Perspectives on Women in American History*, ed. Carol V. R. George (Syracuse: Syracuse University Press, 1975), 72.

18. Blee, *Women of the Klan*, 2, 3.

19. Ibid.

20. White, *Short Sermons*, 79, 119, 198–199.

21. White, *Radio Sermons and Lectures*, 241.

22. Wade, *The Fiery Cross*, 148.

23. White, *The Ku Klux Klan in Prophecy*, 118; White, *Heroes of the Fiery Cross*, 72, 116. The quotation in the section title is from White, *The Ku Klux Klan in Prophecy*, 118.

24. White, *Heroes of the Fiery Cross*, 70.

25. Wacker, "Travail of a Broken Family," 24.

26. David Morgan, *Protestants and Pictures: Religion, Visual Culture, and the Age of American Mass Production* (New York: Oxford University Press, 1999), 19; David Morgan, *The Lure of Images: A History of Religion and Visual Media in America* (New York: Routledge, 2007), 14.

27. Alma White, *The Story of My Life and the Pillar of Fire*, vol. 2 (Zarephath, NJ: Pillar of Fire, 1935), 165.

28. White, *The Ku Klux Klan in Prophecy*, 65.

29. Wade, *The Fiery Cross*, 170–171.

30. Mary Kelley, *Private Woman, Public Stage: Literary Domesticity in Nineteenth-Century America* (Oxford: Oxford University Press, 1984).

31. White, *Heroes of the Fiery Cross*, 75.

32. Dumenil, *The Modern Temper*, 235; Goldberg, *Discontented America*, 120.

33. Alma White, *Klansmen: Guardians of Liberty* (Zarephath, NJ, 1926), 20.

34. See David Brion Davis, "Some Themes of Counter-Subversion: An Analysis of Anti-Masonic, Anti-Catholic, and Anti-Mormon Literature," *Mississippi Valley Historical Review* 47 (Sept. 1960): 205–224; John Higham, *Strangers in the Land: Patterns of American Nativism, 1860–1925* (New Brunswick, NJ: Rutgers University Press, 1955); Timothy W. Bosworth, "Anti-Catholicism as a Political Tool in Mid-Eighteenth-Century Maryland," *Catholic Historical Review* 61, no. 4 (Oct. 1975): 539–563.

35. White, *Klansmen*, 23.

36. White, *The Ku Klux Klan in Prophecy*, 50; White, *Heroes of the Fiery Cross*, 123.

37. White, *Klansmen*, 85; *The Ku Klux Klan in Prophecy*, 8, 91.

38. White, *Klansmen*, 20.

39. White, *The Ku Klux Klan in Prophecy*, 82–83.

40. Ibid., 90.

41. White, *Heroes of the Fiery Cross*, 46.

42. White, *The Ku Klux Klan in Prophecy*, 73–74.

43. Ibid., 118; White, *Klansmen*, 66.

44. White, *Heroes of the Fiery Cross*, 8.

45. White, *The Ku Klux Klan in Prophecy*, 25.

46. Ibid., 128; White, *Heroes of the Fiery Cross*, 8.

47. White, *Klansmen*, 122–123.

48. White, *Heroes of the Fiery Cross*, 70.

49. White, *Klansmen*, 50–56, 42–45; White, *Heroes of the Fiery Cross*, 40, 62–64.

50. White, *Klansmen*, 60.

51. White, *The Ku Klux Klan in Prophecy*, 23, 62; White, *Klansmen*, 39.

52. White, *The Ku Klux Klan in Prophecy*, 6.

53. Brian Levin, "History as a Weapon: How Extremists Deny the Holocaust in North America," in *Crimes of Hate: Selected Readings*, ed. Phyllis B. Gerstenfeld and Diana R. Grant (Thousand Oaks, CA: Sage Publications, 2004), 187.

54. Thomas A. Tweed, ed., *Retelling U.S. Religious History* (Berkeley: University of California Press, 1997), 2.

55. The quotation in the section title is from White, *The Ku Klux Klan in Prophecy*, 130.

56. Dorothy M. Brown, *Setting a Course: American Women in the 1920s* (Boston: Twayne, 1987), 245.

57. Alma White, *The Story of My Life and the Pillar of Fire*, vol. 1 (Zarephath, NJ: Pillar of Fire, 1935), 311.

58. See Davis, "Some Themes of Counter-Subversion"; Harvey Cox, "Myths Sanctioning Religious Persecution," in *A Time for Consideration*, ed. M. Darrol Bryant and Herbert W. Richardson (New York: Edwin Mellen, 1978), 3–19; David G. Bromley and Anson D. Shupe Jr., *Strange Gods: The Great American Cult Scare* (Boston: Beacon Press, 1981).

59. Bennett, "Women and the Nativist Movement," 72.

60. White, *Klansmen*, 127.

61. White, *Heroes of the Fiery Cross*, 171.

62. Ibid., 127.

63. White, *The Ku Klux Klan in Prophecy*, 136.

64. White, *Heroes of the Fiery Cross*, 72.

65. White, *Klansmen*, 64; White, *The Ku Klux Klan in Prophecy*, 65.

66. Kelly Baker, "The Gospel According to the Klan" (PhD diss., Florida State University, 2008), 72.

67. Clifford Putney, *Muscular Christianity: Manhood and Sports in Protestant America, 1880–1920* (Cambridge, MA: Harvard University Press, 2001), 4. See also Baker, "The Gospel According to the Klan," 71–91; and Betty A. DeBerg, *Ungodly Women: Gender and the First Wave of American Fundamentalism* (Minneapolis: Fortress Press, 1990).

68. Bederman, "'The Women Have Had Charge of the Church Work Long Enough,'" 435.

69. White, *The Ku Klux Klan in Prophecy*, 18, 32.

70. White, *Klansmen*, 109, 45, 23, 64, 116–117.

71. Ibid., 19.

72. Ibid., 121.

73. White, *Radio Sermons and Lectures*, 246.

74. Diane Lipstadt, *Denying the Holocaust: The Growing Assault on Truth and Memory* (New York: Free Press, 1993), 7–8.

75. Goldberg, *Discontented America*, 51.

76. Helen Jackson, *Convent Cruelties* (Toledo: Helen Jackson, 1919).

77. White, *The Ku Klux Klan in Prophecy*, 130.

78. White, *Heroes of the Fiery Cross*, 23.

79. Jackson, *Convent Cruelties*, 8.

80. White, *Heroes of the Fiery Cross*, 70; White, *Klansmen*, 131, 147; White, *The Ku Klux Klan in Prophecy*, 120.

81. White, *Klansmen*, 131–132.

82. White, *Heroes of the Fiery Cross*, 58; White, *Klansmen*, 127, 131.

83. White, *The Ku Klux Klan in Prophecy*, 136.

84. White, *Heroes of the Fiery Cross*, 70.

85. White, *Klansmen*, 82.

86. White, *Heroes of the Fiery Cross*, 71, 59–60.

87. White, *Klansmen*, 99.

88. White, *The Ku Klux Klan in Prophecy*, 98; White, *Heroes of the Fiery Cross*, 71.

89. White, *Klansmen*, 66; White, *Heroes of the Fiery Cross*, 71.

90. Klansmen Take Notice!," *Good Citizen* 13, no. 8 (August 1925): 5; "A Marvelous Sale," ibid., 10.

91. C. R. Paige and C. K. Ingler, *Alma White's Evangelism: Press Reports*, vol. 2 (Zarephath, NJ: Pillar of Fire, 1940), 32–33.

92. Paige and Ingler, *Alma White's Evangelism: Press Reports*, 2: 91.

93. Chalmers, *Hooded Americanism*, 131, 244–245, 247–248.

94. "Self-Named Bishop Violent in Anti-Catholicity," *Denver Catholic Register*, Feb. 1, 1923, 1, 3.

95. Wiesenthal quoted in James R. Lewis, *From the Ashes: Making Sense of Waco* (Lanham, MD: Rowman and Littlefield, 1994), 213.

96. Melton and Bromley, "Challenging Misconceptions about the New Religions," 42–56.

10

Of Tragedy and Its Aftermath

The Search for Religious Meaning in the Shootings at Virginia Tech

Grace Y. Kao

On April 16, 2007, twenty-three-year-old Seung-Hui Cho killed thirty-two of his fellow students and faculty and wounded many more at Virginia Polytechnic Institute and State University ("Virginia Tech" or VT) before he took his own life in what became the deadliest shooting by a lone gunman in U.S. history.[1] Despite extensive media coverage, left underreported were the various ways in which attempts were made to infuse the tragedy with religious meaning. This chapter attempts to fill that gap by examining the religious significance attributed to the killer's motives, certain jeremiadic attempts to identify the root cause of the suicide-shootings, and the ritualized expressions of public mourning and solidarity across the Virginia Tech community and beyond. The many roles that religion was enlisted to play were premised upon and themselves representative of ongoing debates in American society about religion and its relationship to violence. Some blamed religion for having caused the shooting rampage. Others appealed to religion to explain and even justify it. Still others drew upon religion to comfort and unite the community afterward. This chapter shows how the multiple uses of religion surrounding these shootings belie any simplistic relationship between the powerful forces of religion and violence in American society.

RELIGION AND THE QUESTION OF THE KILLER'S MOTIVES

One early attempt to find religious meaning in the shootings centered upon discussions of the killer's motives. Some commentators immediately suspected Cho was a Muslim acting in the tradition of "Islamic terrorism." But a closer look at Cho's final words, photos, and video suggests that Christianity figured more prominently in his own framing and perhaps even sanctification of his actions.

The first attempt to ascribe religious import to the attack originated in the early days of reporting, when many within and outside of the VT community began speculating about the pseudonym that the killer used on several occasions: "Ishmael" or some variant thereof. The name "A. Ishmael," not Seung-Hui Cho, appeared on the return address of the "multimedia manifesto" that he mailed to NBC between his two sets of killings.[2] "Ax Ishmael" also was scrawled in red ink on Cho's arm when his body was recovered at the second crime scene. On the basis of these two references and some mistaken reporting about its spelling,[3] some journalists immediately theorized that Cho had been a Muslim jihadist.

Jonah Goldberg, editor-at-large of *The National Review Online*, posted on his April 18, 2007 blog, without adding any comments of his own, a third-party blog, the first paragraph of which read: "First it was Johnny Muhammad, now it was Cho Seung Hui aka Ismail Ax [sic]. Precisely how many mass shooters have to turn out to have adopted Muslim names before we get it? Islam has become the tribe of choice of those who hate American society. I'm not talking about people who grew up as Muslims, confident and secure in their faith, good fathers, sons and neighbors. I'm talking about the angry, malignant, narcissist loners who want to reject their community utterly, to throw off their 'slave name' and represent the downtrodden of the earth by shooting their friends and neighbors."[4]

Washington Post columnist Charles Krauthammer not only compared Cho's actions to "Islamic suicide bombing" but also strongly insinuated on national news that Cho had been motivated by Islam: "that picture . . . draws its inspiration from the manifestos, the iconic photographs of the Islamic suicide bombers over the last half decade in Palestine, in Iraq and elsewhere. That's what they end up leaving behind, either on al Jazeera or Palestinian TV. . . . it seems, as if his inspiration for leaving the message behind in that way, might have been this kind of suicide attack. . . . And he did leave the return address . . . 'Ismail Ax.' I suspect ['Ismail Ax'] has more to do with Islamic terror and the inspiration than it does with the opening line of *Moby-Dick*."[5]

Another egregious attempt to interpret Cho as a jihadist came from Richard Engel. One might have expected higher standards from NBC's Middle East bureau chief and a 2006 recipient of the prestigious Edward R. Murrow Award in journalism. Like Krauthammer, Engel compared Cho's video to the many "taped testimonials [that] suicide bombers leave behind to justify their crimes" such as those seen in the Middle East: "an angry young man dressed in battle clothing preach[es] a message of hate in front of a drab background," expresses a "desire to battle injustice and moral turpitude," and offers final words "replete with religious references."[6] Engel also ruminated over the Islamic significance of Cho's pseudonym by discussing Abraham's near sacrifice of his son and the rite of ani-mal sacrifice during the *hajj* (the pilgrimage to Mecca) that commemorates it. Engel then went further than the others did when he observed, in addition to Cho's repeated mentions of "Christ, suffering, and isolation," that there "appear to have also been references to the Koran." This last statement is problematic not only because there were no unique references to the Qur'an in the manifesto, but also because the public lacked any way of verifying his claim.

We will probably never know what Cho meant to imply by his "Ax Ishmael" or "A. Ishmael" moniker.[7] The many comparisons made between his video and those of suicide-bombers probably disclose less about his motivations than about our efforts to catalogue and understand them. Still, the theory that Cho's actions were prompted by Islam or by those who kill indiscriminately in its name becomes less convincing in the face of the following three facts.[8] First, in no instance did Cho spell his alter ego or pseudonym in the purportedly Islamic way; thus, those who based their suspicions on the significance of this alternate spelling began with a false premise. Second, Cho had a Christian (not Islamic) upbringing, and pursued several courses at Virginia Tech that explored biblical (not qur'anic) themes.[9] Nor is there evidence of his embracing or converting to Islam or even involving him-self with Virginia Tech's vibrant Muslim community. Third, and perhaps most importantly, those seeking to ascribe religious meaning to Cho's actions must recognize that the contents of Cho's "multimedia manifesto" resonate more with Christianity than with Islam. Even here, the Christian symbols are rather skewed, probably a result of Cho's mental illness. Nevertheless, consider an enigmatic photo of a drawing that appears twice in the manifesto: a cross enclosed in a heart with two eyes bisected by the cross's vertical beam. More telling are Cho's own recorded words, which were transcribed and widely broadcast:

> Thanks to you I die, like Jesus Christ, to inspire generations of the weak and the defenseless people.

> Do you know what it feels like to be humiliated and be impaled, impaled upon on a cross and left to bleed to death for your amusement?

> Jesus loves crucifying me. He loves inducing cancer in my head, terrorizing my heart, and raping my soul all this time.[10]

The centrality of the cross and the belief that Christ died for the sake of others are basic to Christianity, but are foreign to the Qur'an and Islam (see, for example, Surah 4:157–158). Also alien to the Islamic tradition (and to Christianity as prac-ticed by the vast majority of the faithful) is the idea found in the third utterance—that Christ takes delight in inflicting pain on his followers.[11]

Rather than substantiating a link to Islam, the passages above reveal that Cho deployed powerful and unmistakably Christian imagery to frame and perhaps even legitimate his actions. Some of his final words that were not released to the public (but to which I was granted access) lend additional support to this interpretation. In one passage, Cho repeats the refrain of dying like Jesus Christ and then compares the new life that will emerge thereafter to Easter: "It will be a day of rebirth." In another, Cho offers a peculiar fusion of Christian and Islamic rhetoric with the following instruction: "I say we take up the cross, Children of Ishmael, take up our guns and knives and hammers, and take no prisoners and spare no lives until our last breath and our last ounce of energy."[12] The phrase "children of Ishmael" could refer to Arabs or Muslims, since Ishmael, the son of Abraham and Hagar, is believed to be the ancestor of both peoples. And "take up the cross" echoes Jesus' command to his would-be disciples to do likewise and follow Him (Matthew 10:38, 16:24; Mark 8:34; Luke 9:23, 14:27). What is more, while the Gospel of John narrates that Jesus literally but nonviolently carried his own cross to be killed by others, the inverse idea of figuratively "taking up the cross" in violent pursuit of others has precursors in the history of Christianity; examples include the legend of Constantine conquering under the sign of the cross and the reproduction of crosses on the battle gear of crusaders.

My point in highlighting these Christian themes is to suggest neither that Cho actually was motivated by Christian beliefs to kill nor that the ideas expressed in his final words and video are compatible with Christian orthodoxy.[13] Nor am I implying that the only plausible religious interpretation is a Christian one, since Cho's references to Moses and Ishmael are generic enough to work equally well (or poorly) in Jewish or Muslim contexts.[14] Nevertheless, that Cho deployed explicitly and sometimes uniquely Christian language and symbols (in publicly accessible materials which journalists should have accessed) raises important questions about why there was considerable speculation about his possible Islamic inspiration and scant public speculation about his connection to Christianity.

On one reading, the impulse to link Cho to the tradition of "Islamic violence," by those who either advanced this theory or readily entertained it, was reflexive for a society conditioned to conceptualize America's foes in light of a "war against terrorism." Since the "Islamic extremist" has become the presumed enemy for many Americans, it is not surprising that several commentators quickly folded the perpetrator of such spectacular violence at Virginia Tech into the familiar narrative of Islamists seeking America's destruction. Other additional factors—Cho's use of communication technologies similar to those used by suicide-bombers, the problem of journalistic error and irresponsibility, and the Internet's capacity to disseminate misinformation rapidly—helped this theory to have "legs" for as long as it did.

On a more critical reading, the attempts to dissociate Cho from the dominant culture and religion in America were expressly made to assure a stunned nation that "real" Americans do not commit such horrific acts. The media and even the official Virginia Tech Review Panel Report transformed Cho into a racial and ethnic "other" by drawing upon existing prejudices and stereotypes about Asian Americans.[15] More prominently, certain journalistic decisions to cast Cho into the role of a young Muslim extremist helped conceal Cho's use of Christian symbolism and also prevented citizens from grappling with the distinctly American influences on him. For example, he cited the Columbine High School killers by first name and planted himself firmly in their "martyrdom" tradition. Transforming Cho into a religious other further stigmatized a barely tolerated Muslim minority while strengthening the popular notion that the greatest threats to peace and security are foreign or "outside," not internal and homegrown. But Cho's words and actions reveal the disquieting truth that suicide-murders and self-martyrdom, whether in purported imitation of Christ or as a copycat of other adolescent killers, remain possible in America today, and thus cannot be confined to premodern Christianity, Islam, the Middle East, or the angry young jihadist.

RELIGIOUS JEREMIADS IN RESPONSE TO 4/16

The attempts to infuse Cho's shooting rampage with religious meaning were not limited to those who blamed "Islamic extremism" as the underlying culprit. While many other critics sought to identify the tragedy's root cause in the secular realm (for example, the effects of bullying, violence in popular culture, inadequate mental health services and privacy laws, too much or too little gun control), a small subset of commentators interpreted the calamity either as divine punishment for America's sins or as the inevitable outcome of a nation that had strayed from its religious heritage.

The jeremiad neither originated in America nor is unique to the American experience, but it has played a key role in the self-understandings of Americans since the colonial period. According to Sacvan Bercovitch's classic study, the style of preaching and prophetic interpretation popularized by the Puritans combined lamentations on the present with renewed hope for the future by exhorting audiences to return to their God-given covenantal duties.[16] By interpreting misfortunes that befell the community as a sign of divine disfavor for unfaithfulness and thereafter pleading for the relationship to be restored through remedial action, those who delivered jeremiads elided sacral and secular history in a way that helped to advance the national mythos of American exceptionalism that endures today.

Following Andrew Murphy and Jennifer Miller's more recent work on this genre, we can identify a four-part structure to this rhetorical device: the contemporary jeremiad (1) enumerates current problems in society, (2) posits a root cause for them, (3) identifies the period in which that root cause first appeared, and (4) warns of dire consequences if behavior is not soon reformed.[17] Other common features include a defense of public religiosity as the basis of social order and the American experience, a valorization of the nation's founders and their ideals, and an interpretation of worldly misfortunes as the result of societal unfaithfulness to those foundational values and/or social practices. All these elements can be found in the jeremiadic responses to the shootings at Virginia Tech.

The most strident jeremiad was delivered by the Westboro Baptist Church (WBC) of Topeka, Kansas. This church, led by pastor Fred Phelps Sr., is composed primarily of his relatives and extended family and is unaffiliated with any mainstream or national Baptist organization. The Southern Poverty Law Center has labeled it an extremist hate group. Started in 1955, WBC first gained international notoriety in 1998 for picketing at the funeral of murdered gay college student Matthew Shepherd in Wyoming, as members carried placards that read "God Hates Fags" and "Hell Is Real–Ask Matt." Beginning in June 2005, the group began demonstrating at the funerals of U.S. service personnel killed in Iraq, with signs that read "Thank God for Dead Soldiers" and "Thank God for IEDs" (referring to improvised explosive devices). WBC sees in these deaths God's judgment upon a nation so "debauched" that it allows gays and lesbians to serve in the military and propagates the "lie that it's okay to be gay."[18]

Within this context of antigay vitriol and gross insensitivity to those in mourning, WBC released the following statement only hours after the public had learned of the shootings: "God is punishing America for her sodomite sins. The 33 massacred at Virginia Tech died for America's sins against WBC (Westboro Baptist Church). Just as US soldiers [are] dying in Iraq each day for America's sins against WBC."[19] Phelps later explained why the Lord had sent a "world-class whopper of a massacre" to Virginia Tech, why WBC intended to demonstrate at the funerals of the slain, and why more and worse for America was on the way. To paraphrase, God's wrath was upon America because America had failed to heed WBC's messages and had persecuted them for publicly delivering jeremiads.[20] America may have once been "uniquely . . . brought up by the tender hand of God" to become the greatest nation in the world, but its downward spiral began with the rise of the "modern militant homosexual movement" and reached its nadir on June 26, 2003, when the Supreme Court ruled that "we must respect sodomy."[21]

Curiously, although most jeremiads combine a prophetic call for drastic reform with hope for redemption, WBC did not, even though it had formerly proclaimed that repentance by the humble and contrite would bring about God's "repent[ance] of the evil that he has purposed against you."[22] Instead of exhorting the nation to repent in the aftermath of the school shootings, WBC declared that this "evil sodomite nation is doomed." Marshaling Jeremiah 7:28 and 15:1 for support, WBC declared that America "has sinned away her day of grace," can no longer "receive saving faith for redemption at this hour," and thus "it's too late to pray . . . [or] call on the Lord."[23]

Phyllis Schlafly, the well-known conservative activist, columnist, opponent of feminism, and defender of "traditional family values," offered a markedly different jeremiad. Though likewise critical of contemporary American sexual mores, she theorized that the root cause of the tragedy was not sexual licentiousness per se, but the state of liberal arts education in general and Virginia Tech's course offerings in particular. In an Eagle Forum column titled "What Cho Learned in the English Department," Schlafly conceded that she did not know which courses Cho had taken as an English major but went on to link Cho's interest in "violence, death, and mayhem" to several English professors' use of feminist pedagogy and deconstruction, assignment of poems and books featuring violent themes, and support for "diversity, post-modernism . . . multiculturalism . . . [and] undiluted Marxism." That Schlafly regards Cho's shooting rampage as a case of chickens coming home to roost is strongly implied by her column's concluding words:

> At the campus-wide convocation to honor the victims, Professor Nikki Giovanni read what purported to be a poem. On behalf of the English Department, she declaimed: "We do not understand this tragedy. We know we did nothing to deserve it."
>
> Maybe others will render a different verdict and ask why taxpayers are paying professors at Virginia Tech to teach worthless and psychologically destructive courses.[24]

Schlafly's Virginia Tech jeremiad can best be understood in the context of her extended critique of the American public educational system. The Eagle Forum, the conservative grassroots public-policymaking organization of which Schlafly is founder and president, opposes "liberal propaganda in the curriculum" and the "dumbing down of the academic curriculum" through "courses in self-esteem, diversity, and multiculturalism."[25] According to their declensionist narrative, U.S. public education took a decisively wrong turn in the 1960s under the influence of "John Dewey and his Columbia Teachers College acolytes" when they opposed "objective truth, authoritative notions of good and evil, religion and tradition." Today, the wages of their sins can be seen in the supposed right of public schools to "indoctrinate students in Muslim religion and practices . . . force students to attend a program advocating homosexual conduct . . . censor any mention of Intelligent Design . . . [and] force students to answer nosy questionnaires with suggestive questions about sex, drugs and suicide."[26]

The Eagle Forum prophetically calls for America to reclaim its pre-1960s teaching of "traditional family values" and the "greatness of our heroes and successes" instead of the "values of situation ethics . . . [and] the doctrines of U.S. guilt and multiculturalism." Citing a selection in the *American Citizens Handbook* published by the National Education Association in 1951, Schlafly and the Eagle Forum encourage public schools to cultivate a "common mind—a like heritage of purpose, religious ideals, love of country, beauty, and wisdom to guide and inspire"—and to draw instruction from "Old and New Testament passages, the Ten Commandments, the Lord's Prayer, the Golden Rule, the Boy Scout oath, and patriotic songs."[27] Thus, while not made explicit in Schlafly's column about the shootings, her jeremiadic warning is clear enough: because Virginia Tech's English department is representative of the "weird" and "leftwing" tendencies of faculty in higher education today, we should not be surprised if another "already mixed-up kid" conducts another shooting rampage after taking similarly "worthless and psychologically destructive courses" elsewhere. In contrast to WBC, Schlafly does not so much interpret the murderous rampage in terms of divine punishment for America's sins as she judges them to be the inevitable result of a society that has strayed too far from its "Judeo-Christian" roots.

Though different, each of these jeremiads captures features common to the genre—nostalgia for purportedly simpler and more righteous times and a reduction of complex social problems. The events of April 16, 2007, may have inspired a new wave of jeremiads, but it is worth mentioning that WBC and Phyllis Schlafly's messages were poorly received. American society may be divided on issues of sexuality and civil rights for gays and lesbians, but Americans on either side of those debates expressed great disgust for both WBC's tactics and its theology of divine retribution. WBC did not carry out its planned pickets at VT funerals. Had it done so, it would probably have been the most despised group among the flood of proselytizers who descended upon the campus in the aftermath of the tragedy.[28]

Something comparable can be said about Schlafly's jeremiad. Heated debates in multiple venues will no doubt continue about the curriculum in public schools as well as about the meaning and value of a liberal arts education. Nevertheless, while researching this chapter, I found no other organization (including conservative "pro-family" groups) that blamed Cho's suicide-shootings on the course offerings or pedagogy of Virginia Tech faculty. Many Americans still believe that a divine blessing rests upon the nation, but most seem to have lost their taste for the notion of divine rebuke or judgment for wayward behavior.

RELIGION IN PUBLIC EXPRESSIONS OF GRIEF AND SOLIDARITY IN THE WAKE OF 4/16

The question remains whether there were more responsible and widely embraced ways of responding religiously to the tragedy. As a scholar writing about these events and as a member of the community who lived through them, I conclude that there were. While local religious communities offered services in liturgically distinctive ways and many individuals wrestled existentially with questions of meaning, faith, and theodicy, there also were shared public responses to the tragedy that were interreligious in spirit and often nationalistic in form. Ecumenical and patriotic expressions of mourning and solidarity appeared in three distinct venues: the student-initiated makeshift memorial to the dead, the official Virginia Tech Convocation (memorial service) on the day following the shootings, and the White House response.

Issues of memorialization often have strong religious dimensions. They raise questions about the meaning of life and death, as they also make statements about community responsibility and belonging. Memorials involve choices about who and which values will be honored, and what form the remembrance will take.[29] By evening on the day of the shootings, members of the student-driven volunteer organization Hokies United had placed thirty-two "Hokie Stones," one for each slain victim, in a semicircle on the Drillfield in front of Burruss Hall at the center of campus. (The Hokie is the school mascot, and Hokie Stones are pieces of dolomite limestone that, quarried locally, feature in nearly all campus buildings). This impromptu and makeshift memorial became one of the most recognizable and powerful images of Virginia Tech following the shooting and an immediate gathering place for reflection and prayer. It even became a site of pilgrimage. Two aspects of this memorial merit further comment.

The first was the placement of an American flag at each stone. The "Stars and Stripes" stood out prominently amidst the growing pile of remembrances because of their identical size, comparatively greater height, and iconic symbolism. Aesthetically speaking, the maroon and orange of the "Hokie Nation" had been supplemented—even overpowered in some cases—by the red, white, and blue of the United States of America. While it is not known who placed those flags there and why, Virginia Tech political scientist Timothy Luke compared it to the aftermath of 9/11, when all the dead were transformed posthumously into "lost Americans . . . even if they were perhaps Korean, Canadian, Israeli/Romanian, Peruvian, Indian, Egyptian, or Indonesian beforehand."[30] For me, this series of flags on memorial markers evoked images of flag-draped coffins of the American war dead and thus the associated civil religious conceptions of honor and sacrifice.

The second distinctive feature of this impromptu shrine was the (initially anonymous) addition of a thirty-third stone (for Cho) in the early hours of April 19, 2007. When the stone later mysteriously disappeared, an undergraduate student "outed" herself as the one who had placed it. She stated in her letter to the student newspaper that she intended to restore it—repeatedly if need be—for as long as the makeshift memorial remained. In writing that "we did not only lose

32 students and faculty members that day, we lost 33," Katelynn Johnson reasoned that all VT students, faculty, and alumni remain members of the "Hokie family" regardless of their problems, criminal history, political or religious views, or mental health status. Neither she nor anyone else was in a position to judge "who has value and who doesn't," she went on, for Cho's family and loved ones also grieved his loss.[31] The stone was then anonymously restored, though Johnson insists not by her doing. Reports differ as to how many more times the stone was anonymously removed and restored (if at all), but the physical space left for remembering Cho continued to amass its own share of flowers, candles, American flags, and even cards about regret and forgiveness. (In the end, the pile of mementos made it nearly impossible to tell whether there was an actual stone buried beneath them.)

The act of symbolically remembering the killer alongside his victims was not universally supported. The VT administration certainly emphasized thirty-two instead of thirty-three victims in all official memorial dedications and other actions (for example, in the ringing of bells, release of balloons, deliverance of eulogies, and creation of the permanent April 16 Memorial). Nevertheless, Cho's stone (or the place reserved for it) garnered many onlookers and memorabilia before the official memorial was installed on August 19, 2007. Most Blacksburg-area churches also chose to remember thirty-three victims.[32] The harshest criticism about adding a thirty-third stone came from outside of the VT community. All these indicators point to the community's general acceptance that the tragedy had claimed thirty-three lives. In contrast to some camps who sought to "other" Cho, much of the VT community chose to memorialize all who had died—by acknowledging the killer alongside those he had so senselessly murdered.

Religion also was on display in symbolically nationalistic ways during Virginia Tech's ceremonial response to the shootings. Upwards of 15,000 people attended the April 17, 2007 Convocation, while approximately 20,000 more sat in overflow seating. The Convocation began with the posting of the colors (flags) and the playing of the national anthem by members of the VT Corps of Cadets. Remarks by President George W. Bush, Virginia Governor Tim Kaine, VT officials such as President Charles Steger, and four local religious leaders attempted to acknowledge the pain and provide solace. The ceremony formally ended with the retiring of the colors following Professor Nikki Giovanni's stirring poem, whose last lines read: "We will prevail. We are Virginia Tech." These words cathartically transformed the somber mood of the Convocation and became a popular "secular liturgical formula" in the days and weeks to follow.[33]

Since Virginia Tech is a public state institution, the Convocation's overtly religious elements were clearly designed to be ecumenical and inclusive, but without becoming generic or what some call "nonsectarian." For instance, Governor

Kaine spoke of the importance of Job's story of faith and suffering found in Judaism, Islam, and Christianity. He then referenced "those haunting words that were uttered on a hill on Calvary" to illustrate the natural human tendency to despair and doubt God in the midst of great suffering.[34] President Bush pointed to religion as one of the sources of strength that sustains us and reminded those in attendance that "houses of worship from every faith" across the nation have been praying for us. He also spoke of the comfort and grace that a loving God provides, concluding with the benediction: "May God bless you. May God bless and keep the souls of the lost. And may His love touch all those who suffer and grieve." (Interestingly, this was not the ever-present "May God bless America" refrain of most major presidential addresses since the 1980s.) Several weeks later, on the national day of prayer and remembrance, the president reprised his role as comforter-in-chief when he directed the American people to keep Virginia Tech in their thoughts and prayers.[35]

Although the four leaders representing the Islamic, Jewish, Buddhist, and Christian communities drew more richly and particularly from their own traditions, their remarks reflected sensitivity to the culturally and religiously diverse composition of the audience.[36] Virginia Tech professor Sedki M. Riad, a Muslim, began his remarks with the Bismillah (which he translated, "in the name of Allah, the most merciful and most compassionate") and spoke of the unity in pain that all children of Adam and Eve suffer. He then referenced several qur'anic passages dealing with death and calamity and concluded with "the Islamic greetings of peace: *assalamu alaikum*." Student leader Julie Still, a Buddhist, emphasized the "sacredness and preciousness of life" that she found in all religious teachings, quoted from the Dalai Lama and Daisaku Ikeda about the potential for good in the midst of adversity as well as the importance of maintaining the "courage for nonviolence," and led the audience into a moment of silence. Hillel Executive Director Sue Kurtz drew from the teachings of Ecclesiastes 3:1–8 in Hebrew and English, before urging the community to draw strength from one another in moving "from a time of violence and sorrow to a time of healing and peace." Finally, the Lutheran campus minister William King affirmed the "sovereignty of life over death" without explicitly mentioning the Christian hope of resurrection. He also acknowledged that "the light shines in the darkness and the darkness has not overcome it," though without explicitly mentioning that the words were drawn from John 1:5. His decision to speak *out of* his faith tradition, but not just *to* his community of faith, was apparently one that all the speakers had made.[37]

Weaving interfaith religious elements into official ceremonies like the April 17 Convocation and the official White House response is never easy. My own observation is that these religiously tinged expressions of mourning and solidarity were well received in the Virginia Tech and Blacksburg-area communities, since they played a role in helping the community come together to grieve and to begin the long process of healing.

Nevertheless, I count two notable concerns. First, the national shock and grief over the VT dead, represented and facilitated by the use of the rites and symbols of civil religion (for example, the omnipresent American flag), eclipsed another legitimate cause for national concern and mourning—a particularly violent day in Iraq. On the same day that portions of Cho's final words and video made national and international headlines, five car- and suicide-bomb attacks in Baghdad killed 171 and wounded many others. This was the deadliest day in Baghdad in the two months since the United States had initiated its "troop surge" to secure the city. But those deaths went virtually unnoticed as the nation and even the White House appeared to focus closer to home. President Bush's order to lower the American flag to half-mast at the White House and upon all public buildings and grounds, at home and abroad, came in response to events in Blacksburg, not in Baghdad. Sociologist Ben Agger has argued that this tremendous outpouring of national support and concern for Virginia Tech, but not for either foreign nationals or U.S. service personnel killed in Afghanistan or Iraq, emerged from and contributed to a "narrative of undeserved death." According to this narrative, death as a result of war—even of noncombatants—is regarded as normal, tragic-but-necessary, or otherwise justifiable, while a homicide on a college campus is understood as violating everyday expectations of how things ought to be and therefore is newsworthy.[38] If Agger is right, one might conclude that the American people's generous outpouring of support and concern for Virginia Tech, though deep and sincere, should be considered alongside general indifference to or complacency about the massive loss of life and suffering in the Iraq and Afghanistan wars. Shocking and painful as they are, tragedies like the killings at VT seem easier for American society to confront and to mourn than the myriad tragedies of modern warfare.

The second major concern was the enmeshment in ongoing controversies about the proper role of religion in the public sphere, including whether and how religion should be articulated by state officials in public settings of state-sponsored institutions. Bracketing potential vulnerability to First Amendment establishment clause concerns, both Virginia Tech, as the sponsor of the Convocation, and President Bush waded into contentious theological territory when they implied that the "God" of wisdom and comfort so frequently invoked by the various political dignitaries and the Jewish, Christian, and Muslim leaders was one and the same.[39] The Convocation also left unclear how to square the respect it showed to the Buddhist community, by including the remarks of its representative, with the ceremony's otherwise overtly monotheistic framework and assumptions (for example, in the playing of certain hymns such as "Amazing Grace" and in the content of several of the speeches). Finally, some theological exclusivists were appalled that the Muslim representative had freely invoked Allah and qur'anic passages in his address, while the Christian minister had not even mentioned Jesus or God by name. While Reverend King later explained that he was bound by his responsibility to provide "pastoral care for the whole university community" and not by any personal or university-imposed "political correctness," it is clear from the many pieces of hate mail he received that his critics would have preferred him instead to have boldly preached the Gospel or at least prayed "in Jesus' name."[40]

Fortunately for his critics, someone in the audience was on hand to provide an explicitly Christian response during the Convocation. After the four religious leaders finished speaking, and after a mournful version of "Amazing Grace" ended (but just before the officials at the podium had a chance to resume the program), an unknown man from the floor gave an impromptu shout to the effect of "Now let us all pray in the beautiful words that Jesus our Savior has taught us." After a brief moment of confusion, thousands of people stood up and recited the Lord's Prayer in unison. The unidentified person, whom many believe to have been an outsider to the community, obviously saw no problems—legal, theological, ethical, or otherwise—with calling a religiously diverse audience during an official ceremony of a public university to a collective recital of Christianity's most basic confessional prayer.

Clearly, some see in the design of an explicitly interfaith environment the implicit endorsement of an inclusivist or pluralist theology that, contrary to its intent, is neither shared nor appreciated by all. Convocation planners would have been hard pressed to please everyone or fully harmonize the service's various incongruous elements. Convocation participants themselves became vulnerable to criticism by those who would have handled the religious aspects differently. Finally, no matter how carefully planned a demonstration of interreligious solidarity may be, it can always be disrupted by intervening forces with their own agendas to pursue. All these irrefutable realities point to the highly fraught and ambivalent project of public religion wherein both well-intentioned and self-serving elements inevitably combine.

CONCLUSION

This chapter has explored several attempts to infuse the Virginia Tech shootings with religious meaning. These diverse dimensions reveal the highly varied ways in which religion was brought to bear in order to explain and respond to a seemingly inexplicable tragedy: the trope of the "young angry Muslim" for those habituated to see "Islamic extremism" behind acts of spectacular violence; a decadent culture in decline in the eyes of those primed to interpret America's calamities as a sign of divine disfavor or broken covenant; and the power of public religion for those seeking to bring healing and unity in tragedy's wake. All three responses framed the shootings as more than a local event affecting the Virginia Tech community: they drew from familiar ideas in the American psyche to interpret or make sense of the shootings, thus transforming the tragedy into a national event that both implicated and made an impact on American identity and culture more broadly.

Although I have written positively about the displays of religion in the official ceremonies to remember the victims, legitimate concerns remain about the propriety of employing nationalistic and religiously pluralistic rituals or rhetoric as aids to communal solidarity and healing. Still, it is difficult for civil society in general, and a secular public university in particular, to know how to deal with religious meaning and symbolism, especially when many of its constituents feel that some sort of religious response is called for in a horrific and tragic situation. With that in mind, we should be heartened that the majority of those in the extended Virginia Tech community who turned to religion in the aftermath of the tragedy did so as a source of unity and healing, and not intentionally as a way to exclude, *other*, or condemn. Perhaps we can see in the VT community's response an approximation of what interreligious solidarity might look like, what it might achieve, and some of the obstacles that remain.

NOTES

I thank friends and colleagues in the Virginia Tech community who spoke candidly about their personal reflections: Alex Evans, Bernice Hausman, Elizabeth Hahn Chancey, Jaime Williams, Peter Schmitthenner, Shannon Turner, Scott Russell, William King. Others—Brent Jesiak, Guy Sims, Jong Min Lee, Larry Hincker, and Tom Tillar—provided research assistance, while Brian Britt, Benjamin Sax, Elizabeth Struthers Malbon, Jerome Copulsky, and Matthew Gabriele provided valuable feedback on earlier drafts.

1. The deadliest mass murder in a U.S. school occurred at Bath, Michigan, on May 18, 1927, when a series of bombs killed forty-five people and injured fifty-eight others. Carla Bank, "Worst US Massacre?" *San Francisco Chronicle*, May 2, 2007.

2. Christine Hauser, "Gunman Sent Photos, Video and Writings to NBC," *New York Times*, April 18, 2007.

3. See Jerry Markon, "Did Cho Make Dry Run at Va. Tech?," *Washington Post*, Aug. 11, 2007. Cho also had written "I am Ax Ishmael" near the end of his manifesto, but this instance was not released to the public and received no comment from NBC or the official August 2007 VT Review Panel Report (hereafter VTRPR); http://www.vtreviewpanel.org/report/index.html.

4. Jonah Goldberg's April 18, 2007, blog "Ismail Ax & Cho," http://corner.nationalreview.com/post/?q=MWJlNDUxODE4NjQ5NGY3NjlmMGY4MWIoOGRkNjJhODE=. His reference to Johnny Muhammad is to the "D.C.-area sniper," the person who killed ten people and critically wounded three others during three terrifying weeks in October 2002. Goldberg's blog included a hyperlink to Jerry Bowyer's April 18, 2007, blog, "The Shooter was Another 'Son of Sacrifice,'" http://www.tcsdaily.com/article.aspx?id=041807B.

5. Charles Krauthammer, "Special Roundtable Report" with Brit Hume, *Fox News*, April 18, 2007.

6. Richard Engel, "Cho's 'Religious' Martyrdom Video," April 19, 2007, http://worldblog.msnbc
.msn.com/archive/2007/04/19/157577.aspx.

7. Some parties theorized that in light of Cho's choice of major (English), the allusion might
have been to American literature instead—perhaps to the narrator of *Moby-Dick* (Ishmael) or to
James Fenimore Cooper's novel *The Prairie*, with its ax-wielding outlaw character (Ishmael Bush).
Other suggestions included a misspelling of the Turkish hip-hop artist Ismail YK, computer code
language, and perhaps a different biblical figure named Ishmael than the son of Abraham (see, e.g.,
2 Kings 25:22–26 and Jeremiah 40:7–41:16; 1 Chronicles 8:38; 2 Chronicles 19:11, 23:1; Ezra 10:22).

8. Admittedly, one of Cho's files is titled "am al qaeda," though NBC senior investigative producer Robert Windrem notes that all Cho's titles are "varied and hard to match with their content."
See his "Va. Tech Killer's Strange Manifesto," *NBC News*, April 19, 2007, http://www.msnbc.msn
.com/id/18187368/. Moreover, while terrorism is one of the manifesto's recurring themes, Cho portrays himself as terrorism's *victim*, who is leading fellow "Crusaders of Anti-Terrorism" in violent
opposition to it, because he is "the Anti-Terrorist of America."

9. In his youth, Cho regularly attended the Korean Presbyterian Church of Centreville,
Virginia—a church of the Presbyterian Church of America (PCA) denomination—with his sister
and mother. See "Cho's Mentor Cannot Reconcile Shooter Images, *Star-Ledger*, April 22, 2007; and
"Reasons for Cho's Rampage Might Never Be Explained," Associated Press, April 28, 2007; VTRPR,
33–34.

10. These first two utterances were posted on http://www.msnbc.msn.com/id/18185859/. The
third was reported on *NBC News* (April 18, 2007, evening broadcast) and on CNN's *American Morning* (April 19, 2007).

11. While notions of discipline, sacrificial suffering, and persecution can be found in Pauline
theology and in various biographies of Christian saints, they do not generally suggest a combative
relationship to Christ. See Galatians 6:14; 1 Corinthians 5:5; 11:32; 2 Corinthians 12: 7–10; and
Hebrews 12:5–11, quoting Proverbs 3:11–12. See also Matthew Gabriele, "Cho's Violent Crusade
Ripped from the Middle Ages," *Roanoke Times*, June 2, 2007.

12. Cf. "Thanks to you, I die, like Jesus Christ, to inspire generations of the Weak and Defenseless people—my Brothers, Sisters, and Children—that you fuck"; VTRPR, 8, 12. This text appears
below a photo of Cho as a militarized Christ-like figure: he is sternly facing the camera with arms
outstretched and a gun in each gloved hand.

13. For example, Cho refers in one passage of the manifesto to a "power greater than God"—a
technical impossibility under the traditional understanding of God's omnipotence. Cho might also
be rejecting Christ's ontological uniqueness when he says, "I say we're the Jesus Christs, my Brothers, Sisters, and Children. Jesus Christ exists in us all: Ax Jesus Christ, John Jesus Christ, Jane Jesus
Christ, Seung Jesus Christ. . . ."

14. In one video clip, Cho claims: "Like Moses, I split the sea and lead my people, the weak, the
defenseless, the innocent children of all ages." He repeats this comparison in a slightly altered form
in the manifesto.

15. I briefly discuss the racialized and exoticized coverage of Cho in the press and the VTRPR in
Grace Yia-Hei Kao, "Prospects for Developing Asian American Christian Ethics," *Society of Asian
North American Christian Studies* 3 (2011): 91–102. The upshot was a reinforcement not only of the
perception of Asian Americans as perpetual foreigners, but also of nativist anxieties about
immigrants.

16. Sacvan Bercovitch, *The American Jeremiad* (Madison: University of Wisconsin Press, 1978).

17. Andrew R. Murphy and Jennifer Miller, "The Enduring Power of American Jeremiad," in
Religion, Politics, and American Identity: New Directions, New Controversies, ed. David S. Gutter-
man and Andrew R. Murphy (Lanham, MD: Lexington Books, 2008).

18. These quotes and other material about WBC appear on the websites of the Southern Poverty Law Center such as http://www.splcenter.org/intel/intelreport/article.jsp?sid=184. See WBC's own website for their sign-movies: http://www.signmovies.net/videos/news/wmv.html.

19. Quoted in "Protesters Threaten to Interrupt Funerals of Virginia Tech Victims," *Daily Press* (Newport News, VA), April 19, 2007. See also David Miller, "Group Plans to Picket Va. Tech Funerals," *CBS News*, April 18, 2007.

20. Cf. "They shall put on sackcloth, horror shall cover them. Shame shall be on all faces, baldness on all their heads" (Ezekiel 7:18). See also WBC's video news release, "Virginia Tech Massacre–God's wrath–4-23-07," http://www.signmovies.net/videos/news/wmv.html.

21. WBC, "God Is America's Terror," http://www.signmovies.net/videos/news/wmv.html.

22. WBC, "God Hates Fags," http://www.adl.org/special_reports/wbc/wbc_on_america.asp.

23. See WBC, "America Is Doomed" "Too Late to Pray," www.godhatesfags.com.

24. Phyllis Schlafly, "What Cho Learned in the English Department," http://www.eagleforum .org/column/2007/may07/07-05-09.html.

25. See http://www.eagleforum.org/misc/descript.html.

26. These passages are taken from a description of the importance of education on the Eagle Forum at http://www.eagleforum.org/education/ and at http://www.eagleforum.org/education/in dex2.html.

27. Joy Elmer Morgan, ed., *American Citizens Handbook*, 4th ed. (Washington, D.C.: National Education Association of the United States, 1951), 313.

28. Largely in response to the public outcry regarding WBC's pickets at U.S. military funerals, the Respect for America's Fallen Heroes Act made it illegal to protest or demonstrate within 300 feet of national cemetery entrances (Public Law 109-228, 120 Stat. 387). WBC won a legal victory on March 2, 2011, when the Supreme Court affirmed their First Amendment rights to free speech by ruling against a grieving father's lawsuit against WBC for the emotional pain it caused when members picketed at his Marine son's funeral. (WBC had complied with police instructions to stand 1,000 feet away from the church where the funeral took place.) See *Snyder v. Phelps*, 562 U.S. ___, 131 S. Ct. 1207 (2011).

29. See Jerome Copulsky, "Civil Religion, Mourning and Memorials," Boisi Center for Religion and American Public Life, Boston College, Sept. 19, 2007, 3, http://www.bc.edu/centers/boisi/pub licevents/browse_events_by_date/f07/virginia_tech.html.

30. Timothy Luke, "April 16, 2007 at Virginia Tech—To: Multiple Recipients: 'There is a Gunman on Campus . . . ,'" *Fast Capitalism* 3, no. 1 (2007), http://www.uta.edu/huma/agger/fastcapital ism/3_1/luke.html.

31. Katelynn Johnson, Letter to the *Collegiate Times*, April 25, 2007, http://www.the33rdstone .com/. Several reactions to her letter also appeared there. See also Tim Thornton, "Student Takes on Heavy Responsibility: Appropriateness of Cho's Stone," *Roanoke Times*, April 26, 2007; and Kerry O'Connor, "Permanent Memorial on Drillfield," *Collegiate Times*, April 16, 2008.

32. Tony Campolo, the keynote speaker for the Blacksburg Ecumenical Worship Service for "Celebrating, Healing, and Serving" that was held on November 4, 2007, at Cassell Coliseum, repeatedly emphasized thirty-three in his remarks. The Apostolics of New River Valley, located in Blacksburg, placed on its grounds a memorial that reads: "Remembering VT 33: Families, Students & Faculty." See also Bill King, "Reflections on Last Spring's Tragedy at Virginia Tech—and the Ongoing Challenge to Heal and Forgive," *Furman* 50, no. 4 (Winter 2008): 15.

33. The phrase "secular liturgical formula" comes from King, "Reflections on Last Spring's Tragedy," 17. Variations of "We will prevail. We are Virginia Tech" soon appeared on VT's website and in official e-mails by the administration to the VT community, were reproduced on signs at local shops and businesses, and even made their way into the engravings of the official April 16 Memorial.

34. Tim Kaine, "Transcript of Gov. Tim Kaine's Convocation Remarks," April 17, 2007, http://www.remembrance.vt.edu/2007/archive/kaine.html.

35. George Bush, "President Bush Offers Condolences at Virginia Tech Memorial Convocation," April 17, 2007, http://georgewbush-whitehouse.archives.gov/news/releases/2007/04/20070417-1.html; and "National Day of Prayer, 2007: A Proclamation by the President of the United States of America," April 20, 2007, http://georgewbushwhitehouse.archives.gov/news/releases/ 2007/04/20070420-4.html.

36. For a video stream of the entire April 17, 2007 Convocation, see http://www.hokiesports.com/convocation.html. Many of the Convocation speeches were reproduced in the memorial issue of the *Virginia Tech Magazine*, 29, no. 3 (May 2007), http://www.vtmagazine.vt.edu/memorial07/index.html.

37. For William H. King's Convocation remarks and reflections on his experiences speaking at the memorial service, see his "Naming the Pain, Speaking of Hope: Considerations for Religious Address in Time of Crisis," *Journal of Lutheran Ethics* 7, no. 5 (May 2007). http://www.elca.org/What-We-Believe/Social-Issues/Journal-of-Lutheran-Ethics/Issues/May-2007/Naming-the-Pain-Speaking-of-Hope-Considerations-for-Religious-Address-in-Time-of-Crisis.aspx.

38. Ben Agger, "Cho, Not Che? Positioning Blacksburg in the Political," in *There Is a Gunman on Campus: Tragedy and Terror at Virginia Tech*, ed. Ben Agger and Timothy W. Luke (Lanham, MD: Rowman and Littlefield, 2008), 243–250; quote from p. 245.

39. The use of religious elements such as clergy-led prayer or moments of silence in public schools has been subjected to legal scrutiny and even prohibited in some contexts. While I suspect that Virginia Tech would have been able to defeat any legal challenge to its use of religion in the aftermath of 4/16 in light of the extraordinary and extenuating circumstances, I do find it significant that Virginia Tech has made the written transcripts and even podcasts of many of the speakers at the Convocation available in several venues (e.g., the May 2007 memorial issue of the *Virginia Tech Magazine*, the Virginia Tech: We Remember website, http://www.vt.edu/remember/multimedia/), though not any of the remarks of the four religious leaders (although these have been made available in other venues unaffiliated with Virginia Tech).

40. King, "Naming the Pain, Speaking of Hope."

PART THREE

The Ethics of Violence and War

11

A Just or Holy War
of Independence?

The Revolution's Legacy for Religion, Violence,
and American Exceptionalism

John D. Carlson

In his 2009 Nobel Peace Prize acceptance speech, President Barack Obama sharply distinguished the notion of just wars from holy wars and crusades. In reminding his audience "that no Holy War can ever be a just war," the president censured those who use religion to justify violence. He appealed to prominent just war criteria to describe his position: *jus ad bellum* concerns, such as the view that war must be a "last resort," waged for a just cause such as self-defense, and declared by governments responsible for protecting their citizens (legitimate authority); and *jus in bello* tenets that force must be proportional and must discriminate between combatants and noncombatants. As illustrations, Obama cited certain American wars such as World War II, the 1990 Persian Gulf War, and the battle against al Qaeda (all of which have been distinguished by strong international alliances). Holy wars, by contrast, are characterized by belligerents who lack restraint and "kill in the name of God." While clarifying that religious ideas are not incompatible with peace (having invoked Gandhi and Martin Luther King elsewhere in the speech), Obama nevertheless reinforced a pervasive modern, post-Enlightenment assumption that just wars are predominantly secular, whereas holy wars are "warped," irrational holdovers from a premodern era: "the cruelties of the Crusades are well-recorded."[1] Such assumptions concerning "just/secular" or "holy/religious" categories are hardly confined to presidential rhetoric. They dominate popular opinion, modern scholarship, and even historical understanding of the American Revolution.

The context of Obama's Peace Prize address is significant for several reasons. For one, it followed his address at the U.S. Military Academy ten days earlier in which he announced a major U.S. troop surge to defeat the Taliban insurgency in Afghanistan. The incongruence of awarding the Peace Prize to a commander-in-chief escalating a war, Obama himself admitted, required explication. More importantly, the president situated his remarks squarely within a twenty-first-century milieu of globalization. Forces such as the global extension of human rights, the growing reliance upon international alliances and institutions, and the increasingly important role of international law have served to create global norms that govern political behavior, including the use of force. Obama was keenly aware how this internationalist approach had been upset by his predecessor's controversial decision to invade Iraq in 2003 and the costly, lengthy war that followed. Thus his speech sought to reclaim for America the mantle of international consensus that, critics argued, the Iraq War and a militant—often religiously tinged—form of "American exceptionalism" had undermined.[2] Obama sought to do so by returning his audience's attention to shared, ostensibly universal, secular ideas about war. He also went on to observe how homogenizing forces, such as the "cultural leveling of modernity," globalization, and secularization, are challenged by those who "fear the loss of what they cherish in their particular identities—their race, their tribe, and perhaps most powerfully, their religion." These comments, flowing directly as they did into his discussion of holy war, crystallize how contestations between secular universalism and religious particularism play out in the recent wars that Western and Western-backed nations wage against terrorists and insurgents. Obama's pivot away from the excesses of religious particularism served to distinguish his vision of war from both religiously inspired terrorism and George Bush's version of American exceptionalism.

Nevertheless, in his Oslo speech (and others), Obama has sought to preserve America's special role in the world through a different account of American exceptionalism, one perhaps more precisely called *exemplarism*. The president's rhetoric has fit within a long, distinguished political heritage that emphasizes universal values such as representative government, legitimate authority, individual rights, and the cause of freedom. Since the War of Independence (1775–1783), the United States has invoked such principles to justify the resort to arms. As subsequent revolutions around the world attest (most recently in the Middle East), these are enduring, global, and, say many, universal human aspirations. And they are values that America, at its best, exemplifies and defends.

In light of such claims, though, it would be rather awkward if it turns out, as some scholars suggest, that the American Revolution (an insurgency, no less!) turned out not to be a just war after all. In fact, some go so far as to claim that it bears greater affinities with holy war and the excesses of the religious particularism that Obama condemns. Such discoveries would undercut the president's efforts to situate America's political heritage within a predominantly secular just war framework and cause one to question whether the broader universal principles the United States champions through its wars comport with the historical realities of the war that founded the nation. Absent a historical connection, it becomes easier to second-guess America's commitment to these moral and political principles that continue to define America's place in the world today. In short, it seems hard to square an unjust revolution or a holy war of independence with President Obama's stirring rhetoric and conviction that the United States—through its values and its wars—offers a model for other nations and peoples to follow.

This chapter considers the role that certain religious ideas played in efforts to justify the American Revolution in response to the perceived violence and illegitimate authority of the British Crown. Examining the sermons of Revolution-era minister Josiah Stearns and situating this discussion in light of contemporary just war discourse, I contend that the Revolution does not fit within binary just war/holy war categories as commonly conceived, whether by historians or presidents. Rather, secular and religious elements of just war thought converged in revolutionary formulations of what would later be identified as "American civil religion." This served to foster coherence between the universal and particularist qualities in civil religion and in just war thought as well. The usefulness of religious particularism in just war thought is very much in doubt today, though, given efforts to secularize and universalize the tradition. Yet, as with civil religion, both such elements must be preserved—not simply the aspirations for universalism but the underappreciated insights of religious particularism as well. This is vital if just war thought is to overcome an artificial religious/secular divide and to continue to guide ethically America's use of force. Just war ideas also bear directly upon issues of American exceptionalism concerning the unique roles, responsibilities, and exemptions that America claims for itself in the world. A richer account of religious particularism, including the religious forms, ideas, and rhetoric used in war, can aid efforts to shape how such exceptionalism is conceived and how American exemplarism can be restored.

JUST WAR AND THE QUESTION OF REVOLUTION

"Just war" is a long-standing tradition of ethical, religious, and political inquiry in Western thought for reflecting on the moral justifiability of war.[3] As such, it is an appropriate starting place for considering the question of when, if ever, revolution can be justified. For those looking to classical accounts of the just war tradition, the principle of legitimate authority holds a central place. It is where Thomas Aquinas begins his discussion of war (before considering two other just war principles—just cause and right intention):

> In order for a war to be just, three things are necessary. First, the authority of the sovereign by whose command the war is to be waged. For it is not the business of a private individual to declare war, because he can seek for redress of his rights from the tribunal of his superior. Moreover it is not the business of a private individual

to summon together the people, which has to be done in wartime. And as the care of the common weal is committed to those who are in authority, it is their business to watch over the common weal of the city, kingdom or province subject to them.[4]

Aquinas comments that political authorities are empowered (as attested by scriptural passages such as Romans 13) to use the sword against both "internal disturbances" and "external enemies" that jeopardize the common weal. This reverence accorded to public authorities long precedes and succeeds the thirteenth century, when Aquinas wrote, and can be found among Catholics and Protestants of various persuasions (including pacifists). Some Christian thinkers, such as Martin Luther, are remembered for overextending deference to governments to use coercive force against their own citizens when peace and order are threatened.[5] It is thus no small hurdle to identify resources within just war thinking that would authorize revolution—the wholesale overthrow of a political authority and, in the U.S. case, its replacement with another.

For Aquinas the question of sedition (which is the closest he came to discussing revolution) is linked critically to legitimate authority. Aquinas sees sedition as both similar to and distinct from war, involving those who, intending to fight, are "opposed to a special kind of good, namely the unity and peace of a people." Unlike war, though, sedition cannot be morally justified. Sedition is "a special sin" that sacrifices the common good for the sake of a private good. Whereas war can serve as an instrument of justice, sedition is so opposed to justice and the laws and institutions that preserve the common good that it is "a mortal sin."[6]

Only after issuing this robust condemnation does Aquinas then raise the question of tyranny. While allowing that "disturbing a government of this kind" might be justifiable under certain circumstances, there are two significant caveats. First, he clarifies that tyranny represents a failure of legitimate authority. Tyrants rule for their own private good, not for the common good of the polity; as such, they commit "injury" against the multitude. Consequently, it is the tyrant who is guilty of injustice and sedition. Thus does Aquinas preserve the notion that sedition is *never* justifiable. Second, as to the proper recourse to tyranny, Aquinas grants that no sedition is involved in "disturbing" a tyranny. Nevertheless, such action cannot be justified if "the tyrant's rule be disturbed so inordinately, that his subjects suffer greater harm from the consequent disturbance than from the tyrant's government."[7] Aquinas offers no concrete guidance about how this judgment would be reached or whether the great "consequent disturbance" of revolution could ever be justified. For that matter, "disturbing" a government is hardly the same as overthrowing it. Thomas probably had in mind altering or replacing a specific officeholder who had overstepped his authority—not dispensing with the entire office itself (for example, of monarch or sovereign). Even John Calvin, who was much closer to the modern turn when he defended lower magistrates' divine commission to rise up against a tyrant, never condoned popular revolution: "For though the correction of tyrannical domination is the vengeance of God, we are not, therefore, to conclude that it is committed to us"—meaning "private persons" for Calvin—"who have received no other command than to obey and suffer."[8] At the end of the day, revolution was foreign not only to Aquinas but to just war tradition and political thought through the late Middle Ages. As Hannah Arendt and others have argued, revolution was a concept born in the modern Anglo-American world.[9]

Beyond this general backdrop that tilts against revolution, distinguished scholars of American religious history have greeted specific just war arguments for the American Revolution with skepticism. Historian George Marsden avers of the revolutionaries, "their claim that they faced a case of extreme tyranny seems extravagant. In retrospect it is difficult to believe that [the] British government of America was designed to create utter despotism" as the Declaration of Independences states. "In fact," he continues, "most people of the world, both then and now, have lived with much less freedom than the Americans enjoyed under the British."[10] Mark Noll comments that purported travesties such as the Stamp Act were "nothing but a modest plan for the colonists to share in the expenses of defending the western frontier against the Indians and to do their fair share in easing the crush of Britain's war debt."[11] Back then, Brits paid much higher taxes than Americans as remains true today.[12]

This is not to say that colonists believed the dissolution of government could be undertaken casually. The Declaration did stipulate, "Prudence, indeed, will dictate that Governments long established should not be changed for light and transient causes." Revolution was a special case, even Marsden admits. Given Christian doctrine counseling obedience to public authorities, colonists felt compelled to justify the Revolution "as carefully as any strict just war theorist might desire." Indeed, they invoked reasoning akin to that offered by Aquinas and Calvin as well as John Locke. Nevertheless, after reviewing their case for revolution, Marsden remains unmoved, infused as it was by "partisanship" and "enthusiasm for war." He wonders of American founders, "How could they honestly have believed that they were acting in one of those rare instances of opposition to extreme tyranny such as they described?"[13] Marsden goes on to indict revolutionaries' religious sensibilities, which had the effect of raising "their perceptions of the American national cause to the level of a crusade" and, in turn, establishing a pattern and a "mythology that determined America's behavior in subsequent wars."[14] For his part, Noll explicitly calls out pastors who delivered their sermons as if preaching an actual crusade.

Here, Noll and Marsden join company with other leading lights of American religious history who find just war reflection less germane than the rubric and rhetoric of holy war. Some claim that colonists expected the Revolution to bring

holy history to culmination, ushering in biblical prophecies and eventually leading to the millennium itself, right in America. Asserts Marsden, commenting on
one 1776 election-day sermon by Rev. Samuel West: "The approach of the millennium is identified with the advances of the Continental Army; the American
Revolution is seen as part of God's redemptive plan. The people, the new Israel, is
no longer even simply the elect of the church as it was for the Puritans; it is the
entire American nation."[15] Millennial interpretations also appear in the work of
Americanist Sacvan Bercovitch, who distinguished the religiously significant revolution in America from the secular rebellions of Old World Europe: "Revolution
in America was the vehicle of providence. It took the form of a mighty, spontane-
ous turning forward, both regenerative and organic, confirming the prophecies of
Scripture as well as the laws of nature and history. And in all this, it stood dia-
metrically opposed to rebellion. The Revolution fulfilled the divine will." Whereas
rebellion had signified disobedience, revolution augured divine progress.[16]

Other scholars claim that religious ardor and aspirations for salvation became
indistinguishably enmeshed in the cause of overthrowing tyranny. Puritan
thought internalized America's special calling in the world while externalizing
politically a collectivized pursuit of righteousness. Nathan Hatch puts it this
way: "America would become [liberty's] permanent sanctuary since God would
not allow liberty to be banished from the earth. And because the future of liberty, the cause of God, depended entirely upon the war's outcome, the conflict
assumed all the emotional intensity of a crusade of heaven and hell. Americans
were not fighting for themselves, but for the well-being of the whole world."[17]
Hatch, like Marsden and Noll, looks to Revolution-era sermons to buttress his
views, for they "extended the canopy of religious meaning so that even the cause
of liberty became sacred."[18]

Historians claiming that politics and war were sacralized can point to the
widespread rhetorical outbursts of those who equated religious liberty with political liberty from Britain; who compared King George to the Anti-Christ; and
who, likening their cause to the Protestant Reformation, viewed the possibility of
establishing an Anglican bishop in the colonies as religious coercion and the
suppression of true faith. Given this heady religious brew (following the already
intoxicating revivalism of the First Great Awakening), one rightly begins to wonder how a sober case for a just revolution—rather than a holy one—can be made
at all.

HOLY WAR REVISITED

There are other historians, however, who contest militant religious interpretations of American revolutionaries.[19] Melvin B. Endy, in a thorough and thoughtful essay, critically examines the just war / holy war debate. Unlike other histori-

ans, Endy finds that colonists' rationale for war was more political than religious; that just war reasoning outweighed holy war overtures; and that religious idioms and arguments for revolution were more seamlessly and harmoniously integrated into "commonsense" political reflection than many historians have claimed. Like other historians, Endy draws from Revolution-era sermons. His findings are backed by a review of more than two hundred sermons, mostly by Congregationalist ministers, including some whom other historians identify with holy war ardor. Endy certainly acknowledges the prominence of religious ideas and tropes—these are sermons, after all—but he does not find untrammeled zealotry and millennialism everywhere dominating and sacralizing political causes. In this regard, the Revolutionary War aligns more neatly with just war heritage than holy war crusading. Endy summarizes, "While it is true that holy war themes are marked in the writings of about one-fifth of the ministers, including a number of prominent men, the Revolutionary clergy for the most part presented themselves not as priests of a holy people but as the religious and moral leaders of a body politic fighting what they perceived to be a just war."[20] Interestingly, Endy reaches this conclusion even though several historians he critiques do not discuss "holy war" explicitly. To understand this move and Endy's methodology requires returning briefly to the Middle Ages.

When Thomas Aquinas codified the central criteria of a just war, he could not have anticipated that, five centuries later, non-Catholic Christians would use them to justify the overthrow of a divinely instituted king and to initiate arguably the most important political experiment in modern history. Nor could Aquinas have anticipated that, another two centuries later, historians would commemorate the U.S. bicentennial by returning again to these criteria to debate the justness of the American Revolution. Endy makes his case against a holy War of Independence by showing how other historians misapply holy or sacred modifiers to transform the traditional principles of legitimate authority, just cause, and right intention set out by Aquinas.[21] First, Endy challenges portrayals, by Bercovitch and others, of revolutionaries who went beyond the traditional legitimate authority criterion to proclaim "sacred authority," presumably out of a belief in national election or a God-given commandment to wage battle. Endy counters: "Historians who believe that the clergy justified the war primarily by reference to America's divine calling or sacred status tend to regard all references to biblical history and all assertions of similarity between Israel and America as signifying an intention to sacralize the American experience. The evidence suggests, however, that the Bible provided primarily a set of sagas and heroes that served to reinforce and legitimate the Real Whig ideology and its application to the war but without granting it the status of revealed truth."[22]

Second, in Aquinas the principle of just cause typically permits use of force to prevent or respond to some wrong or injustice. Endy challenges others' arguments that ministers boosted the colonists' cause to a holy or sacred level; instead he foregrounds the importance of British Real Whig influences that emphasized natural law, natural rights, representative government, and limited govern- mental powers. These principles led colonial ministers and their congregants to believe they were waging a defensive war in direct response to concrete injuries and injustices. The belief in universal rights, Endy argues, actually mitigated the strong millennialist interpretations that others have seen in America's chosen status and thus "precluded the kind of subordination of human rights to divine causes of which holy wars are made. If all human beings have certain *inalienable* rights, one cannot use a religious rationale to justify forfeiture of those rights . . . . [I]n the Revolutionary era reliance on natural rights served as a brake on the crusading mentality. There is little evidence that large numbers of the Revolu- tionary clergy era idolized their cause to a significant extent."[23] Endy does not dispute Hatch's claim that divergent streams of millennialism and Real Whig thought converged during the Revolution. Rather, he simply disagrees that the two tributaries emptied into a rushing river of holy war fervor whereby a sacred cause overtook the more tempered stream of republican political thought.

Finally, and perhaps most important, Endy does not find that Revolution-era sermons were suffused with righteous zeal approaching a crusade. The just war tenet of right intention requires that war be approached for the sake of "securing peace" and with proper inner motives; invoking Augustine, Aquinas contrasted such motives with "the cruel thirst for vengeance" or "lust of power." While this is surely a difficult criterion to evaluate in any war, Endy asserts that the revolu- tionary ministers' generally mournful attitudes toward fighting places them firmly in the just war tradition; only a small minority exhibited a "crusading zeal." In spite of just war's strong Catholic heritage, which some scholars distin- guish from Puritans' crusading mentality,[24] Endy's study shows that Protestant (mostly Congregationalist) colonial ministers specifically referenced just war principles in ways that undercut this generalization. Thus does the narrative of a holy revolution begin to fade in the light of countervailing evidence. A brief, more detailed look at one pastor's sermons reveals not only the texture of just war reasoning but also how profoundly it penetrated the Protestant mind.

JOSIAH STEARNS AND THE MORAL CASE
FOR REVOLUTION

On January 29, 1777, the Reverend Josiah Stearns preached two sermons to his congregation in Epping, New Hampshire, during a public fast occasioned "on Account of the Unnatural and Distressing War with Great Britain in Defence of Liberty."[25] The sermons remind congregants (and readers of the published ver- sions) that, under certain prescribed circumstances of a just war, Christians are morally justified in taking up the sword (or musket). For Stearns, the current "War with Great Britain" clearly meets such conditions. But even a preacher cannot simply assert that a war is just. Rather, each person must undertake "a fair, impartial, often-repeated enquiry into the right of it [war], that we may act with a safe conscience, and be able to justify our proceeding." Stearns's sermons presume there is a deep-seated, even natural antipathy toward war. "War, indeed, is an awful scene; that mankind, all made of one blood, should kill and devour one another, and by the destroying sword, make even rivers of human blood to flow—how horrible the thought!"[26]

To make his case for revolution, Stearns uses the rhetorical form found in Aquinas and other Catholic just war scholastics, which includes *objectiones* and *responsiones*. When presented with the objection that Christians are taught to renounce fighting, Stearns *answers that* "Christians should never give occasion for the use of the sword; nor should they lightly and hastily take occasion to use it." But, he goes on, "where Christians are required to give up their liberty, and submit to slavery," the violations of the same rights they hold "in common with the rest of mankind" permit them "to defend themselves by the sword."[27] Stearns discusses several prudential *jus ad bellum* considerations. For example, he specifies that recourse to force is not authorized for "inconsiderate matters" but only when absolutely necessary; after "milder measures have been tried and pursued" (last resort); when there is a "rational hope" and reasonable "prospect of success." Like early just war forbearer St. Augustine, who lamented the misery of war, Stearns counsels that such "an awful scene" as war "is a matter of too solemn, and weighty importance, to be lightly and hastily engaged in"—and never without "the greatest reluctancy" and the "most serious enquiry" into its lawfulness and necessity.[28]

The bulk of Stearns's argument centers upon the three primary *jus ad bellum* criteria advanced by Aquinas centuries before. He does not address them as distinct conditions, as Aquinas had; rather, the Revolution provided the context in which legitimate authority, just cause, and right intention converged in a moral-political-religious argument against "violence" broadly speaking and against British violence in particular.

To begin with, perhaps no distinction in Western political thought is as important as the authority that public officials possess in lieu of private citizens. Individuals who use force but lack public authority participate in violence. The distinction, crucial to Christian ethics and steeped in scriptural references, lies behind both Aquinas's and Stearns's articulations of *legitimate authority*. Stearns starkly lays out prohibitions against "private violence" as well as "private revenge," both of which magistrates and public authorities possess divine mandates to restrain. Though he contests the medieval notion of divine right, Stearns maintains that magistrates possess a "divine right to rule well; but not to oppress the people." Stearns offers this "sober, qualified" view: "I believe that magistracy is of divine right; but I believe withal, that God has left it with the people to choose their form of Government, and appoint and constitute the magistrate." Referencing biblical notions of covenant, he reminds congregants that each party has certain duties: public authorities to rule well and private citizens to obey. When, however, the magistrate "wantonly tramples on their most important rights," this covenant is broken, and the people incur the right to "renounce their allegiance" and "recall the delegated power."[29] Stearns here draws critical distinctions between a magistrate's lawful use of force for the sake of the public good and a tyrant's "violence" against his subjects (namely, violating their God-given, rights that all people enjoy), which erodes the sovereign's authority.

Stearns actually backs into the notion of *just cause* through this understanding of legitimate authority that is forsaken through violence. The violations of subjects' individual rights is an injury—an injustice that must be challenged. (Note here that the Latin root *jus*, often translated as "right," is also the basis of "injury" and "injustice." Similarly, *violence* and *violate* share a common stem: *violare*.) In terms that Aquinas put forth, a tyrant rules for his or her own private good rather than for the common weal. Acting as if a private individual, a tyrant forsakes the public authority that otherwise legitimates the use of force and distinguishes it from private violence. Throughout his sermons, Stearns repeatedly denounces the violence of the Crown's oppression and abuse of power. In such extreme cases, a people's resort to force becomes justified, even a duty: "Self-preservation, self-defense from extreme violence and wrong, is the great and universal law of nature, which I dare say the gospel does not disannul."[30]

Finally, Stearns's deep concern with *right intention* also flows out of this discussion of legitimate authority and his understanding of violence. According to Aquinas (following Augustine), in order for a war to be considered just, a just cause alone is insufficient. Proper motives also must be present and violent ones avoided such as lust for cruelty, aggrandizement, and revenge. Indeed these are the violent dispositions that public authorities are ordained to restrain and that individuals are assumed to overcome when acting in their public capacity as soldiers or officials. It follows that those declaring a just revolution must not arouse internal violence. Stearns struck this Augustinian chord of Puritan piety when, warning against the lusts that war stirs up, he called for "mourning, and deep humiliation before the Lord, and a ferocious concern to obtain pardon and reconciliation with him." In response to the objection that the gospel forbids revenge and requires forbearance, Stearns answers, "When there is great necessity for using the sword, it must not be from malice and a desire for revenge: Wo to them that use it thus, be it even so just a cause: Its just and lawful use, even on the weightiest occasions, is to obtain peace and quietness on terms of reason and right, which cannot otherwise be had."[31] Here just war's traditional focus on right intention is reinforced by the Puritan heritage of spiritual introspection and discernment; for early Americans, this entailed detailed diaries documenting concerns about inner motive, intentionality, and ordering of the soul. Viewed within a just war frame, such private matters are neither irrelevant nor impervious to public life.

While much of Stearns's (and Aquinas's) discussion of just war can be couched in secular terms, it is also replete with different religious, scriptural, and spiritual themes. Stearns's sermons instruct congregants that, in the case of the war with Britain, reason and revelation point in the same direction. Indeed, "the voice of reason, is always the voice of God."[32] Stearns makes extensive use of religious allegory and biblical allusion. The sermon's opening passage from Judges 20:26–28 references Israel's misgivings and assurance from God that battle against one's brother, the children of Benjamin, can be justified—an obvious reference to the reticence of many colonists to wage war against their English kinsmen. Yet this religious language strikes the attentive reader far less as an appeal to holy war than as an explanatory device common to Puritan thought that draws parallels from the Bible (especially the Hebrew scriptures) to illustrate how political principles of government applied to the particular context of the American colonies. Stearns's sermons make clear—more so than is acknowledged by historians working with holy war categories—that pivotal just war tenets provided important moral and religious resources for preachers and their audiences during the Revolution. The explicitly religious elements of Stearns sermons, we see later, remain important for other reasons as well. In the remainder of this chapter, I move beyond adjudicating the historical debate over a just or holy revolution to consider the relevance to contemporary debates and how Stearns offers helpful insights and resolutions to them.

JUST WAR AND CIVIL RELIGION: FORMATIONS OF THE UNIVERSAL AND THE PARTICULAR

In spite of different interpretations of the Revolution, the historians discussed above generally agree that intellectual justifications for the revolution drew from two distinct yet often overlapping sources: from republican political theories about self-evident truths, reason, human equality, natural law, inalienable rights, and theories of legitimate government; and from biblical traditions emphasizing God's providential workings in human history, early Americans' understandings of chosenness, and their commitments to piety and religious liberty. The extent to which historians accent religious or republican elements helps explain how they have plotted the Revolutionary War at different points along a just war–holy war spectrum. For example, historians who associate the revolution with crusade charge that, in spite of having legitimate political grievances, revolutionaries "vastly inflated [their cause's] importance by sanctifying it with biblical imagery."[33] Meanwhile, those emphasizing just war's influence highlight biblical history's allegorical role as a complement to republican political philosophy.

Perhaps more important than adjudicating whether the Revolution was more holy than just (or more religious than political) is understanding the roles these different intellectual strands have played—and perhaps still play—in moral debates about war. For as President Obama's Peace Prize address illustrates, holy war and just war often stand in for subtler tensions between the particular and the universal, between religion and the secular. Obama's speech epitomizes modern thought, which generally assumes that universal and secular principles (including those associated with just war) constructively serve to check extreme or violent religious particularism.

Sermons such as Josiah Stearns's, however, suggest that just war reflection during the Revolution was more synthetic—more so than historians of the Revolution have appreciated and more so than just war thought often is today. That is, Stearns seamlessly reconciled universalist and particularist approaches, blending religious and republican reasoning. Again, the dimension associated with Real Whig political thought offered a view of governance that emphasized protection of natural and inalienable rights to which all human beings, so endowed by their Creator, possessed. Such universal truths were "self-evident," knowable by human reason, and entailed deep claims of conscience, as Stearns himself preached. By virtue of a certain view of human nature, the rights that human beings require for their flourishing include life, liberty, property, and other pursuits on which human happiness rest. As the Declaration of Independence itself suggests, a government that violates what is natural and good for human beings—as enshrined in the "Laws of Nature and of Nature's God"—becomes "destructive of these ends" and loses its legitimate authority, or, to use Stearns's language, performs "violence" against its people. Such a government is worthy of neither obedience nor even preservation. The Declaration goes on to list a long train of abuses specific to the American colonies: imposition of standing armies, unfair taxes, denial of habeas corpus. Yet the signers perceived clearly the need to appeal to (if not set forth) broader ideals that could justify, morally and politically, overriding the well-established presumption against sedition and rebellion.[34]

The explanatory power of universal moral and political principles, of course, still requires attentiveness to the cultural, religious, and political context of early America. Thus colonists also justified their resort to arms in prose that was tailored to their particular identity, circumstances, and religious character. Here biblical religion and history come into play. Many colonists viewed themselves as citizens of a "new Israel": Winthrop's "city on a hill," chosen by God for special purposes, and guided by providence to exemplify a new form of governance wherein liberty (both religious and political) as well as personal and collective righteousness could be assured. Historians of colonial America have emphasized the special calling colonists felt as well as the sense of celestial possibility in the new America. This view of the American self, deeply imbued with Puritan piety, relied less upon rationalism, universal laws of nature, and the laws of nations to justify independence. Cogent precedents found in the Bible, particularly the Hebrew scriptures detailing the Israelites' escape from slavery under Egypt's Pharaoh, spoke directly to the religious mind. Colonists, seeing themselves similarly enslaved, staged their escape from, and revolt against, British tyranny.

The two modes of revolutionary justification, the republican/Whig and the biblical/Puritan strands, were mutually reinforcing and often indistinguishable even within the same voice. A prime example: chief republican articulator and author of the Declaration, Thomas Jefferson, supported as the new national emblem an image of the Israelites' flight from captivity, featuring the motto "Rebellion to tyrants is obedience to God." The convergence of republican and biblical strands also characterizes Stearns and other Protestant ministers of the era who understood that revolution could not be justified lightly (especially given Calvinists' intense preoccupation with order) or undertaken simply by appealing to providence, divine mission, or a sense of American chosenness. Some claim to broader principles of universal moral law, natural rights, and proper governance also was necessary—an appeal knowable by reason and not dependent upon any particular religious identity. The multiple influences converged indistinguishably for some, such as "New Divinity" ministers for whom "nothing would have seemed so inherently spiritual . . . as the moral dimensions of political events."[35] In short, the Revolution provided an occasion on which the threads of universalism and particularism, of rationalism and pietism, of republicanism and religion became woven into the warp and woof of the new American civil religion. In this sense, the Revolution marked a crucial moment in the development of a new mindset in the emerging American nation.[36]

Crosscutting both republican theories of governance and Puritan forms of piety was the political concept of legitimate authority. As a just war tenet, the mutual reinforcement that legitimate authority offered to and received from both strands of American civil religion has shaped American formulations of just war thought in ways that many contemporary just war theorists, whether working from religious or secular frameworks, often have overlooked. Yet clearly, just war reflection during the Revolution provided the early American conscience with a mode of religious and ethical reflection about violence by which the solemn decision to recall one's delegated power—by force of arms—could be evaluated and ultimately justified. Just war arguments for the war with Britain successfully bridged the universal and particularist elements of early American thought in ways that contemporary just war reflection in the United States and beyond seems unable to do. The present inability to preserve such unity between formations of the universal and the particular has become a liability that under-cuts perceptions of American legitimacy and action in the global arena.

JUST WAR AND AMERICAN EXCEPTIONALISM
IN CONTEMPORARY CONTEXT

From colonial to contemporary contexts, American civil religion's political and religious strands not only have shaped historically the nation's identity; these for-mations of the universal and the particular have influenced how Americans today perceive their nation's place in the world—and, in turn, how other peoples and nations perceive the United States. Nowhere has it been more important than in deliberating on U.S. wars and their moral legacies. Whether looking to historians of American religion reflecting on the Revolution during the nation's bicentennial (which occurred significantly as the nation was considering the legacies of the Vietnam War), or to President Obama's global address contrasting his philosophy of war and peace to the allegedly messianic approach of his predecessor[37]—both cases would seem to caution against allowing ardent, religiously infused, particu-larist approaches to war to overtake more secular, limited approaches based upon universal ideals that can be defended on rational, consensually shared political grounds.

Such reservations about religious particularism also emerge in two related debates in contemporary life: one involving an internal crisis within just war thought over how the tradition should be conceived; and, second, a broader crisis about what is often called "American exceptionalism." Situating these debates together within the context of the American Revolution suggests how the Revo-lution's legacy might still be instructive. I am arguing that the universal and particularist strands of American civil religion *each* must be sustained if Ameri-can just war thought is to overcome its internal divisions and cohere as a moral-political theory to which the United States—as a leading actor on the global stage—can lay strong, compelling, and exemplary claim. Contrary, though, to those who conceive religious particularism as a recurring source of hubris, ex-tremism, or messianism that secularism must contain, preserving vital religious elements, such as those found in Josiah Stearns's sermons, can serve to counsel humility and restraint.

That the United States has become the seat of just war reflection today is not unrelated to the fact that, as the foremost military power in the world, it has en-gaged in war numerous times during the twentieth and twenty-first centuries. Speeches by Presidents George H. W. Bush and Barack Obama specifically in-voking just war tenets sufficiently demonstrate this connection.[38] Another sign of just war's renaissance is the growth in scholarly engagement, including inter-nal debates between rival approaches to the tradition. One important division among these scholars is whether and how just war thinking should reinforce American particularism and exceptionalism (including how restrictive or permissive just war reasoning should be). These divisions are related to the ways in which different just war camps conceive violence and the role of just war to restrain violence—a discussion that connects back to both Aquinas and Stearns.

Archbishop of Canterbury Rowan Williams epitomizes one way of thinking about the American just war context through what he calls just war's "presumption against violence." Invoking Aquinas, he defines violence as an external action that violates claims of nature and justice. It is a force imposed against the will, in violation of goods that human beings hold in common and pursue by nature. Williams, again following Aquinas, distinguishes such violence from coercion, including the state's use of force, which can be used legitimately to protect human beings' pursuits of the common good. Whereas private individuals use violence in the wrongful furtherance of their own ends, governments employ justifiable coercion to preserve public goods (including the protection of individual rights). This mandate requires that governments offer public reasons, based upon consensual (international) norms, for their actions. When a state acts against such norms, however, as Williams argued that the United States did when invading Iraq, it commits violence "in a way analogous to a private person."[39]

Williams represents a school of just war thought I call *presumptionism*, which holds that the "presumption against war" is a foundational principle that all states should share, and that this presumption should be overridden only in extreme circumstances, when all or the most vital just war criteria are met in consensually held ways. This just war approach—as a shared, ostensibly universal theory, girded in moral foundations of human reason, natural law, and *jus gentium* (the law of nations); codified politically in international law and institutions; and administered through the prudence and virtue of political leaders—prevents any one state from losing "the power of self-criticism" and becoming "trapped in a self-referential morality."[40] Not surprisingly, most just war presumptionists opposed the Iraq War. Those concerned that the United States exerts undue exceptionalism in the world—exempting itself from shared norms because of its unique history, chosen status, presumed importance, unparalleled power, or national interests—can look to this more restrictive just war approach to check a nation's particularist tendencies.

The other dominant school of just war thought rejects the presumptionist starting point. Better, its advocates argue, to propose that just war begins with a presumption *for* justice. Because the world is a violent place, there should be no presumption against using force to counter aggression. These just war *classicists* (again, my term) argue that the primary *ad bellum* criteria set out by Aquinas (and others)—especially the mandate of legitimate authority—affirm this view and provide statesmen with ethical guidance in the resort to war.[41] As George

Weigel states, in an exchange contrasting his view with Williams's, just war provides "context-setting moral judgment about the obligation of public authority to pursue the peace of right order—which includes the obligation of providing for the security of one's people against aggression."[42] Sometimes dubbed "just war as statecraft," this view is less concerned than presumptionism with developing a universal moral-legal framework of war than with shaping a political ethic for how governments should—in moral fashion—fulfill their mandate to protect the common good, defend citizens against violence, and establish order and justice. This camp defends a more permissive approach that allows, and may even require, a government to make moral-political arguments, the legitimacy of which do not depend upon the consent of other nations and international organizations. Just war as statecraft appreciates the role of international law but recognizes it is subject to divergent interpretations and significant limitations regarding its enforcement. Just war statecraft is a more self-referential position, which confers a state's leaders with the moral prerogative to use force even when it conflicts with the "prudential judgments" of international lawyers, religious leaders, or other just war critics. Leading just war thinkers who supported the Iraq War such as Weigel often fall in this camp, with some invoking a particularism that extols America's exceptional roles and responsibilities in a violent world, including protecting victims of aggression in other nations.[43]

We have, then, two accounts of just war: one aspires to a universal moral-political theory entailing rational agreement and international consensus on how just war principles are to be applied; the other views the obligations of security, self-defense, and a right order of justice as essential moral responsibilities that a particular nation's citizens can expect from their government (or that oppressed citizens in other parts of the world can expect from a particular nation such as the United States). The locus of accountability differs: the former conceives of a moral-political community above or beyond the state; the other locates moral and political accountability in one's citizens (or even in oppressed citizens of other countries). Both approaches speak the language of justice, and both decry violence: just war presumptionism is concerned especially with the violence and injustices states commit when they act outside of a shared moral vocabulary of war; just war statecraft is most concerned with the violence and injustices that can befall people when states fail to protect them. The former extols a universal standard that would contain the excesses of American particularism; the other accommodates—and, at times, extols—American exceptionalism, noting the evil and violence that would prevail in the world if the United States failed to use military force—even without international consensus.

Recalling Stearns's just war argument for the Revolution helps us close the distance between these two rival positions, since his sermons offer intellectual support for both. For example, recall how Stearns's case for revolution draws upon classical just war reasoning, as found in Augustine and Aquinas, especially the primary *ad bellum* criteria of legitimate authority, just cause, and right intention. Such "classical" intellectual underpinnings ground the just war statecraft approach. Interestingly, Stearns unifies his discussion of these three criteria under the rubric of violence to which a just war (or a just revolution) responds: the violence of a tyrant who squanders his legitimate authority by acting against the common good; the abuse and violation of people's natural rights; and the violent dispositions that must be avoided even when defending a just cause. In so doing, though, Stearns articulates a rather stark "presumption against violence," including the necessity of avoiding violence in one's office, actions, or motives. Even classicist advocates of just war statecraft would do well to concede this point, though they will still quite understandably differ with presumptionists on how violence is conceived (especially with respect to the U.S. invasion of Iraq).

While the debate between Williams and Weigel (and those they represent) may strike some as inside baseball, these just war differences also provide a lens through which to view the universal and particular elements of American exceptionalism. Again, Josiah Stearns can be said to bat for both teams. On one hand, his and other revolutionary ministers' appeals to force were justified with respect to universal principles of governance, especially republican/Whig views that a government's legitimate authority rests upon its protection of its citizens' individual rights—natural rights guaranteed to all people to pursue basic human goods. When, however, a government acts as an "external force" to hinder citizens' rights, it commits violence against them. The presumption against violence in Thomas Aquinas and Rowan Williams lends warrant to Josiah Stearns's portrayal of revolution as a people's effort to "defend themselves from violence, and right themselves from extreme wrong."[44] Universal notions of legitimate authority, individual rights, and violence do not depend upon national particularity. Rather, they are based upon beliefs about natural equality and human nature—knowable by reason, conscience, and experience. One certainly can find evidence of such universal aspirations in sermons of the American Revolution, and one can observe them in the chants and placards of those who participated in the Arab Spring of 2011.

Of course, one also can conceive Stearns's sermons as an early articulation of "just war statecraft"—a particularist position that yields latitude to a particular people to conceive how their specific history, grievances, religion, and identity inform their reflections and decisions about war. Stearns invokes in morally meaningful and religiously resonant ways the Puritan distinctiveness and emerging national character of many early Americans. This particularist thrust of Stearns's just war statecraft allows space for citizens to lay claim to their collective experiences, values, identity and culture on which the work of politics vitally depends. Such an approach recognizes that nations often make moral-political arguments using their own distinctive vernaculars, including religious ones. Of course, particularistic idioms and identities can give way to a particularlistic politics that refuses to conform to shared norms and conventions of the day. Certainly for its time, the American Revolution was an extreme deviation from prevailing norms and conventions.

For these same reasons, just war particularism can seem to fall prey to the trap of "self-referential morality" and worrisome forms of exceptionalism—especially when given voice through biblical and religious language. Revolutionary metaphors of America as the "new Israel," we saw, can have a triumphalist ring. Whether found in Revolutionary sermons or more recent "unilateral" foreign policy decisions, American exceptionalism strikes discordant notes in the ears of many. One can understand, then, the concern that such reasoning cannot stand the test of universalization. One might ask whether just war statecraft is too permissive to check religiously exceptionalist impulses so as to prevent a holy war or crusade from taking hold. At a minimum, just war statecraft seemed to authorize what Williams viewed as special exemptions that allowed the United States to bypass "international processes" during the 2003 invasion of Iraq. But is this the only way to conceive American exceptionalism and the religious dimensions thereof?

IN DEFENSE OF RELIGIOUS PARTICULARISM

The struggle to sustain coherence between the universal and particularist elements of American civil religion and of just war thought is surely greater today than it was during the Revolution. There is no simple way to harmonize what have become competing elements within American thought, with scholars, citizens, and even presidents increasingly emphasizing the need to restrain religious particularism. Evidence of this appears in arguments against holy war (and holy revolution), critiques of American exceptionalism, and deep reservations about just war statecraft (which seems to give cover to such views). Secular, universal political principles, it is assumed, serve to limit the damages associated with religious particularism. This is an understandable, if somewhat misguided, assumption. I conclude by proposing a different path, one that addresses these worries by shoring up the particularist strands of American civil religion, just war thought, and American exceptionalism and by binding them back to the more universal elements. Rather than assuming that religious particularism exacerbates violence and war, I want to show briefly how it also can counsel humility and militate against war's excesses.

Much has been made already of the triumphalist variant of American exceptionalism—what Canadian philosopher-statesman Michael Ignatieff dubs "exemptionalism."[45] The view seems to underwrite special claims to preemptive force (some supported by just war statecraft theorists) as well as U.S. deviations from various international treaties and norms. Ignatieff also identifies other forms of American exceptionalism, none of which are particularly laudable. What he does not discuss, however, is what I would call the *exemplarist* variant: the view that, by embracing certain universal norms, the United States can serve as a moral exemplar to be esteemed and emulated by others throughout the world. In this account, the United States possesses a *premier but not exclusive status* with respect to standards shared broadly across the globe.[46] American exemplarism draws our attention to the way in which founding documents such as the Declaration of Independence and the U.S. Constitution have inspired people around the world and served as standards for over a hundred other nations that have adopted similar principles. Or to President Obama's claim about the essential role the U.S. wars have played in securing global peace.[47] Of course, this status also entails special responsibility to live up to high expectations, which, in turn, subjects the United States to acute scrutiny whenever American exemplarity is wanting. Obama seems to have understood the implications of this model for military force when he asserted that "America—in fact, no nation—can insist that others follow the rules of the road if we refuse to follow them ourselves. For when we don't, our actions appear arbitrary and undercut the legitimacy of future interventions, no matter how justified."[48]

Within the exemplarist model I am commending, the embrace of the universal need not exist apart from religious particularism. To illustrate, I return a final time to Josiah Stearns to consider how American civil religion—and, by extension, American just war thought—might continue to draw strength from its biblical roots and pietist offshoots as found in the jeremiad tradition. America's Puritan origins are often decried for cultivating a sense of collective righteousness and chosenness that is perceived to underwrite American arrogance and exceptionalism, especially regarding foreign policy and war.[49] Few, however, consider how biblical sources also seek to mitigate American hubris. What is needed at this point, I would suggest, is a reconnection with jeremiadic thinking that perceives tragedy and war as a call for retrospection, humility, repentance, and, in the words of Reverend Stearns, "reconciliation with God." Puritan jeremiads traditionally sought to convince listeners of their pride, sins, and imperfections. The intent was to deflate self-righteousness—not to stoke it. Stearns did not counsel simply against individual misdeeds but also against political sins. "[T]here is no doubt but that America has been faulty in many things," he implored, reminding his congregants that "there is blame, more or less, on both sides." And even while he casts comparatively more blame on the "aggressor" Britain (whose "violence had risen to such an height, as to make it a matter of plain duty, and indispensable necessity, to take the sword of self-defense") he does not overlook the "rash and unjustifiable" speeches and actions of certain

Americans who overstated their cause and overlooked the collective sins of the community.[50]

Skeptics might question whether Stearns was merely doling out such sermonic platitudes, perhaps to provide moral or spiritual cover for the war. But let us also recall that his sermons were delivered during a public fast (just one of many after the war began) that called the entire community to exercise humility and "moral sincerity." Indeed, he singles out those who feign humility and fail to adopt the rightful attitude and proper piety that fasting, prayer, and humbling before God require. Stearns contrasts these God-provoking feigners with sincere and devout followers who "are mourning before the Lord, for the sins of the Land."[51] This preoccupation with collective humility and collective guilt—even when at war for a just cause—is the culminating message of Stearns's sermon. Returning to his opening passage from Judges, he reminds his listeners that "even when justly called to arms," and even when the Israelites enjoyed God's divine favor against Benjamin, God still uses the enemy to chasten and correct "his people" and bring them to a shared understanding of their failings. His stern rebukes clearly are intended to prevent early Americans' sense of chosenness from going to their heads: "may the goodness of God to so undeserving, and ill-deserving a people, lead us to repentance."[52] If anything, Stearns reminds his congregants and fellow colonists that any exceptional status, divine favor, or blessing they receive is through no doing of their own. Indeed, it accrues in spite of those "sins of the Land" for which they are accountable. An exemplarist form of American exceptionalism, then, entails confessing one's shortcomings, walking humbly before God, and giving an honest public accounting of when exemplarity has been wanting.

It remains to be seen of course whether such pious reflection can function similarly today, when ridicule and contempt are common reactions to Puritan voices of the past. For this reason, it may be optimistic to think that jeremiadic reflection, if more widely appreciated or adopted, could improve America's standing in the wider world. Nevertheless, it would be wiser to preserve than to neglect those moments when Americans have urged humility and contrition in times of war, especially when emanating from deep wells of religious conviction.

To conclude, although Stearns preached his just war arguments as sermons, they rest as much on republican defenses of universal rights, classical just war notions of legitimate authority, and a presumption against violence as on explicit biblical or theological thinking. These more universal elements, so central to American civil religion, are not exclusive to the United States but are found in moral and religious traditions of peoples and nations around the world. Stearns's religious particularism—his extensive use of biblical exegesis and spiritual exhortation—generally serves as a guide to the conscience and a call for humility and reconciliation with God. Alongside jeremiadic tropes of other Revolution-era preachers, such religious reflection reinforces the moral seriousness with which just war thinking, as a guide to the individual and collective conscience, should be approached. For, whether in the eighteenth or twenty-first century, so long as the call to arms remains a vital means of "defending the common rights of mankind" and countering the violence that hinders human beings' pursuit of the common good—as history suggests it does—the United States and other nations of the world will be well served by preserving a broad panoply of ways for deliberating soberly on the ethical dimensions of revolution and war.

NOTES

This chapter builds upon themes first explored in my "Just War, Just Revolution: Self-Evident Truths, Biblical Roots, and the Revolutionary Origins of American Exceptionalism," *Annali di Storia dell'Esegesi* 26, no. 2 (2009): 311–327. I am grateful to Seth Clippard, who provided vital research assistance, and to Jonathan Ebel for his very helpful comments.

1. Barack Obama, "Remarks by the President at the Acceptance of the Nobel Peace Prize" (hereafter "Peace Prize Address"), Oslo, Norway, Dec. 10, 2009, http://www.whitehouse.gov/the-press-office/remarks-president-acceptance-nobel-peace-prize.

2. See Bruce Lincoln, *Holy Terrors: Thinking about Religion after September 11*, 2d ed. (2003; reprint, Chicago: University of Chicago Press, 2006), and Andrew Bacevich, *The Limits of American Power: The End of American Exceptionalism* (New York: Metropolitan Books, 2008).

3. For an excellent history, see James Turner Johnson, *Just War Tradition and the Restraint of War* (Princeton: Princeton University Press, 1981).

4. Thomas Aquinas, *Summa Theologica* II-II, Benziger Bros. ed., trans. Fathers of the English Dominican Province, vol. 3 (Allen, TX: Thomas More, 1948), q. 40, a. 1, pp. 1353–1354.

5. Martin Luther, "Against the Robbing and Murdering Hordes of Peasants," in *Martin Luther*, ed. E. G. Rupp and Benjamin Drewery (London: Edward Arnold, 1970), 121–126.

6. Aquinas, *Summa Theologica*, vol. 3, q. 42, a. 1, p. 1359.

7. Ibid., a. 2, 1360.

8. John Calvin, *Institutes of the Christian Faith*, trans. John Allen (Philadelphia: Board of Presbyterian Church, 1936), bk. 4.31, p. 804.

9. Hannah Arendt, *On Revolution* (1963; reprint, New York: Penguin, 1991).

10. George Marsden, "The American Revolution," in *The Wars of America: Christian Views*, ed. Ronald A. Wells (Macon, GA: Mercer University Press, 1991), 17.

11. Mark A. Noll, *Christians in the American Revolution* (Washington, DC: Christian University Press/Christian College Consortium, 1977), 18.

12. Such economic interpretations lie behind much revisionist history that conceives the Revolution and the American founding as driven by economic interests. For an interesting discussion, see Edmund S. Morgan, "The American Revolution: Revisions in Need of Revising," *William and Mary Quarterly*, 3d ser., 14, no. 1 (Jan. 1957): 3–15.

13. Marsden, "The American Revolution," 22.

14. Ibid., 26, 14.

15. Ibid., 29.

16. Sacvan Bercovitch, *The American Jeremiad* (Madison: University of Wisconsin Press, 1978), 134; Bercovitch, *The Puritan Origins of the American Self* (New Haven: Yale University Press, 1975).

17. Nathan Hatch, *The Sacred Cause of Liberty: Republican Thought and the Millennium in Revolutionary New England* (New Haven: Yale University Press, 1977), 88.

18. Ibid., 3.

19. Jon Butler denies any linkage between the Great Awakening and the American Revolution and qualifies the claims of some evangelical historians in "Enthusiasm Described and Decried: The First Great Awakening as Interpretive Fiction," *Journal of American History* 69, no. 2 (Sept. 1982): 305–325. Mark A. Valeri discusses the overlooked importance of mid-eighteenth-century "Edwardseans," whose influential brand of Calvinism appealed to republican virtue, natural moral law, and theological humility over the preoccupation with national election, covenant, and "civil millennialism" emphasized in other historians' accounts; "The New Divinity and the American Revolution," *William and Mary Quarterly*, 3d ser., 46, no. 4 (Oct. 1989): 741–769. In this chapter, I draw primarily from Melvin B. Endy Jr., "Just War, Holy War, and Millennialism in Revolutionary America," *William and Mary Quarterly*, 3d ser., 42, no. 1 (Jan. 1985): 3–25.

20. Endy, "Just War, Holy War, and Millennialism," 10.

21. Endy draws here from a classic essay by LeRoy Walters showing how just war and the Crusades, while distinct, draw from common patterns; Walters, "The Just War and the Crusade: Antithesis or Analogies?" *The Monist* 57 (1973): 584–594.

22. Endy, "Just War, Holy War, and Millennialism," 12–13.

23. Ibid., 18–19.

24. Michael Walzer, *The Revolution of the Saints: A Study in the Origins of Radical Politics* (1965; reprint, New York: Atheneum, 1971).

25. Josiah Stearns, *Two Sermons Preached at Epping . . . on a Public Fast* (Newbury Port, MA: John Mycall, 1777).

26. Ibid., 6-7.

27. Ibid., 14.

28. Ibid., 8, 23.

29. Ibid., 10-11.

30. Ibid., 15.

31. Ibid., 14.

32. Ibid., 15.

33. Marsden, "The American Revolution," 30.

34. This is not to say that rebellions and uprisings were uncommon features of political life in early America, but few assumed that such revolts would lead to revolution and overthrow of the government.

35. Valeri, "The New Divinity and the American Revolution," 765.

36. See Jerald C. Brauer, ed., *Religion and the American Revolution* (Philadelphia: Fortress Press, 1976), including Robert Bellah's essay on the subject; as well as Robert N. Bellah, Richard Madsen, William M. Sullivan, Ann Swidler, and Steven M. Tipton, *Habits of the Heart: Individualism and Commitment in American Life* (New York: Perennial/Harper & Row, 1985), 28–31. For critical readings of American civil religion, see Catherine L. Albanese, *Sons of the Fathers: The Civil Religion of the American Revolution* (Philadelphia: Temple University Press, 1976). On civil religion's homogenizing tendencies, see Ronald Takaki, *A Different Mirror: A History of Multicultural America* (Boston: Back Bay Books, 1993).

37. One recalls the numerous charges against President Bush's "crusade" in Iraq. See, for example, James Carroll, *Crusade: Chronicle of an Unjust War* (New York: Holt /Metropolitan, 2004).

38. Consider also former president Jimmy Carter's opposition to the 2003 invasion of Iraq, "A Just War—or Just War," *New York Times*, March 9, 2003.

39. Rowan Williams, "Just War: An Exchange," *First Things*, no. 141 (March 2004), http://www.firstthings.com/article/2007/01/war-amp-statecraft-9.

40. Ibid.

41. James Turner Johnson, *Morality and Contemporary Warfare* (New Haven: Yale University Press, 1999).

42. George Weigel, "Just War: An Exchange," *First Things*, no. 141 (March 2004), http://www.firstthings.com/article/2007/01/war-amp-statecraft-9.

43. Jean Bethke Elshtain, *Just War against Terror: The Burden of American Power in a Violent World* (New York: Basic Books, 2003). See also her "Military Intervention and Justice as Equal Regard," which calls upon powerful nations (read: the United States) to lead humanitarian military efforts; in *Religion and Security: The New Nexus in International Relations*, ed. Robert A. Seiple and Dennis R. Hoover (Lanham, MD: Rowman and Littlefield, 2004), 115–130.

44. Stearns, *Two Sermons Preached at Epping*, 14–15.

45. Michael Ignatieff, ed., *American Exceptionalism and Human Rights* (Princeton: Princeton University Press, 2005), 4–7.

46. Harold Koh endorses this view in his chapter "America's Jekyll-and-Hyde Exceptionalism," in Ignatieff, *American Exceptionalism and Human Rights*, 111–143.

47. Rebuffing many countries' "reflexive suspicion of America," Obama affirms, "Whatever mistakes we have made, the plain fact is this: The United States of America has helped to underwrite global security for more than six decades with the blood of our citizens and the strength of our arms." Obama, "Peace Prize Address."

48. Ibid.

49. Andrew Bacevich, for example, draws a direct line from John Winthrop to George W. Bush's agenda to bring freedom to other countries; *The Limits of American Power*, 75–76.

50. Stearns, *Two Sermons Preached at Epping*, 24.

51. Ibid., 25.

52. Ibid., 37.

12
———

Why War Is a Moral Necessity
for America

Realism, Sacrifice, and the Civil War

Stanley Hauerwas

The violence that characterizes the history, political culture, and identity of the United States depends upon the belief that war is necessary. In America, dominant modes of religious and moral discourses of war, such as pacifism, just war, and realism, differ over what it means to conceive war as a necessity. Realists often begin with the view that war is an unavoidable fact of political reality. In a world shaped by realist assumptions, pacifists bear the burden of proof. They do so because, as attractive as nonviolence may be, most people (realists, especially) assume pacifism just will not work. You may want to keep a few pacifists around for reminding those burdened with running the world that what they sometimes have to do is a lesser evil, but pacifism simply cannot and should not be, even for Christians, a normative stance. To call, therefore, as Enda McDonagh and I have, for the abolition of war is deemed an unrealistic proposal made possible by isolation from the "real world."[1] Nonviolence is unworkable, or, to the extent it works, it does so only because it is parasitic on more determinative forms of order secured by violence. Those committed to nonviolence, in short, are not realistic.

In contrast to pacifism it is often assumed that just war reflection is "realistic." It is by no means clear, however, if advocates of just war have provided an adequate account of what kind of conditions are necessary for just war to be a realistic alternative for the military policy of a nation. In the first part of this chapter I will explore that issue. In the second part, I will consider the American understanding of war as sacrifice in order to raise questions about how realistic it is to think war can be limited. The understanding of war as sacrifice, I believe, was forged in the American Civil War and continues to shape how Americans morally comprehend war today, including U.S. wars in Afghanistan and Iraq. For

Americans, war is a necessity for our moral well-being. As a result, it is by no means clear what it would mean for Americans to have a realistic understanding of war. Realism rests on a promise to provide a realistic, practicable outlook, yet American forms of realism fail in this regard.

THE IDEALISM OF REALISM

In Christian tradition, realism is often thought to have begun with Augustine's account of the two cities (that is, the City of God and the city of man), hardened into doctrine with Luther's two kingdoms, and given its most distinctive formulation in the thought of Reinhold Niebuhr, a leading public theologian of the mid-twentieth century. Thus Augustine is often identified as the Christian theologian who set the stage for the development of just war reflection that enables Christians to use violence in a limited way to secure tolerable order.[2] It is assumed, therefore, that just war is set within the larger framework of a realist view of the world.

With his customary rhetorical brilliance, Luther gave expression to the realist perspective, asking:

> If anyone attempted to rule the world by the gospel and to abolish all temporal law and sword on the plea that all are baptized and Christian, and that, according to the gospel, there shall be among them no law or sword—or the need for either—pray tell me friend, what would he be doing? He would be loosing the ropes and chains of the savage wild beasts and letting them bite and mangle everyone, meanwhile insisting that they were harmless, tame, and gentle creatures; but I would have the proof in my wounds. Just so would the wicked under the name of Christian abuse evangelical freedom, carry on their rascality, and insist that they were Christians subject neither to law nor sword as some are already raving and ranting.[3]

Luther is under no illusions. War is a plague, but it is a greater plague that war prevents. Of course slaying and robbing do not seem the work of love, but "in truth even this is the work of love."[4] Christians do not fight for themselves, but for their neighbor. So if they see that there is a lack of hangmen, constables, judges, lords, or princes, and find that they themselves are qualified, they should offer their services and assume these positions.[5] That "small lack of peace called war," according to Luther, "must set a limit to this universal, worldwide lack of peace which would destroy everyone."[6]

Reinhold Niebuhr understood himself to stand in this realist tradition. In 1940 in his "Open Letter (to Richard Roberts)" Niebuhr explains why he left the Fellowship of Reconciliation; he observes that he does not believe that "war is merely an 'incident' in history but is a final revelation of the very character of human history."[7] According to Niebuhr, the incarnation is not "redemption" from history as conflict, because sinful egoism continues to express itself at every level of human life, making it impossible to overcome the contradictions of human history. Niebuhr therefore accused pacifists of failing to understand the Reformation doctrine of "justification by faith." From Niebuhr's perspective, pacifists are captured by a perfectionism that is more "deeply engulfed in illusion about human nature than the Catholic pretensions, against which the Reformation was a protest."[8]

Paul Ramsey understood his attempt to recover just war as a theory of statecraft—that is, that war is justified because our task is first and foremost to seek justice—to be "an extension within the Christian realism of Reinhold Niebuhr."[9] Ramsey saw, however, that there was more to be said about "justice in war than was articulated in Niebuhr's sense of the ambiguities of politics and his greater/lesser evil doctrine of the use of force."[10] That "something more" Ramsey took to be the principle of discrimination, which requires that war be subject to political purposes through which war might be limited and conducted justly: that is, that noncombatants must be protected.

Yet it is by no means clear if just war reflection can be yoked consistently to a Niebuhrian realism. Augustine's and Luther's "realism" presupposed there was another, divine city that at least could call into question state powers. For Niebuhr, realism names the development of states and an international nation-state system that cannot be challenged. Niebuhrian realism assumes that war is a permanent reality for the relation between states because no overriding authority exists that might make war analogous to the police function of the state. Therefore each political society has the right to wage war because, it is assumed, to do so is part of its divinely ordained work of preservation. Realism, for Niebuhr, names the reality that, at the end of the day in the world of international relations, the nations with the largest army get to determine what counts for "justice." But, to use Augustine or Luther to justify this understanding of realism is, in effect, to turn a description into a recommendation.

In their article "Just War Theory and the Problem of International Politics," David Baer and Joseph Capizzi admirably try to show how just war requirements as developed by Ramsey can be reconciled with a realistic understanding of international relations. They argue that even though a certain pessimism surrounds a realistic account of international politics, such a view of the world is not necessarily amoral. To be sure, governments have the right to wage war because of their responsibility to a particular group of neighbors, but that does not mean that governments have carte blanche to pursue every kind of interest. "The same conception that permits government to wage war also restricts the conditions of legitimate war making. . . . Because each government is responsible for only a limited set of political goods, it must respect the legitimate jurisdiction of other governments."[11]

Yet who is going to enforce the presumption that a government "must respect the legitimate jurisdiction of other governments"? Baer and Capizzi argue that Ramsey's understanding of just war, as the expression of Christian love by a third party in defense of the innocent, requires that advocates of just war should favor the establishment of international law and institutions to better regulate the conduct of states in pursuit of their self-interest.[12] Yet they recognize that international agencies cannot be relied on, because there is no way that such an agency can judge an individual government's understanding of just cause; they write: "absent effective international institutions, warring governments are like Augustine's individual pondering self-defense, moved by the temptation of inordinate self-love."[13] Baer and Capizzi argue that a more adequate understanding of just war will combine a realist understanding of international politics with a commitment to international order by emphasizing the importance of just intention.[14] In other words, a war can be undertaken only if peace, which is understood as a concept for a more "embracing and stable order," is the reason a state gives for going to war. The requirement that the intention for going to war be so understood is an expression of love for the enemy to the extent that a lasting order encompasses the interests of the enemy.[15]

And pacifists are said to be unrealistic? The idealism of realist justifications of just war is nowhere clearer than in these attempts to fit just war considerations into the realist presuppositions that shape the behavior of state actors. Ramsey, Baer and Capizzi, and Oliver O'Donovan are to be commended for trying to recover just war as a theory of statecraft, that is, as an alternative to the use of just war as a checklist to judge if a particular war satisfies enough of the criteria to be judged just.[16] Yet by doing so they have made apparent the tensions between the institutions necessary for just war to be a reality and the presumptions that shape international affairs.

What would an American foreign policy determined by just war principles look like? What would a just war Pentagon look like? What kind of virtues would the people of America have to have to sustain a just war foreign policy and Pentagon? What kind of training must those in the military undergo in order to be willing to take casualties rather than conduct the war unjustly? How would those with the patience necessary to ensure that a war be a last resort be elected to office? Those are the kinds of questions that advocates of just war must address before they accuse pacifists of being "unrealistic."

To put the challenge more concretely: Why was it possible for the United States to conduct the second war against Iraq? The answer is very simple. Because America had a military left over from the Cold War, a war that was fought according to an amoral realism. America could go to war in Iraq because nothing prevented America from going to war in Iraq—a war that has been justified as part of a "war against terrorism." Yet, in spite of the title of Jean Bethke Elshtain's book, *Just War against Terror*, it is not clear that it is possible to fight a just war against terrorism.[17] If one of the crucial conditions of a just war is for the war to have an end, then the war against terrorism clearly cannot be just, because it is a war without end.

I think the lack of realism about realism by American just war advocates has everything to do with their being American. In particular, American advocates of just war seem to presume that democratic societies place an inherent limit on war that more authoritarian societies are unable to do. While such a view is quite understandable, I want to suggest that democratic societies, or at least the American version of democracy, is unable to set limits on war precisely because it is democratic. Put even more strongly, for Americans war is a necessity to sustain our belief that we are worthy enough to be recipients of the sacrifices made on our behalf in past wars. Americans are a people born of and in war, particularly the Civil War, and only war can sustain our belief that we are a covenanted, chosen people worth sacrificing ourselves and others for.

"UPON THE ALTAR OF THE NATION"

In his extraordinary book *Upon the Altar of the Nation: A Moral History of the Civil War*, Harry Stout tells the story of how the Civil War began as a limited war but ended as total war. He is quite well aware that the language of total war did not exist at the time of the Civil War, but he argues that by 1864 the *spirit* of total war had emerged and "prepared Americans for the even more devastating total wars they would pursue in the twentieth century."[18] Stout's story of the transformation of the Civil War from limited to total war is also the story of how America became the nation we now know as America. Stout documents how during the Civil War the flag became the central symbol of American patriotism. Before 1860 the flag was barely visible, flying primarily on ships, but after 1861 the flag was flown on churches, storefronts, homes, and government buildings to signify loyalty and support.[19] According to Stout:

> Neither Puritans' talk of a "city upon a hill" or Thomas Jefferson's invocation of "inalienable rights" is adequate to create a religious loyalty sufficiently powerful to claim the lives of its adherents. In 1860 no coherent nation commanded the sacred allegiance of all Americans over and against their states and regions. For the citizenry to embrace the idea of a nation-state that *must* have a messianic destiny and command one's highest loyalty would require a massive sacrifice—a blood sacrifice.... As the war descended into a killing horror, the grounds of justification underwent a transformation from a just defensive war fought out of sheer necessity to preserve home and nation to a moral crusade for "freedom" that would involve nothing less than a national "rebirth," a spiritual "revival." And in that blood and transformation a national religion was born. Only as casualties rose to

unimaginable levels did it dawn on some people that something mystically religious was taking place, a sort of massive sacrifice on the national altar. The Civil
War taught Americans that they really were a Union, and it absolutely required a
baptism of blood to unveil transcendent dimensions of that union.[20]

The generals on both sides of the Civil War had been trained at West Point to
embody American might and power, but they had also been taught to be gentlemen. The title "gentlemen" carried with it expectations not only that the bearers
would be honorable, but also that they would pursue their profession justly. They
imbibed the code of limited war, which demanded that they protect innocent
lives and minimize destructive aspects of war. According to Stout, they were
even taught by Dennis Mahan, a professor of civil engineering, to use position
and maneuver of interior lines of operations against armies rather than engaging
in crushing overland campaigns that would involve civilian populations.[21]

Stout argues that Lincoln realized as early as 1862—before his generals—that
the West Point Code of War would have to be abandoned. After Bull Run and
frustrated by McClellan's timidity, Lincoln understood that if the Union was to
be preserved it would be necessary to escalate the war and to wage war against
both citizens and soldiers. In response to Unionists in New Orleans who protested Lincoln's war policy, Lincoln replied, "What would you do in my position?
Would you drop the war where it is? Or would you prosecute it in future with
elder-stalk squirts charged with rose water? Would you deal lighter blows than
heavier ones? I am in no boastful mood. I shall not do *more* than I can, and I
shall do *all* I can, to save the government, which is my sworn duty as well as my
personal inclination. I shall do nothing in malice."[22] Grant and Sherman are the
two men most associated with pursuing a brutal strategy in the war, but Stout
makes clear each was, in quite different ways, doing Lincoln's bidding. In a letter
to General Halleck about his destruction of Atlanta, Sherman concluded, "If the
people raise a howl against my barbarity and cruelty, I will answer that war is
war, and not popularity-seeking. If they want peace, they and their relatives must
stop the war."[23]

Crucial to Lincoln's strategy for the prosecution of the war against the population of the South was the Emancipation Proclamation, which Lincoln signed
on September 22, 1862. Lincoln's primary concern was always the preservation of
the Union, but the Emancipation Proclamation made clear to both sides that a
very way of life was at issue, and that required a total war on all fronts. On August 22, 1862, Lincoln sent a letter to Horace Greeley that was printed in the *New
York Tribune* in which he made clear his primary purpose in pursuing the war:
"My paramount object in this struggle *is* to save the Union, and is *not* either to
save or to destroy slavery. If I could save the Union without freeing *any* slave I
would do it, and if I could save it by freeing *all* slaves I would do it, and if I could

save it by freeing some and leaving others alone I would also do that. What I do about slavery, and the colored race, I do because I believe it helps to save the Union; and what I forbear, I forbear because I do *not* believe it would help to save the Union. . . . I have here stated my purpose according to my view of *official* duty; and I intend no modification of my oft-expressed *personal* wish that all men every where could be free."[24] Emancipation blocked any attempt that an accommodation between the North and South could be found, because now the war by necessity stood for moral aims that could not be compromised. Stout quotes Massachusetts' abolitionist senator Charles Sumner, who supported the Emancipation Proclamation as a "war measure" in these terms:

> But, fellow-citizens, the war which we wage is not merely for ourselves; it is for all mankind. . . . In ending slavery here we open its gates all over the world, and let the oppressed go free. Nor is this all. In saving the republic we shall save civilization. . . . In such a cause no effort can be too great, no faith can be too determined. To die for country is pleasant and honorable. But all who die for country now die also for humanity. Wherever they lie, in bloody fields, they will be remembered as the heroes through whom the republic was saved and civilization established forever.[25]

Stout's book is distinguished by his close attention to what religious figures on both sides were saying about the Civil War. Ministers of the Gospel supplied the rhetoric necessary for the war to achieve its mythic status. To be sure, the South represented a more conservative form of Christianity than the North; Christianity was recognized as the established religion in the Confederacy's constitution, but for both sides "Christianity offered the only terms out of which national identity could be constructed and a violent war pursued."[26]

Stout provides ample examples of how Christians narrated the bloody sacrifice of the war, but Congregationalist minister and theologian Horace Bushnell's contribution is particularly noteworthy for no other reason than that his Christianity was liberal. Early in the war, Bushnell suggested that, morally and religiously speaking, a nation was being created by the bloodshed of war. According to Bushnell, through the shed blood of soldiers—soldiers of both sides—a vicarious atonement was being made for the developing Christian nation.[27] Such an atonement was not simply a metaphor, "but quite literally a blood sacrifice required by God for sinners North and South if they were to inherit their providential destiny."[28] Shortly after Gettysburg, Bushnell identified those who gave their lives in the war, with the martyrs, writing: "How far the loyal sentiment reaches and how much it carries with it, or after it, must also be noted. It yields up willingly husbands, fathers, brothers, and sons, consenting to the fearful chance of a home always desolate. It offers body and blood, and life on the altar of devotion. It is a fact, a political worship, offering to seal itself by martyrdom in the field."[29]

The language of laying lives on the altar is repeated often in sentiments expressed by wives on hearing of their husbands' deaths as well as soldiers reflecting on the deaths of their friends.[30] Stout quotes a pastor who at a funeral for two soldiers cried out: "We must be ready to give up our sons, brothers, friends—if we cannot go ourselves—to hardships, sufferings, dangers and death if need be, for the preservation of our government and the freedom of the nation. We should lay them, willing sacrifices, upon the altar."[31]

As the toll of the war mounted, the most strident voices calling for blood revenge came from the clergy. Thus Robert Dabney at the funeral of his friend Lieutenant Carrington, who had served in the Confederate army, told his listeners that Carrington's blood "seals upon you the obligation to fill their places in your country's host, and 'play the men for your people and the cities of your God,' to complete vindication of their rights."[32] One Confederate chaplain even prayed, "We should add to the prayer for peace, let this war continue, if we are not yet so humbled and disciplined by its trials, as to be prepared for those glorious moral and spiritual gifts, which Thou designest it should confer upon us as a people."[33] Such a prayer makes clear that the war had become for both sides a ritual they had come to need to make sense of their lives.

Stout's account of the religious character of the Civil War is best illustrated by the most celebrated speech ever given by an American, the Gettysburg Address. Stout observes that something "emerged from Gettysburg that would become forever etched in the American imagination. A sacralization of this particular battlefield would mark it forever after as the preeminent sacred ground of the Civil War—and American wars thereafter."[34] Stout's observation is surely correct, rendering these words all the more chilling:

> It is for us the living, rather to be dedicated here to the unfinished work which they who fought here have thus far so nobly advanced. It is rather for us to be here dedicated to the great task remaining before us—that from these honored dead we take increased devotion to that cause for which they gave the last full measure of devotion—that we here highly resolve that these dead shall not have died in vain—that this nation, under God, shall have a new birth of freedom—and that government of the people, by the people, for the people, shall not perish from the earth.

A nation shaped by such words, such elegant and powerful words, simply does not have the capacity to keep war limited. A just war can be fought only for limited political purposes and using limited means, which cannot and should not be understood in terms shaped by the Gettysburg Address.[35] The Civil War led Americans to think they must go to war to insure that those who died in our past wars did not die in vain.[36] Thus American wars are justified "to end all wars" or "to make the world safe for democracy" or "to defend freedom." Whatever may be the realist presuppositions of those who lead America to war, those presuppositions cannot be used as the reasons given to justify the war. To do so would betray the tradition of war established in the Civil War. Wars, American wars especially, must be wars in which the sacrifices of those doing the dying and the killing have redemptive purpose and justification. War is America's altar. Confronted by such a tradition of war, the attempt to justify war using just war considerations, no matter how sincerely done, cannot help but be ideological mystification

In an essay on Martin Luther King, Timothy Jackson distances himself from King's pacifism, observing: "in a fallen world, at any rate, I believe that protecting the innocent may move some Christians, properly, to take up the sword against evil, as in the American Civil War."[37] I would like to know what "evil" Jackson assumes the sword was taken up against in the Civil War. Was it the evil of secession? Was it the evil of slavery? Does the true "cause" of the war even matter for Jackson-like appeals to the Civil War to justify the use of the sword? I think Jackson's appeal to the Civil War to justify Christian participation in war exemplifies the presumption that finally pacifism just will not do. Yet show me how, in the light of Stout's history, the Civil War can be used as a justification for limited war that just war reasoning requires. Of course I think slavery should have been brought to an end. I think, moreover, that pacifists should have been more prominent in that struggle. John Wolmann and other "Friends" worked tirelessly to convince slaveholders of the evil of slavery, but overall slavery was (and still is) a judgment on Christians. Nevertheless, to say that war is the only alternative form of faithfulness is surely a mistake.

In his book *The Civil War as a Theological Crisis*, Mark Noll asks why the Civil War, in contrast to past wars, produced no "deep theological insights from either elites or the masses."[38] At least one of the reasons, as Noll documents, is that religious thinkers in America assumed that the people of America had a covenantal relationship with God.[39] America identified with the tribes of Israel in which it was assumed that the federal union "created a higher bond than the bond constituted by the unity of all Christian believers in the church."[40] This typological view of history and the widespread Enlightenment confidence in the ability of the common man to read and understand scripture apart from any other authority made it a simple matter to read God's providential will out of political events.[41] The war did not force American Christians to deeper theological insights since the nation was the church, and war was the altar on which the religion of America was born.[42]

PACIFISM AS REALISM

Where has all this gotten us? I think it helps us recognize that we live in the worst of all worlds. Realism is used to dismiss pacifism for being unrealistic and then to underwrite some version of just war. But it is not clear that the conditions for the possibility of just war are compatible with realism. In other words, just war is an unrealistic alternative. It is not clear that just war considerations can be constitutive of the decision-making processes of governments that assume that might makes right. Attempts to justify wars begun and fought on realist grounds in the name of just war only serve to hide the sacrificial reality of war.

Yet war remains a reality. War not only remains a reality, but if Stout's account of the enduring significance of the Civil War is close to being right, war remains for Americans our most determinative moral reality. How does one get people who are taught that they are free to follow their own interest to sacrifice themselves and their children in war? Democracies by their very nature seem to require that wars be fought in the name of ideals that make war self-justifying. Realists in the State Department and Pentagon may have no illusions about why American self-interest requires that a war be fought, but Americans cannot fight a war as cynics. It may be that those who actually wage war, because they have actually faced the reality of war, may have no illusions about the reality of war, but those who would have them fight justify war using moral categories that require there be a "next war." These are the categories of idealists, not realists.

Pacifists are realists. We have no reason to deny that the "realism" associated with Augustine, Luther, and Niebuhr has much to teach us about how the world works. Indeed, they help us see why we do not trust those who would have us make sacrifices in the name of preserving a world at war. Christians believe a sacrifice has been made that has brought an end to the sacrifices of war. Augustine and Luther thought Christians might go to war because they assumed that the church could provide an alternative to the sacrificial system that a nation at war always threatens to become. If the Civil War teaches us anything, it makes clear what happens when Christians no longer believe that Christ's sacrifice is sufficient for the salvation of the world. As a result, Christians confuse the sacrifice of war with the sacrifice of Christ.

If a people does not exist to be Christ's people, war will always threaten to become a sacrificial system. War is a counter-church. War is the most determinative moral experience many people have. That is why authentic Christian realism requires the disavowal of war. Christians should not disavow war because it is often so horrible, but because war, in spite of its horror, or perhaps because it is so horrible, can be so morally compelling. That is why the church does not have an alternative to war. Rather, the church is the alternative to war. When Christians lose that reality, that is, the reality of the church as an alternative to the world's false reality, we abandon the world to the unreality of war.

NOTES

1. For the text as well as a justification of our "Appeal to Abolish War," see Stanley Hauerwas, "Reflections on the 'Appeal to Abolish War,'" in *Between Poetry and Politics: Essays in Honour of Enda McDonagh*, ed. Linda Hogan and Barbara FitzGerald (Dublin: Columba Press, 2003), 135–147.

2. Niebuhr's use of Augustine to justify war in the name of realism is a simplification of Augustine. Robert Dodaro provides a much more complex understanding of the two cities in his *Christ and the Just Society in the Thought of Augustine* (Cambridge: Cambridge University Press, 2004).

3. Martin Luther, "On Temporal Authority: To What Extent It Should Be Obeyed," in *Luther: Selected Political Writings*, ed. J. M. Porter (Philadelphia: Fortress Press, 1974), 56.

4. Luther, "Whether Soldiers, Too, Can Be Saved," in ibid., 103.

5. Luther, "On Temporal Authority," 58.

6. Luther, "Whether Soldiers, Too, Can be Saved," 103. For a fuller account of Luther on the ethics of war, see Joel Lehenbauer, "The Christological and Ecclesial Pacifism of Stanley Hauerwas: A Lutheran Analysis and Appraisal" (Ph.D. diss., Concordia Seminary, St. Louis, 2004).

7. Reinhold Niebuhr, "An Open Letter (to Richard Roberts)," in *Love and Justice: Selections from the Shorter Writings of Reinhold Niebuhr*, ed. D. B. Robertson (Louisville: Westminster / John Knox Press, 1957), 268.

8. Robertson, *Love and Justice*, 269.

9. Paul Ramsey, *The Just War: Force and Political Responsibility* (1968; reprint Lanham, MD: Rowman and Littlefield, 2002), 260.

10. Ibid.

11. Helmut David Baer and Joseph E. Capizzi, "Just War Theory and the Problem of International Politics: On the Central Role of Just Intention," *Journal of the Society of Christian Ethics* 26, no. l (2006): 167–168. George Weigel argues in a similar fashion in his article "World Order: What Catholics Forgot," *First Things*, no. 143 (May 2004): 31–38.

12. Baer and Capizzi, "Just War Theory and International Politics," 164–166.

13. Ibid., 168.

14. Baer and Capizzi argue that this means that going to war requires increasing reliance on international agencies. Weigel, in the article mentioned above, argues exactly the opposite. Indeed Weigel wrote his article in response to the Vatican's deferral to the United Nations concerning the legitimacy of the war against Iraq. Weigel defends the preemptive war strategy of the Bush administration in the name of preserving a more nearly just world order.

15. Baer and Capizzi, "Just War Theory and International Politics," 170–171. One wonders what empirical tests might exist to test this requirement of enemy love. Would the "enemy" need to say after being defeated that they were glad to lose the war?

16. Oliver O'Donovan, *The Just War Revisited* (Cambridge, UK: Cambridge University Press, 2003).

17. Jean Bethke Elshtain, *Just War against Terror: The Burden of American Power in a Violent World* (New York: Basic Books, 2003). The subtitle of Elshtain's book is revealing to the extent it suggests that America's role in the world, a role shaped by a realistic foreign policy of American self-interest, is the necessary condition for fighting a just war.

18. Harry S. Stout, *Upon the Altar of the Nation: A Moral History of the Civil War* (New York: Viking, 2006), xv. The following account draws extensively upon Stout's book. Stout is to be commended for his courage as a historian to make candid that he is writing a "moral history" of the Civil War. He does not elaborate in this book upon what it means methodologically for him to assume a moral stance other than to accept just war as normative for the story he tells. We can only hope that in the future he will tell us more about what it means for a historian to acknowledge that

history is a moral endeavor. Though he ends his book making clear that he does not think the experience of the Civil War justifies pacifism, he remains deeply ambivalent about the reality of war. It remains true for him that "at its most elemental, war is evil. War is killing. War is destroying. War may be a necessary evil, and in that sense 'right,' but it is nevertheless lethally destructive" (xii).

19. Ibid., 28. The title of Stout's book as well as his understanding of the flag as a totem is supported by Carolyn Marvin and David Ingle, *Blood Sacrifice and the Nation: Totem Rituals and the American Flag* (Cambridge: Cambridge University Press, 1999). They argue "that violent blood sacrifice makes enduring groups cohere, even though such a claim challenges our most deeply held notions of civilized behavior. The sacrificial system that binds American citizens has a sacred flag at its center. Patriotic rituals revere it as the embodiment of a bloodthirsty totem god who organizes killing energy," 1. See also Ernest Tuveson, *Redeemer Nation: The Idea of America's Millennial Role* (Chicago: University of Chicago Press, 1968); and Michael Northcott, *An Angel Directs the Storm: Apocalyptic Religion and American Empire* (New York: I. B. Tauris, 2004). Tuveson's book is essential reading if we are to understand the rhetoric that has shaped American foreign policy after September 11, 2001. Northcott offers an astute and informative analysis of that rhetoric.

20. Stout, *Upon the Altar of the Nation*, xxi.

21. Ibid., 21.

22. Quoted in ibid., 139. Italics added.

23. Quoted in ibid., 369. For a depiction of the complex character of Sherman, see E.L. Doctorow, *The March* (New York: Random House, 2006). *The March* is a novel, but it may give us a better sense of the anarchy of Sherman's march across the South than many of the histories on the same subject.

24. Quoted in Stout, *Upon the Altar of the Nation*, 184.

25. Quoted in ibid., 174–175. See also Tuveson, *Redeemer Nation*, 197–198. Tuveson calls attention to the significance of Julia Ward Howe's "Battle Hymn of the Republic" for giving the war its apocalyptic cast. What makes Howe's hymn so significant is her identification with such liberal thinkers as Theodore Parker, Ralph Waldo Emerson, and Oliver Wendell Holmes. Tuveson observes that though Howe had no use for faith in a special revelation she could still write lines like these: "I have seen Him in the watch-fires of a hundred circling camps; / They have builded Him an altar in the evening dews and damps; / I can read His righteous sentence by the dim and flaring lamps: / His day is marching on."

26. Quoted in Stout, *Upon the Altar of the Nation*, 43.

27. Lincoln shared Bushnell-like sentiments most clearly articulated in the Second Inaugural. Yet Stout quotes Lincoln reflecting as early as 1862 on the imponderable purpose of God in relation to the war. "In the present civil war it is quite possible that God's purpose is something different from the purpose of either party—and yet the human instrumentalities, working just as they do, are of the best adaptation to effect this purpose. I am almost ready to say this is probably true—that God wills this contest, and wills that it shall not end yet." Stout also observes that Lincoln's sense of destiny "provided for Lincoln a Christlike compassion for his foes; in death, it would render him a Christlike messiah for the reconstituted American nation" (*Upon the Altar of the Nation*, 146).

28. Ibid. Stout quotes from a sermon preached after Lincoln's assassination by N. H. Chamberlain concerning the flag. Chamberlain said: "Henceforth that flag is the legend which we bequeath to future generations, of the severe and solemn struggle for the nation's life. . . . Henceforth the red on it is deeper, for the crimson with which the blood of countless martyrs has colored it; the white on it is purer, for the pure sacrifice and self-surrender of those who went to their graves up bearing it; the blue on it is heavenlier, for the great constancy of those dead heroes, whose memory becomes henceforth as the immutable upper skies that canopy our land, gleaming with stars wherein we read their glory and our duty" (454).

29. Quoted in ibid., 251.

30. Ibid., 200, 340.

31. Quoted in ibid., 341.

32. Quoted in ibid., 201.

33. Quoted in ibid., 197.

34. Ibid., 269.

35. Ramsey, *The Just War*. Paul Ramsey insists that at the heart of the just war was the requirement that a war have a recognizable political purpose. From Ramsey's perspective a failed nation is one unable to fight a "good war," that is, "a war in which force begins and ends in subordination to national purpose and policy, even the purpose of the arbitrament of a civil war waged to determine what a national purpose shall be"; 15. Accordingly, Ramsey thinks a nation's "self-interest" should be constitutive of any reason given for going to war. Therefore Ramsey argues that the goal of American foreign policy should be the creation of a system of free and independent nations (8).

36. Ramsey recognizes that war has a sacral quality. He writes: "who can deny that there is a strong feeling for the sacred in the temporal person at work delaying and weakening political resolve until a more inclusive entity is vitally challenged—the nation which is felt to be immortal and transcendent over the individual in value and in the perdurance of its life? Thus the nation affords a provisional solution of the ambiguity of finite sacrifice, and only if this is the case does the nation or any other political entity become the 'subject' of political agency capable of legitimating finite sacrifice"; ibid., 15. But Ramsey does not tell us what keeps finite sacrifice finite. I suspect one can keep the sacrifice of war finite only if one had a church strong enough to discipline a nation's ambition. Which presents an interesting challenge to just war thinkers; do they think the church in America has the strength to keep the finite finite? Though I am critical of "Constantinianism," at least the Constantinian churches once had the power to keep the finite finite by reminding those who ruled that they were destined to die. Once "the people" are said to rule themselves, the church in America seems to have lost that ability.

37. Timothy Jackson, "Martin Luther King," in *The Teaching of Modern Christianity on Law, Politics, and Human Nature*, ed. John Witte and Frank Alexander, vol. 1 (New York: Columbia University Press, 2006), 456.

38. Mark Noll, *The Civil War as a Theological Crisis* (Chapel Hill: University of North Carolina Press, 2006), 15.

39. Ibid., 18.

40. Ibid., 61.

41. Ibid., 19. I argued a similar case in *Unleashing the Scripture: Freeing the Bible from Captivity to America* (Nashville: Abingdon Press, 1993).

42. Stout's illuminating account of Civil War generals, who were seen as "saviors" at the time, reinforces this view. Stonewall Jackson especially became a "messianic figure" who could "never die" because he incarnated the Confederate civil religion through a violent atonement; *Upon the Altar of the Nation*, 229.

13

Contemporary Warfare and American Efforts at Restraint

James Turner Johnson

SETTING THE SCENE

A front-page story in the *New York Times* on October 7, 2007, focused on the "rape epidemic" of the war in Congo—the systematic and widespread use of rape and sexual abuse as a preferred means of carrying on this armed conflict. According to the story, the worst perpetrators were Hutu militias, gangs of armed men who participated in the Rwandan genocide of 1994 and subsequently fled to Congo to escape punishment. But the article also noted that other armed forces in this conflict were guilty of similar practices. The women who were the targets of this abuse were members of ethnic groups other than those of the perpetrators, and the attacks were neither incidental nor forms of sexual release: the women were targeted directly, and the mode of attack was aimed at leaving the victims alive but so damaged physically that they could never reproduce, and so damaged emotionally that their lives would be a burden on their own societies.

There is, in a sense, nothing exceptional about this story, though the horrific nature of what it reports turns the stomach. The same front page carried a story about the risks borne by Iraqi civilians who worked for the Americans in Iraq and had to adopt elaborate subterfuges so that they and their families would not be targeted by insurgents. A story inside the front section described a roadside bomb attack in Afghanistan that killed one American soldier as well as four Afghan civilians who happened to be in the way of the blast. I could, in fact, choose the stories of almost any day's newspaper from the last two decades to depict the issue I treat here. Namely, much recent warfare throughout the 1990s and the first decade of the twenty-first century directly and intentionally seeks to harm those people whom the moral traditions of the West and of other cultures have sought to protect. Too often, contemporary warfare erodes to the vanishing point the legal restraints laid out in the law of armed conflict and violently rejects any notions of fundamental human rights. This widespread pattern constitutes a direct assault on the idea that war can and should be restrained in its targets and methods, and it undermines efforts at defining and imposing restraints as prescribed in international law and various moral traditions. U.S. individuals and institutions (among others) historically have played an important role in developing and promoting restraints that limit the use of force and rein in wanton, gratuitous forms of violence. This chapter highlights some of those vital contributions and offers a counterview to those who see the United States and its military as the source of excessive violence in the world. I discuss how some American just war reflection has been central to such efforts to limit unnecessary human suffering, namely through efforts to regulate the justice of war's conduct (*jus in bello*). Interestingly, though, other U.S. just war thinkers, by strictly limiting the occasions for resorting to war (*jus ad bellum*), unwittingly have helped to marginalize concern for its restraint.

The history of armed conflict over the past half-century is a steady diet of front-page stories about rebellions, wars, and terrorism: in recent years the subjects have included reports of car bombings aimed at civilians in Iraq; attacks aimed directly and intentionally at civilians in Darfur; suicide bombings at a Jordanian wedding and in Israeli shopping centers; the train, subway, and bus bombings claimed by al Qaeda affiliates in Spain and England; the 9/11 attacks in this country; similar tactics used by the Tamil Tigers in the civil war in Sri Lanka; and rape during the Balkan wars. The kinds of conflicts reported on here, and the behaviors characteristic of them, have largely been ignored in recent moral debates about war. Since the 1950s there has been much in those debates about nuclear weapons, much about the inherent destructiveness of contemporary conventional weapons—and a good deal of animosity toward states, especially toward the United States—but next to nothing about the other face of contemporary warfare. Here, I do not mean the warfare of states but that of groups, usually inflamed by ideological, religious, or ethnic causes. Such warfare is carried out by direct, intentional harm to ordinary persons in the course of their everyday lives, often by the most horrific means available.

Two factors have contributed to the indiscriminateness and destructiveness of such warfare: first, the failure of states, mirrored by the proliferation of armed groups under the direction of leaders who shoulder no responsibility for public welfare; and, second, the influence of attitudes and assumptions that minimize or demonize the entire population of enemy groups, which results in treatment of them as worthless or evil and deserving of cruel treatment and death. Typically, the weapons of choice in this targeting of civilians have been of the most primitive kind: knives, clubs, machetes, and the use of sexual assault as a weapon of social destruction. The most advanced weapons in such conflicts have been light rockets and mortars, land mines, explosives fashioned into IEDs (improvised explosive devices), and automatic rifles, these last often in the hands of children.[1] Warfare conducted in this way constitutes a concerted and extended attack on the existing restraints on the conduct of war. It is important to understand these restraints, why they have collapsed, and how they might be reestablished effectively.

I will examine the United States' key role in establishing, enforcing, and, ironically, weakening restraints on the conduct of war from three angles: first, a brief history of the effort to define and impose restraints on armed conflict (which began in the Middle Ages but has evolved significantly in the twentieth century); second, a closer look at the issue in terms of the law of armed conflict, focusing on the shift in assumptions that developed from the 1949 Geneva Conventions to the 1977 Protocols to those Conventions; and, third, the shape of recent just war discourse (particularly in the United States) and its failure to come to terms with the changed nature of contemporary war. I will conclude with some thoughts on how to counter the erosion and collapse of restraints on armed conflict.

DEVELOPING RESTRAINTS ON THE CONDUCT OF WAR

Two major issues are at stake in efforts to restrain conduct in the use of armed force: distinguishing those who are proper targets from those who are not; and identifying means of war that should be restricted or entirely prohibited. Both are central to modern efforts to preserve justice in war's conduct. In Western cultural contexts two medieval developments stand as the first focused treatment of these issues: the Peace of God movement from the late tenth and eleventh centuries, which produced the first formal lists of noncombatants (prohibiting direct, intended attacks against them and their property); and the ban issued by the Fourth Lateran Council in the mid-eleventh century on weapons that were especially deadly and indiscriminate. Both these restraints became part of the consensus on the idea of just war, which came together about a century after them, with the coalescence of the Code of Canon Law (1150–1250) and the chivalric code (1300–1450). While other major cultures have produced similar conceptions of permissible use of armed force, the development of international law on this subject, particularly contemporary understandings of noncombatant immunity and proportional use of force, historically grew out of the just war tradition thus defined.

The same approach to restraint found in medieval efforts has characterized subsequent developments toward restraining conduct in the use of armed force. In the medieval and early modern periods, the just war tradition was developed principally by canon law, theology, and (for the *jus in bello*) the chivalric code. From the publication of Grotius's *De Jure belli ac pacis* (1625) and the Peace of Westphalia (1648), though, the just war tradition was principally carried, used, and developed as an element within the emerging secular field of international law (including theoretical legal writings, the "laws and customs of war," and positive international law on war) and, to a limited but real extent, military theory and practice.

With the transition from the medieval to the modern age came a shift away from war conducted primarily, and sometimes solely, by members of a knightly class toward war conducted by armies made up of common men. The former group had aspired to restraint by an internalized code; the latter required external restraint in the form of military discipline. Increasingly, commanders became the locus of responsibility for the conduct of their subordinates. Ultimately this trend sharpened the focus on the responsibility of the monarch, the supreme commander of his military forces, and in fact the first codes on military discipline bore the names of the monarchs who issued them to their armies. At the same time, however, the idea of an internalized code of conduct persisted, especially among the officers, who in many cases were members of (or aspired to emulate) the knightly class. The overall result has been, in Western armies, a mixture of external restraints such as rules of engagement for specific conflicts and international law, and internalized codes of conduct. In the U.S. military today, for example, both these strands have a robust presence. In those conflicts most characterized by the sorts of violence described at the beginning of this chapter, however, there is no external authority able to impose and enforce restraint, while the internalized code (so far as there is one) is to kill, maim, and destroy without restraint.

The idea of restraint in war evolved such that the rules of war applied regardless of the moral status of the belligerent. By extending this way of thinking about inter-state war to civil wars, jurists and strategists fomented further changes in the idea of restraint. The older tradition had assumed that rebels had no rights, and warfare against them did not have to honor the same concerns about restraint as applied in wars between or among states. Simultaneously, only members of organized armed forces—uniformed soldiers and sailors under the authority of a head of state—were, on the established conception, to be treated with honor if taken prisoner; others could be summarily denied quarter and put to death if captured.

The U.S. Civil War brought change in both these respects. Two figures bear much of the credit for these changes: Henry W. Halleck, general-in-chief of the

Union Army during the first years of the war; and Francis Lieber, the German-American political theorist. Both were lawyers and legal scholars. Both had written books on international law in which they referred to the body of consensually accepted restraints known as "the laws and customs of war." Finally, both played central roles in extending that body of restraint to the waging of the Civil War. There were general issues of war-conduct, and these were addressed definitively by General Orders No. 100 of 1863, issued by Halleck's authority but composed largely by Lieber. Earlier, though, these men had addressed two specific issues that changed the direction of the existing "laws and customs of war."

One general problem was how to treat those taking the Confederate side. In a letter to a general under his command, Halleck laid out rules that essentially ignored the older tradition on treatment of rebels and extended the "laws and customs of war" governing interstate armed conflicts to the civilians and soldiers of the Confederacy. Another, more acute problem was the proliferation of partisan forces on both sides in the war. Halleck commissioned Lieber to clarify the situation. Lieber responded with a short treatise in which he defined several rules that partisans must follow in order to be treated as legitimate soldiers (and which, if they did follow these rules, meant that they should be treated as regular combatants). The Union Army's treatment of Confederates as legitimate belligerents provided a powerful precedent that effectively replaced the older consensus on behavior in civil wars.[2] Lieber's rules on partisans were adopted by the 1907 Hague Conference and were written into the 1949 Geneva Conventions. They include rules that partisan bands must operate under the discipline of a commander who himself is under discipline of the army on whose behalf they are operating. They also must wear a sign of recognition distinguishable at a distance, carry their weapons openly, and follow the established laws and customs of war.

Finally, the greatest change regarding the rules for conduct in war has been the coalescence of customary consensus into positive law. This development began in the American Civil War. Contemporaneously, in 1864 the first Geneva Conference resulted in the First Geneva Convention, which focused on the protection of wounded soldiers and the medical personnel treating them. The first and second Hague Conferences, held in 1899 and 1907, produced a number of resolutions binding their signatories in matters of restrictions on the means of war. Later Geneva conferences produced new Geneva Conventions, broadening the categories of protected persons and enlisting increasingly broader ranges of international signatories.

What began in the Middle Ages, then, in efforts initiated by the church, enforced by temporal authorities, and incorporated into the code of conduct of the medieval professional military class has developed into the modern-day system of positive law. This law is codified and enforced by signatory states, with parallel developments in domestic law. The internalization of these restraints is part of the modern military code in professionalized militaries. The United States has played a vital role in this development. But in those conflicts today in which restraint in war is most conspicuously lacking, there is no state strong enough to impose and monitor the rules of international law, no military discipline to enforce behavior in line with these rules, and no professional code of conduct to help internalize restraint. All three of these aspects need to be addressed in the effort to reach a solution to the problem.

Unfortunately, the path to doing this through positive international law has been made more difficult by the 1977 Protocols to the 1949 Geneva Conventions, the intent of which was to extend the reach of the law of armed conflict over national or civil armed conflicts and to change the rules for conduct to level the playing field between insurgent forces and government forces in civil wars. On paper, the Protocols achieved both these aims; in actuality, though, the redefinitions and other changes necessary to do this undermined elements in the older law of war that had been a source of effective restraint on conduct in the use of armed force.[3]

The Protocols extend the rules of restraint on armed conflicts to nonstate actors by shifting the focus of responsibility from states to individuals. The original pattern in the positive law directly reflected its nature as an agreement among states: states were responsible for enforcing the agreements among their own people (and on each other by the exercise of reciprocity during armed conflicts); these same states, or their leadership, could be held accountable for nonenforcement. But building on the precedent of the Nuremberg and Tokyo war crimes trials, which held individuals accountable not only for crimes of war but also for crimes against humanity, the Protocols extended accountability for observation of the rules for conduct in armed conflict to individuals. The state could no longer be specified as the necessary intermediate entity charged with enforcing the rules, because in civil wars doing so could lead to one-sidedness in judgment and behavior. The Protocols ultimately shift this charge to the international community, resulting in a layered system that has subsequently been institutionalized in the International Criminal Court. Yet where everyone is responsible, no one is. Something is clearly gained by clarifying that the rules for armed conduct apply both to nonstate actors and to states; yet something is also clearly lost when accountability cannot be enforced.

The displacing of state responsibility toward individuals on the one hand and the international community on the other creates more problems than it solves. Responsibility and accountability of states still must be seen as the central issue. Though individuals should certainly be held to account for their behavior in an armed conflict, doing so through an international body—whether an ad hoc war crimes tribunal or the new International Criminal Court—still requires state compliance in order to be effective. Furthermore, punishing wrongful behavior after the fact by judicial process is difficult if such conduct occurred during an armed conflict. Gathering forensic evidence is extremely difficult, witness testimony is often biased or otherwise unreliable, and the means for taking suspects into custody may be frustrated by the opposition of states or powerful groups within states. Since states remain central to the process of imposing and enforcing restraint in the conduct of armed conflicts, it seems reasonable that efforts should be directed earlier on—proactively, not reactively—to strengthen state commitments to impose and enforce restraint.[4]

THE AMERICAN RECOVERY OF JUST WAR DEBATE

The recovery of the idea of just war as a frame for specifically moral analysis and argument regarding justified resort to, and conduct of, armed force traces back to three major influences: the work of Paul Ramsey in the 1960s, including two books, *War and the Christian Conscience* and *The Just War*; Michael Walzer's *Just and Unjust Wars* from the next decade; and the United States Catholic bishops' pastoral letter, *The Challenge of Peace*, in the early 1980s.[5] While all these authors saw themselves engaged in a recovery of the just war idea, they also redefined this idea on their own terms, since none of them directly engaged the earlier just war tradition in its classic form that traces its lineage to the Middle Ages. Of these three, Ramsey and the Catholic bishops explicitly developed their conceptions of just war on bases in Christian theology. Both of these positions have been highly influential in subsequent religiously based reflection on war and other uses of armed force. As well, both developed their conceptions of just war in the context of thinking specifically about nuclear weapons and their possible use.

Ramsey articulated his conception of just war through reflection on the ethical meaning of the Christian moral ideal of love of neighbor. In the first place, he argued, neighbor love—what Ramsey also describes as charity, other theologians have termed *agape*—obligates one to defend one's neighbor against an unjust threat or attack; from this obligation comes the permission to use force in such defense. At the same time, love sets limits on the permitted use of force (since love of neighbor also extends to love of enemies) by, first, specifying who may and may not be the object of such force (the idea of discrimination between combatants and noncombatants) and, second, requiring that the kind and amount of force employed be no greater than necessary to protect the neighbor being unjustly threatened or attacked (the principle of proportionality as Ramsey defined it). In developing his just war theory on this moral basis, Ramsey intentionally emphasized *jus in bello* but said little about the *ad bellum* decision to use force, because he regarded this as belonging to the province of statecraft and not that of moralists.

Rejecting the widespread nuclear pacifism found in American Christian thought when he entered the nuclear debate, Ramsey sought to lay out the limits within which nuclear weapons might be used. Working from the principles of discrimination and proportionality, he found the limits to a moral use of nuclear weapons first in the strategy of *counterforces* targeting, by which the use of nuclear weapons would be restricted to defensive purposes against the enemy's armed forces of any kind, including both conventional and nuclear forces. Later he embraced a narrower strategy of *counterforce* targeting, by which nuclear weapons would be used against the enemy's nuclear forces *only*. On Ramsey's understanding, both these conceptions (especially the latter) could satisfy the *in bello* principles of discrimination and proportionality and were significantly distinct from *counterpopulation* strategies.[6] The key moral difference he stressed here rests on the principle of discrimination, though proportionality enters the picture in the form of the decision regarding how much noncombatant harm will be produced by a particular strike, and whether such harm is proportionate to the good that might be achieved.

Elements of Ramsey's thinking can be found in the U.S. Catholic bishops' *The Challenge of Peace*, but there is considerable daylight between the bishops' and Ramsey's conceptions of just war. While Ramsey regarded the use of force as good or bad depending on whether or not it served the obligations of neighbor love, the bishops argued that just war theory begins with a "presumption against war" and that its various moral criteria serve only to show when this presumption can be overridden. The result of the bishops' statement was a "dirty hands" theory of just war: a view that the use of armed force is itself morally wrong but can be overridden under circumstances defined by the various criteria provided. The bishops developed an elaborate conception of *jus ad bellum* that included (but significantly redefined and reordered in terms of priority) the classic requirements of right authority, just cause, and right intention while also adding several new criteria (for example, last resort, probability of success, proportionality, and "comparative justice"). The result was—and remains for many today—a just war theory that is heavily consequentialist, by contrast to the deontological nature of Ramsey's just war theory, which is closest to the classic approach of much of the just war tradition.

Why did the bishops put forward a theory that shifts the meaning of just war? *The Challenge of Peace* was in part a response to Catholic antiwar and antinuclear activists, including some among the bishops themselves who wanted the bishops (if not the church itself) to take a stand against nuclear weapons, for nuclear disarmament, and against war in general. They were particularly concerned by the ongoing strategic relationship of mutual assured destruction between the United States and the Soviet Union and by the Reagan administration's effort to achieve nuclear superiority over the USSR. The committee formed to draft a

statement for the National (U.S.) Conference of Catholic Bishops included pacifists and nuclear pacifists as well as members who identified themselves (and
Catholic tradition) in relation to just war terms. Several drafts of a possible pastoral ensued. The second draft, which most fully took the position of the pacifist
and nuclear pacifist wing among American Catholic bishops, met with such an
immediate and overwhelmingly critical reaction that a third, more balanced
draft was generated.[7] The "presumption against war" conception of just war was
a central element in draft three: the idea was that both just war theorists and
pacifists could agree on this presumption.

In fact, though, the argument in *The Challenge of Peace* as well as subsequent
statements by representatives of the U.S. Conference of Catholic Bishops and
moralists seeking to draw out the implications of the bishops' position have
tilted toward at least a functional or de facto pacifism. The pastoral itself particularly reveals that the bishops' major goal is the prevention of war. While they rejected any use of nuclear weapons as inherently immoral—both indiscriminate
and disproportionate—they accepted the continued possession of nuclear weapons for the sole purpose of deterrence of war. At the same time, they ignored or
rejected any technological efforts toward making nuclear weapons (or any other
weapons, for that matter) more capable of discriminate and proportionate uses
(for example, by increasing the accuracy of targeting or weapons delivery systems or by lowering the yield of nuclear warheads). Such efforts were cast as increasing "war-fighting" capacity and, thus, efforts that accepted the possibility of
a war. While one might frame the "presumption against war" as capable of being
overridden, these provisions in the pastoral rendered avoidance of war as a moral
norm if not a moral absolute.

This same aim dominates later statements by representatives of the Catholic
bishops' conference. In 1990–91, during the debate over the use of force to respond to the Iraqi invasion of Kuwait (despite there being a clear violation of the
provisions of the United Nations Charter), the bishops' representatives strongly
cautioned against use of force against Iraq, citing the "presumption against war"
and painting a dire picture of how such use of force might well lead to a confla-
gration of war that would engulf the entire Middle East.[8] Similar arguments were
offered on other occasions, up to and including the debate over the use of force to
overthrow Saddam Hussein in 2002–03. Some might say that the bishops were
right to oppose this last use of armed force. My concern, though, is with their
reasoning.[9] The bishops' spokesmen have systematically shaped their arguments
in such a way that the use of force could never actually satisfy the requirements
for overturning the "presumption against war." This is a functional pacifism, not
a just war position. It leaves little room for any moral discussion of methods in the
use of armed force, and indeed, with the bishops' past rejection of technological

improvements as means of "war-fighting," it is not clear what they could say about efforts to achieve discrimination and proportionality in practice.[10]

The relevance of all this for efforts to limit war's conduct or to restrain the use of force is that the Catholic bishops have simply taken no note of such efforts. Their priorities have focused on avoidance of war as such and on seeking to prevent the use of armed force by the United States. *The Challenge of Peace* is shaped around an antiquated conception of mid-twentieth-century warfare. In recent official statements by the U.S. Conference of Catholic Bishops, *jus in bello* in other wars, particularly involving nonstate actors and lower levels of weaponry, simply does not appear on the agenda.

Though Ramsey's initial thinking about just war emerged in the context of debate over nuclear weapons, he came to different conclusions from the Catholic bishops regarding both what is moral in the use of nuclear weapons and the application of just war thinking to low-level, nonnuclear armed conflicts such as Vietnam. In this second context he developed two especially significant ideas. First, Ramsey argued that one cannot depend upon the international community in dealing with such threats for a variety of real-world reasons, including a fundamental precept of politics: the international community, even in an institutionalized form such as the United Nations, is not a state. The UN does not have the authority of a state, the power of a state, or a body of citizens for whom it bears responsibility, as a state does. Rather, in the final analysis, states must bear the burden of dealing with threats to fundamental ethical values, and force is sometimes necessary for this task. In this regard, Ramsey argued, the United States, with its exceptional power and global reach, is charged with this moral and political burden in a special way.[11] Second, he developed an argument for nonlethal means as possibly more discriminate and proportionate than lethal ones—a position he spelled out in an essay on the use of incapacitating gases against Vietcong combatants in tunnel complexes.[12] His moral analysis and argument on this topic remain interesting and relevant. He returns to his unwillingness (also central to his discussions of nuclear weapons) to think of the weapons of war in black-and-white terms such that some types of weapons are always or inherently evil; rather, for Ramsey, the use of a particular means of war must be decided in context by reflecting on the requirements of discrimination and proportionality.

How might we make use of Ramsey's insight today? His fundamental point is that there is a moral responsibility to make the means of war as discriminating and minimally destructive as possible, consistent with the moral justification of force in the first place. Ramsey's preference for counterforce warfare as the upper moral limit for the use of nuclear weapons further illustrates this same point. While he did not specifically address the issue of the kinds of technological developments the Catholic bishops rejected as "war-fighting," we might extrapolate

Ramsey's views in reflecting on recent technological developments in the means of war. I believe his views would have come out substantially where my own have: that taking seriously the moral obligations of restraint in the use of armed force means not only considering how to use the weapons at hand but also focusing on developing the technology for more accurate weapons; lowering the yields needed for particular types of targets; and revising tactics, training, and command and control processes so as to use much more discriminate and less destructive means effectively. This is, in fact, what the U.S. military, significantly more than any other warfighting force, has done.

Evidence of this approach can be seen in contemporary theories and practices of counterinsurgency warfare in Iraq and Afghanistan. (Such strategies and tactics were also part of "surges" that made use of increased U.S. and allied troop levels.) Even where aerial bombardment is practiced, it is nothing like the horror of high-altitude "carpet bombing" such as the bombing of Dresden or Tokyo or the atomic bombing of Hiroshima and Nagasaki. Aerial strikes today make use of precision-guided munitions that achieve more discriminating effects (even if human error can never be fully eliminated). Predator drones' use of low-yield warheads lowers the threshold of collateral damage. Finally, the possibility of having to resort to nuclear warfare has been vastly diminished by the development of targeting and delivery technologies of theater ballistic missile defense that obviate the need for nuclear strikes. These new realities, which greatly reflect the obligations of discrimination and proportionality in the use of armed force, could not have emerged from the U.S. bishops' rejection of "war-fighting."

REESTABLISHING RESTRAINT IN ARMED CONFLICTS

I turn now to the failure of recent just war thinking to engage seriously the problem of how force may be used for positive purposes, such as in humanitarian intervention and peace stabilization efforts. If the problem I outlined at the beginning of this essay is a real one—and compelling evidence suggests it is—then just war analysis should be directed to reversing the erosion of restraint in contemporary armed conflict. This involves thinking about the uses of military force that were discussed in the 1990s under such rubrics as humanitarian intervention, peacemaking, and peace-stabilization. It also involves taking a new look, from a just war perspective, at the responsibilities of states, the relationship of states to the international order, and the institutional organization of the international order.

The first thing to say is that, from a just war perspective, Ramsey basically got it right in his 1968 thoughts on the responsibilities of states, especially the United States, and the international community when facing major manifestations of injustice in other states. His position was that it is among the responsibilities of states, depending on their actual ability to act decisively and effectively, to respond to such injustices, including through the use of military force. The international community, he argued, cannot be relied upon to do so. The other version of just war reasoning set out by the U.S. Catholic bishops rests on problematic assumptions about contemporary war that historically are at odds with the just war tradition. Depicting the use of armed force as so inherently morally problematic—to be avoided in itself—shifts the focus to avoiding the use of armed force in nearly every instance. The effect is to diminish systematically both the possibility of using such force to respond to injustice and to minimize the importance of thinking about restraints in the use of such force. This ostensibly "just war" position eventuates functionally in pacifism: the idea that modern war is inherently immoral. Such a position leaves little room for discussion of restraints on war. Interestingly, though, the bishops' own reliance upon *jus in bello* has been used repeatedly to argue that contemporary war can never measure up to the demands of these criteria, so that it will never be moral to use force. Such appropriation of the *jus in bello* for purposes of denying *jus ad bellum* fundamentally warps the historical purposes of both arms of the just war tradition.

What is needed is a resumption of the debate that began in the 1990s in the context of thinking about how to respond to the indiscriminate and highly destructive conflicts in former Yugoslavia, parts of Africa, and other regions. That debate should have been engaged, and could perhaps have produced some useful thinking in response to President George W. Bush's summaries of the crimes of the Saddam Hussein regime as one of the justifications for use of military force to overthrow that regime.[13] Yet this opening was systematically disregarded, when first offered and since, by those who used just war thinking to no purpose other than to oppose the use of force as a matter of policy. Some may never be able to move beyond such functional pacifism, but at least their position can be recognized as such so that others, with a view of just war more faithful to the nature and purposes of just war tradition, can reengage the issues that were on the table in the debates over humanitarian intervention in the 1990s.

In the arena of international law, *The Responsibility to Protect* had an immediate influence on thinking within the United Nations context, though more broadly the effect is well rooted in developments in human rights law since World War II. One of the most important implications of these developments is a shift in the conception of sovereignty away from the formalistic definition assumed in the Westphalian system, which focuses on the inviolability of territorial borders and—in the name of self-determination—effectively gives a ruler a free hand in dealing with the state and all who live inside its borders. The emerging conception of sovereignty coming out of human rights law focuses on sovereignty as the exercise of responsibility for the welfare of the populace within a state and, more broadly, for upholding an international order in which such responsibility is the norm. This principle is wholly consistent with both Ramsey's just war thought and notions of governance assumed in early formulations of the just war tradition.

As to the particular role of states versus the role of international institutions, both this conception of sovereignty in terms of a moral responsibility held by governments and the experience of history serve as reminders of the importance of well-functioning, morally responsive, and morally responsible states as well as the need for robust engagement in common purposes by such states. (The United States has an important but no means exclusive role to play here.) The obverse of this is the recognition that the erosion and collapse of restraint in warfare has taken place most strikingly in weak or failed states. Classical just war theorists conceived the ends of political life in terms of the three Augustinian ends of order, justice, and peace. In an ideal political system, these are all reciprocally related, so that there is no true order that is not just and peaceful, no real peace without a just order, and so on. Those in the current debate who conceive the use of armed force as an inherent evil to be avoided tend to prioritize the value of peace defined as the absence of conflict, including the absence of armed force. As the slogan says, "Say no to war. Give peace a chance." But peace in the Augustinian sense involves a good deal more than the absence of war, and just war reasoning is rooted in the realization that the use of force may be necessary to produce order so that a just and peaceful society might emerge. This is a key lesson of recent history that was realized in places like Bosnia and Kosovo but not in places like Rwanda in 1994 or Congo today.

Restoration of order to disordered political systems is thus the first step toward reestablishing restraint in armed conflict. But who can, in fact, provide order where there is none? Where the United Nations is concerned, the record does not promote optimism. Aside from this, the UN itself is not a sovereign entity but one that rests on consensus. Both these institutional facts serve as limiting factors on the UN's exercise of power. At the other extreme, individual states have coherence and capabilities that correspond to their political systems, their wealth (or lack thereof), and the values held by their populaces. From this, many assume that the United States, as the world's leading superpower, will (if not should) always step in to address the gaps of international political authority. But this need not always be the case. For a state to be able to respond effectively to breakdown of civil order or unrestrained warfare, it is not necessary that it be a major power: consider Vietnam's intervention in Cambodia during the slaughter perpetrated by the Khmer Rouge under Pol Pot, Tanzania's intervention in Idi Amin's Uganda, or Uganda's later intervention in Rwanda in response to the 1994 genocide. Surely, though, one should not insist that such unilateral interventions be purely altruistic, unmotivated by the national interest of the intervening state. To make this stipulation when the intervener shares a border with the failed state is especially absurd, as it is very much in the common interest of both states to restore order where it has broken down catastrophically and to make possible both justice and peace.

Between individual states and the United Nations lie both formal regional alliances of states and ad hoc alliances that coalesce to meet a particular need. The U.S. invasion of Iraq in response to Saddam Hussein's tyranny shows that ad hoc "coalitions of the willing" can be controversial, with much of the ire directed at the United States. Some authors who entered the debate over intervention in the 1990s insisted that states should never act alone and that international approval and cooperation is always necessary to ensure that the state in question is not exploiting a crisis for predatory purposes. Although I think this view is mistaken, there are real advantages to cooperative actions within the framework of either treaty-defined or ad hoc alliances. Such cooperation tends to insulate the action in question against charges that it is predatory. Further, spreading the involvement among a number of states symbolizes importantly that the action in question proceeds from shared norms and commitments. Still further, it spreads actual costs and responsibilities of armed conflict while allowing the best use to be made of various national contributions. The United States has learned all these lessons during its extended counterinsurgency operations in Afghanistan and Iraq.

Finally, in action within a specific region by an alliance centered within that region, the states in the alliance have strong reasons to want to resolve the crisis successfully for their own welfare individually and for the welfare of the region as a whole. NATO's involvement in Bosnia and Kosovo comes to mind; so does the continued involvement of the OSCE (Organization for Security and Cooperation in Europe) in rebuilding Kosovo, the African Union's involvement in the Darfur region of Sudan, and the Arab League's support for new regimes and reforms in Libya and Syria. While the United States has often played organizing roles in such conflicts, the importance of regional bodies and international norms cannot be underestimated.

An effective response to the erosion and collapse of restraints in warfare in contemporary armed conflicts and just war theory, thus, turns out to draw moral analysis back to the subject of humanitarian intervention, the proper understanding of sovereignty, and the relations of states to regional alliances and the United Nations. Fundamentally, all these lines of concern point to the importance of a robust conception of the state within an international context. Within this context, the responsibilities of states for protecting and advancing order include efforts to establish order in failed societies and to enforce, by their own military power, an end to armed conflicts characterized by direct, intentional harm to enemy noncombatants. Respecting these ideas is still a considerable way from actually stemming the erosion and collapse of restraint in contemporary armed conflict, but this provides a place to begin.

NOTES

1. What has resulted is total war (or indiscriminate war), even if the means typically employed have not themselves been totalistic. Given the motivations of those waging such warfare, there is no reason why weapons of mass destruction will not be brought into use, given the opportunity.

2. Contrast this with the Confederate policy of killing black soldiers taken alive.

3. While the 1949 Geneva Conventions were accepted and formally adopted nearly universally by states (and universally among major states), the Protocols never have won such universal acceptance or adoption. The list of states that have not formally agreed to the Protocols includes the United States, even though it is U.S. military policy to abide by provisions in the Protocols that reflect customary international law. Exactly what the customary law is, though, and how to define it differ markedly from society to society. Traditionally the customary law has been understood as defined by the actual behavior of states, a conception reflected in the nineteenth-century term "the laws and customs of war." Moving from this conception, the emergence of positive international law was understood as the codification of what was agreed to as customary law. The standard view among continental European international lawyers today, reflecting their legal roots in positivistic understandings of law, turns this historical relationship around, so that the positive law, once adopted, should be seen as a statement of the customary law. In the United States, the United Kingdom, and the British Commonwealth in general, all reflecting the heritage of a common-law understanding of law, actual behavior represents what the law is. Given the nature of international law as based on compacts among states to be bound by the provisions of the law, it matters how the law is interpreted by each state. How the states actually behave matters in explaining the nature and binding power of the law; and if a state has not agreed to be bound by it, it is not at all clear that it is so bound. Thus whether a state has signed the Protocols matters, and the fact that the Protocols have not won universal acceptance not only undercuts their authority but signals a problem with their substance.

4. The Protocols also change the rules regarding irregular soldiers—"partisans," in the standard earlier legal usage, "guerrillas" or "insurgents" in everyday usage. The 1949 Geneva Conventions uses the rules as stated originally by Lieber and as included in the 1907 Hague Conventions governing the status of such fighters, which requires them to carry their arms openly and wear a sign that is recognizable at a distance. In the Protocols, though, these provisions are rewritten so that it is only during an actual attack that such irregulars must do so. The practical implications are illustrated strikingly by the behavior of Iraqi *fedayeen* during the drive toward Baghdad by American forces in 2003. On different occasions, *fedayeen* fighters approached lightly defended supply columns wearing ordinary Iraqi peasant clothing, including robes that covered their bodies, under which they carried their weapons. They shed their robes and revealed their weapons only upon attack. Such behavior is clearly not in accord with the rules laid out in the 1949 Geneva Conventions, which both Iraq and the United States had signed.

If the 1977 Protocols are taken as the standard, though, the situation is different. Arguably the *fedayeen* behavior was in accord with the rewritten rules in the Protocols. Though neither Iraq nor the United States had signed the Protocols, if these rewritten rules are taken as specifying customary international law on this matter, the rules apply in this case. As this behavior illustrates, the rewritten rules make it easier for insurgents and paramilitary units like these *fedayeen* to hide among the civilian populace until they are actually engaged in an attack. Given the danger posed by such an attack, this puts the civilian population among whom irregular soldiers are hiding—or suspected of hiding—at greater risk, since normal civilian behavior itself could be perceived as the beginnings of an attack.

5. Paul Ramsey, *War and the Christian Conscience* (Durham, NC: Duke University Press, 1961) and *The Just War* (Lanham, MD: Rowman and Littlefield, 1968); Michael Walzer, *Just and Unjust Wars* (New York: Basic Books, 1977); National Conference of Catholic Bishops, *The Challenge of Peace: God's Promise and Our Response* (Washington, DC: United States Catholic Conference, 1983).

6. Ramsey recognized that even restricted, legitimate forms of counterforce targeting could produce harm to noncombatants, since military targets may be found in or near population centers. Still, he made use of the Thomistic rule of double effect to draw the morally significant distinction between direct, intentional attack on noncombatants (as found in counterpopulation strategy) and a direct counterforce attack against a legitimate military target that causes only indirect and unintended (even if foreseeable) harm.

7. These developments are discussed further in George Weigel, *Tranquilitas Ordinis: The Present Failure and Future Promise of American Catholic Thought on War and Peace* (Oxford: Oxford University Press, 1987).

8. See examples of statements by spokesmen for the American Catholic bishops in James Turner Johnson and George Weigel, *Just War and the Gulf War* (Washington, DC: Ethics and Public Policy Center, 1991), 102, 126–128.

9. I explore this at length in Johnson, *The War to Oust Saddam Hussein: Just War and the New Face of Conflict* (Lanham, MD: Rowman and Littlefield, 2005).

10. The reluctance to accept any use of armed force recurs in a tension between two parts of the Catholic bishops' statement *The Harvest of Justice Is Sown in Peace* (Washington, DC: United States Conference of Catholic Bishops, 1993), which marked the tenth anniversary of *The Challenge of Peace*. *Harvest* reiterates in slightly broader form the "presumption against war" argument. But the language of "presumption against the use of armed force" stands in tension with later parts of the statement in which the bishops justify humanitarian intervention in the face of gross violations of fundamental human rights. The result, once again, seems to be de facto pacifism. Interestingly, the 2002–03 statements from the bishops against using force to remove Saddam Hussein completely ignore the humanitarian intervention argument put forward by President Bush on three occasions (the first and most prominent of which occurred in Bush's November 2002 United Nations speech— before the Catholic bishops' statements were issued).

11. There was great debate in the 1990s over humanitarian military intervention and what kinds of forces—national, regional, or international—are best positioned to respond. The most thoughtful and thorough treatment of the issues has been produced by the ad hoc International Commission on Intervention and State Sovereignty (ICISS), including both the widely known report *The Responsibility to Protect* (Ottawa: International Development Research Centre, 2001) and the lesser-known but highly substantive volume of supporting essays, *The Responsibility to Protect: Research, Bibliography, Background* (Ottawa: International Development Research Centre, 2001). What emerges from this is a new, if only suggestive, conception of the needs of international order, the nature of state sovereignty, and the relation of states to one another and the institutions of the United Nations.

Nothing comparable has come from those engaged in the just war debate or those who address the ethics of military force from within a religious frame. The somewhat tentative efforts found in *The Harvest of Justice* were marred by the bishops' continued commitment to the "presumption against the use of armed force" such that, in the end, they were unable to think seriously about the justified use of armed force in response to the gross human rights violations they condemned. The situation was much worse in a resolution adopted by the General Convention of the United Presbyterian Church, which allowed humanitarian intervention by military force only if there was no national interest involved.

12. Ramsey, *The Just War*, 465–478.

13. Some authors have argued that just war reasoning during the Iraq War should have focused more heavily on humanitarian concerns. See, for example, John D. Carlson, "The Morality, Politics, and Irony of War: Recovering Reinhold Niebuhr's Ethical Realism," *Journal of Religious Ethics* 36, no. 4 (2008): 631–636.

14

Enemies Near and Far

The United States and Its Muslim Allies
in Radical Islamist Discourse

Sohail H. Hashmi

Jeremiad and jihad have a venerable tradition in Islamic history and have been prominently on display during the past century in the broad phenomenon labeled "political Islam." In Islamic tradition, the jeremiad, understood simply as a bitter and sustained lament for or denunciation of the fallen state of society, finds expression and religious sanction in the moral duty of *amr bi al-maʿruf wa nahy ʿan al-munkar* (commanding the right and forbidding the wrong).[1] This duty can be performed, in the opinion of scholars, noncoercively and coercively. Thus, it parallels the concept of jihad (struggle), which also may be performed through both nonviolent and violent means. The Islamist challenge to postcolonial Muslim states, to politics generally, and to modernity even more generally deploys jeremiads and jihads of all sorts, ranging from righteous example and purely moral suasion to advocacy and acts of extreme violence.

Since the end of World War II, the United States has become more and more implicated in Islamist jeremiads and jihads. This was inevitable as the United States replaced European powers not only as a major political, economic, and military influence in Muslim countries, but also as a dominant cultural and intellectual trendsetter. Few Islamist writers have had much good to say about the United States—its politics, its culture, and its role in the world—but the vast majority of them have confined their anti-Americanism to verbal attacks and sometimes more elaborate jeremiads. Even among the ranks of so-called radical Islamists, those who espouse and practice violent jihad, the United States historically has not figured all that prominently as a target.

That changed in 1998, when the World Islamic Front, consisting of al Qaeda and its affiliates, issued the notorious "Declaration of Jihad against the Jews and the Crusaders."[2] Few analysts appreciated the significance of this declaration at the time or for the next three years. It wasn't until al Qaeda took its jihad to the American homeland on September 11, 2001, that the full import of the 1998 statement became clear. Simply put, what al Qaeda did in 1998 was to buck a consensus among radical Islamist groups, which held that the United States, though an enemy, was too powerful to attack directly, at least in the foreseeable future. In the dominant trope of radical groups, the United States was the "far enemy," and any challenges to it should be indirect and limited so as not to provoke a full-scale American retaliation. The immediate target of the radicals' jihad had been the "near enemy," the ruling regimes of the Muslim world, who were thwarting the realization of the true Islamic order in politics and society. Al Qaeda's most enduring achievement has been to insist and to act upon the claim that jihad against the far enemy cannot be postponed pending the completion of the jihad against the near enemy, that both the near and far enemies must be combatted simultaneously. Far from establishing a new consensus, however, al Qaeda unleashed an intra-jihadist controversy over which enemy, near or far, should be the primary target of the Islamist struggle. The controversy has been animated and reanimated repeatedly by al Qaeda's war against America and by America's "war on terror." It continues to rage today.

This chapter explores how the United States became implicated in the Islamist trope of the near and far enemy during the past quarter-century. Unlike previous studies of this topic,[3] I examine the theological groundings of this trope in the Qur'an and its classical interpreters before considering how contemporary Islamist writers appropriated and applied it to their own ideological and programmatic ends. I analyze the historical developments that pushed the United States into the center of radical Islamists' agendas, and conclude by reflecting on the implications for American foreign policy of the ongoing jihadist controversy over whether to target the near or the far enemy.

No understanding of the Islamists' worldview and motivations is possible without delving into their theological justifications and controversies. There are undoubtedly a number of motivations, sacred and profane, that drive their militant agenda. But to dismiss their use of religion as merely instrumental or disingenuous is to fail to understand the main driving force behind these groups and individuals. They view themselves as sincere Muslims, called by God to undertake resistance to the corrupt order around them. They justify their actions, including the use of extreme violence, by citing the Qur'an and the actions of the prophet Muhammad. They are careful to situate themselves in the classical tradition of Qur'anic exegesis and Islamic jurisprudence. All of this does not mean they are slavish imitators of tradition. Despite their generally conservative and literalist approach to Islam, the radicals demonstrate a willingness to finesse the Qur'an and *hadiths* (records of the prophet Muhammad's sayings and actions) to suit their needs. In short, the role of Islam in radical Islamism demonstrates fully all the complexities and ambiguities of the relationship between religion and violence.

NEAR AND FAR ENEMIES: ORIGINS OF A TROPE

The concept of the near versus the far enemy is of relatively recent coinage in jihad discourses. It does not seem to have roots in the classical juridical literature on the laws of war or in Muslim manuals on warfare. It seems to have originated—or at least was first popularized—in a pamphlet written by a young Egyptian engineering graduate named ʿAbd al-Salam Faraj. The pamphlet, titled *al-Farida al-ghaʾiba* (The Neglected Duty), was written probably in 1980 or 1981 as a justification for the assassination of Egyptian president Anwar Sadat. It was in all likelihood meant only for internal consumption to resolve any lingering doubts within Faraj's group, Tanzim al-Jihad, as to the Islamic validity for killing Sadat.

In the first part of the pamphlet, Faraj tackles what he realized was the most contentious issue: whether Sadat and other Egyptian officials could under Islamic law be treated as enemies. In the name of political necessity and social stability, classical jurists and political theorists generally proscribed rebellion against Muslim rulers, even those who had usurped power; "sixty years of tyranny is preferable to one day of civil strife (*fitna*)," according to one widely quoted tradition. This quietist attitude was challenged by a few "revisionist" scholars of the twelfth and thirteenth centuries, prompted by the Crusades and the Mongol invasions. The most prominent was Ibn Taymiyya (d. 1328), who in certain writings suggests that jihad could be waged against both infidels and those who made infidel rule over Muslims possible. Among infidels he included Mongol rulers who claimed to be Muslim yet did not observe the requirements of the faith or enforce the *shariʿa*. As for those who helped infidels come to power over Muslims, Ibn Taymiyya made it clear that he meant primarily the Shiʿa and other non-Sunni groups. What Ibn Taymiyya and other jurists of his period did was to introduce into mainstream Sunnism the idea that nominal Muslims—including rulers—could be the object of jihad, and fighting this internal enemy was as important as fighting the external enemy.[4] This was the intellectual tradition within which Faraj positioned himself. Ibn Taymiyya is copiously cited to provide legal support for his argument that Sadat was not a Muslim ruler but, rather, an apostate at the head of an un-Islamic regime. Removing him and his regime from power had become not just permissible, but obligatory according to Islamic law.[5] Indeed, Ibn Taymiyya has emerged as a patron saint of sorts for all radical Islamists.[6]

In the second part, Faraj deals with objections and "false" notions of jihad. One of the sources of dissension within the ranks of the radicals was whether priority should be given to attacking the Egyptian government or Israel. Faraj's generation had imbibed from childhood the Egyptian state propaganda that the state of Israel was the Arabs' (indeed, all Muslims') primary enemy. The Islamic dimension to the Arab-Israeli conflict had risen dramatically in salience following the Six-Day War of June 1967, when Israel seized East Jerusalem, with the Dome of the Rock and al-Aqsa Mosque at its center. Then, in November 1977, Anwar Sadat became the first Arab leader to visit Israel and address the Israeli Knesset, opening the way for the U.S.-sponsored Camp David Accords of September 1978 and eventually the Egyptian-Israeli Peace Treaty signed in March 1979. The treaty was bitterly denounced by Islamist groups, and it contributed importantly—though not singularly—to Sadat's assassination. As *The Neglected Duty* indicates, some radicals needed convincing that the jihad against the Egyptian government now trumped the jihad against Israel.

In a section titled *al-'Adu al-qarib wa al-'adu al-ba'id* (The Near Enemy and the Far Enemy), Faraj writes: "It is said that the battlefield of jihad today is the liberation of Jerusalem since it is (part of) the Holy Land. It is true that the liberation of the Holy Land is a religious command, obligatory for all Muslims, but the Apostle of God—may God's peace be upon him—described the believer as 'sagacious and prudent,' and this means that the Muslim knows what is useful and what is harmful, and gives priority to radical definitive solutions."[7] Faraj then expounds on what sagacity and prudence require at the moment: Fighting the near enemy (Sadat's regime) takes precedence over fighting the far enemy (Israel). Curiously, Faraj does not elaborate further on this point. He may have based his argument on Qur'an 9:123 and simply assumed his readers would understand the reference: "O you who believe! Fight the unbelievers near to you, and let them find firmness in you. And know that God is with the pious."

This verse is found in the ninth chapter of the Qur'an, which is believed to be one of the last revealed to Muhammad shortly before his death in 632. During the twelve years Muhammad preached Islam in Mecca (610–622), the Qur'an is silent on the subject of war. Jihad during these years meant exclusively forbearance and patient, nonviolent struggle against the persecution of the Muslims' enemies. Following Muhammad's move to Medina (622–632), some qur'anic verses continue to extol jihad as a nonviolent struggle but others add a military dimension to it. Initially, the verses suggest self-defense as the legitimate grounds for violent jihad. But by the time verses from the ninth chapter were revealed, especially the "verse of the sword" (9:5) and the "verse of the poll tax" (9:29), the "jihad of the sword" could be interpreted as having acquired more expansive goals, namely, to overthrow ungodly social and political systems in order to establish a righteous Islamic order. The majority of later qur'anic exegetes favored the latter view of jihad, interpreting it as a divinely ordained responsibility of Muslims to spread the blessings of Islamic law and civilization—peacefully if possible, forcefully if necessary.[8]

Q. 9:123 is one of many verses from the Medinan period that both exhorts Muslims to fight their enemies and offers advice on how to do so. The fact that there is no consensus on its "occasion of revelation" (that is, the approximate time and historical context when the verse was revealed) led the great commentators of the classical period to speculate on the identity of the "near enemy" mentioned in it. Some commentators read into the verse a general command regarding the conduct of jihad. The influential exegete al-Tabari (d. 923) interprets the verse as requiring Muslims to fight "the unbelievers near them before those far from them." He adds the caveat, however, that the duty to assist Muslims under attack—perhaps in a remote region—trumps this directive.[9]

Another prominent commentator, Ibn Kathir (d. 1373), writes:

> God the most Exalted ordered the believers to fight the unbelievers closest to the territory of Islam. Therefore, the Messenger of God (peace and blessings be upon him) began by fighting the polytheists in the Arabian Peninsula. When he was victorious over them and God gave him control over Mecca, Medina, Ta'if, Yemen, Yamama, Hajr, Khaybar, Hadramawt and other areas of the Arabian Peninsula and the various Arab tribes entered Islam in waves, he started fighting the People of the Book. He prepared to fight the [Byzantine] Romans who were the closest to the Arabian Peninsula and the first to be called to Islam because they were People of the Book.[10]

Ibn Kathir then relates the ever-widening geographical scope of jihad during the caliphates of Abu Bakr, 'Umar, and 'Uthman, in whose reign "the pure monotheist faith reached its fullest aims, and whenever Muslims overcame one group, they moved to the next and then the next of the impudent transgressors." After the first three generations, however, the Muslims became divided internally, allowing their enemies to march into the very capitals of Muslim realms and seize the land. Ibn Kathir ends with a plea for Muslim unity: "Whenever a just Muslim king rose up and obeyed God's orders, all the while trusting in God, God helped him regain control over some Muslim lands and take back from the enemy according to his obedience and support to God. We ask God to help the Muslims gain control over His disbelieving enemies and to raise high the word of Muslims over all lands."[11]

Ibn Kathir lived in Syria in the fourteenth century. The immediate backdrop for his work was the turbulent period of the Crusades from the west followed by the Mongol invasion from the east. His gloss on Q. 9:123 is an elegy to the Muslims' faded glories and a jeremiad against their present corruptions. This pattern is all too familiar in the works of modern Islamists.

Among modern commentators on the Qur'an, two deserve particular attention because of their influence on Islamic radicals. Abu al-A'la Mawdudi (d. 1979), the founder of the Jama'at-i Islami, the most active and influential Islamist party in South Asia, writes that some may read Q. 9:123 as placing the responsibility to fight the enemy on those Muslims living in territories closest to enemy territory. This reading is inaccurate, Mawdudi avers, for the context of this verse establishes that the intended enemy are the hypocrites within the Muslim community. Q. 9:73 opens this theme by commanding: "O Prophet! Strive against the unbelievers [kuffar] and the hypocrites [munafiqin], and be severe with them." This verse orders the believers to struggle (jahidu) against the hypocrites, whereas Q. 9:123 specifies that the believers must fight (qatilu) them.

Mawdudi's argument that the verse refers to internal hypocrites and not external unbelievers faces the difficulty that unlike Q. 9:73, where both hypocrites and unbelievers are mentioned, Q. 9:123 refers only to unbelievers (kuffar). He addresses this problem by declaring that by the time Q. 9:123 was revealed, the enmity of the hypocrites had become clearly exposed so that the Qur'an no longer validates in any way their formal profession of faith but treats them simply as unbelievers along with all those who openly rejected Islam. At this stage, the jihad against the hypocrites moved from a nonviolent to an openly violent phase.[12]

Mawdudi's qur'anic commentary was written and published in Urdu, and although parts had been translated into Arabic, English, and other languages by the mid-1970s, Faraj and his contemporaries in Egypt would most likely have been exposed to it only indirectly, through selective quotations in Arabic sources. Mawdudi's interpretation of Q. 9:123 accords with Faraj's claim that the enemy at home must take priority over the enemy abroad. Yet Mawdudi never went so far as to sanction violence against successive Pakistani governments, no matter how corrupt or un-Islamic he felt they were. The Jama'at-i Islami has remained a loyal opposition in Pakistani politics.

Faraj was certainly familiar with the second major modern exegete, Sayyid Qutb (d. 1966), the most important ideologue of the Muslim Brotherhood. Qutb's pamphlet Ma'alim fi al-tariq (Milestones) is justifiably considered the manifesto of modern jihadist movements, but his magnum opus is his multivolume qur'anic commentary, Fi zilal al-Qur'an (In the Shades of the Qur'an). Qutb uses his commentary on Q. 9:123 to advance his general critique against Muslim "defeatists" who contend that jihad can be pursued only for defensive purposes. The example of the Prophet and the rightly guided caliphs, Qutb argues, completely contradicts this view, for they all undertook jihad proactively in order to free people to hear the Islamic call. "What we find here [in Q. 9:123] is an order to fight those unbelievers who are near to the Muslim state, without specifying whether these have launched any aggression on Muslims or their land." Since it is one of the last verses on jihad to be revealed, Qutb argues, it is not restricted by any conditions that may have attached to previous verses. Following the classical exegetes, Qutb understands the verse as coming directly after the successful conclusion of military action against remaining polytheist tribes in the Arabian Peninsula. It directs the Muslims to fight next the Byzantines, who were the closest unbelievers to the Islamic state at that time.[13]

But Qutb interjects into his discussion another theme familiar to his (and Mawdudi's) work: Muslim societies today are in a state akin to that of the Arabs at the beginning of the Prophet's mission, namely, *jahiliyya*, or "ignorance."[14] They are, therefore, Muslims in name only. There is no true Islamic state, only states led by corrupt and hypocritical rulers who have replaced God's law, the *shari'a*, with man-made laws. The import of Q. 9:123 for Muslims today, Qutb suggests, is that "they have to start again at the beginning, with the declaration that 'There is no deity other than God, and Muhammad is His Messenger.' They will have to move forward on the basis of this declaration until they reach, in their own good time and with God's help, the final stage."[15]

As he does in *Milestones*, so here in his qur'anic commentary, Qutb never openly declares war against Muslim rulers, but his meaning is clear. The jihad against infidels abroad cannot resume after its centuries-long hiatus unless the vanguard of true Muslims first brings the jihad against the infidels at home to a successful conclusion. Faraj and his compatriots saw themselves as acting on Qutb's injunctions; they were waging jihad against those who were waging war against Islam in their own society. Near the end of *The Neglected Duty*, Faraj quotes Qutb in a final challenge to the "defeatists" who deny the necessity of jihad: "Many are those who shirk hardship and flee from effort, and prefer cheap comfort to noble toil, base safety to sweet danger, and they collapse exhausted behind the marching fighting ranks who are in earnest."[16]

In sum, Q. 9:123 seems to provide a general and important directive on how to conduct jihad. This is the reading given by some of the most cited classical commentators. Yet, aside from the exegetical literature (*tafsir*), the verse does not figure significantly in other classical literatures on jihad, most importantly in the jurisprudential sources (*fiqh*) or in military manuals (*adab al-harb*). No general principle was adduced from it by jurists and military strategists. The verse appears from time to time in modern arguments about jihad, but here too it remains relatively underutilized. Not only Faraj, but most participants in the near versus far enemy debate fail to reference Q. 9:123 explicitly. Given the interpretation of this verse by such influential commentators as Mawdudi and Qutb, Faraj could credibly have adduced it as a qur'anic proof-text for his argument that jihad begins with the enemy at home.

After tersely declaring that fighting the near enemy takes priority over fighting the far enemy, Faraj goes on to list two other reasons why the jihad to liberate Jerusalem ought to be postponed. First, fighting the far enemy requires the shedding of Muslim blood, he notes, and the beneficiaries will be the infidel regime, not the Islamic movement. The infidel rulers use nationalist ideas and false calls for jihad against external enemies to divert attention from their own malefactions. Second, Faraj argues, imperialism in the lands of Islam exists because of infidel rulers. "To begin by putting an end to imperialism is not a laudatory and not a useful act. It is only a waste of time. We must concentrate on our own Islamic situation. We must first establish God's law in our own country and make God's word supreme."[17] Faraj does not directly refer to the United States in this brief mention of imperialism or anywhere else in *The Neglected Duty*. But again he did not need to be specific for the audience he was addressing. His reference to imperialism and the occupation of Jerusalem clearly signaled who was in his mind the far enemy—the United States and its agent in the region, Israel.

By 1980 the United States had clearly come to occupy the role of chief imperialist power in the Arab and Muslim world in the ideologies of radical Islam. Anti-Americanism had trumped anti-British and anti-French sentiments as the dominant strand of anti-imperialism. This had been a slow process of evolution. The driving ideological force behind rising anti-Americanism in the Arab world during the 1950s and early 1960s was secular Arab nationalism. The rallying cry of secular Arab nationalists was opposition to the remaining colonial presence of Britain and France in Arab countries and to the state of Israel, which they castigated as nothing more than a colonial outpost created to divide and weaken the Arab heartland. The United States' central role in successfully promoting the partition of Palestine in the UN General Assembly tarnished its standing among Arabs, but subsequent policies adopted by Harry Truman during the 1948–49 Arab-Israeli war and by Dwight Eisenhower during the 1956 Suez crisis to some degree rehabilitated the U.S. image as an evenhanded international power. Arab nationalist opinion turned decisively against the United States after the Eisenhower Doctrine was issued in 1957, and when, acting on it the following year, the United States intervened militarily in Lebanon, along with Britain in Jordan. The United States emerged as the chief prop for conservative, atavistic regimes that stood in the way of Arab unity, populism, and progress.[18]

Islamic groups during the 1950s and 1960s shared many aspects of the anti-Americanism espoused by secular Arab nationalists. To the secular Arab critique of American political and economic imperialism the Islamists added the condemnation of American cultural and spiritual imperialism. The groundwork for this critique was undeniably laid by Sayyid Qutb. In 1948 the Egyptian education ministry sent Qutb, who was already established as a writer, literary critic, and inspector of schools, to study American methods of education. He lived in Washington, D.C., Colorado, and California before returning to Egypt in 1950. Before his American tour, Qutb was moving toward Islamic activism in response to what he saw as a deepening malaise in Egyptian society. In some of his published works, he had expressed disillusionment with American support for Zionist ambitions in Palestine. His visit to the United States seems to have intensified and radicalized his views. He became active in the Muslim Brotherhood shortly after his return to Egypt.

In 1951 Qutb published his notes and letters from the United States in a booklet titled *Amrika allati ra'itu* (The America I Have Seen)—arguably the first Islamist jeremiad directed at the United States. One characteristic dominates his description of the American people and their culture: "<u>primitive</u>" (*bida'a*). America exhibits, Qutb writes, a seeming paradox: It is a nation that has reached the height of economic, scientific, and technological prowess without commensurate refinement in its morals, sensibilities, and tastes. The paradox is resolvable, he suggests, by studying America's origins: It is a nation created by "groups of adventurers and groups of criminals" whose one ambition was to tame the virgin land for the sake of material prosperity.[19] As they tamed the land, Americans ruthlessly warred against those originally inhabiting it. "The American is, by his very nature, a warrior who loves combat."[20] Qutb argues, in so many words, that America's material prosperity has been bought by spiritual impoverishment.

Qutb sprinkles his critique with anecdotes of personal experiences purporting to demonstrate the materialism, alienation, and moral laxity of American culture. The sexual promiscuity of American women dominates the narrative, sometimes in lurid detail. On more than one occasion he expresses his disdain for fellow Arabs who have succumbed to the lures of American females while he himself managed to resist because of his strong Muslim faith.[21] His fixation on this subject can be interpreted on many levels. He may perhaps have been developing a metaphor of America as the seductive temptress, whose charms could readily ensnare the spiritually bankrupt but were ineffective against the morally pure.

Yet, having made the West the mortal enemy of true Islamic civilization, Qutb does not suggest any concrete course of action to repel it. His entire oeuvre is devoid of a practical political agenda, opening the door to dissension and real controversy on how the Muslim vanguard ought to combat the new *jahiliyya*. Should it challenge the far enemy—the source of *jahiliyya*—or should it focus first on the near enemy that propagates the *jahiliyya* within Muslim societies?

Clearly, these issues were being debated by Tanzim al-Jihad in the early 1980s when 'Abd al-Salam Faraj wrote *The Neglected Duty*. The Iranian Revolution, which had just swept away the shah, provided a boost for those, like Faraj, who argued that the near enemy could and should be targeted first. The failure of the United States to rescue its agent, the shah of Iran, indicated to them that U.S. support for tyrants in Muslim countries was shallow and fickle. The United States was unwilling, it seemed, to commit its troops and treasure to keep in power one of its staunchest allies. If the shah could be brought down, then why not the pharaoh, as Sadat was called by Egyptian radicals. On October 6, 1981,

Faraj's call to action was realized when Sadat was assassinated. Yet the hoped-for Islamic revolution in Egypt failed to materialize, as Hosni Mubarak moved quickly to crush Islamist opposition. Faraj was executed in 1982. One of his compatriots, a physician named Ayman al-Zawahiri, was also arrested and imprisoned. But al-Zawahiri survived Mubarak's prisons and went on in the mid-1990s to help build al Qaeda.

STRAIGHTENING THE ROD: AL QAEDA ATTACKS THE FAR ENEMY

American policy in the Middle East began to shift in the late 1980s and early 1990s as the United States, for the first time in its history, committed large-scale military forces to the region. The shift began with Ronald Reagan's decision in 1987 to make the U.S. Navy the guardian of the Persian Gulf at the height of the Iran-Iraq War. George H. W. Bush's decision in 1990 to send 500,000 American troops to Saudi Arabia to reverse the Iraqi invasion of Kuwait dramatically escalated America's military presence in the region. In the span of four years, the United States went from being a superpower content to project power in the Middle East from outside the region or indirectly through regional proxies to the dominant military force in the region.

The entry of the United States into the Persian Gulf had the greatest impact upon Arabs from the Arabian Peninsula who had gone to Afghanistan in the 1980s to wage jihad against the Soviet Union. In their eyes, just as they were on the brink of defeating one superpower, the other superpower was engaged in occupying their homeland. In Islamist discourses after 1987 distinctions between the far enemy and the near enemy began to blur. Still, radical groups did not rush to declare jihad against the United States, certainly not one targeting the American homeland or civilians. Most groups in the mid- 1990s were fully mired in struggles both political and military with their homegrown enemies. This was not the case with the leaders of the group that would become al Qaeda. Safely ensconced in Taliban-ruled Afghanistan, Osama bin Laden, Ayman al-Zawahiri, and their followers had the luxury of time and space to plot more ambitious undertakings.

From 1994 onward, the leaders of al Qaeda issued a number of statements on why jihad must now be taken directly to the United States. These came as the U.S. military presence in Saudi Arabia continued after the Gulf War, and after the failed attempt to destroy the World Trade Center in 1993, the first large-scale attack conducted by a radical Muslim group on American soil. In August 1996 bin Laden released a lengthy, rambling statement of al Qaeda's goals and strategy. It was published in the London-based Arabic newspaper *al-Quds al-'Arabi* and later translated into English and posted on the Internet in October 1996 as the "Ladenese Epistle: Declaration of War (Parts I–III)." The document charges the

"Zionist-crusader alliance and their collaborators" with waging a war against Muslims all over the world. Muslims are being persecuted, robbed of their land and possessions, and massacred in Palestine, Kashmir, the Philippines, Eritrea, Chechnya, and other places, all while the United States and its allies, under the cover of the "iniquitous" United Nations, block means of assistance for them. "The latest and the greatest of these aggressions . . . is the occupation of the land of the two holy places—the foundation of the house of Islam, the place of the revelation, the source of the message and the place of the noble Ka'ba, the *qibla* [direction of prayer] of all Muslims—by the armies of the American crusaders and their allies."[22]

Much of the statement focuses on the crimes of the near enemies, the Muslim allies of the "American crusaders." The Saudi regime in particular is lambasted for opening the sacred land of Islam to infidel troops during the Gulf War. King Fahd had promised Muslims that all foreign troops would leave in a few months, as soon as the emergency under which they arrived had passed. Yet, the statement observes, foreign troops remain on Saudi soil years later. Instead of evicting the Americans, the Saudi government rebuffs appeals from the ulema (religious scholars), jails religious dissidents, and lies about American intentions in Saudi Arabia.[23]

By doing nothing to expel the American "occupiers," the current Saudi leaders continue a pattern established by the founder of the kingdom, 'Abd al-'Aziz, who permitted, under British urging, the loss of Palestine. Now his son, Fahd, had committed the ultimate betrayal of the Muslim community (*umma*) by calling a "Christian army to defend the regime. The crusaders were permitted to be in the land of the two holy places [that is, Mecca and Medina]. . . . The country was widely opened from the north to the south and from the east to the west for the crusaders. The land was filled with military bases of the USA and the allies. The regime became unable to keep control without the help of these bases." When the Saudi rulers permitted the violation of the sanctity of the Arabian Peninsula, the statement charges, they in effect renounced their Islamic identity and joined forces with the infidels.[24]

Yet bin Laden does not explicitly call for the overthrow of the Saudi regime in this statement. In an interview published at roughly the same time, he holds open the possibility of reconciliation between the Saudi government and its people, but only after it effects "essential changes, the most important of which is to bring back Islamic law, and to practise real consultative government." Without such fundamental change, bin Laden warns, the Saudi regime faced escalating confrontation "between the Muslim people and the American occupiers. . . . Its most important goal would be to change the current regime."[25] Thus, in both his epistle and the interview, bin Laden states, in so many words, that the Saudi regime cannot survive unless it transforms itself into a righteous Islamic state, and it cannot become an Islamic state without first purging itself of American political, economic, and military influence.

In its condemnation of the Saudi regime, al Qaeda's statement is hardly distinguishable from Faraj's declaration of war against the Egyptian government and countless other radical Islamist attacks against allegedly apostate regimes that had become nothing more than American stooges. What is novel about this statement is the proclamation that to fight the tyrants ruling over Muslims, jihad has to be taken directly to their imperialist backers: "Everyone agrees that the situation cannot be rectified (the shadow cannot be straightened when its source, the rod, is not straight) unless the root of the problem is tackled. Hence it is essential to hit the main enemy who divided the *umma* into small countries and pushed it, for the last few decades, into a state of confusion."[26]

In hindsight, the 1996 statement was a seminal document, the first significant justification for al Qaeda's attempt to refocus jihadist strategy away from near enemies to the far enemy. The document itself does not dwell on the reasons why the United States must be the primary target, but other sources suggest the following explanations.[27]

By the mid-1990s bin Laden and al-Zawahiri had concluded that their intermittent guerrilla warfare against Arab regimes, especially the Saudi and the Egyptian, had little chance of success so long as these regimes enjoyed the military and economic backing of the United States. They could continue to attack U.S. political and military interests in the Middle East, but so long as the American public itself did not feel the costs of its government's policies, the policies would not change. The way to force the United States out of the region was to punish the American people.

In addition, al Qaeda's leaders understood that the near enemy strategy had failed to win popular support among ordinary Muslims. The attacks against government targets usually took place in crowded urban areas where civilian casualties were inevitable. Arab governments had become adept at using their media to turn public opinion against terrorism. For example, in 1993 al-Zawahiri's group, Islamic Jihad, killed a young Egyptian girl outside her school during an assassination attempt on Prime Minister Atif Sidqi. Al-Zawahiri later went to great lengths to explain that the child's death was a tragic, unintended consequence of Islamic Jihad's action, and he noted bitterly that the government had exploited the event for its own benefit.[28] Taking their war to the far enemy, bin Laden and al-Zawahiri reasoned, would tap the latent anti-Americanism of Muslim masses and galvanize a rejuvenated jihad effort at home.

Finally, the strategic shift seems to have been driven by the personal ambitions of bin Laden himself. Bin Laden emerged from the Afghan war against the Soviets with a grandiose view of himself and his organization. He had begun to see himself as a freelance *mujahid* (one who wages jihad) with a transnational mission. When Iraqi forces invaded Kuwait in August 1990, he offered the Saudi government his "Afghan Arabs" as a fighting force ready to take on the Iraqi army. Bin Laden was stung by the government's rebuff. The Saudi government, which had previously used bin Laden and his network, now began to view him as a potential threat. It seized bin Laden's passport and increased surveillance on him and his supporters.[29] It was the beginning of the break between bin Laden and the regime. By 1996, when he issued his epistle, bin Laden's disdain for the Saudi royal family and his self-image as a legitimate challenger to their rule were in plain view.

At the heart of bin Laden's disaffection with the Saudis lay his conviction that they were now fully controlled by the United States. Bin Laden had developed strong anti-American sentiments at an early age, but such emotions were prevalent in Saudi society.[30] When the Saudi ruling establishment turned against him in the early 1990s, bin Laden was convinced that Americans were dictating the action. In his epistle, he blames the United States for the "injustices" visited upon him in Saudi Arabia and for pursuing him in Pakistan, Sudan, and Afghanistan.[31] The United States had, in bin Laden's mind, already declared war against him. Consequently, he was now an international player, and his jihad was a global effort. Al Qaeda informants confirm that bin Laden was the driving force behind the decision to target the far enemy. He personally lobbied Ayman al-Zawahiri and his Egyptian fighters to focus on the United States, and once the idea for the 9/11 attack was proposed to him, he embraced it wholeheartedly.[32]

Al Qaeda declared war against the United States in the 1996 "Ladenese Epistle," but it was vague on how the war was to be waged. The ambiguity was removed in a terse document published in *al-Quds al-'Arabi* on February 23, 1998. In a proclamation of "Jihad against Jews and Crusaders," bin Laden, al-Zawahiri, and their associates in the World Islamic Front list three "crimes and sins committed by the Americans" that amount to "a clear declaration of war on God, His Messenger, and Muslims." The first is that which was discussed at length in the 1996 statement: the American "occupation" of the most sacred of Islamic lands, the Arabian Peninsula. The second is the United States' continuing war against Iraq, "despite the great devastation inflicted on the Iraqi people by the crusader-Zionist alliance, and despite the huge number of those killed, which has exceeded one million." The third American crime is support for Israel and Israel's occupation of Jerusalem and repression of the Palestinians. At the end of the statement we find what al Qaeda's war against the United States—what "straightening the rod"—requires: "To kill the Americans and their allies—civilians and military—is an individual duty incumbent upon every Muslim in all countries, in order to liberate the al-Aqsa Mosque and the holy mosque [in Mecca] from their grip, and in order for their armies to move out of all the lands of Islam, defeated and unable to threaten any Muslim."[33]

The list of grievances against the United States in the 1998 declaration—as it had been in the 1996 statement and in virtually all other al Qaeda pronouncements—is singularly political, not ideological, cultural, or theological. This is an important point given the claims of George W. Bush and his administration that al Qaeda attacked because "They hate our freedoms: our freedom of religion, our freedom of speech, our freedom to vote and assemble and disagree with each other."[34] Al Qaeda may have no use for American-style democracy, and it undoubtedly shares much of Sayyid Qutb's loathing for American culture. But these were not the fundamental reasons for its decision to wage war against the United States. In the scores of statements issued by bin Laden and other al Qaeda leaders, jeremiads against American society are not prominent. A letter "To the Americans" posted on the Internet on October 6, 2002, is an exception. In it bin Laden claims to clarify two questions: "Why are we fighting and opposing you?" and "What are we calling you to, and what do we want from you?" In answering the first question, he rehashes the familiar reasons given in the 1996 epistle, the 1998 declaration, and many other statements and interviews. The reasons are all political: "Because you attacked us and continue to attack us."[35]

In answering the second question, bin Laden begins by calling Americans to embrace Islam and to "stop your oppression, lies, immorality, and debauchery that has spread among you." A litany of American immorality and debauchery follows, including usury, alcoholism, sexual promiscuity, consumerism, greed, the spreading of AIDS, and environmental destruction. At the root of America's sins is that it is a nation divorced from religion, where laws are based not on divine guidance but on human inventions.[36]

Separation of religion from law and politics is, of course, not a uniquely American characteristic, nor are other societies—especially other Western societies—free of the vices listed in this letter. Indeed, in the radical Islamist polemic, the anti-American jeremiad could have been directed against most societies, including those that purport to be Muslim but are in fact steeped in *jahiliyya*. What distinguishes the United States, according to this statement, is the extent of the American iniquity ("You are the worst civilization witnessed in the history of mankind") coupled with the self-delusion of greatness and the arrogance to impose its will on peoples around the world.[37] By the end of the letter, bin Laden returns to familiar political grievances: the United States preaches peace, but it is the most aggressive nation; it touts human rights and democracy, but only when it suits its interests; it champions international law, but it is the worst violator.[38]

The reasons why bin Laden felt compelled to issue this letter are unclear. Bruce Lawrence suggests that in calling Americans to Islam, bin Laden may have been responding to Muslim criticisms that al Qaeda had not followed Islamic law, which requires that before an attack the enemy must first be summoned to embrace Islam.[39] Bin Laden could very well have fallen back on the legal argument that his jihad was a defensive war against American aggression, and therefore the call to Islam is not applicable. But perhaps he was "going through the motions" to placate Muslim critics. His call for Americans to convert to Islam is perfunctory, and his polemic against American vices is formulaic. At the end of the letter, bin Laden himself acknowledges the futility of his jeremiad: "Take an honest stance with yourselves—and I doubt you will do so—in order to discover that you are a nation without principles or manners."[40]

NEAR IS NEAR AND FAR IS NEAR: THE UNITED STATES IN AFGHANISTAN AND IRAQ

The far enemy strategy developed by al Qaeda aroused controversy within radical Islamist circles even before 9/11, for reasons both practical and ideological. Some opponents feared the implications of arousing a full-scale American military response, which they argued would be inevitable following an attack on the American homeland. Bin Laden and al-Zawahiri reportedly dismissed such fears, arguing that as demonstrated by the short American intervention in Somalia, the United States was unwilling to commit to a war in the Middle East.[41] Others opposed the strategy on dogmatic grounds. The jihadist movement had been predicated for decades on the argument enunciated clearly by 'Abd al-Salam Faraj: the near enemy takes priority. One of al-Zawahiri's mentors, 'Abd al-Qadir ibn 'Abd al-'Aziz (known as Dr. Fadl), authored an influential treatise on jihad in which he stated categorically, "It is obligatory to begin fighting the nearest enemy."[42]

The American response to 9/11 greatly intensified the internal debate over near versus far enemy targeting. The invasion and occupation of parts of Afghanistan and later Iraq by American forces further blurred the distinction between near and far enemies. Subsequent Islamist discourses on this trope evince confusion and deep divisions.

A senior scholar named Abu 'Amr 'Abd al-Hakim Hasan composed a legal treatise in the months after the overthrow of the Taliban that attempts to reframe the near/far enemy categories in light of the new realities in Afghanistan. The treatise opens with the question: "Are jihad operations in the territories of infidels, such as America, preferable to those in Muslim territories now occupied by infidels, such as Afghanistan?" After a long excursus on the priority that defensive jihad should be given over a jihad to call infidels to Islam, the author asserts that in Islamic law, the treatment of apostates is much harsher than the treatment of "original" infidels. Muslims may not fight the latter if they are "people of the book," namely, Jews and Christians, and they pay the *jizya*, the poll tax. Moreover, Muslims may not fight them once they conclude a treaty or truce with them. The apostates ruling in Muslim lands, in relation to the inhabitants of that land, are the near enemy, and the original infidels in their own lands are the far enemy. "It is necessary to begin with the nearest before the farthest," states Hasan. "If we examine these tyrants who rule over Muslim lands, we find that all the conditions making them the first to be fought are present in them: they are apostates from Islam, they are the closest infidels to those living in their midst, and they are warring against Islam and the Muslims in every way. . . . Jihad against them rather than against foreigners is the priority." He concludes: "Jihad operations in lands that once were under Islamic rule and then were occupied by the enemy, such as Afghanistan, are obligatory and take precedence over such operations in lands of the original infidels that Muslims never conquered and in which Islamic rulings never applied, such as America. Preserving the capital takes precedence over new profit, especially when those imposing their rule in Islamic lands are apostates."[43]

The author of this treatise is an Egyptian scholar sympathetic to al Qaeda if not actively a member. Ayman al-Zawahiri praised his writings for encouraging jihad against the United States.[44] But in this document, Hasan seems to be at odds with bin Laden and al-Zawahiri. He comes as close to condemning the 9/11 attacks as jihadist etiquette would permit. By attacking the far enemy, al Qaeda had in fact lost its "capital"—Taliban-ruled Afghanistan—as it launched a risky campaign for new "profits." Hasan's argument regarding defensive jihad does not rule out attacks on American troops occupying Afghanistan, but his focus is clearly on fighting the apostate usurpers, the government of Hamid Karzai.

In Iraq, the dispute over which enemy to target was much more public and vituperative. This was so because of the personal ambitions and hatreds of the man bin Laden deputized to lead what became known as al Qaeda in Iraq, the Jordanian Abu Mus'ab al-Zarqawi. The relationship between al-Zarqawi and the core al Qaeda leadership was strained from the beginning. Al-Zawahiri sent a much-publicized letter to al-Zarqawi in October 2005 politely but pointedly criticizing him for his indiscriminate attacks on Iraqi civilians because they threatened to erode Iraqi popular support for the insurgency.[45] Rather than relent, al-Zarqawi continued his murderous campaign and broadcast in detail the reasons for his disagreement over targets.

Two months before he was killed in June 2006, al-Zarqawi released a four-hour-long videotaped message titled *Hal ataka hadith al-rafida?* (Has Word of the Traitors Reached You?). *Rafida*, meaning "turncoats" or "renegades," is a derogatory term historically used by Sunnis in anti-Shi'a polemics. It was a term regularly used by Ibn Taymiyya in his attacks on the Shi'a following the sack of Baghdad in 1258 by the Mongols. Not surprisingly, al-Zarqawi finds a direct parallel between his situation and that of Ibn Taymiyya and draws abundantly upon the medieval scholar for theological and legal support. Al-Zarqawi's purpose in this long tirade against the alleged historical and contemporary villainies of the Shi'a is to do in Iraq what Hasan had done in the treatise discussed above in Afghanistan and what Faraj had done in *The Neglected Duty* in Egypt: establish the primacy of fighting the local "apostates" over their foreign backers. In al-Zarqawi's case, all Shi'a are heretics and enemies of true Islam. All Iraqi Shi'a are, in addition, traitors and enemies of the *mujahidin* in Iraq because they are openly aiding in the American-led invasion and occupation of this Muslim land.

Muslims will have no chance for victory over their Jewish and Christian enemies, al-Zarqawi declares near the end of his statement, until they have destroyed the apostates who work with them, the most dangerous being the Shi'a. To buttress his position, he appeals to his own version of Islamic history. Jerusalem fell to the crusaders in 1099 with the assistance of the Fatimids, an Isma'ili Shi'a dynasty, he claims. Two celebrated Muslim warriors, Nur al-Din al-Zangi and Salah al-Din al-Ayyubi (Saladin), both battled the crusaders. Al-Zangi was the fiercest fighter against the foreign invaders, yet God did not give him the ultimate victory, the recapture of Jerusalem. That achievement went to Saladin, who focused first on overthrowing the *rafida*, the Fatimids. Only after he had defeated the Shi'a, al-Zarqawi avers, was Saladin granted victory over the crusaders and the restoration of Jerusalem to Muslim control. "This important lesson that history gives us should never be forgotten," al-Zarqawi declaims. "We will never have victory over the original infidels [*al-kuffar al-asliyyin*] until we fight the apostate infidels [*al-kuffar al-murtadin*] along with the original infidels."[46]

By September 2007 al Qaeda's core leadership felt the need to enter directly the doctrinal fray over near versus far enemy targeting. Chosen to respond to critics of its "far-enemy-first" strategy was Abu Yahya al-Libi, a prominent lecturer on juridical matters in videos produced by al-Sahab, al Qaeda's media outlet.[47] Al-Libi opens his comments by quoting Qur'an 9:123, indicating that this verse did in fact figure in the intra-jihadist controversy, even though it does not appear as regularly as one might expect in documents or formal statements. Initially, his interpretation of the verse seems to accord with those who had criticized al Qaeda's far enemy strategy. He states:

> As God has said: "O you believe, fight the unbelievers near to you and let them find harshness in you." . . . Yes, we believe all of earth must be under the rule of Islam, with no exception made for the smallest part of it, because our Messenger was sent to all the people without exception. But this in no way means that we will fight all the peoples of earth at one go, to subjugate them to the Islamic *shari'a*. Islam didn't order us to do that, but rather ordered us to fight the nearest, then the next nearest of those who refuse to submit to Islamic rule, and begin with the closest and then the next closest. And in this way the circle widens until all submit to God's rule. And we are now at the first step and the beginning of the road as we are striving to recover our territories taken over by the infidels: the Jews and Nazarenes and their apostate helpers, the traitorous rulers. And this is the duty of the Muslims today, to find a foothold where they can establish their state which will rule by Islam and under which they will be shaded and in whose justice they will bask.

An unseen questioner then sets al-Libi up to respond squarely to al Qaeda's critics: "Speaking of the issue of priorities in fighting, there are some who propose beginning with the apostate governments because they are the enemies closest to the Muslims instead of the Americans and the other infidel coalitions." Al-Libi responds: "Without a doubt, the original confirmed ruling laid down by the noble verse and attested to by the biography of the Prophet and practice of the Companions after him is that we begin fighting the nearest then the next nearest." But this ruling applies, he avers, when jihad is being performed under its "normal" or ideal circumstances, with the *mujahidin* moving in their conquests from the nearest territories to those adjoining them.

Nevertheless, al-Libi continues, the jurists who spoke about this issue and clarified its ruling (he does not specify which jurists) stipulated that there are numerous situations in which it is better to start by fighting the farther enemy and giving priority to it over the others. Among those situations is if the farther enemy is more harmful and dangerous to the Muslims and their religion. Assessing the relative threat is the job of the commanders of the *mujahidin*, who decide—after consultation and review—which of the enemies must be fought first. The issue, al-Libi states, is not a definite textual directive in Islamic law but one open to discretion, study, and preference according to reality, need, ability, and interest.

When weighed in light of modern conditions, al-Libi continues, the question of spatial nearness and farness does not have the same significance it had when the Qur'an was revealed. Modern weapons, especially aircraft and missiles, cross continents and oceans, and target the Muslims as they sit in their homes with their families. Moreover, in contemporary international politics, the "major infidel powers" are closely tied at all levels with the "apostate regimes"—political, military, economic, and even cultural. "So in general they are a single entity, a single enemy, and a single army. They are a single hand against us, and the battle they are waging against us is a single battle which either the infidel crusader states adopt themselves or is taken up by their traitorous proxies who reign over the Muslim peoples."

The major infidel powers—foremost among them America—are no longer a distant enemy, al-Libi notes. "They are on the soil of the Muslims, killing, sabotaging, and destroying, and violating their sanctities, plundering their treasures, and imposing on them their policies and laws. And these apostate regimes with these states are like troops with their commanders, or rather like slaves with their master, making not a sound and speaking not a whisper." By defeating the infidel powers, the *mujahidin* will simultaneously topple the apostate "statelets" that are dependent on them. Therefore, for the clear-thinking *mujahidin*, al-Libi concludes, disputes over targeting the near or the far enemy are irrelevant.

The *mujahidin* today are in the situation of repelling the enemy and stopping his fierce attack on the Muslim land, and thus the option of beginning fighting with this enemy or that doesn't really have much meaning now. And even the one who wants to begin by fighting the apostate regimes dominating the Muslim lands will find himself after a little while—if not from day one—confronting in one way or another the crusader forces, foremost among them America. And thus he will stand face-to-face with the enemy he used to consider the farther and avoided fighting first. So with our enemies today, their near is near and their far is near. The part the *mujahidin* play in choosing the time of the confrontation is to try as much as they can to enter the decisive battle that suits their abilities, has the factors for success, saves them from a lot of effort, and leads to the elimination of the greater enemy, which spreads corruption and ruin and under whose wings the regimes of tyranny and torture develop and prosper.

ASSESSING THE TROPE AND ITS IMPLICATIONS FOR U.S. POLICY

The trope of the near and far enemy illuminates much about the radical Islamists who developed it and continue to deploy it. On the discursive level, it sheds light on how they use religious texts, hermeneutical devices, and legal reasoning to justify acts of violence. On the ideological level, it illuminates important aspects of their motivations and goals. And on the practical, strategic level, it demonstrates a keen appreciation for the material constraints under which they wage their jihad.

All the Islamist writers and commentators considered in this chapter profess to be Salafis; that is, they claim to follow the example of the first three generations of Muslims. These generations exemplify for them pristine Islamic faith and practice, untainted by innovations and heresies that crept in later. The Salafism of the radical Islamists often takes a particularly rigid, literal approach to qur'anic interpretation that is deeply informed by Wahhabism, the conservative ideology of Saudi Arabia. But as we have seen in the controversy over near versus far enemy targeting, basic religious texts such as Qur'an 9:123 are subject to quite different interpretations. As Abu Yahya al-Libi asserts in the video discussed above, the matter of targets is left to the discretion of the *mujahidin* on the basis of their own determination of their situation and interests. In short, the Salafists claim to be waging violent jihad because of clear texts in the Qur'an, and they condemn as "defeatists" those who interpret the same texts in less bellicose, more nonviolent ways. Yet the same Salafists, when it suits their needs, embrace creative, often utilitarian interpretations of the Qur'an. Religion plays as complex and malleable a role in justifying violence in the radical Islamist universe as it does in any other context.

The trope also indicates that ideologically the intent of the radicals' jihad (at least for the foreseeable future) is not conquest of non-Muslim lands in order to spread Muslim hegemony or the Islamic faith. Most Islamist groups are fixated on combatting the near enemy, by which they understand the traitorous, "apostate" governments that impede the establishment of true Islamic states. The far enemy, most importantly the United States, was once the object of attack mainly because it propped up the near enemy. But today the United States is no longer the far enemy. Its military presence in Muslim lands and the global "war on terror" have made it the most powerful of the radicals' near enemies. Accordingly, new categories have been coined to describe the United States in relation to its Muslim allies, as seen in the statements of 'Abd al-Hakim Hasan and Abu Mus'ab al-Zarqawi. The United States is now the chief power among the "original infidels" who prop up the "apostate infidel" regimes.

Islamists of all stripes inveigh against the moral corruption of the United States, in jeremiads public and private. But there is little evidence in the trope of the near and far enemy to indicate that these jeremiads are linked directly to jihad against the United States. Even al Qaeda, which became the first major Islamist group to declare war on the United States, does not emphasize spiritual or cultural motivations for its jihad. Instead, its stated motivations are overwhelmingly political. The difference between it and its critics lies in their strategy for achieving an American disengagement from the Muslim world.

On the practical level, debates over whom to target reflect an understanding by the radicals that their resources are limited, their numbers relatively small. They need to choose targets carefully to maximize their impact. Al Qaeda's leaders thought they were doing precisely that when they decided to attack the American homeland. Their shift in focus was criticized before 9/11 and vociferously denounced after it by other radical groups and by dissidents within al Qaeda's ranks because it recklessly aroused a full-scale American military response against them. One attack on the far enemy set back decades of struggle against the near enemy.

The implications of all this for American policy in the Muslim world is that a diminished American military presence in the region will weaken al Qaeda's position in this ongoing debate because it will lessen the conflation of the United States as both the near and the far enemy. Of course, it will not end this conflation, because the United States is unlikely to withdraw entirely from the region or to end its support for pro-American regimes or the state of Israel. Still, the smaller the military footprint of the United States in the Muslim world, the greater the chances that opponents of al Qaeda's "far-enemy-first" strategy will gain ground in this internal debate.

Finally, two unfolding developments promise to affect profoundly the future of radical Islamist strategies and American engagement with the Muslim world. First is the Arab Spring, which threatens to further marginalize the radical Islamists, especially in Egypt. Unarmed protestors in Tahrir Square effected the overthrow of

Hosni Mubarak over the course of weeks where armed militants had failed over the course of decades. Not even the United States could or would rescue its ally. The challenge now for both al Qaeda and the United States is to respond to the democratic aspirations unleashed in Egypt and elsewhere by the Arab Spring.

Second is the killing of Osama bin Laden on May 1, 2011, and the appointment of Ayman al-Zawahiri as his successor. The death of the chief proponent of the far enemy strategy may well result in a return to an emphasis on the near enemy. That battle, in places like Afghanistan, Pakistan, Yemen, and Saudi Arabia, promises to continue in an internecine fashion for some time to come.

NOTES

I thank John Carlson, Jonathan Ebel, and Samah Jafari for their helpful comments on earlier drafts of this chapter. Thanks also to Jeffry Halverson for helping track down difficult-to-find transcripts of al-Zarqawi's statements.

1. See the detailed study by Michael Cook, *Commanding Right and Forbidding Wrong in Islamic Thought* (Cambridge: Cambridge University Press, 2000).

2. Osama bin Laden, *Messages to the World: The Statements of Osama bin Laden*, ed. Bruce Lawrence, trans. James Howarth (London: Verso, 2005), 58–62. This declaration came five years after al Qaeda's first and largely unsuccessful attack against the World Trade Center in 1993.

3. See, for example, Fawaz A. Gerges, *The Far Enemy: Why Jihad Went Global* (New York: Cambridge University Press, 2005); David R. Springer, James L. Regens, and David N. Edger, *Islamic Radicalism and Global Jihad* (Washington, DC: Georgetown University Press, 2009).

4. For translations of relevant writings by Ibn Taymiyya, see Richard Bonney, *Jihad: From Qur'an to bin Laden* (New York: Palgrave Macmillan, 2007), 424–425; and Yahya Michot, *Muslims under Non-Muslim Rule* (Oxford: Interface Publications, 2006), 63–100. For a broader discussion of jihad ideology in Ibn Taymiyya's age, see Suleiman A. Mourad and James E. Lindsay, "Ibn 'Asakir and the Radicalization of Sunni Jihad Ideology in Crusader-Era Syria," in *Just Wars, Holy Wars, and Jihads: Christian, Jewish, Muslim Encounters and Exchanges*, ed. Sohail H. Hashmi (New York: Oxford University Press, 2012).

5. 'Abd al-Salam Faraj, *al-Farida al-gha'iba*, in *al-Fatawa al-Islamiyya min Dar al-Ifta' al-Misriyya*, vol. 10 (Cairo: Ministry of Awqaf, 1983), 3762–3771; cf. Johannes J. G. Jansen, *The Neglected Duty: The Creed of Sadat's Assassins and Islamic Resurgence in the Middle East* (New York: Macmillan, 1986), 160–179.

6. The appropriation of Ibn Taymiyya by contemporary radicals has been strongly challenged by some Muslim and non-Muslim scholars. See Bonney, *Jihad from Qur'an to bin laden*, 121–126; Michot, *Muslims under Non-Muslim Rule*, 101–122. For a summary of Ibn Taymiyya's work that emphasizes the ambivalence in his approach to rebellion and political violence generally, see Khaled Abou El Fadl, *Rebellion and Violence in Islamic Law* (Cambridge: Cambridge University Press, 2001), 271–279.

7. Faraj, *al-Farida al-gha'iba*, 3776; cf. Jansen, *Neglected Duty*, 192.

8. For a short overview of the qur'anic ethics of jihad, see Sohail H. Hashmi, "Interpreting the Islamic Ethics of War and Peace," in *Islamic Political Ethics: Civil Society, Pluralism, and Conflict*, ed. Sohail H. Hashmi (Princeton: Princeton University Press, 2002), 194–216.

9. Muhammad ibn Jarir al-Tabari, *Jami' al-bayan fi ta'wil al-Qur'an*, vol. 6 (Beirut: Dar al-Kutub al-'Ilmiyya, 1999), 517–518.

10. Isma'il ibn 'Umar ibn Kathir, *Tafsir al-Qur'an al-'azim*, vol. 2 (Beirut: Mu'assasat al-Riyan, 1996), 525–526.

11. Ibid.

12. Abu al-A'la Mawdudi, *Towards Understanding the Qur'an*, trans. and ed. Zafar Ishaq Ansari, vol. 3 (Leicester, UK: Islamic Foundation, 1990), 274–275.

13. Sayyid Qutb, *In the Shade of the Qur'an*, trans. and ed. Adil Salahi, vol. 8 (Leicester, UK: Islamic Foundation, 2003), 265, 309.

14. For a detailed study, see William E. Shepard, "Sayyid Qutb's Doctrine of *Jahiliyya*," *International Journal of Middle East Studies* 35 (2003): 521–545.

15. Qutb, *In the Shade of the Qur'an*, 308–309.

16. Faraj, *al-Farida al-gha'iba*, 3791; cf. Jansen, *Neglected Duty*, 226.

17. Faraj, *al-Farida al-gha'iba*, 3776; cf. Jansen, *Neglected Duty*, 192–193.

18. Robert W. Stookey, *America and the Arab States: An Uneasy Encounter* (New York: Wiley, 1975), 127–159; Ussama Makdisi, "'Anti-Americanism' in the Arab World: An Interpretation of a Brief History," *Journal of American History* 89, no. 2 (Sept. 2002): 548–550.

19. Sayyid Qutb, *Amrika allati ra'itu: Fi mizan al-qiyam al-insaniyya*, in *Amrika min al-dakhil*, ed. Salah 'Abd al-Fattah al-Khalidi (Algiers: Dar al-Madani, 2002), 131–138; cf. Sayyid Qutb, "The America I Have Seen: In the Scale of Human Values," trans. Tarek Masoud and Ammar Fakeeh, in *America in an Arab Mirror: Images of America in Arabic Travel Literature*, ed. Kamal Abdel-Malek (Gordonsville, VA: Palgrave Macmillan, 2000), 11–14.

20. Qutb, *Amrika allati ra'itu*, 140; cf. "America I Have Seen," 14–15.

21. Qutb, *Amrika allati ra'itu*, 147–155; cf. "America I Have Seen," 19–24. See also John Calvert, "'The World Is an Undutiful Boy!': Sayyid Qutb's American Experience," *Islam and Christian-Muslim Relations* 11, no. 1 (2000): 87–103.

22. "Ladenese Epistle: Declaration of War (Parts I–III)," at http://www.washingtonpost.com/ac2/wp-dyn/A4342-2001Sep21 (accessed Sept. 28, 2001), I: 1–2. An abbreviated version is in bin Laden, *Messages to the World*, 23–30.

23. "Ladenese Epistle," II: 2–3; cf. bin Laden, *Messages to the World*, 25–26.

24. "Ladenese Epistle," II: 2–3; cf. bin Laden, *Messages to the World*, 28. For further details on the sanctity of the Arabian Peninsula in Islamic tradition, see Sohail H. Hashmi, "Moral Communities and Political Boundaries: Islamic Perspectives," in *States, Nations, and Borders: The Ethics of Making Boundaries*, ed. Allen Buchanan and Margaret Moore (New York: Cambridge University Press, 2003), 186–194.

25. Bin Laden, *Messages to the World*, 38–39.

26. "Ladenese Epistle," I: 6.

27. Gerges, *Far Enemy*, 119–184; Springer, Regens, and Edger, *Islamic Radicalism*, 57–76; Michael Scheuer, *Through Our Enemies' Eyes: Osama bin Laden, Radical Islam, and the Future of America* (Washington, DC: Potomac Books, 2006), 181–203.

28. Ayman al-Zawahiri, "Knights under the Prophet's Banner," in *His Own Words: A Translation of the Writings of Dr. Ayman al-Zawahiri*, trans. Laura Mansfield (Old Tappan, NJ: TLG Publications, 2006), 102–103.

29. Steve Coll, *The Bin Ladens: An Arabian Family in the American Century* (New York: Penguin, 2008), 372–377.

30. Ibid., 289–290.

31. "Ladenese Epistle," I: 1–2; cf. bin Laden, *Messages to the World*, 26.

32. Gerges, *Far Enemy*, 119–150; Coll, *Bin Ladens*, 508–509; Nick Fielding, "Bin Laden's Key 9/11 Role Revealed," *Sunday Times*, Nov. 2, 2003, at http://www.timesonline.co.uk/tol/news/world/article1101581.ece (accessed June 24, 2011).

33. "Jihad against Jews and Crusaders," at http://www.washingtonpost.com/ac2/wp-dyn/A4993 -2001Sep21 (accessed Sept. 28, 2001), 2; cf. bin Laden, *Messages to the World*, 58–62.

34. George W. Bush, address to Congress, Sept. 20, 2001, at http://www.washingtonpost.com/ wp-srv/nation/specials/attacked/transcripts/bushaddress_092001.html (accessed June 23, 2011).

35. Bin Laden, *Messages to the World*, 162.

36. Ibid., 166–168.

37. Ibid., 166.

38. Ibid., 168–171.

39. Bruce Lawrence, introductory comments in ibid., 160–161. On this point of Islamic law, see Majid Khadduri, *War and Peace in the Law of Islam* (Baltimore: Johns Hopkins University Press, 1955), 94–101.

40. Bin Laden, *Messages to the World*, 170.

41. Scheuer, *Through Our Enemies' Eyes*, 149.

42. Quoted in Springer, Regens, and Edger, *Islamic Radicalism*, 67.

43. Abu 'Amr 'Abd al-Hakim Hasan, "Is Jihad in the Lands of the Original Infidels Preferrable?" 19–20, at http://www.jihadica.com/shaykh-isa-on-near-enemy-vs-far-enemy (accessed June 25, 2011).

44. See Will McCants, "Important al-Qaeda Scholar Identified," June 4, 2008, at http://www.ji hadica.com/important-al-qaeda-scholar-identified (accessed June 25, 2011).

45. Al-Zawahiri, *His Own Words*, 250–279.

46. Abu Mus'ab al-Zarqawi, *Hal ataka hadith al-rafida?* June 1, 2006, 593–594, at http://www .archive.org/stream/Abu-Musab-Zarkawi-Speechs/AMZ-Ver1#page/n524/mode/2up (accessed June 25, 2011).

47. Abu Yahya al-Libi, "Far and Near Enemy in the Present Reality," videotaped interview posted on the Internet by al-Sahab Media, Sept. 10, 2007.

15

Varieties of "Violence"

Thinking Ethically about the Use of Force in the War on Terror

Jean Bethke Elshtain

American moral thought is vexed by the problem of violence. By this I do not mean that conversations about how Americans ought to act as individuals or how the United States ought to act in the world frequently devolve into fisti-cuffs. Rather, many who reflect on America's place in the world have lost their ability to distinguish violence from other actions involving force or to think clearly about quite distinct concepts or phenomena. Ironically, by "seeing" vio-lence everywhere—transferring the substantial moral force of the word *vio-lence* into contexts where it fits poorly—scholars have hampered themselves and others in locating it anywhere.[1]

When we hear of "violence," we conjure up images of deadly force, bodily harm, war, torture, physical destruction, egregious violations such as rape, and other horrific matters. It is simply an empirical fact to say that all of these can or do entail violence. But we cannot speak of violence without also invoking ethical concepts such as violation, injustice, injury, excessiveness, vehemence, and other related terms.[2] The word *violence* brings together these two modes of description and evaluation; fact and value; the empirical and the ethical. Yet, not everything labeled violence should be understood as such, particularly when speaking about the United States' use of coercive force in the "war on terror."

This chapter takes up the seemingly simple question of whether and when the United States has responded to acts of violence with force in the war on terror. I frame the question in this way to provoke deeper consideration of the words—and the often-flawed moral judgments they have carried—that have been used to describe many efforts to defeat al Qaeda and other militants plotting against the

United States and its allies. Language can either help clarify or obscure vital moral distinctions. My concern is that by overusing and conflating terms such as *violence, torture,* and *war,* we have impaired our critical thinking about the use of force and lost our ability to distinguish—intellectually, morally, and emotionally—among uses of force that are permissible and forbidden. There lies as well between these two categories a large and morally ambiguous realm, in which certain forms of coercion might be deemed justifiable (or not) depending on the moral argument and circumstances of the case.

MORAL LANGUAGE AND CLARITY

Language does not simply describe or designate; it also assigns meaning and value. We make such assignments of value daily without reflecting on them, but they pop into focus as soon as language is flagrantly misapplied. For instance, we do not speak or write of the "Massacre of Gettysburg" or the "D-Day Massacre." Such language is jarring because it is historically and morally inaccurate. For the same reason, one who wrote of the "My Lai Battle," the "Battle of Columbine High School," or the "Virginia Tech Battle" would be rightly dismissed as obtuse. As Michael Walzer writes in his classic work *Just and Unjust Wars,* terms such as aggression, self-defense, and massacre render judgments while also connecting to quite different realities.[3] To be sure, people are killed in each instance; indeed, in a massacre the entire point is to slaughter as many people as possible, including civilians or noncombatants. Massacre implies that those killed have been murdered. They were innocent. Or, it was not a fair fight; they had no way to defend themselves. They—the victims—were set up and mowed down. It would be incoherent to speak of a "just massacre."[4] But a battle is something else factually and morally. Here we find strategic deployment of force pitting armed combatants against one another in an environment where the rules of war prohibit certain kinds of behavior. These rules are not always observed, of course, but we can rightly condemn those who do not abide by such norms. A battle is not something we condemn a priori—unless we are pacifists. Far more commonly, though, we are just terribly careless in our use of evaluative language.

There is something in the word *violence* itself that names an act as that which should be eschewed and condemned. *Violence* is and should be a strongly pejorative term. Why? To parse this question, one needs to be sensitive to the ways in which words are embedded in traditions, ways of thinking and living. The dictionary provides some clarification by defining *violence* as actions and attendant passions that are immoderate and furious; that injure or damage; that entail excessive or unlawful use of force. We call the action of a street gang violent. We do not call a police response violent, unless the police violate (a term from the same root as *violence*) their own procedures and turn rogue and anarchic. The actions of the police and military are rule-governed and consist in restraint in the use of force and minimal use of force, not unleashing men and women in uniforms to kill anyone in sight, to generate mayhem, to plunder and to rape. But talk of violence conjures up all these things. By proclaiming *any* deployment of coercive physical force "violence," we put our thumbs on the scale and short-circuit moral reflection before it can even begin.

The linguistic waters surrounding the term *violence* have been muddied further by widespread use of the phrase "structural violence," which suggests that violence is somehow encoded into structures with predictably violent outcomes. The problem with this use of *violence* is that there is no agency, which means no one can be assigned responsibility. The term has become a kind of all-purpose form of condemnation, and, as such, it is recognizable as a general ideological plaint. Reclaiming and relimiting the term *violence*, then, is an important first step in the careful consideration of the moral application of force.[5]

Fortunately, we have traditions that help us to make the necessary distinctions between violent actions, those that should always be forbidden, and the vast range of acts that fall outside that category but still require deep moral deliberation. We distinguish aggression from self-defense; violent criminality from the restrained deployment of force by police; terrorism from revolution; torture from other forms of coercive interrogation; and so on. The burden of this chapter is to clarify these important distinctions. It is sloppy thinking that shoves all physical or empirical forms of force into one generic category of "violence." In turn, such linguistic imprecision permits us to be intellectually lazy and ethically muddled. There is a great deal at stake when we make critical distinctions, as I shall claim, particularly when it comes to the ethical evaluation of U.S. policies pertaining to the war on terror.

When we erode distinctions among moral categories we risk, on the one hand, acquiescence in the face of evil and, on the other, an amoral approach to force in which the ends always justify the means.[6] For some, no use of force is ever permissible or morally justifiable. Period. This sort of *prohibitionism* is unhelpful ethically, as it effaces the distinctions that have challenged men and women for centuries and to which so many have devoted so much care and thought. Given that the United States has always faced and will continue to face decisions involving self-defense, efforts to confront aggression, and the deployment and projection of force on behalf of U.S. interests, the defense of allies, or humanitarian concerns, it behooves us to think and speak cogently about these matters. Yet we also know that force can and has been used excessively and, as such, can usher in its own forms of violence. Let's work through these categories first.

THE FORBIDDEN AND THE PERMISSIBLE:
RESPONDING TO AGGRESSION WITH FORCE

Not all actions that entail force or coercion are violent. Consider a few examples: a parent who roughly grabs a child running into a busy street; a student defending herself from an assault; a homeowner who takes on an intruder to protect family or home. Laws within and beyond the United States have long recognized as permissible such obvious forms of self-defense. Likewise, the actions these efforts seek to thwart—rape, robbery, assault, murder—are and *always* must be forbidden because they amount to violence. No one—at least no one worth taking seriously—can morally defend them.

Within the realm of political affairs, there are similar categories of permissible and forbidden actions that build upon such notions of self-defense. What is unique in the political context is that the foremost responsibilities of states and governments are to provide basic security for their citizens, to protect private property, and to preserve civic peace and order. In other words, governments exist to prevent or respond to violence. This notion is central to the thought of theologians such as Augustine, Thomas Aquinas, Martin Luther, Reinhold Niebuhr, and many others, which explains why Christian teaching has long deemed government a "legitimate authority" and, as such, authorizes polities to use force to protect citizens and mete out justice in the wake of violence. It is primarily in the absence or inadequacy of such authority that individuals or groups may legitimately resort to force in self-defense. Otherwise, governments themselves become agents of violence (as opposed to force) or revenge (as opposed to retribution). It should also be said that while war may be authorized by a government, governmental authorization does not per se make war legitimate, for legitimacy or illegitimacy are assessed along the vectors of both political authorization and moral justification, as I shall explain below.

Much religious reflection about permissible and forbidden uses of force has emerged within, and been codified by, the "just war" tradition. Anyone who has considered problems involving violence and force has some passing familiarity with just war's constitutive categories: the *jus ad bellum*, or justifiable occasions for resorting to force; and the *jus in bello*, or justifiable forms of force deployed in fighting a war. The behavior of states and militaries is assessed by the moral standards of these broad conceptual frameworks. Within each category, there are a number of prerogatives, rules, and restrictions. For this discussion, the most important *ad bellum* norms are those of "legitimate authority," as noted above, and "just cause" for the resort to force (such as self-defense, deterrence, or response to aggression). When considering *jus in bello*, the most critical norm is "discrimination" (or noncombatant immunity), which requires those using force to distinguish combatants from noncombatants and expressly forbids targeting noncombatants. As well, "proportionality" forbids using excessive force that causes unnecessary harm or destruction.

In *Just and Unjust Wars*, Michael Walzer claims that aggression is the one crime that a state can commit against another state. An aggressive war is one whose ends are illegitimate and whose cause is unjust: to acquire territory, to gain pelf, or to further some other agenda by inflicting injury, death, or physical destruction. We do not hold two states culpable of committing violence when one crosses the territory of the other in the dead of night, or sends aircraft to bomb cities, or perpetrates some other unjustifiable activity, such as North Korea's 2010 sinking of a South Korean ship or its bombing of Yeonpyeong island. If the state committing aggression claims to be responding to "provocative behavior," one's critical antennae come out immediately. For one must distinguish so-called provocation and pretext from a nigh-certain attack, against which self-defense is authorized. Similarly, too, in clear-cut cases of aggression, such as the German and Soviet invasions of Poland in 1939, it would be odd to condemn all three nations for engaging in violence when it was Germany and the Soviet Union that committed the acts of aggression and Poland that responded, such as it could, in self-defense. These examples remind us that aggression remains the most prominent form of violence against which governments must be prepared to use force in order to defend themselves and their citizens.[7]

What we learned from the attacks of September 11, 2001, is that nonstate actors also can commit aggression. When terrorists attack a nation and its people so as to instill fear or influence their actions, we rightly consider it a political act of aggression and injustice—in other words, violence. When al Qaeda attacked the United States, it acted without the legitimate authority to use force that accrues to governments charged with protecting specific citizens and territory. No people elected Osama bin Laden to defend them. No international body such as the United Nations recognizes al Qaeda's right to use force. Nor can al Qaeda claim a "just cause" in the widely understood sense of the term, no matter the extensive list of grievances it invoked to justify its actions, primarily having to do with Western decadence.

In the dark days following 9/11, there were many who inveighed against a "rush to war" and urged the U.S. government not to "respond to violence with violence." The notion that the United States was hell-bent on vengeance and rushed headlong into war is not borne out by the facts. The United States waited, weighed alternatives, gave the Taliban ample time in which to turn over Osama bin Laden, and took the matter to the United Nations. The United Nations authorized the operation in Afghanistan by invoking Chapter VII collective security provisions, as it had only done during the Korean War, the Persian Gulf War, and some prominent peacekeeping missions.[8] The U.S. war in Afghanistan did not begin with a tantrum. It began when the international community and the

United States acted as they ought to have acted in response to an act of violence that used innocent civilians as weapons against innocent civilians. In other words, as legitimate authorities, they acted on behalf of a just cause to respond to aggression.

The other arm of the just war tradition, *jus in bello*, also helps us distinguish between violence and force. Even if al Qaeda had been a sovereign government or legitimate authority, and even if its grievances were sufficient to warrant the use of force, it still committed morally forbidden and violent acts by intentionally targeting civilians and seeking to cause as much damage as it could. Such violent actions must be distinguished from other insurgent groups that have targeted military installations. Al Qaeda's indiscriminate and disproportionate attacks are rightly placed in the pantheon of the world's worst violence, as the term is properly understood. Compare this, then, to the so-called violence that the United States was accused of when it responded.

In Afghanistan the measured use of force was brought to bear against those who had perpetrated egregious acts of terror—unrestrained violence—and their supporters. The United States did not recruit suicide hijackers to fly commercial airplanes in an attempt to kill as many Afghan civilians as possible. Rather, from the initial invasion throughout the troop surge in Afghanistan, the U.S. military and its NATO partners have been committed to heeding the demands of *jus in bello* and the internationally recognized laws of war. Indeed, some critics claim that the United States has been too reticent about its use of force. In any case, counterterrorist efforts do not intentionally target civilians, and they make every effort to avoid loss of innocent life. This is not to say there have not been many accidental deaths and rogue acts of violence, but there is a crucial distinction between targeting civilians and unintentional killing by stray bombs. Yet there are those who insist on seeing these activities—the terrorist attacks of September 11, 2001, and the war in Afghanistan—as morally equivalent, often by conflating terrorism and counterterrorism under the broad rubric of violence. It is particularly alarming to observe how many of these and related calls emanated from American pulpits and religious organizations.[9]

Violence violates not only human bodies (battles do that as well) but long-established rules of conduct in warfare. The fact that rules of war are sometimes violated, as has been done by a small number of U.S. forces fighting in Iraq and Afghanistan, is not to say that rules don't exist or that they will cease to exist if breached repeatedly. These unfortunate cases have received extensive media coverage, recounting the incarceration and trials of those accused of war crimes under the Uniform Code of Military Justice. What is critical in the war on terror is that we erect and preserve the most solid ethical barriers possible *against* the violence of unlawful and excessive use of force. For this distinction is what separates terrorism from the lawful and morally justifiable use of force.

Massacres, excessive force, and the targeting of civilians are all war crimes and acts of violence. Not all violence or war crimes result in death. Other forbidden activities include the soulless torture of a helpless prisoner (no matter how fiendish his activities may have been prior to being taken prisoner), such as ripping out fingernails, applying cattle prods to genitalia, rape, burning with cigarettes, or amputating body parts. Other forbidden acts include less extreme but similarly abusive acts such as the scandalous conduct by U.S. prison guards against Iraqi detainees at Abu Ghraib. These heinous misdeeds, though certainly less vicious than the routine cruelties that occurred there as a matter of policy under Saddam Hussein's regime, nevertheless were egregious violations of legitimate authority. As such, we properly label them violence. Where the ethical rubber really hits the road is in determining what lies between the easily justifiable, permissible, or legitimate, on one hand, and the clearly forbidden and violent, on the other. This means that there may be morally ambiguous actions that yet might be justifiable or even necessary under certain circumstances. Indeed, moral ambiguity is unavoidable in these matters, which is why careful consideration is called for. One might visualize this typology as two clear ends of a spectrum. Between these forbidden and unproblematically permissible poles lies a gray area—a morally ambiguous terrain—to which we now turn our focus.

COERCIVE INTERROGATION IN EXTREMIS

Having clarified that torture falls into the category of the absolutely and always forbidden, what, then, of coercive interrogation? I have discussed this matter at great length elsewhere and expand upon it here.[10] Is a shouted word torture? An insult? A slap in the face? The mere threat of violence? That which is undeniably torture—those horribles enumerated above—is forbidden. But many now call any form of coercion "torture." This rhetoric guts the category and makes it very difficult for us to make critical ethical distinctions. Surely sleep deprivation does not belong in the same category as amputating a body part. A shouted insult is a far cry from slicing off an ear. This is not so mysterious. We make such distinctions all the time. To call an insult, sleep deprivation, or beating someone nearly to death "abuse" is of little use in helping us, as moral beings, to evaluate the degrees of harm that one charged to protect citizens might employ against a would-be perpetrator.

But is coercive interrogation violent and per se forbidden, or might it under certain circumstances be morally justifiable if still not entirely unproblematic? Again, let me be clear: that which is per se violent is forbidden and distinguished from forms of coercion and force that are clearly permissible. Between these categories, then, is a more ethically complex and problematic realm in which, under certain circumstances, something short of violence but more than routinely permissible force might be morally justifiable and even necessary to carry out if a government is to live up to its most fundamental mandate to protect its citizens.

The matter of coercive interrogation forces us to confront this moral ambiguity. Discussions about coercive interrogation are tragically relevant in the midst of the war on terror in which the United States has used coercive interrogation and gained vital intelligence from the process. In my earlier work on torture, I argued that deontological moralism and legalism make it nearly impossible for us to plumb the problem of morally ambiguous activities such as coercive interrogation, for the entire aim of such an approach is to eradicate all such ambiguity.[11] The deontological approach presumes that all political action can and must be *either* clearly permissible *or* strictly forbidden. Such either/or thinking often relies on an approach that effaces any distinction between that which is legal and that which is moral. Morality and law are conflated. Indeed, if it can be shown that an action violates some aspect of law—whosoever's law it might be, however multiple the range of legal interpretations entailed—it can be claimed that the action must be immoral as well.

Deontological approaches seek to overcome the problems of consequentialism, which makes it altogether too easy to do whatever one has to do to "get results." A strictly consequentialist approach would deem the process of interrogation acceptable—without limits—simply on the basis of the information expected to be gained and the attendant outcome. Whereas for the consequentialist potentially high levels of human violation are defensible if the result is the prevention of, say, a suicide bombing, the deontologist makes all applications of coercive interrogation equivalent to torture and thus forbidden. In this context a slap to the face is no different from mutilation. To the foreign policy "realist" consequentialist, nothing is as important as "national interest." There are no limits to protecting society. The deontological moralist, however, is so committed to keeping his or her hands clean that the safety of the collective is correlatively downgraded.

The form of moral reasoning that drove the just war tradition historically is casuistry. One begins with a rule-governed activity—and when "violence" is rule-governed, it ceases to be "violence" and becomes something else—the measured use of force, the taming of "violence," if you will. To a large extent, these are the norms that have governed—or held to account—U.S. foreign policy decisions and military action in the war on terror, including wars in Afghanistan and Iraq. A similar moral logic applied to a different set of circumstances, such as the detention of a high-level terrorist in a nonmilitary facility, could be expected to produce a different outcome.

But how do we navigate this complex, morally ambiguous terrain? Such moral ambiguity recognizes that coercive interrogation relies upon techniques that many deem ethically problematic; yet forswearing them also could be problematic. Straddling the two horns of this dilemma, moral casuistry invites us to consider the exigencies of the threat; the nature of the organization, including one's role within it; the circumstances in which a prisoner is taken; and so on. With these rough-and-ready considerations in mind, we turn to the case of Khalid Sheikh Mohammad, the so-called mastermind responsible for planning the attacks of September 11, 2001. He was apprehended in Pakistan in 2003 and has been in U.S. detention ever since. Khalid Sheikh Mohammad was taken prisoner in the midst of a conflict initiated by a nonstate terrorist organization of which he was not only a member but in which he played a vital leadership role. Al Qaeda—having declared war against the United States, the United Kingdom, and any nation allied to them; having committed violent attacks not only against Europe and the United States but against civilians in Jordan, Indonesia, Pakistan, Spain, and elsewhere; and having declared its intent to commit future attacks—shows a clear pattern of aggression and poses an exigent threat to the protection of many nations' citizens.

In the effort to prevent future attacks and apprehend or kill those who plan them, counterterrorist branches of legitimate authorities can and should be prepared to use techniques of coercive interrogation if determined to be necessary. Given that Khalid Sheikh Mohammad was captured in the midst of a conflict and had planned operations against the United States, it is reasonable to assume that he possessed knowledge of additional operations to inflict as much violence as possible on as many people as possible. With all of this in mind, violence (ripping out fingernails, beating, electric shock) against him would still be beyond justification. But might other forms of coercive interrogation short of that be justifiable as a last resort? If intimidating Khalid Sheikh Mohammad into sharing information about his organization can be directly linked to preventing other attacks and rendering al Qaeda incapable of plotting against commuters in Spain or holiday travelers in the air over the Atlantic Ocean then, however morally distasteful, coercive interrogation tactics may be, it could be even more problematic if the nation's authorities responsible for protecting fellow citizens refuse to apply such forms of coercion. This does not mean that harsh forms of interrogation should be normalized in the moral sense of the term, even if they yield potentially life-saving information. This is what moral ambiguity entails—resisting the tendency to normalize (for example, through "torture warrants") that which is not otherwise permissible use of force in the ordinary sense.

Again, though, this does *not* mean that "anything goes," as consequentialism allows. Moral casuistry invites limits. Just war thinking makes use of certain criteria, which can be helpful in these circumstances as well. "Discrimination" would prohibit *ever* harming—or threatening to harm—the innocent as a means of extracting useful information, which would put Khalid Sheikh Mohammad's family off-limits. Prudential criteria such as "last resort" also have a place. One should not launch right into the "rough stuff" but rather recognize its assigned place only when other provisions have failed. Finally, it should be noted that Khalid Sheikh Mohammad's ability to provide useful information diminishes over time; as such, the range of permissible coercive actions would narrow accordingly.

In addition to helping us see how challenging these waters are to navigate, the case of Khalid Sheikh Mohammad helps us to see what was so wrong about the actions perpetrated by the U.S. prison guards at Abu Ghraib. In the former case, coercive interrogation techniques were applied for the sake of life-sparing information. Lamentably, in the latter case, violence and abuse were applied to an entirely different category of prisoner without authorization, without oversight, and without any clear sense of the ability of prisoners to provide timely information. If we are to judge from the now infamous photos of those who carried out these activities, this was a case of loving violence for its own sake. This must always be forbidden and cautioned against.

Wartime killing can never be sanctioned as a morally normative activity: it is never an unqualified good. But it may be a necessary and justifiable one—permissible but lamentable. To accept that an activity is justifiable is not to condone or to sanction it as universally acceptable, even laudable. We rightly associate Augustine with the mordant recognitions that enter into the tragedies of statecraft, political judgment, and soldiering. Augustine's "melancholy soldier" is the soldier who understands that a war is just but that even in a just war, killing is a terrible thing.[12] Even more stringent precautions pertain with coercive interrogation. Physical coercion that goes beyond detaining and questioning someone can never be lifted up as salutary or morally unproblematic, but it may be defended as necessary.

Over the years, respected ethical and political theorists have written of the moral guilt incurred by stateswomen and statesmen in the pursuit of their office. We are not talking about the guilt that a Hitler, Stalin, or bin Laden incurs, but that of, let's say, a democratically elected war leader. Furthermore, in the thick of a justifiable struggle against an aggressive foe who has perpetrated one horror after another, suppose the leader permits or even orders what, under ordinary circumstances, would be morally dubious at best and perhaps criminal at worst? This is no hypothetical possibility but a set of conditions encountered frequently in the war on terror.

Facing up to this sort of problem often troubles religious believers, especially many Christians who recall that their Lord came to bring peace on earth and goodwill to all men and women. Anti-Nazi German theologian and pastor Dietrich Bonhoeffer warned against this kind of "private virtuousness," by which moral actors pride themselves on keeping their hands clean.[13] The privately virtuous launch condemnatory thunderbolts against those who "dirty" their hands in the legitimate pursuits of statecraft, including foremost the charge to protect citizens and the common good. For there can be no common good of any kind if a people is defeated, pillaged, and massacred. Bonhoeffer respected civil authorities and their divine "mandate" to protect their citizens. Yet he also recognized that the Nazi regime had forsaken this solemn responsibility under God. This tragic realization ultimately drew him into the plots to assassinate Hitler. These were deeply conflicting, morally ambiguous positions to hold simultaneously. How did he reconcile his recognition of the necessities of political authority and his conviction that Nazism had betrayed its mandate? It is notable that Bonhoeffer never offered an apologia for the actions that would cost him his life and brand him a traitor. To do so would have suggested that his actions were ethically permissible and unproblematic. However defensible, courageous, or necessary Bonhoeffer's actions may have been, they were not clear-cut "self-defense." His actions, legacy, and moral reflection stand within a grayer realm of moral ambiguity.

Torture remains a horror and a tactic that is forbidden. There are moments, though, when a rule forbidding what some have wrongly labeled "torture" may be overridden to permit certain forms of physical and psychological coercion and pressure. Coercive interrogation should always remain in a zone of moral ambiguity. If we overlegalize and overmoralize the matter—forcing the gray to become either black or white—then we will have done violence, so to speak, to the complexities of the issues involved.

CONCLUSION

Ethical reasoning is largely about how we make critical distinctions. Whether we are to criticize or to laud, to oppose or to endorse, to emulate or to repudiate, turns on the ways in which we reflect upon and describe what it is we face when we take up arms, protect the public, or interrogate hostile prisoners. If all force becomes "violence" or all violence reduces to "force," matters become too easy for us—too easy to endorse or to condemn. We soothe our consciences as we twist our intellects. The key distinction with which our reasoning about violence and the use of force begins is to acknowledge from the outset that there *is* a distinction to be made; that not every instance when force is used is a moment of violence. Violence is by definition unrestrained and morally unjustifiable. It reaches toward the extreme where there are no rule-governed limitations to its exercise. By contrast, force may be deployed to justifiable or unjustifiable ends. If it is unjustifiable, illegal, and immoral, we properly call it violence. If we eschew this vital distinction, we have nothing to reason about at all.

NOTES

1. Jon Pahl, *Empire of Sacrifice: The Religious Origins of American Violence* (New York: New York University Press, 2010); Rosemary Radford Ruether, *America, Amerikka: Elect Nation and Imperial Violence* (London: Equinox, 2007).

2. On the meanings of violence, see John D. Carlson, "Religion and Violence: Coming to Terms with Terms," in *The Blackwell Companion to Religion and Violence*, ed. Andrew R. Murphy (Oxford: Wiley-Blackwell, 2011), 7–22.

3. Michael Walzer, *Just and Unjust Wars: A Moral Argument with Historical Illustrations* (New York: Basic, 1977), 3.

4. Another unambiguously forbidden form of violence is genocide. Even those who perpetrate genocide deny they are doing so, or have done so, because of the universal revulsion conjured by the term and the reality it names.

5. See Pahl, *Empire of Sacrifice*.

6. In the case of the former, Joseph Loconte reminds us of the sad story of calls for appeasement made on religious grounds in his *The End of Illusions: Religious Leaders Confront Hitler's Gathering Storm* (Lanham, MD: Rowman and Littlefield, 2004), which includes dozens of editorials, essays, and excerpts from sermons that, in making exculpatory arguments and flattening out the moral horizon, advocated for isolationism and U.S. nonintervention in the face of Nazi aggression. In the case of the latter, Machiavelli's *The Prince* is still the reigning illustration of how readily violence can be used to political advantage.

7. Morally unambiguous scenarios such as this are increasingly few and far between. Since the 1990s, we find more frequent cases of internal strife, the violent fragmenting of a once civil order, cross-border violence by nonstate actors, and unjust peace brutally maintained by self-serving tyrants. These scenarios raise different sets of questions for all who seek to think ethically about violence and for those who would seek to promote peaceful human flourishing. As a result, humanitarian military intervention has been given an international imprimatur with the articulation of the norm "responsibility to protect"(R2P), which holds that the United Nations or a member state or states are authorized to respond with the use of force to systematic, egregious, and continuing violence by a state or group within it. See Jean Bethke Elshtain, "International Justice as Equal Regard and the Use of Force," *Ethics and International Affairs* 17, no. 2 (2003): 63–75.

8. As well, for the first time in its history, NATO invoked Article 5 of the Washington Treaty, which states that an attack on one member nation will be viewed as an attack on all member nations.

9. See chapter 8 in my *Just War against Terror: The Burden of American Power in a Violent World* (New York: Basic, 2003).

10. Jean Bethke Elshtain, "Reflections on the Problem of 'Dirty Hands,'" in *Torture*, ed. Sanford Levinson (New York: Oxford University Press, 2004), 77–89.

11. Ibid.

12. Augustine's classic work *The City of God* is the great text that takes up the burdens of statecraft. Michael Walzer, in his pathbreaking essay "Political Action: The Problem of Dirty Hands," reprinted in Levinson, *Torture*, 61–76, repeats Augustine's discussion of the melancholy soldier.

13. Dietrich Bonhoeffer, *Letters and Papers from Prison*, ed. Eberhard Bethge (1953; reprint New York: Collier/Macmillan, 1972), 5.

CONTRIBUTORS

JOHN D. CARLSON is Associate Professor of Religious Studies at Arizona State University, where he is Associate Director of the Center for the Study of Religion and Conflict. He is coeditor of *The Sacred and the Sovereign: Religion and International Politics* (2003) and *Religion and the Death Penalty: A Call for Reckoning* (2004).

JOHN CORRIGAN is the Lucius Moody Bristol Distinguished Professor of Religion and Professor of History at Florida State University. His books include *The Oxford Handbook of Religion and Emotion* (2008); *Religious Intolerance in America: A Documentary History* with Lynn Neal (2010); and *Religion in American History*, coedited with Amanda Porterfield (2010).

JONATHAN H. EBEL is Associate Professor of Religious Studies at the University of Illinois. He is the author of *Faith in the Fight: Religion and the American Soldier in the Great War* (2010).

JEAN BETHKE ELSHTAIN is the Laura Spelman Rockefeller Professor of Social and Political Ethics in the Divinity School of the University of Chicago, with appointments in Political Science and on the Committee on International Relations. Her books include *Sovereignty: God, State, and Self* (2008) and *Just War against Terror: The Burden of American Power in a Violent World* (2003).

EDDIE S. GLAUDE JR. is the William S. Tod Professor of Religion and African American Studies in the Department of Religion and the Chair of the Center for African American Studies at Princeton University. He is the author of *Exodus! Religion, Race, and Nation in Early 19th Century Black America* (2000), *Is It Nation Time? Contemporary Essays on Black Power and Black Nationalism* (2002), and *In a Shade of Blue: Pragmatism and the Politics of Black America* (2007).

285

ELIZABETH HANSON is a Ph.D. candidate in English at Loyola University Chicago. She is working on a dissertation exploring asexuality and narrative in Victorian and modernist fiction.

SOHAIL H. HASHMI is Professor of International Relations at Mount Holyoke College. His publications include *Islamic Political Ethics: Civil Society, Pluralism, and Conflict* (2002) and *Ethics and Weapons of Mass Destruction: Religious and Secular Perspectives,* coedited with Steven P. Lee (2004).

STANLEY HAUERWAS is the Gilbert T. Rowe Professor of Theological Ethics at the Duke University Divinity School. His publications include *A Cross-Shattered Church: Reclaiming the Theological Heart of Preaching* (2009) and *Hannah's Child: A Theologian's Memoir* (2010).

JAMES TURNER JOHNSON is Professor of Religion and Associate Member of the Graduate Department of Political Science at Rutgers–The State University of New Jersey. His publications include *Morality and Contemporary Warfare* (1999), *The War to Oust Saddam Hussein* (2005), and *Ethics and the Use of Force: Just War in Historical Perspective* (2011).

GRACE Y. KAO is Associate Professor of Ethics at Claremont School of Theology and Associate Professor of Religion at Claremont Graduate University. She was Assistant Professor of Religious Studies and Women's Studies at Virginia Tech from 2003 to 2009. She is the author of *Grounding Human Rights in a Pluralist World* (2011).

TODD M. KERSTETTER is Associate Professor of History and Director of Graduate Studies at Texas Christian University. He is the author of *God's Country, Uncle Sam's Land: Faith and Conflict in the American West* (2006). He has published articles in *Western Historical Quarterly, Great Plains Quarterly, American Journalism*, and *Nebraska History*.

MARTIN E. MARTY is the Fairfax M. Cone Distinguished Service Professor Emeritus at the University of Chicago, where he taught for thirty-five years. He is the author of over fifty books and the recipient of seventy-five honorary doctorates, the National Humanities Medal, the National Book Award, and the Medal of the American Academy of Arts and Sciences.

ANDREW R. MURPHY is Associate Professor of Political Science at Rutgers University. His books include *Conscience and Community: Revisiting Toleration and Religious Dissent in Early Modern England and America* (2001) and *Prodigal Nation: Moral Decline and Divine Punishment from New England to 9-11* (2008).

LYNN S. NEAL is Associate Professor of Religion at Wake Forest University. Her publications include *Romancing God: Evangelical Women and Inspirational Fiction* (2006) and *Religious Intolerance in America: A Documentary History* with John Corrigan (2010).

NED O'GORMAN is Associate Professor in the Department of Communication at the University of Illinois. He is the author of *Spirits of the Cold War: Contesting Worldviews in the Classical Age of American Security Strategy* (2011).

S. BRENT RODRIGUEZ-PLATE is Visiting Associate Professor of Religious Studies at Hamilton College. His books include *Blasphemy: Art That Offends* (2006) and *Religion and Film: Cinema and the Re-Creation of the World* (2009). He is co-founder and managing editor of *Material Religion: The Journal of Objects, Arts, and Belief.*

STEPHEN H. WEBB is Professor of Religion and Philosophy at Wabash College. His books include *American Providence: A Nation with a Mission* (2006), *Dome of Eden: A New Theory of Evolution and Creation* (2010), and *Jesus Christ, Eternal God: Heavenly Flesh and the Metaphysics of Matter* (2012).

INDEX

Abbey, Edwin, 68

Abel, 50, 54, 57, 58

abolitionism, 25n33, 130, 132, 226; militant forms of, 1–2, 9, 13, 130; religious grounding of, 13. *See also* Brown, John; Garnet, Henry Highland; Garrison, William Lloyd; slavery; Walker, David

abolition of war, 220

abortion, 22, 39, 40

Abraham, 111, 179, 180, 191n7

Abu Ghraib, 22, 279, 282

Adams, Samuel, 165

Afghanistan: war in, xvi, 106, 233, 261–62, 264–65, 278

African American, 20, 43; churches, 128; experience in America, 140–41; freedom for, 98–99, 129, 130–32; lynching of, 167; national identity, 131; violence against, ix, 16. *See also* slavery. *See also under* jeremiad

African Episcopal Church, 128

al Qaeda, xvi, 259; attacks of, 10, 234, 251, 277–78, 281; "Declaration of Jihad against the Jews and the Crusaders," 250–51, 262–63, 270n2; declaration of war against the United States, 259–70; internal disputes of, 21, 251; opposition to Saudi regime, 259–62; Seung-Hui Cho's invocation of, 191n8; U.S. military force against, 197, 273. *See also* bin Laden, Osama; Islamism, radical; jihad; al-Zarqawi, Abu Musʿab; al-Zawahiri, Ayman

Amalekites, ix, 19; biblical story of, 111–12; Catholics as, 112–19; and genocide, 111, 112, 115; Mormons as, 119–23; Native Americans as, 112–16

American Civil Liberties Union (ACLU), 40

American exceptionalism, 21, 85, 93, 101–2, 107n5, 181, 197–99; and civil religion, 214–17; just war and, 210–14, 219n43, 242; variants of, 214–15. *See also* "city upon a hill"

American Expeditionary Force (A.E.F.), 71, 72, 75

American Federation of Labor, 66–67

American Home Missionary Society, 122

American identity, x, xvi, 2, 7, 12, 14, 18, 19, 48–49, 59, 64, 129, 131, 190; and civil religion, 210; early formation of, 39, 44; enforcement of, 155; mythic origins of, 52–58; and providence, 91, 93, 96; threats to, 144; violence of, 220, 226

American Legion, 19, 68, 73–76

American Protective Association, 118

American Revolution, 10, 15, 20, 21, 35, 50; and American exceptionalism, 212–16; and civil religion, 207–10; and doctrine of providence, 94–95; and Exodus story, 131, 209; and holy war, 191, 202–4; and just war, 10, 15, 95, 191, 201–14; and Ku Klux Klan, 165; and

289

diversity, 2, 36, 71; critique of, 183; ethnic, 92; racial, 92, 183, 187; religious, 3, 7, 8, 14–17, 40, 72, 92, 96, 187, 189
Du Bois, W. E. B., 141
Dulles, John Foster, 19, 78–88
Durkheim, Emile, xii
Dyer, Mary, 15

Eagle Forum, 183–84
Eddy, Sherwood, 75
Edmunds Act of 1882, 146
Edmunds-Tucker Act of 1887, 146
Edwards, Jonathan, 113–14
Eggleston, Edward, 115
Egypt: America as pharaonic, 132, 134, 137; and Arab Spring, 269–70; as context for Islamist discourse, 252–70; government of modern day, 252–53, 259, 261; Israelites' exodus from, 63, 93, 98, 105, 111–12, 122, 131–32, 137, 209 (see also Exodus). See also Faraj, Abd al-Salam; Qutb, Sayyid; Sadat, Anwar; al-Zawahiri, Ayman
Egyptian-Israeli Peace Treaty, 253
Eisenhower, Dwight D., 78–79, 85, 257
Eliot, John, 114
Elshtain, Jean Bethke, 223, 230n17
Emancipation Proclamation, 37–38, 46n39, 225, 226
Emerson, Ralph Waldo, 9, 231n25
Endy, Melvin B., 202–4
Engel, Richard, 178
England, 201–2, 204, 205, 207, 209, 215, 257
Episcopalianism, 115, 148. See also African Episcopal Church
Esau, 57–58, 111
Ethiopia, 98
evolution, 90n13, 100, 161
Exodus: African American interpretations of, 99, 105, 107, 113, 130–37, 137–41; biblical story of, 93, 105, 111, 140; Book of, 63–64, 76, 113; politics, 131, 140–41; rejection of "Exodus politics," 137–40

Falwell, Jerry, 11, 40–42
Faraj, 'Abd al-Salam, 252–66
Federal Bureau of Investigation (FBI), 151–52
Federal Council of Churches of Christ, 73, 82, 84
femininity, 166
feminism, 40, 160, 183
Field, Kate, 145

film, 48–60
Findlay, James, 40
Finney, Charles Grandison, 113
force: external, 213; physical, 5, 43, 211, 275. See also coercive force
Fourth Lateran Council, 235
France, 14, 50, 66, 71, 96, 257
Franklin, Benjamin, 94, 97
freedom, 9, 36, 42, 73, 81, 82; African American struggle for, 129–30, 132, 134–35, 137, 140; America's commitment to, 41, 87, 100, 105, 129, 144, 198, 202, 224, 227; attacks against America's, 41, 263; earning of, 70, 84; exported to other countries, 104, 219n49; fight to gain, 137–39; as gift from God, 42, 92, 96, 97, 98–99, 104, 202; Ku Klux Klan and, 165; new birth of, 227; political, 36, 104, 201, 208; and providence, 103; religion and, 95, 98, 155, 202; religious, 2, 12, 16, 93–94, 96, 145, 165, 202, 207; from slavery, 99, 101; and the West, 144, 155; for women, 167, 170. See also African American; civil rights; Exodus; slavery
French and Indian War, 117
French Revolution, 50, 95
fundamentalism, xi, 40, 66, 75, 84, 161–63
Fundamentalist Church of Jesus Christ of Latter-Day Saints (FLDS), 144, 152–55

Garnet, Henry Highland, 20, 129–30, 132, 137–41
Garrison, William Lloyd, 9, 13, 25n33
Garvey, Marcus, 141
Gates, Merril E., 155
Geertz, Clifford, 29–30
Geneva Conventions (1949), 235, 237–38; Protocols to (1977), 235, 238, 247nn3–4
genocide, 111–12, 115, 173, 233, 245, 284n4
Germany, ix, 14, 56, 67–68, 277
Gerson, Michael, 104
Ghost Dance, ix, 20, 144, 146, 148–50
Gildrie, Richard, 44n9
Gilgamesh, 57
Gillman, Neil, 82
God: and America, 41, 91, 92, 113; blessings of, 29, 31, 39, 41, 68, 94, 97, 102, 104, 133, 184, 187, 216; City of, 221, 284n12; covenant with, 29, 30, 36, 41, 44n3, 64, 70, 94, 228; displacement of, 55, 58, 256; favor of, 30, 31, 33, 36, 48, 216; grace, love, or mercy of, 34, 35, 65, 133, 187; hand of, 68, 104, 182; in Hebrew

TEXT

10/12.5 Minion Pro

DISPLAY

Minion Pro

COMPOSITOR

Westchester Book Group

PRINTER AND BINDER

Maple-Vail Book Manufacturing Group